"SOMEBODY IS LYING"

"SOMEBODY

THE STORY OF DR. X

GARDEN CITY, NEW YORK   1982

IS LYING"

by MYRON FARBER

DOUBLEDAY & COMPANY, INC.

Library of Congress Cataloging in Publication Data

Farber, Myron.
"Somebody is lying".

1. Jascalevich, Mario. 2. Trials (Poisoning)—New
Jersey—Hackensack. 3. Farber, Myron. 4. Confidential
communications—Press—New Jersey. 5. Forensic toxicol-
ogy. 6. Curare—Toxicology. I. Title.
KF224.J37F27   345.73′02523
347.3052523   AACR2
ISBN: 0-385-12618-2
Library of Congress Catalog Card Number 81–43851

To
Sabine Victoire

Acknowledgments

For having extended themselves in so many ways during the preparation of this book, I thank the following persons: Blanche Abrams, Floyd Abrams, Paul and Natalie Abrams, Lawrence K. Altman, Peter G. Banta, George Barrett, Marc Bernheim, David Bird, Roland and Elizabeth Brave, Leonard and Renee Buder, Katharine Darrow, Olive Evans, Paul and Wendy Farber, James Ingo and Hermine Freed, Keith and Lois Gasser, Arthur Gelb, James Gleick, Tom Goldstein, James Goodale, Mariana Gosnell, John A. and Julie Guzzetta, Donald A. Klein, Lucy Kroll, Paul Kurland, Marga Land, Mitchel Levitas, Kenneth D. McCormick, Peter Millones, Benno and Nathalie Robinson, Ted Rohrlich, A. M. Rosenthal, Stanley Rothenberg, Sydney H. Schanberg, Eugene R. Scheiman, Catherine Shea, Arthur O. Sulzberger, Seymour Topping, Mary Trone, Leonard and Judith Wachs, and Joan Ward. For being themselves, and for trying to be quiet when it counted, I thank my two wonderful children, Delphine and Christophe. For a lifetime of love, I thank my mother, Ruth Brave Cohen. And for his lessons in constancy and integrity over the years, I thank my uncle, Sam Abrams.

CONTENTS

PROLOGUE

I got off the bed and leaned against the little basin next to the toilet. As always, the cold-water tap was leaking, and I increased the pressure, lowering my face to the rust spot in the sink. There was no need to hurry on this August afternoon in 1978. The water was exquisite and I stood there awhile, soaking my head and thinking about the fellow upstairs who, a few days earlier, had hanged himself. His mother had come to see him on Sunday and had been turned away; Sunday was not a visiting day. On Monday he had been allowed to make a phone call but no one had answered. Then he had reached for the sheet.

"You ungrateful son of a bitch—they're fooling you too, you fucking disease. I'm fasting now, Paul. Jesus is the rock, Peter was the rock—got it straight? Ask not what you can do for your country. Did you ever hear that, you cocksucker? Don't play games with me."

"Boris, please," I shouted, beating the steel wall that separated us. "Not now."

"Myron, I'm dying from the heat. What's going on in this fucking place? One day they give you the food without the spoons, and the next day they give you the spoons without the food."

"Boris, please. Leave Paul alone. Please, we need some quiet."

I always said the same thing to Boris, and eventually they would come and pin him to his mattress and give him a shot of something and he would calm down. But not for long. He would soon be spouting half-remembered passages from Shakespeare and Byron, Pushkin and Poe, or he would be taunting Paul. All Boris could see of Paul, through the barred, foot-high opening in the door of each of their cells, was Paul's face—the uneven teeth, the rubbery mouth, the thick glasses that magnified dark eyes. Paul seldom answered Boris, and he never spoke about the sex charges that had landed him among us. Unlike Boris. Boris explained his own case over and over—how he had been provoked, forced really into bludgeoning his mother to death.

I sat down at the gray metal table that "Don Ron" had found for me. Bless Ron. He had been manager of a small town before his conviction for fraud, but here he was good company and reliable and even the guards listened to him. I made a mental note to ask Ron about Boris and the spoons. If any of our spoons were missing after dinner, we'd have another of those searches that raised everyone's level of anxiety. More than one spoon had been fashioned into a knife.

I noticed that the roses on the table were dying. The long stems were beginning to droop; and, one by one, the large red petals were forming a pile on the table. I wondered who had sent them. The guard who brought them said they were the first flowers received here in ten years. More amazing was the mail, from California, Utah, Texas, Georgia, Maine, Alaska . . . Each delivery brought more, most of it from strangers. "Just a few words of encouragement in your present situation," the letter on top began. "I heartily endorse your stand and do not feel . . ."

The wailing interrupted.

"Bring her in here, bring her in here! I want to kiss her feet. I want to touch her feet." I went to the window of my cell, overlooking the parking lot and the adjacent courthouse. Two stories below, a man and a woman were crossing the parking lot, arm in arm. From one of the cells along my tier, someone was calling after them. "Stick the tongue in there for me. Stick the tongue in the tunnel of love." The couple was quite a distance away and I doubted they could hear. I stood at the window, watching them disappear. It wasn't easy to see: the sun was glaring and my window had heavy, dirt-covered screens on either side of the bars. But I stood there, too tired to do anything else.

Then I saw the doctor. He was in shirt-sleeves, a light blue shirt that looked fresh and cool. He was standing by a driveway that ran between the buildings and spilled out into the parking lot. I supposed that the trial was over for the day and he was waiting for a lift home.

"Mr. Farber?"

I turned around and a guard was at my door. "One of the secretaries asked if you would autograph this picture for her. I'm sorry to bother you."

"No, it's O.K. Let me have it." I signed the photograph, torn from a newspaper, and went back to the window. But the doctor was gone.

I lay down on the bed and put a rolled towel over my eyes, hoping to sleep. Odd, I thought, how things had worked out for the doctor and me.

"And on the basis of the conversation I had with the doctor I thought it was imperative that we get this thing all ironed out here, because somebody is lying. I mean, there has to be liars here, not necessarily in this room—we are not accusing anybody—or at least there is such a divergence of opinion as to what the truth is that it requires an investigation. And it is my responsibility to find out where the truth lies. So that is why you are here."

—Guy Calissi,
Bergen County Prosecutor,
to the directors of Riverdell Hospital,
November 3, 1966

PART I
The Investigations

1

"Agent Farber."

Mike Levitas' voice boomed the length of *The New York Times* newsroom. It was a long room—too long, ordinarily, for Levitas' voice to carry very far. But the metropolitan desk was equipped with a stainless-steel microphone and from midmorning to early evening, every day of the year, the metropolitan editor or his assistants would use it to summon reporters to "the desk" to pass judgment on a story idea or go over an article before publication, or work out an assignment, or just share an observation on life in the city or life at *The Times*. Mike Levitas—on this morning in late June 1975—was the deputy metropolitan editor of *The Times,* second-in-charge of the paper's coverage of New York state, Connecticut, and New Jersey. Levitas liked to refer to me as "Agent Farber." It was his private joke, the origin long forgotten.

The newsroom was on the third floor of the *Times*'s gray sandstone building on West Forty-third Street, just west of Broadway and Times Square. It was an impressive room, more than an acre of formica-topped desks, with green and yellow pillars supporting a ceiling whose maze of fluorescent lights burned throughout the day and much of the night. From Forty-third Street, where the metropolitan, national, and foreign editors were clustered, the room extended a full block north to Forty-fourth Street, where I had my desk. I liked being away from the bustle up front; in the rear of the newsroom, away from the reporters' mailboxes and the telephone message center, and away from the congregation that was almost always gathered at the metropolitan desk, it seemed easier to function—easier to talk on the phone without interruption, easier to think. I also enjoyed gazing out my window at the Shubert Theater marquee and at the crowds that swirled beneath it most evenings.

Levitas looked impatiently across the newsroom and noticed that I was on the phone. He had received a letter that morning and had just shown the three typewritten pages to Arthur Gelb, the metropolitan editor. Gelb, an irrepressible six-footer who gushed leads for stories faster than they could be scooped up, had agreed that it was "perfect for Farber." Gelb had at his command about 100 reporters, a third of the *Times*'s reportorial staff. Many of them were assigned to "beats" —they regularly covered housing, or transportation, or politics, or some other area. Often these reporters, and others on general assignment, did long, probing articles. But Gelb also had a few reporters who worked almost exclusively on stories that required intensive investigation—stories in which, contrary to the usual circumstances, sources were reluctant to disclose information. I was one of those reporters.

"Take a look at this," Levitas said when I went up front. "If there's something to it," he added, handing me the letter, "it's all yours. No severed heads, mind you. But plenty of bodies."

I scanned the letter on the way back to my desk, where, filling my pipe, I read it again. A hospital was cited, but not identified. Doctors were referred to, but not by name. A prosecutor was mentioned, but not which one. No location was provided. But the charge animating the letter was clear and chilling: the chief surgeon of a hospital had, a decade earlier, murdered thirty to forty patients. Not simple malpractice, according to the letter; not some errors in medical judgment, nor some unfortunate slips of the knife. But murder. Of course the letter might have come from a crank. No newspaper was immune to cranks, and the allegation in this letter was breathtaking. But the tone of the letter, and the fact that it was signed by someone who seemed to have met Levitas, suggested otherwise. Many enticing tips fade upon investigation. But I had learned, over the years, not to dismiss any approach by an informant. Whatever their motives, and they varied from the selfish to the altruistic, people in all walks of life had information that was potentially of public interest or importance.

Right away, I was curious to know the name of the hospital. The letter offered no clue, but it indicated that drugs or chemicals might have been involved in the deaths. I picked up the phone. Having done a number of stories on the New York City medical examiner's office in 1973 and 1974, it now occurred to me that Joe Umberger might be of help. If word had ever gotten around about a case like this, and drugs were involved, Dr. Umberger might know something about it. There weren't that many forensic toxicologists in the country, and Charles J. Umberger, who had recently retired as director of laboratories for the city medical examiner's office, was acquainted with most of them.

I reached Dr. Umberger at his farm, a 200-acre spread about eighty miles north of Manhattan, in Ulster County.

"Doc, let me ask you a question. Have you ever heard of a case where a physician was thought to have murdered a lot of patients in a hospital? Some years back."

"I didn't get you. Can you speak up a little? The line's not very good up here."

I didn't want to shout in the office; I never liked to advertise what I was working on. I pushed my chair away from my desk toward an aisle, stretching the telephone cord as far as it would go. Then I raised my voice. "I said, do you know of a case in which a doctor was believed to have murdered many patients in a hospital but was never prosecuted?"

"In a hospital, huh? Let me think."

I waited, staring at the quotation I had taped to my desk a year earlier. It was something Freud had said during the period in the 1880s when he was experimenting with cocaine: *The temperament of an investigator needs two fundamental qualities. It must be sanguine in the attempt but critical in the work.*

"You know," Dr. Umberger said, "I do remember something. It was a case over in Jersey. Maybe ten or twelve years ago. Let me think . . ." His voice trailed off again. "Yeah, that's it. It was a case in Jersey. Some guy—he was a foreigner—came over and got an M.D., and there were a whole series of deaths in a small hospital. All under very peculiar circumstances."

"Doc, have you got this right? What do you know about it?"

"Well, I know curare was tied in with it. He had curare in his locker at the hospital. I was in the M.E. office at the time. That's it. It was over in Bergen County. People started to die, and the circumstances didn't add up. Somebody—actually it was a bunch of doctors—came to see Milton Helpern [then chief medical examiner of New York City] on it. I did some analytical work."

Dr. Umberger went on to say that his tests, on tissues saved from the body of a woman who had died at the hospital, ended after six weeks. "I found out the prosecutor wasn't going to exhume any bodies and that he had dropped the case. So I just said 'the hell with it.'"

"Wait a minute, Doc. Did you do enough work to know whether the death was suspicious?"

"All I remember now is that it was suspicious. Yes, it was suspicious."

"Doc, I don't believe this. You mean to say that somebody like yourself thought this death was suspicious, and that there were a lot of other deaths and nothing was done?"

"The case was dropped. I'm telling you, the case was dropped after the doctor was before the grand jury. There wasn't anything that I could do about it."

"Look, Doc, do me a favor. Try over the next few hours to think this through. Try to recall anything—*anything*—that has a bearing on this case, whether it was the death of the woman whose tissue you got or any other death. And I'll call you back."

"O.K., but this was a long time ago, and I really don't think I'm going to remember anything else."

"Try, Doc, try. And try to remember who else knows anything about this case. Any aspect of it. Do you remember how many deaths seemed odd?"

Dr. Umberger paused. "Thirteen," he said. "Thirteen is the number that comes back to me. And the hospital was somewhere near Paterson, New Jersey. Was it Riverhead? Or Riverdale? No, that's not it. But it was something like that. *Riverdell*—that's it, I think. Riverdell Hospital. It was a hospital for osteopaths."

"Riverdell. Great work, Doc. Just keep thinking away."

"Tell me,what's going on? Why are you bringing this up now?"

"Doc, I'll have to explain it when I see you. I'll talk to you later."

There it was, I thought. One call and, however thin a lead, I had something to work from. What luck!

I got up and headed for the *Times*'s "morgue." Apart from its 40,000-book library on the tenth floor, *The Times* had a morgue—or clip file—off the newsroom. There were more than 20 million clippings in the morgue, stuffed into manila folders that were arranged alphabetically by name and by subject heading. The folders, in turn, were stacked, from floor to ceiling, in dark green and gray metal cabinets. I loved the morgue; I got a sensual delight from rummaging through the folders and holding the clips. I took one of the morgue forms, wrote down "Riverdell Hospital," and handed it to a clerk. Someone had forgotten to shut off a reader-printer by the morgue desk, and as I stood there, the machine emitted a steady gnawing sound. Inside I was whirring too.

"Sorry," the clerk came back. "Nothing on Riverdell Hospital."

The research desk in the newsroom didn't have what I wanted next —a hospital directory. But the *Times*'s science department did have one, and I flipped through it hurriedly to page 146—"Hospitals, U.S.: New Jersey." On page 149, under "Oradell, Bergen County," I found what I was looking for: "Riverdell Hospital, 576 Kinderkamack

Road." Then, figuring out the symbols underneath, I began to glean a profile of the hospital.

I realized, as soon as I returned the directory to its shelf, that I couldn't pursue the Riverdell matter right away. For months I had been investigating an allegation that President Ford had accepted illegal payments from a maritime union when he was a congressman. And that was one story, especially in the aftermath of Watergate, that couldn't be shoved aside. *The Washington Post* had outdistanced *The Times* on Watergate, and no one at *The Times,* least of all its managing editor, A. M. Rosenthal, wanted it to happen again.

I had never forgotten my own baptism by Rosenthal, an intense man who, whether seated at his desk or prowling the newsroom, seemed always to be smoldering. It was in December 1966, ten months after I had joined the *Times*'s staff as a reporter covering education. A group of parents and civil rights workers had taken over the meeting room of the city's Board of Education in Brooklyn to protest the poor quality of many of the schools. After a few hectic days, the rump board, led by Rev. Milton Galamison, was arrested, and I filed my story from the pressroom in the school board building. I soon received a call from Rosenthal, who was then the metropolitan editor. He didn't like the beginning of my story. He wanted to be able to "feel" and "see" the hand of the policeman on Reverend Galamison's shoulder and the expression on the minister's face. And if I couldn't achieve that, he said, maybe a rewrite man at *The Times* could. That afternoon Rosenthal took my by-line off the story. It was the only time he ever did that. But he had made his point.

I hadn't set out to be a journalist. After graduating from the University of Maryland in 1959, I worked for a year as a reference librarian and then enrolled in the graduate history department at Northwestern University. I hoped to earn a Ph.D. and teach American history, but ill-suited to the cloistered life of an academic, I dropped out. In 1963, I landed a job as a reporter for *The Hartford Courant,* in Connecticut. My first story was almost my last. Malcolm X had come to Hartford to give a speech, and I was sent to cover it. Unfortunately, the Black Muslim leader was late, and he wasn't anywhere near the close of his talk when I had to get back to *The Courant* to write a piece for the early edition. At my typewriter, my notes laid before me, I went cold. I didn't know how to start, and I couldn't stop looking at the clock. But then, in an act of charity that constituted my first real lesson in journalism, an elderly editor suggested that I "sit back and do it like you were writing a letter home." And much to my surprise, it worked.

When I came to *The Times* two years later, I acquired a taste for putting together stories that examined complex disputes and that required considerable patience to do. I found, too, that I enjoyed the pursuit of a good story as much as I liked the actual writing of it. In the fall of 1972 I left the education department to help cover the United Nations General Assembly session. Six months later I was in Albany to write about the 1973 session of the New York state legislature. One of the bills passed by the legislature in that session was the tough anti-drug-abuse measure personally developed by then Governor Nelson A. Rockefeller. Many people wondered what the effect of the legislation would be, and *The Times* assigned me to find out and to cover drugs generally. Inevitably, my drug assignment led to the subject of death, and it was during this period that I was tipped off to the case of the severed head.

The severed head story, which I wrote at the close of 1973, concerned not drugs but the handling of a woman's body. A female corpse was found in New York's East River and was taken to the medical examiner's office by the city police. It remained in the morgue for twenty days and, not having been identified, was sent to a potter's field for burial. No autopsy was done, and the death was ascribed to drowning. Simple enough, perhaps. Except in this case, the head of the body had been removed by someone in the medical examiner's office, and was scheduled to be preserved in the morgue museum or displayed on a desk. While he was cleaning up the skull, the museum curator inadvertently came upon a hole and shook the head. Out fell a bullet. The body was exhumed, the head put with it, and the woman was quickly identified as Mrs. Laura Carpi, a thirty-seven-year-old Princeton, New Jersey, housewife who was once a clerk at the White House.

The story, which emphasized that the true cause of death was discovered only by chance and then through bizarre handling of the body, made for grisly reading. It also brought me call after call from people who had had bad experiences over the deaths of relatives or friends. I wrote a detailed account of how a retired Army lieutenant colonel was nearly buried in a pauper's grave because a number of city agencies, particularly the police, failed to notify his frantic family of the death. That article was followed by three similar case studies. And those pieces led me to investigate and disclose a body-snatching scheme by undertakers who were burying people at public expense with the ostensible approval of "friends" of the deceased. The "friends," I discovered, appeared not to have known the deceased or not even to have existed. Some of their addresses were actually vacant lots or street intersections.

Those were the stories that Mike Levitas had in mind when, on that morning in June 1975, he handed me the three-page letter about hospital deaths. Except for another brief conversation with Dr. Umberger, I had laid the Riverdell matter aside while I completed my investigation of President Ford. But then I saw the article.

It was on the morning of August 21, 1975, and I was skimming *The Times* at breakfast in my garden apartment in Greenwich Village. As I turned from page 22 to 23, my eyes caught the words "mysterious deaths" in the eight-column headline. It took a few seconds for me to grasp that the story was not about Riverdell at all, but about a series of unusual deaths at the Veterans Administration Hospital in Ann Arbor, Michigan. Still, there seemed to be a marked resemblance. More than a score of patients had been seized with cardiac arrests or breathing failures, and some had died. "The physicians at the hospital and the outside experts from the Veterans Administration who are conducting the investigation suspect that if a drug is involved, it probably is a muscle relaxant such as curare, pancuronium, or succinylcholine chloride—all of which are used in the hospital here." Unnerved, I reread the sentence. Somehow, I would have to get moving on the Riverdell story.

Through Dr. Umberger I had obtained the name of a woman who had been secretary to Guy Calissi, the Bergen County prosecutor from 1954 to 1970. Hoping now that she could tell me more about Calissi's handling of the case, I tracked her down, by phone, to Cape Cod, where she was vacationing.

Gloria Rowland had a clear memory, if limited knowledge, of the Riverdell affair. I listened closely as she described how five directors of Riverdell Hospital had barged in on Calissi in November 1966 and had told him they had a problem that couldn't wait. " 'This better be important,' " Mrs. Rowland recalled Calissi saying. "He didn't like being interrupted. He had steam coming out of his ears." Calissi conducted an investigation, Mrs. Rowland confirmed, and the target was a doctor at the hospital. "I suppose there wasn't any conclusive proof," she added. "Just a lot of facts. I know that after the whole thing died down, I put a card in my wallet saying that if anything ever happened to me, I didn't want to be taken to Riverdell Hospital. That's how I felt about it then, and that's how I feel about it now." Mrs. Rowland gave me the names of detectives who had worked on the case, mentioning that many of them had left the prosecutor's office since 1966. For some of those who had moved on, she had current addresses. "Why don't you talk to Calissi about it?" Mrs. Rowland asked. "He's a judge now, you know, but he'll probably talk to you. Also Freddy Galda. He was the first assistant prosecutor then, and I think he actually handled most of the case. He's a judge now too."

Three days later, on a rainy Sunday afternoon, I drove out to Ridgewood, New Jersey with my wife and two children. Judge Calissi lived in a big white and red brick house on the corner of Manor Road and Highland Street. It was an affluent residential neighborhood with neatly manicured lawns and shrubbery, and a profusion of flowers. I parked in the side driveway of the house and, taking my kids with me, rang the bell by the kitchen door. An elderly woman answered and, frowning at the intrusion, led us into the judge's living room. At first Calissi—a tall man with a bald pate and pointed ears—seemed befuddled. I had interrupted him while he was writing an opinion. But he was gracious and asked how he could help me. I handed the judge the *Times*'s story on the Veterans Administration Hospital in Michigan and asked whether this reminded him of anything. Calissi read the article carefully. "Riverdell Hospital," he said. "It sounds like Riverdell Hospital, but do you know anything about that?" For forty-five minutes, while my year-old son was laboring to rip the buttons from Calissi's ornate sofa, the judge explained that a situation that seemed similar to the one in Michigan had occurred in Bergen County. He didn't want to be too specific, he said, "but we had many suspicions" that the Riverdell patients had been murdered. "I strongly suspected the guy you're probably thinking about," Calissi remarked, "but we had no hard evidence. He said he was doing these experiments with the curare, and we had no hard evidence that he was up to no good. God, if we had had that, do you think I would have stopped? Although I'll tell you this. My first assistant thought I was riding the doctor too much. He thought I was being too hard on him."

"What about the grand jury?" I asked, remembering my conversation with Umberger.

"The grand jury? What grand jury?" Calissi replied. "We didn't put this before the grand jury."

2

A few days after talking to Calissi, I went to see the current Bergen County prosecutor. He was short, compactly built, and looked, in his modish blazer and plaid slacks, considerably younger than his fifty years. He clutched my hand and motioned me to a couch in his office. "I'm Joe Woodcock. What can I do for you?"

"It's about an old case out here," I began. "I don't think you'd know anything about it; it was when Guy Calissi was prosecutor. The case concerned a number of deaths at a hospital in Oradell—Riverdell Hospital—and Calissi investigated. No one was charged with a crime. But *The Times* is interested in the case now. In fact, we'd like to see the file on the case, to verify a few points."

I had taken a long shot. It was futile to depend on Umberger's memory. Or Calissi's. Or anyone's. Too much time had passed, and if I was going to reconstruct the events of 1966, to try to make sense of them, I would need a contemporaneous record.

Woodcock, I had learned, had been prosecutor since 1973, and he was regarded as one of the "cleanest" officials in a state described by a political almanac as "the nation's most corrupt." I suspected the prosecutor was also a cautious man, and I thought it best not to seem too anxious for the file. The more important the file appeared to be, the more protective Woodcock would probably become. If, of course, there *was* a file after ten years.

"Naturally I'd use the file here and under whatever security conditions you'd want," I said, getting up from the couch and wandering over to the arched windows. On the Hackensack Green I could see a statue of a colonial soldier whose sword blade had been shorn off near the handle. "I went to see Judge Calissi on Sunday, and we talked about the case. He has no objection to my going through the file. If you want to call him, I'm sure he'll confirm that."

Woodcock didn't feel the need. The previous week Richard Kikkert, the county's chief of detectives, had shown him the article from *The Times* about suspicious deaths at the Veterans Administration Hospital in Michigan. Kikkert wondered whether any of the doctors from Riverdell had moved out to Michigan. The same thought had occurred to Cono Delia, another of the county's long-time detectives. "Don't worry about it," Kikkert had told Delia. "I've already spoken to the prosecutor and we've sent for the file. We'll have it here if the FBI wants it."

To Woodcock, the Riverdell case was inactive, with no reason or prospect of revival. He had never even heard of the case until Kikkert brought it up. Woodcock mistakenly assumed that I was simply one step ahead of the FBI in checking any possible connection between the Riverdell and Michigan cases.

"I think we can arrange for you to see the file," Woodcock said. "But first I'd like my chief of detectives to go over it and make sure there isn't anything privileged in there. Why don't you get back to me in a couple of days. A couple of days won't make any difference."

I didn't argue. I just wanted to get out of Woodcock's office before the prosecutor changed his mind.

On the afternoon of August 29, 1975, I was shown into a bleak room in the office of Bergen County's narcotics task force, across the street from the gold-domed courthouse. Built into one wall of the room, which was ordinarily used for interrogating suspects, was a two-way mirror, and I concluded that I was going to be watched by detectives on the other side. There were no windows and only one chair, with a hard seat and a straight back. In the center of the tiny room was a rectangular table covered in a black material. And on the table was the Riverdell file, a yard-long reinforced cardboard box weighing about forty pounds. There were more than a score of manila folders sloping against each other in the file, and most of them, in the way of old clothing that conforms to the body, had lost their sturdiness. I took off my suit jacket and hung it on the chair. One by one, I took out the folders and peeled back their covers. Detective reports on interviews with administrators at several hospitals other than Riverdell and with officials of the Seton Hall School of Medicine in Jersey City. Correspondence between Calissi and the Allied Testing and Research Laboratory in Hillsdale, New Jersey. An application for a search warrant signed on November 1, 1966. Wads of invoices from the General Surgical Supply Company, bound together with rubber bands.

I had seen the company's name a moment earlier, and this seemed as good a place as any to start. I reached back for the memorandum. It was from Investigator George O'Har to First Assistant Prosecutor Fred C. Galda. The date was November 14, 1966.

It read: "In accordance with First Assistant Prosecutor Fred C. Galda's assignment, I went to the General Surgical Supply Company, 444 Sixtieth Street, West New York, New Jersey, to interview the three proprietors in connection with one Dr. Mario E. Jascalevich. The three proprietors are Mr. Michael Abrams, Mr. Leo Abrams, and Mr. Max Seitzman. I spoke to Mr. Michael Abrams and Mr. Max Seitzman as to how Dr. Mario E. Jascalevich bought the tubocurarine [curare]. Both Mr. Abrams and Mr. Seitzman said that he would either stop by the store or he would call up and then they would order it for him, as they do not carry tubocurarine in stock. As to the date, lot, and manufacturer, there is a code number by which the manufacturer could tell the date and lot number and when it was manufactured. Tubocurarine comes in only one strength. Dr. Mario E. Jascalevich never complained to any of the proprietors of the General Surgical Supply Company."

Wondering what the reference to "complaining" was about, I leaned to the floor for my briefcase and removed a yellow-lined legal pad.

"Curare was bought by Dr. Mario Jascalevich," I wrote. "Doesn't seem to be any doubt about it." I flipped through the invoices and some of the other documents, trying to see how much curare had been bought. Apart from the purchase of one vial on May 16, 1964, Dr. Jascalevich paid for twenty-four 10-cc bottles of curare between September 1965 and September 1966. I made another note and picked up two books that were in the file.

They were both human anatomy books. One was in French, the other in Spanish. Perhaps the books once belonged to Dr. Jascalevich or to another of the Riverdell doctors. When I saw the notations in the French work on pages 26, 27, and 32, I decided that the books were probably Dr. Jascalevich's and were related to the experiments Calissi had spoken about. Each of the three pages featured a diagram of the abdomen and, on each, someone had written in English, "MOVE IT UP WITH CURARE!!!" I thought the form and repetition of the curare notation was odd. In each instance, the notation was heavily underlined and followed by two or three exclamation points, almost as if the writer was afraid of forgetting his objective from page to page. Moreover, the curare messages were in pencil and were distinctly legible, while other markings on the pages were in ball-point and were difficult to read.

I laid the books aside when I noticed Dr. Umberger's report on the tissue of a woman who had died at Riverdell in 1966. It was only two paragraphs and was addressed to Calissi on February 19, 1967. At the top it said, "Laboratory Report ⚔103. Case of Eileen Shaw relative to the case of Dr. Mario E. Jascalevich." I jotted down the name of the dead woman, and read it over.

"After a complete analysis, chemical findings in this case must be considered negative. . . . The problem in this case was to separate possible curare from the interfering tissue base. Although findings were suspicious no clear-cut separation was attained. . . . After an extensive study with controls, as well as with the case, it was concluded impossible to detect curare in therapeutic levels in formalin-fixed tissues. The chemical findings in the case should be considered suspicious without sufficient confirmation for definite positive or negative results."

Dr. Umberger appeared to be saying that curare might be present in Eileen Shaw's tissue, but he couldn't be sure because the tissue he worked on was saturated in formalin and the formalin was blocking a clean analysis. But what about tissues from the bodies of others who had died at Riverdell—tissues that might not have been soaked in formalin? Had they been tested?

Already it was approaching 6 P.M., and I had yet to start on the bound, plastic-covered depositions in the file. I pulled them out and arranged them in the order in which they had been taken, at the courthouse, by Calissi and his chief assistant, Fred Galda. The first transcribed session, a brief one, was at 12:45 P.M. on November 3, 1966. Most of the doctors at the session, who were accompanied by a lawyer named Andrew Emerson, were identified as directors of Riverdell Hospital. Calissi, who did most of the talking, reminded the doctors that they had been in to see him two days earlier, November 1, about thirteen "unusual or unexplained" deaths at the hospital over the last year. This, I was sure, was the meeting Mrs. Rowland had told me about. Apparently it had not been recorded. I noticed, too, that the number thirteen was the same number mentioned to me by Dr. Umberger.

"I am talking about foul play," Calissi went on at the November 3 session. "I am talking about the drug curare being responsible for these deaths." Calissi said he had just sent a sample of Eileen Shaw's "fiber or flesh" to Dr. Umberger in New York. He also said that Galda had met with Dr. Jascalevich for about an hour that morning and that he had talked to the surgeon as well, for about five minutes.

"And on the basis of the conversation I had with the doctor I thought it was imperative that we get this thing all ironed out here, because somebody is lying. I mean, there has to be liars here, not necessarily in this room—we are not accusing anybody—or at least there is such a divergence of opinion as to what the truth is that it requires an investigation. And it is my responsibility to find out where the truth lies. So that is why you are here."

Dr. Jascalevich was ushered into the prosecutor's office, and Calissi unwound again. "This is a criminal investigation," he told the surgeon. "We haven't accused anyone, as you can see. Nobody has made a complaint against you or any other doctor, but we are in the process of investigating to determine whether or not this curare was administered to any of these people who died, for the purpose of killing these people." Obviously, the prosecutor went on, "the investigation is being directed in your direction." Calissi advised Dr. Jascalevich that he could remain silent and was entitled to legal representation. "If the hospital has its lawyer present," the surgeon replied, "I would like to have my lawyer too." Dr. Jascalevich was excused, after agreeing that he had been treated "fairly" that morning, and Galda asked that a Dr. Harris be called in at once.

Disappointed that the first deposition had been so thin, I turned to the next statement, taken at 3:50 P.M. on the same day, November 3, 1966. It was from Dr. Stanley Harris, a Riverdell surgeon who lived in Bronxville, New York. "We are not pointing the finger at you as being charged or about to be charged, or being suspected of committing a crime," Calissi said. But, for the next four pages, the prosecutor advised Dr. Harris of his rights. Dr. Harris said he didn't need a personal lawyer and would answer all questions.

"Now, a few days ago, Monday of this week," Calissi continued, "you became suspicious of the number of mortalities connected with the patients that were under your supervision and care at Riverdell Hospital? Is that right?"

"That's right."

"Was it Monday that you became suspicious or were you suspicious before that?"

"Well, it was only Monday when everything seemed to jell."

"Why did it jell on Monday?"

"Because on Monday I went to a postmortem examination on a patient I had operated on, on Friday, at which time I had expected to find some very definite pathology concerning a death."

"You expected something with respect to this particular patient?"

"I anticipated finding a certain pathology in this particular case. I thought this lady had a pulmonary embolus as a cause of death."

"What happened?"

"Well, when I went to the 'post' on Monday there was no pulmonary embolus and there was no organic reason to point to a cause of death at that postmortem on a gross."

"What was the name of that woman?"
"Eileen Shaw."

It was a dark story that Dr. Harris told that afternoon.

Mrs. Shaw, who was thirty-six, had come into the hospital to give birth, her third successive cesarean delivery in five pregnancies. Along with a tubal ligation, or sterilization, the section was performed by Dr. Harris on Friday morning, October 21, 1966. The baby was "a little slow to begin respirations," the surgeon said, "but the baby did well and the baby is well. Following surgery the patient went to the recovery room. There was no difficulty with the surgery involved. She remained completely stable throughout the procedure. We had no excessive bleeding. She required no blood. Surgery was essentially uncomplicated. She went to the recovery room and then from there she went to the ward; and before I left on Friday in the afternoon I stopped downstairs and I briefly saw her and her husband, and she was doing perfectly well. She was quite alert at that time. She said hello and she said she was doing O.K., and she *was* doing O.K., and I said hello to her husband."

Calissi interrupted to ask whether there were other patients in the room—I noticed that the surgeon wasn't sure—and Dr. Harris resumed his account.

On Saturday, about 8 A.M., Dr. Harris said, "I received a call from Dr. Jascalevich, indicating to me that the patient wasn't doing very well. He mentioned something about a little blood from the vagina. He said something about the uterus being high. He said the patient was in shock . . . and he advised that I come down soon." After asking Dr. Jascalevich to do a basic blood test and start a unit of blood if necessary, Dr. Harris began the half-hour drive from Bronxville to Oradell. By the time he got there, Mrs. Shaw had already been seen and resuscitated by Dr. Robert Baba, the anesthesiologist/gynecologist who was her personal physician and who lived near Riverdell. Dr. Jascalevich had called Dr. Baba too.

Dr. Harris's first thought was that Mrs. Shaw was bleeding as a result of the operation—"if the patient was in shock, the likely thing was there might be blood loss." But a blood test came back normal and "when I saw her she didn't look like she was bled out at all. She looked drained out. She looked plethoric. She looked cyanotic, pale . . ."

Neither Dr. Harris nor Dr. Baba, who joined the surgeon in the hospital's cafeteria around 10 A.M., could figure out what had happened to Mrs. Shaw. Dr. Baba had just left for home when Dr. Harris, lingering over his coffee, got a frantic call from a nurse. Mrs. Shaw was "going bad."

"The cafeteria is up on the upstairs level . . . and so I ran downstairs, down the staircase. There is an elevator but I didn't take the elevator, I was in a rush to get down there, and coming up the middle of the staircase was Dr. Jascalevich and he mumbled something about the patient and I better get there and I just kept going and when I found the patient, this time the patient was completely apneic."

Again Calissi interjected. "Completely what?"

"Apneic. A-P-N-E-I-C. She was not breathing at all. She was markedly cyanotic, but she did have a heartbeat."

I stopped and reread the passage, thinking I had gotten it wrong. ". . . I was in a rush to get down there, and coming up the middle of the staircase was Dr. Jascalevich and he mumbled something about the patient and I better get there and I just kept going. . . ." I gazed at the transcript. Where was Dr. Jascalevich going? If he knew the patient was in trouble, why was he going the other way?

Dr. Harris continued, describing the efforts to save Mrs. Shaw. Mouth-to-mouth breathing. Intubation by Dr. Baba, whom Dr. Harris had now summoned. Attaching the patient to a Bennett machine, an artificial respirator. Taking her blood pressure, monitoring her central venous pressure, measuring her urine output. An electrocardiogram. Enzyme and bilirubin tests. Antibiotics and other drugs to combat damage to the lungs from stomach contents inhaled during vomiting. Morphine sulfate to reduce agitation. For hours, Dr. Harris, Dr. Baba, and other doctors ministered to Mrs. Shaw, who showed some improvement. But about 3 A.M. on Sunday morning, October 23, the woman's heart rate fell off. And at 8:20 A.M., the heart gave out. Mrs. Shaw was dead.

"I might mention that Saturday, during the afternoon, I got several calls from Dr. Jascalevich concerned about the patient, how the patient was doing," Dr. Harris related to Calissi. "He also at one time told me that I ought to go home and rest, I shouldn't spend all my effort on one patient, I do have responsibilities to other patients. Shortly after her death, Sunday morning, I had another call from him telling me that he had received a call from a Mr. Mooney, who I had never heard of before, and that Mr. Mooney was a friend of the family and a lawyer and I ought to contact my malpractice insurance carrier, and I was terribly annoyed at all this malpractice bit that he told me and I just, I just rejected the whole idea."

Galda seemed to have heard of Mooney—perhaps from his conversation that morning with Dr. Jascalevich—because the assistant prosecutor broke into Dr. Harris's narrative to identify the firm of Hein, Smith & Mooney. I wrote down the firm's name. Mooney might be of some help.

Calissi asked Dr. Harris to explain why Dr. Jascalevich would have been involved, in the first place, with a patient other than his own.

"Well, what he was doing there now is based upon what I was told by the nurse, Mrs. Darcy. . . . I questioned her several days later because I wanted to know in more detail just exactly what was going on. When she came on at 7 A.M., she took her report, like most nurses do, and then soon afterward she said the trays were coming . . . for feeding for breakfast.

"Now, there are double doors which divide this part of the unit from the other medical-surgical unit, and she was standing at the double doors as the trays were being served—brought in. At that time she said Dr. Jascalevich was in the hall and had asked her how the patient was doing, and she said 'So-so' or the patient was O.K., and he said 'Well, I better check the patient.' So . . . he and she went into the room to check the patient. The next thing she told me was that he had mentioned that the intravenous looked like it was running out and they discussed what should be put up and they said, 'Well, we'll put up some dextrose and water and leave the more specific fluid orders' to myself. Mrs. Darcy said there was a bottle of dextrose and water in the room and she had just replaced that which was running. The next thing that she told me was that he said her [Mrs. Shaw's] color didn't look too good and she [Nurse Darcy] should get a blood-pressure machine. This meant, in essence, that he was attending her at that time by himself. When she brought back the blood-pressure machine . . . he took the blood pressure and she said he reported a blood pressure of 80 over something and also that he examined the patient, he had done a vaginal examination and apparently had withdrawn some blood clots from the vagina.

"Now at about this time she [Mrs. Darcy] mentioned that the patient told her she was having a pain in her chest and difficulty breathing; and then, shortly after, she herself took the blood pressure and found it to be 200 over about 110. At about that time, according to Mrs. Darcy, the patient developed a convulsion and then looked quite blue and appeared to be breathing poorly. Also she mentioned that Dr. Jascalevich suggested that she contact me to let me know about my patient. However, I didn't receive a call from Mrs. Darcy; my call came from Dr. Jascalevich himself."

Dr. Harris said he had had Mrs. Shaw's uterus carefully inspected at the postmortem after no embolus, or blood clot, was found in the lung. The uterus, he said, was well contracted, there was little blood within, and there was no evidence of any infection.

"As a matter of fact," the surgeon said, "I couldn't conceive of anything called sepsis in such a case to occur in this manner. After all, this wasn't the first postoperative and the patient doesn't die from sepsis like this—not often. So, therefore, when I was driving to my office after seeing this postmortem, I was really in a dilly. Because I was just, I was just at a loss to put this together. And then things started to make sense to me."

I looked at my watch. It was nearly 7 P.M. and I would have to go soon. I hadn't finished with Dr. Harris's statement, and the next two depositions on the table were relatively thick. One was from Dr. Allan Lans, a director of the hospital. I skimmed it quickly, hoping to find further discussions of Eileen Shaw. There seemed to be nothing, except a passing reference to Mooney, the Shaw family's lawyer. But the Shaw death was dealt with at some length in the deposition of Dr. Edwin Frieman, another Riverdell director who was the head of the hospital's mortality review committee. Much of what Dr. Frieman had to say about Mrs. Shaw was based on what was in her hospital chart and what Dr. Harris had told him after the woman's death. But some of it was not. For one thing, Dr. Frieman recalled being in the hospital about 2 A.M. on the morning of October 22, roughtly six hours before Mrs. Shaw had her first "episode." ". . . I saw Mrs. Shaw. Mrs. Shaw was certainly in no way critical. She was soundly sleeping. She was breathing right."

Then, about a week after Mrs. Shaw died, Dr. Frieman said, he got a call from the pathologist, Dr. Luther Markley. " 'Well, I found the diagnosis, a fatty embolism of the capillary to the liver,' Dr. Markley said.

"I said, 'Dr. Markley, this patient's liver tests were normal the day before. How could she die a liver or kidney death?'

" 'Well, it's a very rare thing. It's written up in the *Journal of the AMA* of October 17 or 18. I'm sure this is it, and I'm going to write away to a doctor or professor at Baltimore who uncovered this illness and discuss it with him.'

"I said, '. . . Dr. Markley, just do one thing: Anything the prosecutor's office wants as far as the hospital is concerned, you cooperate with them.' And I wasn't completely satisfied that this was the cause of death. And I still am not completely satisfied that this was the cause of death."

What a coincidence, I thought. Mrs. Shaw died on October 23 and the explanation for her death appeared in the American Medical Association's *Journal* virtually that same week. I scribbled on my pad: "Get *JAMA* article."

Dr. Frieman's statement was equally interesting on another aspect of the Shaw death. The exchange began on page 128 of the deposition, with Galda questioning the doctor:

"Your explanation is that someone possibly could have injected her twice?"

"It's possible, yes. It's possible."

"Or can you tell me whether or not one dose of curare could have caused the death under the circumstances that you described in the chart? Could a person come out of this curare difficulty and then lapse back into it?"

"Generally speaking, no. If the body would have metabolized the curare enough for this patient to come out of it, there is no delayed reaction. Now I heard a story, again, this was a story, and I don't know who told it to me, whether it was one of the board members or not who told me, that they heard this patient tell Dr. Jascalevich not to give her as strong an injection or as strong a medicine as the first time."

* * *

"This is during the time she was unconscious?"

Dr. Frieman didn't know any more about the "story," and he admitted that the theory of two curare injections—the first metabolized by a healthy, thirty-six-year-old patient—was ". . . not even probability," but more a "possibility."

Calissi seemed irritated. "With a matter of importance that has been attached to this, it would seem that Sklar [Dr. Jay Sklar, another Riverdell director] or whoever heard this would really follow it through and check it out and . . ."

Before the story could be confirmed, Dr. Frieman said, something occurred that threw the directors into a "complete state of panic."

I put on my jacket, placed the depositions in the file, and spoke to the detectives who had been instructed to accommodate the "visitor." The file was carried into the office's evidence room and set down next to the equipment that was used for wiretapping narcotics suspects. The room was relocked. Outside, the August air was stagnant, but the sky was still a soft blue. I was both elated and depressed. Regardless of who had done what to whom, it was a grim story. But I had access to the file; no other newsman did, and I was intent on keeping it that way until I could sort out this affair. I had asked Woodcock not to identify me as a reporter, and I hoped I could count on the prosecutor. But detectives were another matter. Detectives gossiped. And all it took was one detective's asking one local reporter why *The Times* was around and a strong advantage could be lost. I waited in my car for the light on the corner to change. I looked across the street to the Bergen County Jail, adjacent to the courthouse, and back to the building I had just left. I was wondering whether anyone could see my New York press license plate when the light showed green. I swung left on River Road and zoomed north to Route 4 and the George Washington Bridge.

At *The Times,* I picked up my mail and phone messages. Larry Altman, a doctor/journalist who covers medicine for *The Times,* had left me a paper on curare that he had written as part of a planned book on self-experimentation by medical researchers. Underneath the sixteen-page paper was a copy of *The Penguin Medical Encyclopedia* and a note from Altman saying that he would bring in some of the more esoteric literature on curare later. I took the material and went upstairs to the cafeteria. It surprised me that Gelb and Levitas and even my wife, Sabine, who had grown up in Brittany and Paris, knew of curare. Apparently, as kids they had all seen a movie with South American Indians shooting curare-tipped arrows through long, narrow blowpipes. I had gone to the wrong movies.

Crude curare was a dark brown gummy substance extracted from a variety of plants in the Amazon and Orinoco river basins. "Through experience," Altman wrote in his paper, "the Indians knew curare was poisonous only if injected into the body. Curare was harmless if rubbed on unbroken skin or if eaten in small amounts. Accordingly, the Indians ate with impunity the flesh of the animals killed by the arrows they smeared with curare. The Indians also knew that many curare arrow injuries could be treated successfully if the poison was sucked out of the wound. But they knew that if there was a cut or sore in the sucker's mouth, curare would paralyze." I switched to the Penguin encyclopedia: "In 1813, an English naturalist Charles Waterton made the important discovery that a poisoned animal could be kept alive by artificial respiration until the effects of the curare had worn off; for curare kills only by paralyzing the muscles of breathing . . . A pure alkaloid, *d*-tubocurarine, was isolated in 1935. Since 1942 this and other related drugs have been used during surgical operations. Breathing is regulated artificially, and curare provides complete muscular relaxation—a most important aid to the surgeon—while the dose of anesthesia is kept to a safe minimum. This technique has removed one of the principal risks of major surgery—that a large enough dose of a conventional anesthetic to relax the muscles may be dangerously large."

Back in the newsroom, I pulled down the *Directory of Medical Specialists* from the research shelves. On page 2918, under "Surgeons," I found "Jascalevich, Mario E." I noticed Dr. Jascalevich was South American and a graduate of the University of Buenos Aires Medical

School. There was no reference at all to Riverdell Hospital or other institutions at which he might have practiced after his training. I jotted down the surgeon's office address: 435 Sixtieth Street, West New York, New Jersey. I dialed information: Dr. Jascalevich was listed. I called the number and waited while it rang and rang. No answer. I dialed again. Then I heard the name "Jascalevich." The woman also mentioned another name, but I didn't catch it. Again, she said, "Dr. Jascalevich" and something else. "Hello? Hello?" she said. I put the receiver back on its hook, satisfied that Dr. Jascalevich was still around and could, in time, be reached.

During September 1975, I finished up the Ford investigation, finding no evidence to substantiate the allegation against the President. By mid-October, I was free to pursue the Riverdell case on a full-time basis. I had already gone back to Hackensack on a number of occasions and, in the narcotics task force building, I photostated much of the file. Without copies of the depositions and other documents it would have been impossible to pursue such a technical case. Moreover, I had no guarantee that Woodcock might not suddenly withdraw access to the file. The detectives, I later discovered, had thought I was an auditor or analyst of some kind, and gave me unlimited privileges with the office's reproducing machine. It had worked out beautifully.

I was eager, in October, to reach the family of Eileen Shaw—to get their reaction in 1966 to the death and to whatever Calissi or the hospital had said about the investigation. Strangely, there was nothing in the file to indicate that the Shaw family had been interviewed. Or any of the thirteen families, for that matter. Yet surely they had been advised, if only in retrospect, that the deaths were eventually considered suspicious. And questioned, too. Perhaps some of the family members had been at Riverdell when the deaths occurred.

According to Mrs. Shaw's hospital chart, which was in the file, her husband's name was René and the family lived at 709 Saddle River Road in Saddle River, New Jersey. Information had no listing for a René Shaw. So I drove out to Saddle River, only to find that there was no 709 Saddle River Road in Saddle River and the local police, tax collector, and post office had never heard of René or Eileen Shaw. The hospital chart had a number for Mr. Shaw at the "Department of Defense" in Teaneck, New Jersey, another Bergen County community. But the operator told me that the "TE-4" exchange didn't exist in Teaneck, and the Defense Department said it had no installation there. Then I thought of Mooney, the Shaw family's lawyer and friend. Whatever the errors on the chart—after all, the Shaws hadn't been invented —Mooney would probably know the family's whereabouts. Hein,

Smith & Mooney, the firm cited by Galda in Dr. Harris's deposition, had changed its name in 1975. It was now Hein, Smith & Berezin. Mooney was John T. Mooney, and he was now a County Court judge in Hackensack. Judge Mooney came on the line, and I introduced myself.

"I'm trying to reach an old client of yours, Your Honor. René Shaw. His wife, Eileen, you may remember, died in 1966. I believe you were a friend of the Shaws at that time."

"René Shaw, you say? I'm afraid I don't know a René Shaw. Or an Eileen Shaw. They were clients of mine?"

I was puzzled. Could Galda have had the wrong Mooney? "Excuse me, Judge, but have you ever heard of Riverdell Hospital or Dr. Mario Jascalevich?"

"Why, yes. I'm quite familiar with Riverdell Hospital. The doctor's name sounds like I might have heard it before, but nothing more."

"Well, could you have been interested, back in 1966, in possibly bringing an action against Riverdell or its doctors for malpractice? On behalf of people named Shaw?"

"I don't think so. I did a lot of malpractice work, but on behalf of the hospitals usually. I don't even remember a Riverdell case. But I tell you what I can do, if it's important to you. My entire client records are across the street, at the firm, and I could go and check them under Shaw. I think I'll be wasting my time, but I could go."

Judge Mooney went. And as he had predicted, wasted his time.

Mooney's name had come up twice—in Dr. Harris's statement and in Dr. Lans's. But on rereading Dr. Lans's deposition, I came upon another, longer reference to Mooney—one that I had overlooked in August. It was at the end of the deposition, and it was in the context of Dr. Lans's saying that he thought Dr. Jascalevich was a "liar." On the Sunday morning that Mrs. Shaw died, Dr. Lans explained to Calissi, he received a call at home from his answering service, saying that he should phone Dr. Jascalevich immediately at Christ Hospital in Jersey City. "When I called him there, he told me that a lawyer, Mr. Mooney, had just called him and asked him about this case, and I couldn't understand why would Mr. Mooney—who was Mr. Mooney?—why would he call Dr. Jascalevich, how would he get through to Dr. Jascalevich?"

"Yes, sir."

The prosecutor seemed bewildered. "But what reason would Dr. Jascalevich have to call you to tell you to call him so he could tell you that Mr. Mooney called him and asked him about the progress of Mrs. Shaw?"

"Well, he said he thought it was very important for us to notify our malpractice carriers."

"Who told you this?"

"Dr. Jascalevich."

"Why?"

"Because of this Mr. Mooney questioning the case."

When Calissi said there appeared to be a logical reason for Dr. Jascalevich to have called Dr. Lans, the Riverdell director objected. "No, no. It was logical if you could believe that Mr. Mooney had called him."

"Do you have any doubt in your mind that Mr. Mooney called him?" Calissi asked.

"Yes, I do have that doubt," Dr. Lans replied. "You know, it's very difficult to let it all sink in, and to think and to reconstruct this, it's a difficult thing. There is a far cry between a guy being a liar and a guy being a murderer. But I can't understand why the man lied. I can't understand it. There is no reason. I can't understand any reason for the man to lie."

"When do you think he lied?"

"I think he lied about this Mooney situation."

"Did you ever ask Mooney?"

"No, why would I ask Mooney? Who is Mooney? I don't even know who he is."

I didn't know either. But I was determined to find out, and the key was René Shaw. I took the Metroliner down to Trenton, New Jersey, the state capital, and hopped a cab for the state Health Department's offices. René Shaw must have paid for his wife's funeral, I thought. The death certificate would have the name of the mortician, who might have another address for the widower. I completed a form at the Health Department and gave the clerk two dollars. Ten minutes later I had the death certificate, identifying the undertaker as the Vander Platt Funeral Home in Paramus. But as I scanned the document, I realized that I didn't need Vander Platt. I saw where I had gone wrong. The Shaws had never lived in Saddle River, as the hospital chart had said. The street address was right. But the town was Saddle Brook. I turned back to the clerk. "I'm going to want some other certificates," I said.

I almost missed the house. It was set back from the road, a modest stone ranch house with a wide picture window and a massive oak tree on the front lawn. A woman, blond and in her late thirties, came to the front door as I got out of the car. She had a black and white border collie by her side.

I took a few tentative steps and called out. "Hello. I'm looking for René Shaw or anyone who might know him. Can you help me?"

The woman came nearer. "René's in Florida. He doesn't live here anymore. But this was his house. We're friends of his."

The woman was Marcia Collins, and she and her husband, Dave, had known Eileen Shaw as well. In fact, there didn't seem to be very much that the Collinses didn't know about the Shaws.

"I wouldn't say that Eileen was saccharine sweet," Dave Collins said, offering me a beer. "She was just very straightforward. If she thought you were stepping on someone, she'd tell you right off. She liked everybody until they gave her a reason not to. Half of my memory of her is her piddling around the kitchen here . . . I remember that when she died, it was like being hit by a two-by-four. She had been worried about going into the hospital again, but nobody expected anything like this. We thought she was doing well at the hospital. Then, out of nowhere, she was dead. It didn't fit. They told us that she had died of her own body fluids, whatever that means. René named the baby Suzanne; she's a big girl now."

I asked Dave Collins if I could call René Shaw, and Marcia got out the number in Big Pine Key. Shaw was home. I didn't quite know how to begin. But in a moment I realized that Shaw was unaware of the investigation in 1966 and unaware that the directors of the hospital in which his wife had died had gone to the prosecutor. As for Mooney, Shaw had never heard of him. Nor, he said, had he ever threatened the hospital with a malpractice suit.

Using the death certificates I had obtained in Trenton, I was soon able to reach relatives of some of the other thirteen patients whose deaths at Riverdell had come to seem suspicious. But like René Shaw, none of these relatives knew that the hospital's Board of Directors had initiated a prosecutorial investigation. And none had been interviewed by Calissi or his staff. Now, in the early fall of 1975, they were stunned and furious. Even disbelieving. They had been jolted by the deaths, and some had been uneasy long after the funerals. But few of the relatives had had substantial reason, in 1966, to challenge the official medical pronouncements. René Shaw had fought with Riverdell to get a copy of his wife's autopsy report, Mrs. Shaw's sister recalled. "It took him months and months but they finally released it and, of course, it wasn't very enlightening. Who knew anything about Calissi?" A relative of another patient remembered that his family doctor had thrown up his hands after the death. "'Sometimes these things happen,' he said. And I accepted that. What else was I to do?"

While I was talking to the families—and taking care not to assert

that anyone had been murdered—I was drawing a bead on the Riverdell affair from the hundreds of pages of documents I had photostated
in Hackensack. From these materials and other sources, I was also
learning a good deal about Bergen County and Riverdell Hospital and
the principals in Calissi's investigation.

In 1969, the year that René Shaw and his children moved south to
join his mother in the Florida Keys, Bergen County's official boosters
took up the theme that "Bergen has the best of everything . . . it's the
best of all possible worlds." At that time, the population explosion that
had so altered the county after the opening of the George Washington
Bridge in 1931 was drawing to a close and Bergen was both looking in-
ward and showing off. The county, 235 square miles that sprawl west-
ward from the Hudson River Palisades opposite Upper Manhattan, the
Bronx, and Westchester, had become the quintessential American suburb. Many of its 900,000 residents might have agreed that it was "the
best of all possible worlds." Murder, violence, serious crime were all
part of what the new immigrants to the county had meant to leave
behind in New York City or in the decaying urban centers of New Jersey—Newark, Paterson, Jersey City, Elizabeth. Bergen's population
had doubled after World War Two, giving it more people than many
states. Pastures, apple orchards and truck farms, and great estates were
plowed under in a rush to lay out tract homes, ranch houses, gardens,
high-rise apartments, schools, sewers, and superhighways. Fields that
once produced luscious Hackensack melons and grainy stalks of celery
encased in black muck now yielded to office buildings, motels, restau-
rants, and massive shopping centers crowned by branches of the fan-
ciest New York department stores. A leading New Jersey banker called
Bergen the "Golden Lake" in the middle of the Boston-to-Washington
megalopolis, and the abundance was reflected in family incomes that,
on the average, were the highest in New Jersey. In terms of purchasing
power, the county planning board proclaimed, "the typical Bergen family can afford the life-style of the middle-class American."
And that was what the average Bergen family was after. Forty percent of the county's population had either been born abroad, in Italy or
Poland or Germany or Russia, or were the children of at least one par-
ent who had been born abroad. In Bergen, they had secured their iden-
tities as middle-class Americans. They were, for the most part, politically conservative, well-educated, white-collar workers. And they were
decidedly white. Blacks accounted for less than 3 percent of the
county's population and, while there were no real slums in Bergen, the
vast majority of the blacks, like many of the county's Jews, were con-

centrated in three or four of Bergen's larger communities. Oradell, the home of Riverdell Hospital, was not one of those communities.

The citizens of Oradell (population 8,600) have not elected a Democrat to local public office in a half century. But there was an occasion in the mid-1960s when some newcomers to Oradell from New York tried to foist a Democrat on the Town Council. Their audacity prompted a statement from Mayor Fred Wendel reminding Oradellians of all that the Republicans had achieved since the town had been incorporated in 1894. And, unfortunately for the Democrats, it was hard to quarrel with Mayor Wendel's assessment. Oradell, the mayor said, was "an outstanding, well-administered residential town, fiscally sound, clean, orderly, with complete municipal services and a respectable tax rate and, above all, with several excellent school systems." It was a model of "commonsense government" and " 'do-for-yourself' Americanism."

Wendel put particular emphasis on the words "order" and "orderly" and "orderly growth," and wisely so. Those were dear words to most Oradellians and had been since the days when the Lenni Lenape Indians cultivated maize and squash in the area. Unlike many of Bergen's seventy, fervently independent communities—all but one of which had fewer than 40,000 residents—Oradell made a concerted effort through zoning and other means to control its expansion, to keep the two-square-mile town "orderly" in character as well as appearance. And it had succeeded. Oradell called itself "the family town," and it was precisely that: a quiet, sober bedroom community for people whose incomes and educations were on the high side, even for Bergen County. A safe community, too. The steady stream of cars that passed through town on the way to and from the shopping malls in Paramus and elsewhere was considered to be the most serious threat to life in Oradell, because no one, or almost no one, died an unnatural death in town unless it was the result of an accident.

Oradell had known only two murders in this century. One was easily solved. The other, which took the life of a thirty-five-year-old realty office employee named Eleanor Saia, still remains a mystery. At 1:30 P.M. on March 14, 1960, an elderly client stopped by the office and found Mrs. Saia seated on a couch, her sweater and brassiere ripped away. He asked her if she needed help, but Mrs. Saia, who had a fractured skull and couldn't speak, merely slumped sideways. The client left. At 2:00 P.M. Mrs. Saia's employer returned from lunch and asked her if she was sick and wanted a piece of chewing gum. When Mrs. Saia didn't reply, the employer phoned the police; she was rushed to Bergen Pines Hospital, a county institution in Paramus, where she soon died. For some reason, the police bypassed the osteopathic hospital that had just opened in Oradell, a mile up the road from the realty office.

Riverdell Hospital might never have been built in Oradell had the veterans been luckier. The Oradell Veterans Memorial Building Association had been full of hope and ambition when, in 1952, it had paid $8,000 for a vacant piece of land on the east side of Kinderkamack Road, at the foot of Soldier Hill Road. The veterans intended to build the meeting place themselves, but by 1954 they had discovered that there weren't many carpenters or masons among them and they were running out of funds, with only a cinderblock foundation having been laid. So several years later, the association sold the property for $26,000 to a group of young osteopathic physicians led by Dr. L. Melvin Elting. Dr. Elting had tried for three years to get a hospital started, but nothing had materialized until the Riverdell venture. At that time there was only one osteopathic hospital in Bergen—the sixteen-bed New Jersey Osteopathic Hospital in Dumont—and, with few exceptions, osteopathic physicians were not accepted on the staffs of the half-dozen major allopathic, or regular "M.D.," hospitals in the county. Although the situation improved in subsequent years, allopathic hospitals, in the 1950s, tended to look upon D.O.'s as cultists who lacked proper medical training and qualifications. Compounding that problem for Dr. Elting, who specialized in surgery, was the fact that his privileges had been removed at the New Jersey Osteopathic Hospital in December 1956, allegedly over a disputed operation. Dr. Elting sued the hospital, charging that his privileges were really taken away because of "professional jealousy" by some staff physicians who wanted to "conduct the hospital in such manner as they saw fit and for their own private gain." But the suit died without adjudication.

Shortly after Riverdell was dedicated in the fall of 1959, a bronze scroll was hung in the lobby as a testament to the "foresight, inspiration, and untiring efforts" of Dr. Elting, who had become the largest stockholder in the proprietary hospital, the president of its board of directors, and the chief—and only—general surgeon at Riverdell. The hospital seemed off to a promising start.

With forty-two rooms—a number that doubled within a few years— the red-brick hospital was built on a split level and was laid out like a flattened T. From the front door, at the foot of the T, a 300-foot corridor stretched to the rear of the hospital. On either side of the corridor were the lobby, the admitting and administrative offices, a laboratory, a cafeteria, the emergency room, a suite of three operating rooms, a small locker room adjacent to the operating suite, and a recovery room. At the top of the T, where this central corridor ended, was the main nursing station. To the left and right of this station were patients' rooms. A second tier of patients' rooms, hidden from the road and known as the hospital's "downstairs" level, was directly underneath. Beyond the parking lot at the rear of the hospital was a border of tall hedges, seldom-used railroad tracks, and the placid Oradell Reservoir.

The hospital's professional staff consisted initially of some thirty-five osteopathic physicians, including specialists, and a dozen M.D.'s who consulted in such fields as urology, orthopedics, and internal medicine. All of the physicians, the hospital's bylaws said, were to be "conscientious and faithful" doctors of "upright character, sound morals, and good reputation." If there was any real distinction between the osteopaths and the regular physicians on the staff, or between Riverdell and any other general hospital of its size, it wasn't readily apparent. Osteopathic medicine had come a long way since the days of its founder, Dr. Andrew T. Still, a Civil War physician who was later called the "Lightning Bonesetter." Most osteopaths continued to believe that manipulation of the body's musculoskeletal system could correct misalignments and contribute to recuperation from many internal ailments. But by the 1960s, most D.O.'s were also using the full diagnostic and therapeutic regimen of other physicians, including X rays and drugs. The education of D.O.'s, in colleges of osteopathic medicine had been vastly upgraded and, in most states, D.O.'s and M.D.'s took the same licensing examination and had the same professional rights and responsibilities. In New Jersey, as elsewhere in the nation, less than 10 percent of the physicians were osteopaths, and most of the D.O.'s, unlike the M.D.'s, were general, or family, practitioners.

Riverdell Hospital, from its beginning, drew its patients from throughout Bergen and neighboring counties. It emphasized, in its brochures, "good patient care" and "friendly well-being." But, in fact, all was not harmonious within the hospital.

In January 1963 the executive committee of the hospital's board of directors removed Dr. Elting from Riverdell's medical staff. The action capped a long series of disagreements between Dr. Elting and other board members, two of whom had been associated with the surgeon in the founding of the hospital. And it led Dr. Elting to sue the other directors—Dr. Jay Sklar, Dr. Irwin Rhine, Dr. Marvin Wisch, Dr. Allan Lans, and Dr. Edwin Frieman—for restoration of his privileges. By November 1963 the suit had been settled out of court. Dr. Elting was paid more than $100,000 for his equity in the hospital, and he left Riverdell. In the papers that were filed in connection with the suit, much was said about the hospital's condition in its infancy. It was evidently a tumultuous period, full of recriminations and suggestions of medical malpractice. As he had in his suit against the hospital in Dumont, Dr. Elting alleged in the Riverdell matter that various of the defendants had conspired against him and plotted his ouster for their own personal gain. He accused some or all of his co-directors of diverting corporate funds through fees and salaries to themselves and of slandering him by implying that he had received kickbacks from the construction of the hospital. He said that he had been illegally voted out as president of the hospital in 1960 and illegally suspended for thirty days in April 1962 for sterilizing a man, supposedly without the required consultation of another doctor. Most of the hospital's medical staff signed affidavits in 1963 supporting the renewal of Dr. Elting's privileges. But the controlling directors wouldn't relent. They denied all of Dr. Elting's accusations and went on to say that the surgeon's leadership had nearly crippled the hospital just when it was getting started.

Dr. Elting, who later helped write a book entitled *The Consumer's Guide to Successful Surgery,* was replaced at Riverdell by Dr. Mario Jascalevich. Dr. Jascalevich was an M.D. recommended to the hospital by a urologist who was acquainted with the surgeon's practice in Hudson County, south of Bergen. At the time Dr. Jascalevich was granted privileges at Riverdell, in late November 1962, he was thirty-five years old—a good-looking man of medium height with an oval face, full mouth, green eyes behind horn-rimmed glasses, and a wide forehead topped by dark brown hair combed straight back. Everything about Dr. Jascalevich seemed impeccable: the refined manners, the suits well fitted to his narrow shoulders, the slim frame, the fastidious surgical style. The operating room was his domain. There, under the lights, he was fast and sure and cool. In May 1963, Dr. Jascalevich became chairman of Riverdell's surgical department, which included a half dozen M.D.'s doing specialized surgery; and for two years he was the hospital's only active general surgeon with full privileges.

In the spring of 1965 a second general surgeon, Dr. Robert Briski, joined the staff. Dr. Briski, who was two years younger than Dr. Jascalevich and who had been on the staff of the Flint (Michigan) General Hospital, was an osteopath. A number of Riverdell's doctors had been lobbying for the appointment of an osteopathic surgeon. But there was another reason for bringing in Dr. Briski. To the concern of some doctors on the staff, the busy chief surgeon was unavailable at times for consultations. Dr. Jascalevich had never opened an office in the Riverdell area. He had kept his home, and a varied medical practice, in West New York, fifteen to twenty miles south of Oradell. What surgery he performed away from Riverdell was down there, in Hudson County hospitals, and especially in Jersey City.

Dr. Briski didn't do well at Riverdell. Some of his patients had difficulties after surgery, some died, and within a year his privileges were restricted to hernia, hemorrhoid, and other minor surgery. But if

Dr. Briski was a disappointment, the hospital was hopeful about the addition of yet another general surgeon to the staff. That was Dr. Stanley Harris.

In the summer of 1965 Stanley Harris and his wife, Rena, drove out to Bayshore, Long Island, to have dinner at the home of Dr. Walter Pinsker, who had been an undergraduate with Harris at the University of Rochester in the early 1950s. Dr. Harris was pleased that another of the dinner guests was Dr. Nathan Wisch, a New York internist who had also been at Rochester. It was a leisurely evening, with the physicians recounting their collegiate escapades and remarking on the careers of some of their former classmates.

Several weeks after that dinner Nathan Wisch received a call from his brother, Marvin, who was a director of Riverdell Hospital. Marvin said the hospital needed a surgeon for a possible appendectomy on an eleven-year-old boy, and Dr. Jascalevich was not available. Could Nathan recommend anyone? Immediately Nathan thought of Stanley Harris. Dr. Harris hurried out to Oradell from the Bronx, performed the operation, and made enough of an impression that he was asked whether he would be interested in joining its staff.

Dr. Harris was surprised by the overture, but the more he thought about it, the more appealing it seemed. He wasn't really very happy in the Bronx, and at thirty-three he was thinking ahead. Stanley Harris had grown up in the Sheepshead Bay and East Flatbush sections of Brooklyn, where his father had an automotive repair shop. He had won a scholarship to the University of Rochester, an academically prestigious private university, and after graduating *summa cum laude* in 1954, had gone on to Yale University Medical School. The medical school did not give grades or determine class standing. But in a letter to Riverdell Hospital in the fall of 1965, Thomas R. Forbes, the school's associate dean, summed up young Harris's performance. "Department reports indicate that his work was of good to excellent caliber," Dr. Forbes wrote. "He showed that he had a fine mind. He was thorough, dependable, interested, and alert. He was awarded a summer fellowship in 1956 for research in pharmacology, and in 1957 he received the Perkins Prize for the excellence of his work in the preclinical period. I knew Harris well and I am glad to testify to his maturity, balance, perseverance, determination, and resourcefulness. He is a pleasant, well-adjusted person."

Dr. Harris did his surgical internship and residency at the Bronx Municipal Hospital Center from 1958 to 1964. Affiliated with Jacobi Hospital and the Albert Einstein College of Medicine—Dr. Harris would later hang a huge portrait of the physicist on his living room wall—the 2,000-bed center was one of the largest and best of the city's medical complexes and teaching institutions. In 1961–62, Dr. Harris developed a subspecialty in vascular surgery, aided by a research grant from the American Heart Association and the U. S. Public Health Service. Dr. Harris's chief of surgery, Dr. David State, remembered Dr. Harris as having "average ability among the senior residents" at Bronx Municipal. "Of course you would never have gotten through if you couldn't operate well. Harris was a very bright young man but a bit laconic; an introspective type of person who was somewhat off the beaten path in that he was inclined to have strong opinions that he didn't give up easily. He had a tendency not to go along, and at times he was right." After his residency, the thin, black-haired surgeon and his new wife, who was also a New Yorker, took a cross-country trip to California. In Los Angeles a physician friend suggested that Dr. Harris consider establishing his practice out there. But while the Harrises liked the West, neither Stanley nor Rena wanted to be so far from their parents, and they returned to New York.

In 1965 Dr. Harris was certified by the American Board of Surgery and joined the staffs of Bronx Municipal, the Hospital for Joint Diseases, Fordham Hospital, and a number of smaller institutions, mostly in the Bronx. And he became a clinical instructor in surgery at Albert Einstein. But he soon discovered that relatively few young physicians, who might have referred surgical cases to him, were setting up practices in the Bronx and that the older doctors were inclined to send patients to surgeons of their own generation. He was beginning to feel that a long-term commitment there was not in his professional interest and not in the interest of his family. So the Riverdell invitation, when it was tendered by the board of directors in early 1966, looked good to Dr. Harris. It was a chance to be "a big fish in a little pond," he told himself. He would keep his house in Bronxville temporarily and continue to practice in the Bronx. And he would see how things went in Oradell where, coincidentally, his sister lived.

At first Dr. Harris thought that Dr. Jascalevich did not want him to come to Riverdell. But when the two met, Dr. Harris mentioned to Prosecutor Calissi the following November, Dr. Jascalevich "spoke pretty gently and kindly, spoke in terms of the fact that there was a lot of surgery there and that maybe one day we could entertain a partnership type of arrangement." Dr. Harris asked the chief surgeon whether he would be interested in sharing office space near Riverdell, as a starter. But Dr. Jascalevich said no, and the matter was dropped.

Harris was confident of his surgical skills and eager to demonstrate them to new patients and new colleagues. His first opportunity at Riverdell came on Saturday, March 19, 1966, when he was asked to operate on four-year-old Nancy Savino.

3

The lives of Michael and Martha Savino had barely stabilized when, on October 27, 1961, their daughter Nancy was born. Martha Savino, though only eighteen, was already a divorcée with a two-year-old son. Mickey Savino, who was twenty-seven, had spent five years in the Navy after graduating from high school and was just getting his bearings in a job with the New York Telephone Company.

In October 1963, the growing family had moved to Bergen County to a stucco house on North Vivyen Street in Bergenfield. North Vivyen was a quiet side street arched by shade trees. Nearby was a sprawling public field with a baseball diamond and wooded groves for picnicking and foraging. Nancy and her parents spent much time in this park, but Nancy's life revolved around her house. There, and in the little backyard with its white picket fence and climbing tea roses, Nancy Savino played out her life. Teasing the family's shepherd. Lining the top of her blue and white baby carriage with pebbles. Rocking her dolls in the pink plastic cradle that had been given her by Mickey's aunt on her fourth birthday, when Nancy dressed up in a red velvet outfit and cardboard tiara with silver sprinkles. For hours she would swing in the backyard, brushing against the branches of the small pear tree and singing "Jesus Loves Me." It was a song she had learned in Bible school, and it was her favorite. She often invoked Jesus. "Jesus wouldn't like that," she would say to neighboring children. "You better not fight."

Except for a tonsillectomy in December 1965, Nancy had never been hospitalized. But when she woke up on the morning of March 19, 1966, she wasn't feeling well.

"Mommy, my tummy hurts," she said as she came into the kitchen, where Mrs. Savino was fixing breakfast. Mickey had already gone to work.

"Well you sit down there and we'll see how you feel soon," Mrs. Savino said. "You don't have to eat any breakfast." Martha was worried. Nancy had complained off and on for a month that her stomach was bothering her. Later that morning Nancy again said she didn't feel well, and Mrs. Savino took her temperature. It was over 100. With that, Martha called Allan Lans, an osteopath who was a director of Riverdell Hospital. "Bring her down," Dr. Lans said, so Martha asked a neighbor to watch her two other children and she and Nancy drove over to Dr. Lans's office, across from the Bergenfield High School.

Martha liked Dr. Lans. When she and Mickey had moved into town it was hard getting a doctor to make house calls. But Dr. Lans, who was just getting his practice started, had come, even in bad weather. At first Martha didn't realize that Dr. Lans was an osteopath, not an M.D. When she heard about that, however, she had asked around about osteopathy. While some people said that D.O.'s were no good, others said osteopaths knew even more about treating because they had to know not only what "regular doctors" knew but also "what every bone in your body was like." Why, even Nelson Rockefeller's physician was an osteopath! Martha was satisfied. Dr. Lans, she thought, was "firm but he was gentle and informal."

Nancy was feverish and nauseous when Dr. Lans examined her on March 19, and the physician thought she might be suffering from acute appendicitis. He told Martha to take Nancy over to Riverdell for observation. He would contact Stanley Harris, a new surgeon on the staff whom he wanted to try. That afternoon, Nancy continued to have crampy abdominal pain, and by evening Dr. Harris had agreed with Dr. Lans's diagnosis and decided to operate. The surgery lasted an hour and a half, but the problem was not acute appendicitis. Mesenteric cysts that Nancy had been born with had grown larger and were affecting the small intestine. One cyst had ruptured. Dr. Harris removed the portion of the ileum where the cysts were located and sutured together the edges. He also did an appendectomy, a common practice at that time during abdominal surgery.

A little after 10 P.M., Nancy was wheeled into Room 211, a private room at the end of the short hallway off the main corridor. She was wan and unconscious, but by midnight her color had returned and she was awake periodically. Her parents, who had been at the hospital throughout the evening, went home. From 11 P.M. to 7 A.M. Irving Hall, a special duty nurse, watched over the child. Nancy slept much of the night; now and then she would awaken and cry and say that her belly and throat hurt. She also wanted to "go home to my own bed." At 3 A.M. Dr. Harris came in from the Bronx and reinserted Nancy's intravenous feeding tube, which had come loose. On Sunday, March 20, Mrs. Savino stopped in Oradell to buy some yellow mums, and a coloring book and crayons for Nancy. She arrived at the hospital between 11 A.M. and noon, and was followed by her husband. Nancy was uncomfortable with the suction tube in her nose, but Mrs. Savino remembered that her daughter was "doing marvelously, coloring and making cutouts. She asked me if her little friends knew that she was in the hospital and I told her they were all fixing up cards and I would bring them over." Around 9 or 10 P.M., Dr. Harris looked in on his patient. At 11 P.M. Irving Hall returned for his second nightly shift. Nancy's vital signs were recorded at midnight and were within normal limits. The child had a "restful night," except for interludes of crying, Hall noted on the chart. But at 6 A.M. Nancy reminded the special duty nurse that she wanted to go home. She was "homesick for mommy."

Hall ended his night tour around 7 A.M. on March 21. During the next hour Irene Price, a morning nurse, observed from the hallway that Nancy appeared to be sleeping. Around 8 A.M. Barbara Spadaro, a twenty-three-year-old laboratory technician, stopped by Room 211 to draw blood from Nancy, a routine postoperative procedure to ascertain whether the blood fluids are normal. As she prepared to take the sample, Miss Spadaro noticed the patient was very still. "Wake up," she said, but Nancy didn't move. The technician ran for the door, looking for help.

Miss Price, who was about twenty feet away, raced down the corridor to Room 211, followed by Irene Nelson, a senior nurse. Mrs. Nelson tried to get a pulse and then massaged Nancy's heart. The first physician on the scene was Dr. Jorge Ortega, an intern. Dr. Ortega was unable to revive the child and neither was Dr. Jascalevich when he arrived moments later. In tears Dr. Ortega handed Dr. Jascalevich a stethoscope, and the surgeon applied it to Nancy's chest. At 8:15 A.M. on March 21, 1966, according to her chart, Nancy Savino was pronounced dead.

Martha Savino was just leaving to visit Nancy when the phone rang.

"Martha, this is Allan Lans. You'd better come right over to the hospital. The baby has taken a turn for the worse."

Mrs. Savino feared instantly that her daughter was dead. "It was instinct, mother's instinct," she said later. "I ran out of the house. My mother-in-law was there, and I left her with the children and ran out of the house and jumped into the car. I must have hit 100 on the way over there. I ran in the front entrance and down that corridor that led to Nancy's room on the main floor. Dr. Lans was there, and he and another doctor caught me; they grabbed me on either side. I remember looking past them, down the hall to the closed door. That's when they took me into one of those small rooms. I was hysterical. 'She's dead, isn't she?' I said. And they said 'Yes, yes, she's dead.' I don't know how long I was in that room, but I said I wanted to see her. They said I could as soon as I quieted down. Then they took me in there and I saw my Nancy and I threw myself over her, telling her to wake up. She looked like she was just sleeping. I begged her to wake up. I kept saying to myself that she couldn't be dead. Not my little girl. And that's all I remember. When I woke up, I was in another room there."

The autopsy on Nancy Savino found that "an anatomical, pathological cause of death is not evident . . . The postoperative course was so smooth that there was no warning and no reason to anticipate the sudden death . . . A definite diagnosis is thus not made and [it] remains a sudden, unexpected death, cause undetermined, possibly due to an unexplained physiologic catastrophe."

The death of Nancy Savino was a profound shock to Dr. Harris and Dr. Lans, who didn't know what to put on her death certificate. "People die from something; they don't die from no cause, not this little baby," Dr. Lans later told Calissi. But none of the Riverdell doctors harbored any suspicions of foul play in March 1966 or even a month later, when Margaret Pearson Henderson died at the hospital. Miss Henderson, a twenty-six-year-old factory machine operator, was admitted to Riverdell at 5:05 A.M. on April 22, 1966. For weeks she had been complaining to her gynecologist, Dr. Robert M. Livingston, of pain in her lower abdomen. The pain passed with treatment but recurred severely on April 21. Early the next morning Dr. Livingston, a thirty-one-year-old graduate of Harvard College and Yale Medical School, admitted her to Riverdell, where he had just obtained staff privileges.

Around 8 A.M. on April 22, Miss Henderson was examined—at Dr. Livingston's request—by Dr. Jascalevich, who recommended that more tests be done before any exploratory operation. But Dr. Livingston wasn't satisfied, and late that afternoon, he asked Stanley Harris to assist him in doing an exploratory pelvic laparotomy on Miss Henderson. The patient's abdomen was opened, but as Dr. Harris eventually told Calissi: "We found nothing on this girl. We merely opened her and closed her because her pelvic organs were normal . . . She was not in any difficulty during the surgery. She was alert postoperatively."

Miss Henderston had a "fairly comfortable night" on April 22–23, her chart said, but she was "tense and apprehensive." Around 7:30 A.M. on April 23, the young woman was bathed in her room by Irene

Price, the morning nurse. Miss Price left the room and at 8 A.M., according to the chart, Dr. Jascalevich came in and started an intravenous solution of glucose and water. The surgeon also called Dr. Livingston and told him to come down to the hospital; his patient wasn't well. Sometime in the next half hour, Miss Henderson apparently complained of an inability to swallow and of pain in her legs and chest. By the time Dr. Livingston reached the hospital Margaret Henderson was dead.

Dr. Frieman later told Calissi that Dr. Vincent Gillson, who had performed the autopsy on Nancy Savino, had phoned him right after the Henderson death and said, " 'Doctor, this is the second death you have had in the hospital that seems unexplained and unwarranted—not unwarranted—but it seemed odd.'

"I said, 'Dr. Gillson, I feel exactly like you do. We have requested and gotten permission for autopsies on both of these patients. You are the pathologist; you tell me. If you have any indications of any problems or any way in which these can be prevented . . . Then he called me back. 'Well, Dr. Frieman, we found this woman had a fatty liver.' I remember I said on the phone, 'Well, Dr. Gillson, she died awfully fast for a liver death.' He said, 'Well, this can happen.' So me being a general practitioner and he being a certified pathologist, certainly it's not my position to start arguing with Dr. Gillson as to why his [Livingston's] patient died. Certainly, as long as he was satisfied fully, I felt that there was no reason for me not to be satisfied."

But by November 1966, when he was recounting this conversation to Calissi, Dr. Frieman had had second thoughts.

"I felt a necrotic liver would have—this patient would have been jaundiced. Why the sudden demise within a half hour? She didn't develop this necrotic liver overnight," Dr. Frieman told the prosecutor, "and I felt this was not a liver death."

Dr. Harris was skeptical, too. He was asked by Calissi whether liver necrosis could have been proven by the tissue slides that were viewed under a microscope after the "gross" physical—or naked eye—examination of Miss Henderson's corpse.

"Yes, I think so," Dr. Harris replied. "If she did indeed have liver necrosis, we should have slides to prove it. I was at the postmortem. Dr. Gillson was impressed, grossly, that this was a soft necrotic liver. I can't feel that strongly about it and I would like to see the slides. I never did see the histology on it."

Dr. Livingston didn't see the report on his patient's tissue slides either. It was ultimately prepared by Dr. Donald E. Brown of Hackensack Hospital, a histologist who was working part-time for the Bergen County medical examiner's office. Having studied tissue from Miss

Henderson's liver—as well as from her heart, lungs, kidneys, brain, internal genitalia, and other organs—Dr. Brown concluded that "there is nothing in the microscopic findings which is clearly indicative of the cause of death."

In the late spring and early summer of 1966, Dr. Briski and Dr. Harris lost several elderly patients postoperatively. But those patients had been very sick and had undergone extensive surgery, and none of their deaths was as surprising as that of Frank Biggs.

Biggs was fifty-nine years old when he died on August 28. He had been born in England and orphaned in Canada, and had come to the United States as a teenager with the help of a Pennsylvania judge whom he met while bellhopping at a summer resort in Ontario. Frank had studied for a while at the Carnegie Institute of Technology in Pittsburgh before taking a series of jobs that landed him, in the 1930s, at National Distillers in New York. He worked for the company for the next thirty years, as an auditor/accountant.

"Frank," a relative summed up, "was a God-fearing, good-living, honorable family man. A hard worker all his life." Margaret Biggs's health, a constant worry to her husband, was more a problem than Frank's. But in 1964 Biggs, who had maturity-onset diabetes, developed a peptic ulcer and was put on a liquid diet. On August 20, 1966, after two brief hospitalizations that did not require surgery, he entered Riverdell for a subtotal gastrectomy—removal of part of the stomach—to relieve the ulcer. Preoperatively, a radiologist recorded, Biggs showed "no gross evidence of recent cardiac or pulmonary disease." The surgery was performed by Dr. Briski on August 23, 1966, and for five days Biggs appeared to be recovering. At 8 P.M. on Sunday, August 28, a nurse noted that the patient was sitting in a chair in his room, his "color very good." An intravenous infusion was running "well and slowly." "Patient states that he feels very good—no pains. Evening care given." The next entry was at 9:10 P.M.: "Patient suddenly became cyanotic—difficulty in breathing."

"All of a sudden, at 9:10, the patient suddenly became cyanotic," Dr. Frieman said to Calissi four months later. "Well, cyanosis is certainly a lack of oxygen in the blood, which shows that . . . there is a difficulty in the respiratory process."

"Do people get bluish?" the prosecutor asked.

"Yes, blue; not getting any oxygen, difficulty in breathing is noted on the chart. Dr. Ortega saw the patient immediately, and help was requested from Dr. Jascalevich, who happened to be in the hospital at this odd hour for him, because I know Dr. Jascalevich's habits, and I don't say he shouldn't have been there, but this is not the usual time for Dr. Jascalevich to be there, at 9:10 at night. It says: 'Help requested from Dr. Jascalevich. Coramine, 4 cc'—which is a respiratory stimulant; the only reason this is used is to combat respiratory problems—'was given intravenously. Adrenalin given by Dr. Jascalevich, external cardiac massage.' And within twenty minutes the patient was pronounced dead. They started at 9:10, and at 9:30 the patient was dead."

At Biggs's autopsy, no anatomic cause of death was found. The pathologist attributed his death to "ventricular fibrillation"—an excessively rapid heartbeat possibly caused by what the pathologist took to be a large amount of urine in the dead man's bladder.

Dr. Jascalevich was out of the country in early September 1966. "During that time," Dr. Harris later remarked to Calissi, "I had no troubles." However, when Dr. Jascalevich returned to Riverdell, ". . . a few days after, this lady patient, Mrs. Arzt, died. I remember mentioning to my wife that while Dr. Jascalevich was away I had no troubles, but as soon as he came back, I was in trouble again . . . But I said it off the top of my head, you know, without really thinking about it."

At seventy, Emma Arzt was a happy, and a happy-go-lucky, woman. The retired librarian loved parties, perfume, dancing, social clubs, stray animals, and her independence. She didn't like hospitals. And apart from having her appendix taken out in 1921 and a polyp on her cervix removed three decades later, she had managed to avoid the operating table. But in 1966 Mrs. Arzt, who was under treatment for hypertension and whose weight had dropped from 142 to 110 in two years, was examined and found to have a gallbladder "chock full of stones." Her daughters implored her to have an operation. Mrs. Arzt resisted until a relative who had been in and out of many hospitals assured her that Riverdell was like "an exclusive hotel where they give you shrimp salad and homemade lemon meringue pie." Mrs. Arzt entered Riverdell on September 18, 1966. On September 22, Dr. Harris removed her diseased gallbladder. True to his patient's instructions, he saved the "stones" for her. The nurse's notes that night said that Mrs. Arzt was "resting quietly. Dressing dry and intact. Color good." Mrs. Arzt seemed at peace. Her daughters visited her and she told them that not having a will, she had left a letter in a desk drawer at home. "Now you can rip it up," she said. Around 7 A.M. the next morning, Mrs. Arzt was examined by an intern and her reddened surgical dressing was reinforced. Dr. Harris changed the bandage around 9:45 A.M. Some twenty minutes later Mrs. Arzt became cyanotic and stopped breathing. Alarms brought several doctors, including Dr. Jascalevich, and the patient's breathing was restored. But at 2 P.M. Mrs. Arzt broke into a profuse sweat. Ten minutes later she was dead.

Mrs. Arzt was not autopsied. Although an electrocardiogram taken after her initial respiratory arrest showed no evidence of a heart attack, she was signed out by her personal physician as having died of "acute circulatory failure due to coronary thrombosis, with myocardial infarction."

4

Shortly after the death of Mrs. Arzt, Dr. Jascalevich was called before Riverdell's Medical Practice Committee, which was concerned with the surgeon's availability to referring physicians. Dr. Jascalevich said he would try to make himself more accessible for quick consultations. But he explained that much of the problem could be remedied by "educating" other doctors to understand that a surgeon could not always appear on a moment's notice; it was physically impossible. The doctors, he said, should learn not to make promises to patients and their relatives that could not be fulfilled.

Dr. Jascalevich also approached Dr. Harris during this period with a proposal for a partnership. Preliminarily Dr. Harris would take first call for emergencies and Dr. Jascalevich would take second. Dr. Harris was not impressed with the offer and asked for time to think it over. But on October 3 Dr. Jascalevich issued a memorandum at Riverdell announcing the imminent formation of a "United Surgical Service" between himself and Dr. Harris. On October 7 Dr. Harris put out a notice countermanding the memorandum and told Dr. Jascalevich that there would be no partnership.

The partnership affair dismayed Dr. Harris. But not nearly so much as the fact that he was losing more patients postoperatively. On October 5 and October 14 there were two elderly patients with abdominal conditions. And then there was Eileen Shaw on October 23. With the death of this woman, who had given birth two days earlier, Stanley Harris reached the breaking point.

Driving back to the Bronx after Mrs. Shaw's autopsy on October 24, Dr. Harris later said he thought not only of the deaths of his own patients but of the deaths of Dr. Briski's as well. He recalled that Dr. Jascalevich had once said to him that "all of Dr. Briski's patients have turned to death." The phrasing had seemed eerie to Dr. Harris at the time; now it terrified him. He could hear, ringing in his mind, the calls he had gotten from the hospital—"Dr. Harris, your patient is not doing well; Dr. Jascalevich is attending your patient." Dr. Harris thought, too, of Pasquale Benvenuto.

Benvenuto had come into Riverdell a week earlier for an elective hernia operation. Dr. Harris had done the surgery and it had gone well. As a matter of fact, when the seventy-four-year-old patient was in the recovery room, his personal physician had phoned Mrs. Benvenuto and said, "Mamma, speak to Papa." Benvenuto told his wife that he was doing fine. Not long after he was returned to his room, Benvenuto suffered a respiratory arrest and Dr. Arthur DeMarco, Riverdell's chief anesthesiologist, came to his aid. Dr. Harris hurried over to Riverdell and examined Benvenuto. The surgeon was surprised that afternoon to hear that before the breathing failure Dr. Jascalevich had been in Benvenuto's room and that he had subsequently called the hospital, asking after the patient. Now, on October 24, it began to add up to Stanley Harris.

From his office Dr. Harris called Luther Markley, who had just done the Shaw autopsy. "Dr. Markley, I suspect something," he said. "I think we should get a toxicology on Shaw's tissues."

That week Stanley Harris also made a decision to confide in Allan Lans. Dr. Lans had been Nancy Savino's physician, and the surgeon figured that Dr. Lans would hear him out. Dr. Lans was indeed receptive when Dr. Harris called, primarily because he himself had recently become uneasy about many of the hospital's postsurgical deaths. "I had vague ideas in my head that something, you know, that something just wasn't sitting right with these cases," Dr. Lans later explained to Calissi. "But I couldn't formulate it until the day that Mrs. Shaw died and Dr. Jascalevich called me, saying that he had gotten a call from an attorney [named Mooney]. At that point I felt, you know, that there must be something that is potentially very seriously wrong with these cases, that they are being interfered with."

Reviewing some of the mortalities together, Dr. Harris and Dr. Lans noticed what they felt were several common elements. All the patients who died had had an intravenous tube running, which could have facilitated a quick, and perhaps unseen, injection of poison into the veins. A number of the deaths had taken place around the same time—8 A.M. —and were sudden and wholly unexpected. Respiratory arrests stood out.

At Harris's request, he met with Riverdell's board of directors on

October 25 at the home of one of them, Dr. Jay Sklar. Most of the five directors were astounded by Dr. Harris's presentation. The directors knew that the hospital's postsurgical mortality rate had soared in the last year, but of course none of them, with the possible exception of Dr. Lans, had imagined the worst. Dr. Harris himself realized that all he had were "suspicions, with no proof." And at that meeting, at least one of the directors—Edwin Frieman—considered the suspicions tenuous. Despite his concern about the Savino and Henderson deaths, Dr. Frieman felt that "emotionalism was replacing rationalism."

"Until you boys come up with some more facts," he said, "I'm going bowling. Don't bother me." But when Dr. Harris came back later that week with more information, the directors decided to study the patients' charts and to keep a close watch on Dr. Jascalevich until they could see him the following Monday night, October 31.

On Friday, October 28, the directors met for lunch. At that stage, according to Dr. Frieman, the board members decided that "we just must stay calm; and unless we have more facts—just [practice] so-called diligent neglect. We were in no way going to act, and in no way going to endanger any patients, ourselves, or the hospital."

Dr. Harris wasn't satisfied with the directors' reaction—things, he later said, were "getting too crazy and tough." At one of the meetings, Dr. Harris and the directors had talked about the possibility that the patients had been killed with succinylcholine chloride, a muscle relaxant that Dr. Carl Coppolino, a New Jersey anesthesiologist, was then being accused of using to murder his wife. Dr. Harris knew that a drug like that could cause fatal respiratory arrests. The surgeon also wondered if Dr. Jascalevich kept anything special in his metal box of surgical instruments or in his locker at Riverdell. Dr. Harris himself had never taken a locker at the hospital, but he often passed through the small, L-shaped locker room on his way to and from the operating room suite.

On the afternoon of October 31, 1966, the young surgeon asked the operating room supervisor to assign him a locker. As she ran down the list, Dr. Harris leaned over and observed that locker number four belonged to Dr. Jascalevich. He memorized the locker's combination. Except for a cleaning woman who soon finished up, the pale green locker room was empty. Quickly Dr. Harris opened locker number four. The inside of the crowded, foot-square locker was a mess. Dr. Harris picked up one of the empty vials that were lying about and read its label. Then he shuddered.

Dr. Harris closed the locker and hurried out of the room. From a pay phone in the hospital he called Allan Lans. Having found vials of curare and a large syringe containing fluid, Stanley Harris was more convinced than ever that his patients' deaths "were actually performed by Dr. Jascalevich." Dr. Lans was dumbstruck to hear about the curare. He took down the combination to Dr. Jascalevich's locker and called Edwin Frieman. "Eddie, please go and see this. I'll meet you at the hospital."

Dr. Lans had planned to look into Dr. Jascalevich's locker with Dr. Harris. Now he thought it was foolish of Harris to have gone ahead on his own. But driving over to Riverdell, Dr. Lans contemplated the incidents in recent days that had made Harris feel he was going to be discredited by the chief surgeon. For one thing, Dr. Jascalevich had told Dr. Lans that he had gone to see Dr. Harris's chief of service at Jacobi Hospital to check on the younger surgeon's mortality rate there. Dr. Lans mentioned this to Dr. Harris and the latter called his chief of service. He was out of town, but his secretary said that she had never heard of Dr. Jascalevich. On another occasion that week, Dr. Jascalevich told Lans that Dr. Harris had operated on a man at Riverdell and had left a sponge in the body, which was subsequently removed by a Dr. Weiss at Holy Name Hospital in Teaneck. Dr. Lans passed this on to Dr. Harris, who called Holy Name Hospital. Dr. Weiss didn't know what he was talking about, Dr. Harris told Lans and, later, Calissi.

Dr. Frieman was waiting when Dr. Lans got to Riverdell around 5 P.M. on October 31. "Do you want to talk to Harris?" Dr. Lans asked.

"No, I don't want to speak to anybody. If you found it, it's true, and we will see."

In the locker room Dr. Lans put down his Polaroid camera and fumbled with the combination to locker number four, missing on the first try. Around again, and the locker opened. The two physicians peered in, aghast at the clutter and the vials of curare and the loaded syringe.

Dr. Frieman caught his breath. "I'm amazed. I don't know what to tell you. I can't say anything. I can't talk."

Frightened, Dr. Lans asked what they should do.

"The first thing you better do, you have to have every board member see this to believe it," Dr. Frieman said. "It is just inconceivable to me to find all this stuff in the locker."

Neither Dr. Lans nor Dr. Frieman wanted to touch anything or leave any trace of their having been in the locker. But they wanted some proof of what they had seen. "If they empty this locker," Dr. Frieman said, "I have to be sure that I've got something so that I know what I saw." From the emergency room Dr. Frieman got a sterile ring forceps. Carefully he removed a vial of the curare from the locker and placed it in a clean white envelope. The envelope was sealed and initialed by him and Dr. Lans. Meanwhile Dr. Lans took some color snapshots of the locker's interior.

The directors canceled the meeting they had scheduled with Dr. Jascalevich that evening to discuss the hospital's mortalities. Instead they gathered at the home of Elliott Wiener, Riverdell's administrator, at about 10 P.M., and Dr. Lans and Dr. Frieman recounted what they, and Dr. Harris, had seen earlier in the day. Shortly before midnight Wiener and the hospital's five directors went over to Riverdell, and again the locker was opened. The administrator took a few photographs with a 35-millimeter camera—Dr. Lans's pictures were only a blur.

"I remember I was going to the forceps again . . . ," Dr. Frieman later told Calissi, "and Dr. Wisch said, 'Don't touch anything, please don't touch anything.' I said, 'All right.' And the lock was put on, and we left."

Not only were the directors alarmed at what they had found, they were also worried about having entered the locker "improperly." And were concerned about what would happen when Dr. Jascalevich next opened it. "We didn't know whether he might try to remove the contents of the locker or maybe he would say, 'What's this doing here?' and not recognize it at all," Dr. Lans explained later. So a plan was devised on the night of October 31. Dr. Jascalevich was scheduled to do a vein stripping with Dr. Lans at 8 A.M. the next morning. Dr. Lans would get to the hospital early and station himself in the locker room when the chief surgeon came in.

Dr. Lans was talking to Dr. DeMarco, the anesthesiologist, when Dr. Jascalevich arrived on the morning of November 1, 1966.

"We were talking, just a natural conversation that we would have any day," Dr. Lans recalled. "Dr. Jascalevich came in. He opened his locker, he stood in front of it . . . Then he stepped aside from the locker for a moment to get something out of a jacket pocket that was hanging on a rack right next to it . . . He made some motions in and out of the locker . . . He closed the door of his locker, as he stepped away from it, but he didn't lock it. He went about the process of changing his clothes. He went back into his locker again, with whatever he was putting in and out. Then," Dr. Lans said, "he closed the locker and we went on into surgery."

Within hours, the five directors of Riverdell Hospital were in Calissi's office. Calissi and Fred Galda were long-time partners, if only part-time prosecutors—bound together by Bergen County's Democratic politics. As Calissi's deputy, Galda had investigated all the half-dozen murders in the county between 1954 and 1966. But what the Riverdell doctors had come to talk about on November 1 of that year was unlike anything either Galda or his boss had ever heard. As soon as the doctors left, Calissi applied for a search warrant. The statutes he cited referred to "murder . . . by means of poison." At 4:30 P.M. Calissi, Galda, and two detectives descended on Riverdell and seized the seventy-one items in Dr. Jascalevich's locker number four. The contents included syringes (some with needles attached), sponges, a copy of Riverdell's rules and regulations, surgical instruments, a shoehorn, a pint bottle of mineral oil and a bottle of silver nitrate, a blue mask, a catheter, a chrome oval holder for personal cards, a roll of toilet tissue, and seven pennies. There were also eighteen vials of curare, each of which had held 10 cc. Now most of them contained only "slight fluid."

That day Calissi also summoned Dr. Lawrence Denson to his office. Although he was an internist rather than a pathologist, Dr. Denson was a part-time assistant medical examiner of Bergen County, charged with determining causes of death in cases of suspicious or unnatural circumstances. The medical examiner's office was then headed by septuagenarian Dr. Raphael Gilady. But Calissi felt that Gilady might no longer have the stamina to handle difficult, protracted cases. Dr. Denson knew very little about Riverdell Hospital, and he was personally familiar with only one of the thirteen deaths the hospital's directors were concerned about. What he had heard of Riverdell, some rumors about "goof-ups" there, had left him with an unfavorable impression of the place. But he couldn't understand why a surgeon would have eighteen vials of curare in a dressing room locker. The more he thought about it all, the more his head throbbed. He walked out to Mrs. Rowland's desk. "If you have any aspirins," he said, "I'll take three."

Early on, Calissi wanted to know why Dr. Jascalevich, or any physician, would murder hospital patients. The prosecutor was himself a director of Valley Hospital in Ridgewood, New Jersey, and he thought he knew a thing or two about doctors and about "professional" people.

"Could you give me or any of us any idea why you feel or think or infer that Dr. Jascalevich would, as you put it, perform these deaths?" the prosecutor asked Dr. Harris on November 3.

"Well, I can't look into his mind," the surgeon replied.

"I'm not asking you to do that."

"I really don't know his basic motive for doing this; but certainly looking at the total picture, I would think that he just didn't want anybody else in that hospital doing surgery except himself." Harris also speculated that "things were getting too much" for Dr. Jascalevich and that perhaps that was the motive behind the partnership proposal. He said, too, that he thought Dr. Jascalevich's interest in Riverdell was waning.

The contradictions disturbed Calissi. How could Dr. Jascalevich be uninterested in practicing at Riverdell and still object to competition there? If he did not want to perform surgery at Riverdell, why would he propose a partnership arrangement that would have continued to tie him to the hospital? And, most peculiarly, what possible motive could he have to kill the patients of the very doctor to whom he had offered the association?

Dr. Frieman told the prosecutor that the Riverdell directors had speculated on two possible motives for the murders—if that was what they were. "There sometimes can be an emotional or psychotic drive that can cause people to do this type of thing, as in any other crime," Dr. Frieman said. "There was also—and, again, I am not accusing or making any implication, but it was honestly discussed there was a financial motive involved here, too. We are dealing in $60,000 or $70,000 worth of surgery. We are talking about big money here, and this was an implication."

"I don't understand that," Calissi said.

"Well, if there are two surgeons dividing $60,000 . . . your net at the end of the year is a little different. But there was the counter, as I pointed out to the board. . . . Dr. Jascalevich told us the day he came into the hospital that he wasn't going to do any sections; he didn't want to do sections, cesarian sections. He said he couldn't do them. Be practical. Where is the logic? Mrs. Shaw is a section. Why is he going to mess around with a section? Of all cases I found it hard to believe. I'll tell you the truth: I still find it hard."

Calissi also put the "motive" question to Dr. Lans.

"The only answer that one can possibly come up with," Dr. Lans said, "is that . . . this is not the product of a sane man . . . there is no sane reason for it."

"All right. Did you make any observations concerning Mr.—I should say Dr.—Jascalevich which would in any way indicate the presence of any such idiosyncrasies or aberrations?" Calissi asked.

Before Dr. Lans could answer, Robert Dilts, an assistant prosecutor, cut in. "From your association and contact with him have you observed anything about him that would lead you to believe that he is off his rocker?"

"No, no," Dr. Lans responded.

"Do you know," asked Calissi, "of any of Dr. Jascalevich's patients who died after an operation, over the past year at Riverdell?"

"No, I don't."

"He has a pretty good record, has he not?"

Dr. Lans had long thought that Dr. Jascalevich was "a bit distant, a bit cold" . . . not the kind of "personality that lends itself to a friendly cup of coffee, or a joke, or the usual intercourse that goes on between doctors at the hospital or people anywhere." But Dr. Jascalevich had operated on Dr. Lans's wife, Joan, and the osteopath had nothing but admiration for the chief surgeon's skill.

"He has an excellent record, sir," Dr. Lans said. "He's brilliant. There's no question about it."

"Dr. Jascalevich's patients never die—it's only the other doctors'," Dr. Harris had observed. But it struck me in 1975, as I went through the old records, that while Dr. Jascalevich had not operated in 1965 or 1966 on any of the patients whose deaths came to be regarded as suspicious, he was, in fact, scheduled to perform surgery on one of them. Among the thirteen, this death was the only one to occur preoperatively, I noted, and the only one to occur before 1966. And in some ways, I felt, this was the most unusual of the deaths.

The patient was Carl Rohrbeck, a retired New York public works employee who entered Riverdell on December 12, 1965, on his seventy-third birthday, for repair of a ventral hernia. Rohrbeck had been operated on twice previously at Riverdell. In March 1961 he had had a ganglion of the wrist excised by Dr. Elting. In November 1964, according to Dr. Frieman, his gallbladder was removed by Dr. Jascalevich, who also inserted a T-shaped tube in the common duct to facilitate drainage from the liver to the intestine. It was a four-hour procedure, but the patient apparently took it well.

Rohrbeck's scheduled hernia repair was "elective" surgery. The operation had been set by Dr. Jascalevich for December 13, and at 6 P.M. on December 12, Rohrbeck was given the customary presurgical examination by the anesthesiologist, Dr. DeMarco. Dr. DeMarco found Rohrbeck's blood pressure, temperature, pulse, respiration, and lungs essentially normal. The patient, he noted on the chart, had no cardiac history and his heart appeared fit, with normal sinus rhythm and no murmurs. At 7 A.M. on December 13, Rohrbeck, who had no history of drug allergies, was given Demerol and atropine in preparation for an 8 A.M. operation. Around 7:30 A.M., however, Dr. Jascalevich visited the patient and canceled the surgery. Then or later—it always remained unclear—he wrote on the chart that "I decided cancellation of surgery on this particular case on the basis of minimal clinical signs of heart failure that I [would] like to have further evaluated before proceeding with [the] operation."

From Rohrbeck's room, Dr. Jascalevich went to the doctors' locker room, where he met Jay Sklar, who was Rohrbeck's personal physician. Dr. Sklar was getting ready for the operation, and he was jarred when the department chairman informed him that surgery had been put off.

According to the account Dr. Sklar gave Calissi, Dr. Jascalevich told him that he had a "premonition" about operating on Rohrbeck that morning and "didn't think he should go ahead."

"Well . . . you just don't cancel a case fifteen minutes before it is to be done," Dr. Sklar remembered saying to the chief surgeon. "Before you make up your mind definitely, I would like to go back down to the floor and check him again." Dr. Sklar put a white gown over his "greens" and went to see Rohrbeck, who he said was sitting up in bed.

Dr. Sklar recalled, "I said, 'How do you feel?' or something to that effect. He said he felt fine [and] 'when are we going to get this thing done with?'" Dr. Sklar, an internist, listened to Rohrbeck's heart and lungs, and took his blood pressure. "By then I was a bit annoyed with Dr. Jascalevich and I walked back down. Everything seemed to be perfectly all right and I said to Dr. Jascalevich, 'Mario, I just don't understand. This isn't the dark ages—you've got to give me a better reason.' He said something now that I recall, 'Well, maybe I think I saw a little jumping in his neck vein,' or something of that sort and I said, 'Gee, I didn't see anything like that. Why don't you take another look before you cancel the case.' Dr. Jascalevich visited Rohrbeck a second time, according to Dr. Sklar, and again returned to the locker room.

"He said, 'I'm definitely not going to do him and you just get these feelings and you're not going to do a case and that's all there is to it,' and he called for the next case. I remember very vividly that I was just going to say to him, 'That's the last patient I'm ever going to send you,' when the nurse came in and said, 'Dr. Sklar, your Mr. Rohrbeck just died.'

"Now, I was flabbergasted and I looked at Dr. Jascalevich with his great insight and all I could say was, 'Well, that's the most unusual thing I ever came across. The man just came in yesterday. I'm going to call the medical examiner on this case. It's just too unusual a set of circumstances.' I had been practicing nine years or so by then, and I had never seen anything like it."

On autopsy by Dr. Denson, Rohrbeck's right main coronary artery was found to be normal. But he had marked atherosclerosis in his left main coronary artery and his death was ascribed to a "coronary occlusion."

Like Dr. Sklar, I was fascinated by the timing of Rohrbeck's death. But it was from Dr. Frieman's statement to Calissi, not from Dr. Sklar's, that I learned that Dr. Jascalevich had started an intravenous infusion—1,000 cc of dextrose and water—in Rohrbeck's right arm when the surgeon revisited him around 7:45 A.M.

"Is that unusual before an operation, intravenous?" Calissi asked Dr. Frieman.

"Well, it's very unusual because he had canceled the surgery already."

"So what was the purpose of the intravenous at this state?"

"According to the hospital chart, sir, I can't explain it. I don't know."

"Do you have any circumstances that led up to the death of this particular person?"

Dr. Frieman studied the documents before him. "According to the chart," he said, "there was no reason for him to die, other than [that] he probably—as it was written out, it was an acute myocardial infarction, but there was no clinical evidence to substantiate this."

The prosecutor asked about Dr. Jascalevich's cancellation note. "How can you arrive at that kind of evaluation about imminent heart failure? What do you do?"

"Well, if you feel, or if you heard, fluid in the lungs or swelling of the ankles, you would say that there is impending heart failure . . . Now it is not logical for a man who is in bed overnight to develop heart failure. If you told me this man was out all night—running around, doing work—and then you listen to him again, he could possibly develop signs. But here is a man who evidently slept all night."

Dr. Frieman also questioned the need for the intravenous infusion. "If you have a man in heart failure, what are you going to give him more water for? He's got too much water already. Right?"

"I don't know. Is that right?" Calissi queried.

"Sure. If a man has heart failure, the first, immediate treatment is Mercurhydrin or any other diuretic that will take water out of him. You would give him digitalis to strengthen the heart. Or you would give him sedation if he had any pain. But the clinical impression of heart failure in giving him 1,000 cc of sugar and water—the medical logic does not suggest itself. You see, he ordered this at 7:45 A.M. It is on the chart clearly. This order was his, no one else's."

In the Riverdell file there were several copies of Dr. Frieman's deposition and of the statements of other Riverdell physicians. But notably absent was any deposition from Dr. Jascalevich. I didn't want to approach the surgeon until I had had a chance to read and analyze what he had said in 1966. Surely Dr. Jascalevich had appeared before Calissi after November 3, when he opted to wait to talk until his lawyer was present. But where was the deposition? Why were there no copies at all? One answer—though it didn't explain the fate of the original transcript—turned out to be Matthew W. Lifflander.

I first came upon Lifflander's name when I saw two letters in the file. One—apparently a copy—was from Calissi to Lifflander, dated January 12, 1967. It identified the recipient as the corporate counsel of Hertz International, Ltd., with an address on Madison Avenue in New York. "Enclosed please find copies of reports from the Bergen County Medical Examiner's office concerning CARL ROHRBECK and MARGARET PEARSON HENDERSON," the one-sentence letter read. The second letter, dated January 20, 1967, was from Lifflander to Calissi. "As you know I have tried to reach you by telephone for the last ten days to no avail," Lifflander began. He then went on to say that he had sent the Rohrbeck and Henderson reports to Dr. Helpern and he would like the prosecutor to check whether any tissue slides had been retained from the Rohrbeck and Henderson autopsies. If so, Calissi could forward them to Dr. Umberger.

The letters seemed important. Dr. Umberger, I recalled, had mentioned some Riverdell physicians who had gone to see Milton Helpern, the chief medical examiner of New York City. The Hertz connection didn't fit in, but perhaps Lifflander was associated with those doctors. In spite of his inability to get Calissi on the phone, the lawer seemed to have had enough clout to obtain materials from the prosecutor pertaining to the Riverdell investigation.

By 1975, Lifflander was no longer with Hertz. When I reached him at the Madison Avenue law firm of Moore, Berson & Lifflander, and outlined what I was doing, he was exultant. "Boy!" he exclaimed, "I've been waiting for someone like you for ten years!" Over dinner, Lifflander explained that he was a friend of Dr. Lans, whom he had met when they were students at New York University. He hadn't seen Dr. Lans in the last five years; they had parted ways over a personal matter unrelated to the Riverdell affair. But in late 1966, Dr. Lans and Dr. Harris had turned to Lifflander for help.

Calissi had abandoned the investigation after two weeks, Lifflander told me, but Dr. Lans and Dr. Harris weren't ready to give up. At first Lifflander tried to interest the New York *Daily News* in the Riverdell deaths. But a *News* reporter told him to hire a private detective and, if the detective "came up with something," to get back to the paper. So, with $2,000 of Dr. Lans's money, Lifflander retained a detective. "He did a background check on Jascalevich but he didn't get much," Lifflander recalled. "Then we went to Helpern." The pathologist reviewed excerpts from the charts of some of the Riverdell patients and, according to Lifflander, read a copy of Dr. Jascalevich's deposition to Calissi.

I was thrilled by the mention of the deposition. "Where did you get a copy?" I asked.

"From Calissi. I still have it somewhere; I'll get it out for you."

Dr. Helpern, Lifflander said, thought that some of the autopsy findings in 1966—viewed in the light of the patients' charts—were "patently erroneous." "We were glad to have someone of Helpern's stature helping us," Lifflander said, "but we soon realized that nothing was going to come of it. I remember we had a meeting down at the medical examiner's, around a long table in a room next to Helpern's office. Umberger was there too. I can still see them in their white outfits. But beyond giving us his opinion, Helpern said there wasn't much he could do."

"Did Helpern ever speak directly to Calissi?"

"I don't know whether he did or not."

"What did Jascalevich say about the curare in his locker?"

"He said he was using it in experiments on dogs. It's all in his deposition. But none of us—Lans, Harris, myself—bought that. Jascalevich may have persuaded some people in the prosecutor's office. But we certainly didn't believe him."

Dr. Lans was a thickset man with an enormous reddish brown beard. I met with him in Lifflander's office on the twenty-ninth floor of a skyscraper at Madison Avenue and Fifty-fifth Street. The office had big windows, and the night lights were blazing in most of the buildings in the area of Rockefeller Center. It was like being aloft in a black and gold canyon.

"Whose side are you on?" Dr. Lans began.

I didn't like the question. I wasn't on anyone's side.

"I don't think that's a fair way to start out," I said, trying to make the point without antagonizing him.

"Look, all I meant was this. I didn't come here to help somebody exonerate Jascalevich. Because I don't think he can be. But I did what I thought was the right thing in 1966, and it got me nowhere. I don't want it to get nowhere this time. Sure I'll help you. But just remember that I've been through all this before. I've been there, my man. Understand?"

"I understand. Just don't ask me to take sides."

"O.K., O.K. Now what do you want to know?"

"What happened at the end of Calissi's investigation?"

"He dropped it. That's what happened."

"Well, what did he say? Did he say why he was giving it up?"

"He did and he didn't. We were at his office. I was, anyway; I'm not sure who else from the hospital was there. Calissi said that Jascalevich was going to resign from the hospital and that we should 'go home and play doctors' and let them be cops. He said that enough time and money—I think he said $40,000—had been spent on the investigation. He said he believed there was 'something here' but he couldn't find it.

He didn't know what it was. He sat there behind his desk, rubbing his hand over his head. 'It sure beats me,' he said."

"Did Jascalevich resign?"

"Yes, he did. Around the beginning of 1967. But, you know, that's not all there was to it. Galda, who was Calissi's assistant, thought we had 'framed' Jascalevich. I'm sure of it. It was madness, I'm telling you. Here we go to the prosecutor and what happens? We become the object of the investigation. It made no sense. Why would we frame Jascalevich? If we didn't like him, all we had to do was not renew his contract or stop referring patients to him. Would Harris kill his own patients to get at Jascalevich? It's sheer lunacy."

"What about Briski?"

"Briski was O.K. . . . But Briski didn't do anything. In 1967 he went back to Michigan."

Before leaving that night, I made arrangements with Dr. Lans to review the thirteen deaths. Dr. Lans would also try to set up a meeting with Stanley Harris. Harris, he said, was now the chief surgeon at Riverdell. I had told Dr. Lans that I understood how he felt. But it was some time before I appreciated the depth of Dr. Lans's disillusionment with the prosecutor's office, and the extent to which the Riverdell affair had left its mark on him.

Allan Lans was thirty-four years old in 1966, and he had nearly missed becoming a doctor. He was born in Brooklyn—his father was a high school teacher; his mother worked in a Manhattan milliner's shop —and he lived there until World War Two, when his father became director of Jewish services for a USO in New Brunswick, New Jersey. After graduating from high school in 1950, Allan enrolled at the uptown Heights campus of NYU. He started out as a pre-med student, but soon switched to philosophy and sociology. By his graduation in 1954, however, his interest in medicine had revived and, on the advice of a cousin at the Des Moines Still College of Osteopathic Medicine and Surgery, Allan flew out to Iowa. He began classes the next day, and four years later he was a doctor.

In 1959, after a year's internship in Iowa, Dr. Lans came back to New Jersey and he and Joan, a Smith College graduate whom he had married, bought a small-frame house/office in Bergenfield. On the day they hung out the shingle, the phone rang and Dr. Lans had his first case: a boy with an upper respiratory infection. "I was so excited I was shaking like a leaf," he remembered. "I was all grubby, and I had to borrow a jacket and a tie from a friend, but out I went. I didn't even have any prescription pads, mind you. I had to call the drugstore."

Dr. Lans had returned to the New York area because he loved the "whole cultural *schmaltz*," with its theater and chamber music and jazz and, particularly, its sculpture exhibitions. But there was another reason: Riverdell Hospital. "It was fantastic," he recalled. "I saw an ad in a journal about the opening of the hospital, and it meshed perfectly with my plans. I was able to get on the staff right away."

In late 1960 Dr. Lans borrowed some money and bought into the hospital, on the condition that he become a director. And by 1965–66 his practice was well established, and he had time for the occasional marathon or canoeing trip that doubled as exercise and pleasure. When Calissi's investigation ended and then his own efforts failed, Dr. Lans considered moving to California or taking a residency in psychiatry or obstetrics. But he had three young children, and it would have meant starting over again professionally. So he stayed. And, as he made the rounds at Riverdell, he thought of Nancy Savino. "All these years," he said to me, "I haven't forgotten her. I've thought of her every day."

Stanley Harris was more austere in manner than Dr. Lans—the two were not close personally—but he, too, agreed to talk with me about the Riverdell affair. It was still "inconceivable" to him that Calissi had dropped the matter.

Dr. Harris had succeeded Dr. Jascalevich as Riverdell's chief surgeon within a year of the latter's departure. During that year, he was hypersensitive about his surgical record. "The hospital had no suspicious deaths in 1967, and it hasn't had any since then," Dr. Harris said. "Believe me, I was watching myself and everybody else was watching me. At the end of the year, I could walk around that hospital and hold my head up, and everyone knew it."

In the years after 1967 Dr. Harris developed a reputation at Riverdell as a superior diagnostician, an exacting, methodical surgeon, and a good manager of postoperative care. On the advice of a consultant, he formed an association with a younger colleague, invested in a medical office building ten minutes from Oradell, and moved to Bergen County. He worked hard, obtained privileges at other hospitals, made a very comfortable living, had two sons in addition to the daughter who was born in 1966, and gradually put the events of that year behind him—until the early fall of 1975. In San Francisco for the annual meeting of the American College of Surgeons, he wandered one morning into a session where the speaker was lecturing on a technique for radical mastectomy. Dr. Harris thought he recognized the voice, glanced at his program, and then at the speaker. For the first time in nearly a decade, he was in the same room with Dr. Jascalevich. And everything came flooding back.

Dr. Briski was not asked to give a deposition during the Calissi investigation in 1966, but in the Riverdell file there was a one-page report on a detective's interview with him. According to the report, Dr. Briski described Dr. Jascalevich as a "jinx" but said that he could not envision the chief surgeon harming a patient. He knew nothing about Dr. Jascalevich's locker and was unaware that curare had been used at Riverdell. "He did not feel that any of the deaths he had came from this drug," the detective wrote.

I called Dr. Briski in Traverse City, Michigan, in 1975, and he became upset. "Whatever happened in those cases was coincidental," he shouted into the phone. "Yes, I may have regarded Jascalevich as a jinx, but nothing was found. Absolutely nothing, do you hear. Now you've made your first point. What is your second point? I demand to know your second point." Dr. Briski's voice came booming through the phone, and I eased the receiver away from my ear. "I think that's enough of this conversation!" the surgeon screamed, and I could hear the click.

Matt Lifflander, as he had promised, located his copy of Dr. Jascalevich's deposition. On my way to Hackensack one morning, I met the lawyer on the broad wharf of the Hudson River docks, at 125th Street. Twenty minutes later I was sitting in the parking lot of the Bergen County Courthouse, opening the black looseleaf binder which held the deposition. It was dated November 11, 1966, 10:30 A.M., and was 209 pages in length. On the cover page were the names of the officials who had been present during the interrogation in Calissi's office, and I noticed that there was no medical examiner in the group, as there had been when Drs. Harris, Lans, and Frieman had given their statements. I flipped the page and was immediately surprised to discover that the deposition had not been requested by Calissi but had been the idea of Dr. Jascalevich's lawyer, James E. Anderson.

The transcript opened with Mr. Anderson, asking to "go off the record" for a few minutes.

"Well," Calissi answered, "I would prefer to have everything on the record."

"Well, some of what I have to say," Anderson went on, "might conceivably be useful to someone at a future date in some sort of civil proceeding; and if your record would be available for that purpose, then I am not going to say anything on the record, nor will I permit the doctor to."

"You mean you don't want to give a statement as far as the doctor is concerned today, then?"

Anderson repeated his reservation.

"Then could you tell me why you requested to come here?" Calissi asked.

"Yes, I'll tell you why. I requested to come here because this entire investigation is obviously a deadly peril to my client, based upon the possibility of publicity. He can be as innocent as a newborn lamb, and publicity of this nature can crush him."

"You haven't seen any publicity, have you?"

The lawyer conceded that the prosecutor's office had been "extremely discreet." "I feel," Anderson continued, "that this entire situation arose when the doctor called for a meeting of the board of directors of the hospital to discuss the surgical mortality rate. I feel that his call precipitated the entire situation which has caused him so much grief, because of his efforts to run the place properly as chief of surgery. I believe, and I am not afraid to put this in the record either, that a person or persons—whether out of malice, fear for their own position, or something else—has made the allegations which are in detail unknown to me . . . and has thus used the office of the prosecutor in an attempt either to evade responsibility or to wreak some petty revenge on the doctor arising out of professional jealousy, or fear of his abilities or his intentions. And this is the reason I called for a meeting with you. Now I think I can go into greater detail if I am permitted to go off the record, because, as I say, my thoughts are mere conjecture."

Calissi refused. "Everything is going on the record now."

"I know this."

"O.K."

"However," Anderson said, "I want to see this matter terminated as quickly as possible."

"You and me both," the prosecutor remarked.

"I can imagine, and I have no fear again of saying on the record . . . [that] the doctor desires to terminate his connection with this hospital and he will not do it, at my instructions, while it is even remotely possible that he is under fire, so to speak. He must retain his connection. I may say further that, since this entire matter arose, every bit of surgery he has done, he has done only after detailed consultation with me . . . I say this to indicate that I am fearful that the doctor is the object of someone's bad intentions. Now if you would like to find out more about this, Mr. Calissi or Mr. Galda, you are at liberty to do so."

"I would like to take a statement from the doctor," Calissi said.

"All right."

Dr. Jascalevich was advised of his legal rights, as he had been during his brief meeting with Calissi eight days earlier, on November 3. The prosecutor also explained the basis for the investigation. Anderson wanted to know whether any "postmortem studies" of the patients were underway, and Calissi said there were. Anderson wanted to know who had set off the investigation, and Calissi filled him in.

"Did these persons indicate to your office, Mr. Calissi, that Dr. Jascalevich had, immediately prior to their appearance here, requested a meeting of the board of directors relative to the surgical mortality rate of the hospital?"

". . . It is my understanding that the meeting you speak about was not asked for by Dr. Jascalevich but by the directors . . ."

"Were the deceased patients all the subject of surgery by the same surgeon or by different surgeons?" the lawyer asked.

"No, by different surgeons."

"May I ask how many?"

"Oh, I remember two or three, maybe four or five. I don't recall," answered Calissi.

"Other than the mere, bald statements, whatever they may have been, which initiated the issuance of the search warrant, does your office have any actual, credible evidence—admissible evidence—that there is in any respect any culpability on the part of the doctor?"

Calissi bristled. "I'm just not going to answer that question because now you are turning this into an interrogation of me, and I'm not being interrogated."

"All right, all right."

". . . The investigation is directed toward the effort of exculpating just as strongly as it is directed toward the effort of inculpating."

"Oh, I'm sure it is. All right, I think I know enough, Mr. Calissi, to advise the doctor that he may, under oath, tell you anything you want to know."

"All right. Will you please stand, Dr. Jascalevich, and be sworn? I presume before you are sworn that you believe in God?"

"Yes."

"And that you are a religious person?"

"Yes, sir."

"And you go to church?"

"Yes, sir."

His faith affirmed, Dr. Jascalevich swore to tell the truth.

In the next five hours, Calissi and Galda covered, or started to cover, four areas. A few of the suspicious deaths. The contents of Dr. Jascalevich's locker number four at Riverdell. The surgeon's explanation of the curare. And Dr. Jascalevich's movements on November 2, 1966—the day he was told curare had been found in his locker.

I marveled at the deposition and read it over and over in the weeks after I received it. Each time, I saw something that had eluded me before—some further contradiction between what Dr. Jascalevich said on one page and what he said on another; between what Dr. Jascalevich said and what others in the case said. "Obviously we are not completed with the questioning," Calissi observed at the end of the November 11 interrogation. But as I soon learned, the deposition was never resumed. This was it. And far from resolving anything for me, it only deepened the mystery of the Riverdell deaths. From the distance of a decade, I had to agree with what Calissi had said on November 3, 1966, and what Dr. Jascalevich's lawyer implied eight days later: somebody was lying.

The first death brought up by Calissi on November 11 was that of four-year-old Nancy Savino. Dr. Jascalevich said he remembered the case.

"This little girl was a patient of Dr. Harris, is that right?" Calissi asked.

"Right sir," answered Dr. Jascalevich, "and Dr. Lans, the referring physician, I think. I think this was the first case, or one of the first cases, Dr. Harris did for us at Riverdell."

"And Dr. Harris was one of the surgeons attached to the staff of Riverdell Hospital?"

"One of our new surgeons . . . Newly appointed to the staff."

"You mean about four or five months, or something like that?" Calissi asked.

"I don't recall the date he came in, and I don't recall the date when this case was done, but I recall . . . I was concerned [that] on one of his first cases, he was already losing."

"He was already losing?" Calissi repeated.

"By losing, I think probably this is the first case that died after an operation by Dr. Harris at the Riverdell Hospital. . . . I'm sure this is one of his first cases at Riverdell Hospital and probably his first death."

Calissi asked Dr. Jascalevich whether he had reviewed Dr. Harris's professional qualifications before the younger man was added to the surgical staff. The department chairman said he had done so, but that, like any director of surgery in a hospital, he had had to make a choice.

* * *

"On this man, and it's my policy, I reasoned this way . . . Let the man show what he can do and stop him when his pyramid of complications reaches a certain point. This is my point of view—laissez-faire, let the man do. All right, we let him do, and the mortality count as I call it is when we have reached a certain number that was really—that needed a discussion."

* * *

The prosecutor handed Nancy Savino's hospital chart to Dr. Jascalevich and asked the chief surgeon how familiar he was with the case.

"I became familiar with this case at the time of this child's death. I was in the operating room ready to operate when a call is made over the phone that is picked up by the nurse in charge of the operating room, who at the moment is no longer in the hospital—Miss Munson. I remember very clearly: she picked up the phone . . . There was an emergency. That was my first contact that I was going to have with that child. I rush in my operating room clothes."

* * *

"So you went from the operating room?" Calissi asked.

"So I went from the operating room in my clothes . . . I rushed into the room and there it was, this creature with the priest at the foot of the bed, the intern Dr. Ortega on one side, and I will be precise, holding the left hand, if you allow me to say so, on the left hand of the patient. And on the right hand, the nurse in charge, who was Mrs. Nelson. There are the three parties I meet in the room with the girl in the center. They give me the stethoscope. I examine the girl. The girl was dead. The intern was crying, and, to complicate, even the priest was going to become my patient, I think the day after. I had to remove his stomach, and I became, I recall, very mad why they called this man before an operation so important. Why not call somebody that covers him? In other words, this poor guy in pajamas, because he was a patient, giving the Extreme Unction."

"Extreme Unction?"

"Right. So this is the picture of the situation. Then I went back. I pronounced her dead. I went back to the operating room. Again they call me to the room, the girl was alive. Back I go. I went into the room, but no, it was dead. I think the intern, very emotionally inclined, thought that he heard some heart sound. The girl was dead."

"Well, had you visited that girl earlier that morning, Doctor?"

"No, sir. My first contact with this patient was the moment I rushed from the operating room and I was called as an emergency. I was going to a place; I didn't know where I was going. I was led into the room, room number so-and-so, in an emergency."

"You had never seen this girl?"

"No, sir."

Calissi asked Dr. Jascalevich to examine the chart for the cause of death.

"Well," the surgeon said, ". . . I don't see here the cause of death."

* * *

"And the girl was improving, was she not, according to the chart, and then all of a sudden she's found dead?"

"I don't . . . this was a case of sudden death, but I don't know the clinical case . . ."

"Could you please refer to the chart with respect to the notation especially made by a male nurse by the name of Hall?"

"You want me to refer to the nurse's notes, sir? Here is the point that I was called and the restful night. It says for brief periods of crying, which is expectable; extremely homesick, which is expectable; slept most of the night, which is a good sign; no untoward symptoms; child sleeping—until the moment. So this is a sudden death. Now the cause, the autopsy, is labeled as a physiological reaction."

"What does that mean?"

" 'Physiological reaction' means that a cardiac arrest has occurred, that the heart has stopped."

"That, in a four-year-old girl?"

"It can happen at any age . . ." Dr. Jascalevich told Calissi that an "undetermined" physiologic reaction could have been provoked by a number of things, such as an allergic reaction to medication or to fluids draining from the intravenous apparatus. Another explanation could be a "very early coronary . . . that hasn't been given the chance to leave an imprint on the heart, on the muscles of the heart—so tiny and right at the spot where you have the main center that contracts, that sends information to the heart to contract. So strategically placed—that attack—that the patient dies and you can't find anything in the heart and still he died of a heart attack." He went on to suggest that ". . . there are conditions called auto-something that is rather new [now] that we are waking up to the possibility of auto-allergy; allergic to yourself for some reason—medications, operation, manipulation, or whatever . . . So it is certainly not a rarity—the negative autopsy—no matter what age is the patient. Of course we always like to have a positive diagnosis, and you know very well my anxieties with the cesarean section, the last one. At this moment we are bringing up the first one."

Little more was said on November 11 about the Savino death. But I was interested, in 1975, in Dr. Jascalevich's reference to a second visit to the Savino bedside. The chart in the file gave no indication that the girl was thought to be alive after she was pronounced dead, and it said nothing about a second visit by Dr. Jascalevich. Nor was a second visit mentioned in the report of detectives who interviewed Dr. Ortega, the intern, three days before Dr. Jascalevich's deposition.

I was also disappointed that Calissi hadn't pressed Dr. Jascalevich on his relations with Dr. Harris, especially in view of Anderson's remarks at the outset of the deposition. The chief surgeon had acknowledged circulating a partnership memo at Riverdell "only a short time ago" and that Dr. Harris had rescinded the memo. But Calissi hadn't asked Dr. Jascalevich why he had proposed the partnership, particularly if he was concerned about Dr. Harris's performance at Riverdell, or why he thought Dr. Harris had rejected it.

The other three patients about whom Dr. Jascalevich was asked on November 11 were Margaret Henderson, the twenty-six-year-old woman who died the day after she was admitted to Riverdell with acute pain in her lower abdomen; Carl Rohrbeck, the seventy-three-year-old man whose scheduled surgery for repair of a ventral hernia was canceled by Dr. Jascalevich just before the patient died; and Eileen Shaw, the thirty-six-year-old mother who, two days before her death, gave birth by cesarean delivery.

Dr. Jascalevich told Calissi that he had examined Miss Henderson three hours after her admission to the hospital at 5:05 A.M. on April 22, 1966. Looking through Miss Henderson's hospital chart for his consultation report, Dr. Jascalevich recalled that he had found the woman in such "extreme pain" that it "limited" his evaluation, "but despite this difficulty I'm fairly certain that I felt no sizable pelvic tumor as such. Neither could I detect it in the X-ray films of the kidneys . . . I think we could run some X rays of the bowel to collect more information about her abdomen and while she is observed for progression of her clinical picture." That, Dr. Jascalevich told the prosecutor, was his finding and his advice on the morning of April 22.

"You were asked to make this evaluation?" Calissi asked.

"Exactly, by [the] referring physician—not the referring physician, but the man in charge, Dr. Livingston. He called me, 'Mario, give me your impression,' and this was my impression."

"Dr. Livingston was one of the surgeons on the staff, was he not?"

"This was his first case."

"But he had been approved?"

"Yes, yes, yes, yes, absolutely, absolutely."

"Without supervision he had the right to operate?"

"Without supervision because he had a very good background . . . So I felt again [about] the policy: let the man do [it] and evaluate him through his results."

"And this woman was operated on, but nothing was found?"

"Nothing was found, sir."

"So they sewed her right up. Is that correct?"

"Right."

"What is the cause of death?"

"Liver failure. Acute liver failure. Massive hepatic necrosis was found in the autopsy. This was a case of liver disease coming in as a pseudo, as a false pelvic or an abdominal condition that Dr. Livingston and Dr. Harris, who later comes into the picture, interpret as a disease of the belly of a surgical nature. That is why they operated on her."

"Is there any inconsistency with respect to the pain and the objective symptoms of this particular patient and the exploratory operation that was performed by Dr. Harris and Dr. Livingston?"

"I think if the director of the department of surgery comes into a case and writes his impression, at least he deserves the courtesy of a call on the part of the second consultant that comes out of the unexpected and tells me: 'Mario, I don't agree with you, I think this lady has something in one ovary or something in the uterus, I'm afraid, I'm sorry, Dr. Livingston called me also and I think I should operate, how about if I operated?' And then I would tell him, 'All right, if you think so, go ahead,' or I would have answered something of that sort. I never knew anything about this case. The only thing I knew is that Dr. Harris came, called by Dr. Livingston, that afternoon, and the case was operated on and she died. She had a massive hepatic necrosis that was found in the organ."

Dr. Jascalevich remembered that "there was no reason to rush" into surgery. If the patient had been "worked up better," her actual trouble might have been discovered, he said. "As a result of my examination I didn't find any signs at that very moment of liver disease, but we know that liver disease can be extremely treacherous."

"Extremely what?"

"Treacherous—and can come with the most varied clinical pictures, being a real banana peel for diagnosis. And the only way is to study the patient and all of a sudden you're surprised. You find some bile in the blood, which is the very first sign of liver disease, and the patient looks quite well."

"So an operation on Margaret Henderson, exploratory as it was—did this in any way make her liver malady more acute?"

"There is no doubt . . . ," Dr. Jascalevich began, but Anderson interrupted him. After conferring with Dr. Jascalevich, Anderson barred an answer. A moment later, Dr. Jascalevich said there had been "no reason to operate" on Miss Henderson. Calissi asked whether it was "not unusual" for doctors to disagree.

"Of course," the surgeon replied. "But the courtesy should be extended to the director of the department of surgery when circumstances —the case should not be operated on or some work-up should be done. At least what I deserve is a call on the part of . . . Dr. Livingston or Dr. Harris to tell me they change[d] their mind and they are going ahead despite my opinion."

"This is your complaint?"

"Exactly."

"As far as this case is concerned?"

"I could have even convinced these people not to do it."

I was struck by Dr. Jascalevich's emphasis on "professional courtesy." First the chief surgeon said he would have given the "go-ahead" for the operation; then he said he could have persuaded "these people" to wait. According to the chart, Dr. Jascalevich had visited Miss Henderson on the morning after surgery and started an intravenous infusion on her shortly before her death. Why hadn't Calissi asked about this? And why didn't he point to the results of the microscopic examination of Miss Henderson's tissues, which showed the liver to be normal.

In questioning Dr. Jascalevich about Carl Rohrbeck, Calissi focused on the half hour before the man's death. Guided by what Dr. Sklar, Rohrbeck's physician, had told him a week earlier, the prosecutor asked whether it was a "premonition" that had caused the chief surgeon to cancel the 8 A.M. operation.

"It was no premonition," Dr. Jascalevich said. "It is my custom to go see my patient before surgery, the morning of surgery, to have a short talk, to make evaluation, explaining what they can expect from surgery, what the pain means, how they should behave right after anesthesia. I think this helps tremendously, and I went to see Mr. Rohrbeck and he wasn't looking good to me."

"What was the matter with him?"

"He . . . was pale, had a fast pulse. I sat him up, listened to his chest, and . . . signs from the lungs were not normal. We call it very early congestion of the lungs. So I advised the operating room that I was not going to operate this case and I am going to talk with Dr. Sklar about it. As a matter of fact, there was a big—I had a little bit of exchange with Dr. Sklar because I did something probably wrong. I called first the operating room telling them I wasn't going to do the case, I didn't want them to prepare everything. I should have called first the referring physician and tell him about it. Anyway, when Dr. Sklar arrived, I told him about my feelings. He went to examine the patient and came back and told me, 'I don't think he's so bad, I think you could have done this case.' And I told him, 'Well, I don't—I think we should wait, do some tests, this is not an emergency, this is a hernia, it's a procedure of certain magnitude and this man may die on the table. We better cancel the surgery and do those further tests.'"

Dr. Jascalevich now suggested that Rohrbeck might have had a "problem of reaction" to his preoperative medication of Demerol and atropine. But Calissi wanted to know whether in 1965, Dr. Jascalevich had "put what you found wrong" on Rohrbeck's chart.

"I didn't put anything in the chart."

* * *

"Let me ask you something. Did you tell all this to Dr. Sklar down in the scrubbing room?"

"Not only that, but to the anesthesiologist."

"Did you tell Dr. Sklar what you are telling me now?"

"Exactly."

"Not what the premonition was—what your professional opinion was."

"I gave my professional—it wasn't premonition; this would carry us into the field of magic and imagination. We got to a point. I told him this man has wet rales in his lungs, very fine wet rales."

"What does that mean?"

Dr. Jascalevich explained that ". . . this is one of the incipient first signs" of a heart attack. He said that he immediately reported the wet rales to Dr. Sklar, but since the internist disagreed with him, Dr. Jascalevich revisited Rohrbeck "to see if I was seeing visions or what." He said he came back downstairs again, telling Dr. Sklar that he refused to change his mind, and suggested a "work-up." He recalled that soon, however, "the phone was ringing to rush to Mr. Rohrbeck . . . He was dead, he was dead and had a coronary. I think the autopsy showed a coronary."

"Did you give him artificial respiration?"

"He was not—no resuscitation possible. This man was dead."

"It's only a couple of minutes?"

"You are right . . . But our evaluation, Dr. Sklar and mine, of the case is that this man was dead and, as a matter of fact, the anesthesiologist, which is a very expert man in resuscitation, was there. And we didn't decide to do anything."

"And you attributed the death to a coronary?"

"To a coronary. A man that starts with rales in the lungs and has sudden death, has 99 percent of a chance to have a coronary, and I think the autopsy showed a coronary."

Did the surgeon remember "pretty clearly" what he had said to Dr. Sklar, Calissi asked.

"Very clearly, because this is a case in which I'm sorry that the man is dead but I have shown my—I'm glad that I behaved this way and it shows again one of the many times at the hospital that I am not going to operate on cases that are not duly—that were not duly prepared or there should be no rush into surgery . . . Mr. Rohrbeck is typical of how you can avoid an operating death in the operating room."

Calissi moved away from the Rohrbeck death. But Galda briefly renewed the subject nine pages later in the deposition, asking Dr. Jascalevich if he had ordered anything to be administered to the patient. The doctor replied that he had indeed ordered an intravenous infusion of sugar and water.

"When you give [an] intravenous to a patient, in effect aren't you giving water to a patient?" Galda asked.

"Water, sugar, vitamins."

"Well, if one thought there might be some coronary problem or the rales, you considered that we now have water about to go into the heart?"

"Yes."

"Wouldn't you be compounding that particular problem?"

"Only if that infusion ascends at tremendous speed and force. If it is just to keep slowly dripping, just to give him nothing by mouth until we reach some decision, no harm can come to him."

I was bothered by the discrepancies between Dr. Jascalevich's recollections and Dr. Sklar's. The intravenous infusion—not referred to by Calissi and only belatedly brought up by Galda—was the thing. Why hadn't Dr. Jascalevich started it the first time he visited Rohrbeck—if there were two visits? Was he right about the utility of an intravenous infusion after he had detected "wet rales"? If a heart attack was imminent, why wasn't more done for Rohrbeck at once? Why didn't Dr. Jascalevich accompany Dr. Sklar when the internist went to look at Rohrbeck? Why didn't Dr. Sklar go with Dr. Jascalevich on his second visit to the patient? None of these questions was really being answered in 1966. Some weren't even being asked.

More than a tenth of Dr. Jascalevich's deposition was devoted to the death of Eileen Shaw, the young woman who gave birth by cesarean section a few weeks prior to the deposition; took ill on October 22, a day after the birth; and was pronounced dead the next day.

"Did you have occasion to see this patient prior to or after the operation?" Calissi inquired.

"Yes, sir, prior to the operation."

"When did you see her?"

"I went to give my O.K. [for a sterilization]."

"How about after the operation?"

"I want you to know this: that there are many facets in this case, but here we go again into an area, I don't know, it may implicate—"

"Don't discuss it," Anderson commanded.

"It's so important too," Dr. Jascalevich remarked.

"You don't answer my question," Calissi said, "and I haven't objected . . . All I want to know from you, Doctor, [is] did you see this woman after surgery?"

"Yes, sir."

"What was the purpose of you going to see this woman after surgery?"

"To check on her condition."

"How was her condition?"

"Her condition [around 8 A.M. on Saturday, October 22] was with a low blood pressure, having cold sweats, perspiring, and in a 'shocky' condition that we call [it]."

"Did you put that in the clinical chart?"

"No, I didn't."

"Why not?"

"I should have done it. As a matter of fact, I didn't write in the chart. I rushed to the phone and called the surgeon. I considered that more urgent than to write in the chart."

"Wait a minute. You what?"

"Immediately called the surgeon."

"Dr. Harris you called?"

"Right."

"But you didn't put anything in the chart?"

"I didn't put anything in the chart."

"What did you tell the doctor?"

"I told him, 'Stanley, this lady you did yesterday has a blood pressure'—I don't recall, it was something like 50, which is very low; I imagine a normal human being has to have 120 or 130—'has a blood pressure of 50 and she looks shocky to me. You better come over, you better come over.' So he said, 'Well, all right; let's, in the meantime, start immediately some blood and let's ask for a blood count."

"Start some blood?" Calissi asked.

"Blood transfusion."

"And start a blood count?"

"And do a blood count."

"He told you this?"

"He told me over the phone, gave me the order."

"What happened?"

Dr. Jascalevich continued, "So we went ahead with this patient, but the patient started getting worse and worse. We started the blood as he said, we did the blood count, but she was getting worse and worse."

"What do you mean, she was getting worse and worse—what were her symptoms?"

"More unresponsive, although it was unresponsiveness combined with restlessness and movement in bed."

"Was she having any tough job breathing?"

". . . we gave her oxygen as first aid."

"Why?"

"She seemed to—well, resuscitation maneuvers [were] included to support the circulation with something in the vein to support breathing with oxygen. You may see that actually to give oxygen to somebody doesn't mean he was really short of breath; it's part of the general resuscitation procedure to secure fluids in the veins so the heart can have something to pump and to give oxygen, to give oxygen."

"This is what you did?"

"This is what we did."

"All right."

Later in the deposition, Calissi revived the matter of Mrs. Shaw's breathing when Dr. Jascalevich saw her on Saturday morning.

"When this woman was first seen by you after her operation, you were in the doorway and she was having trouble breathing, was she not —she had a pain in her chest?"

"I had a patient downstairs that morning, and I went to do rounds."

Answer with a yes or no, Anderson told Dr. Jascalevich.

"Was she having trouble breathing, and did she have a pain in her chest at the time?" Calissi repeated.

"No, the problem was rather changes in her color, the cold sweats, the thready pulse, the low blood pressure. She did not show any signs whatever and difficulty in breathing at the moment when I rushed to Dr. Harris's phone—to the phone to call Dr. Harris, rather. It was when the entire picture developed in which there was a respiratory difficulty, there was an increase in the shocky condition, a restlessness, a state of unconsciousness. But not in the beginning."

"Not in the beginning?"

"Not in the beginning; it would have been . . ."

"Did she ever complain of a pain in the chest to you while you were in her presence?"

"Not at any moment."

"Did she complain to you that she had trouble breathing?"

"No."

"Never?"

"Never."

"You recall this case clearly?" Calissi asked.

"Sir, I recall to the best of my recollection. I don't recall the patient having told me, 'Doctor, I can't breathe,' or 'Doctor, I have a tremendous pain in the chest,' I don't recall."

"I'm not talking about tremendous pain. I didn't use the word 'tremendous.' "

"Pain [in] the chest. I don't recall. Actually this lady couldn't even talk, slowly went—very fast—into a state of—she couldn't; I don't think she could have mumbled a word, a coherent word."

"That is when you first saw her, right, and you called the doctor?"

"No, when I first saw her she did say—I told her, 'Darling, how are you?' and I don't recall what she answered. But she didn't look good to me—she was pale, she had some cold sweats, and I told the nurse, 'Did you take her blood pressure?' She said, 'No, I didn't since I came in'— she comes in at 7 o'clock; she should have checked that."

"Will you take a look at the chart, please," Calissi said to Dr. Jascalevich, "and tell me what her blood pressure was at that particular time you are talking about, the pulse, and everything else?"

"But I didn't write any note myself, so this is a reading that I took and I didn't write it down. So where to look for it?"

"See if anybody else took a reading."

Dr. Jascalevich began to discuss Mrs. Shaw's temperature, but Calissi insisted on knowing the pulse and blood pressure when Dr. Jascalevich called Dr. Harris.

"BP 80 over 60, this is my reading," Dr. Jascalevich said.

Was that his writing on the chart, Anderson asked.

"Yes."

Calissi pursued the matter. "Is this your writing?"

"No, no, no, this is the nurse's, the nurse's writing, 80 over 60. This is right, 80 over 60. Of course the blood pressure immediately came up with the blood transfusion. There is a 40 over 60 here, and then after two pints of blood [it] shot up to 200 over 90. But when I came into the case, it was 80 over 60."

"And she improved after that?"

"This is also consistent with an embolic phenomenon, together with high fever."

"This condition that you described before—when you first saw this woman after the operation and you went to call the doctor—this was prior to giving her oxygen?"

"Well, the nurses were helping; I was the only doctor at the moment when the nurses were rushing with the oxygen tube; I was calling Dr. Harris and Dr. Baba. Then I went back to the room, and of course I helped them with the oxygen and the different resuscitation maneuvers."

Dr. Jascalevich said that Dr. Harris took charge of the treatment of Mrs. Shaw after the younger surgeon arrived from Bronxville about 8:45 A.M. At that time, the department chairman recalled, both he and Dr. Harris felt that the patient had "an emboli, and we were right, at that moment we were right; she did show the emboli, but we were wrong in the kind of embolism. We thought the most common emboli, the one in the legs or the one that builds up inside the belly or pelvis, so-called, that shoots this clot in the lungs—that is the most common emboli.

"So we thought about this so much that I said, 'All right, you stay here; I'll rush to Christ Hospital' [in Jersey City]. I wanted to bring a special instrument that has been used in the last year or two to stop clots. So I called them. I called from Christ Hospital to Dr. Harris. I told him, 'Doctor, I got the instrument, but this [is] between you and me: I don't trust [it] very much. It isn't the last moment. I don't like it very much; it's a little bit traumatic. What are we going to do? How is your patient?' He said, 'Look, she is coming, I think'; he gave me a rather favorable report. 'We're not going to use it.' I said O.K. I told him from Christ Hospital, I'll hold it and 'you let me know.' This is about midday, about noontime, some four hours after the beginning of the crisis on this patient."

Dr. Jascalevich made another reference to the special instrument he called a "clamp" later in his deposition, but this time his recollection varied: "I told Dr. Harris, I said 'Stanley, I'm leaving for Christ Hospital. I'm going to get the clip.' Now, we use a clip that clamps the main vein and stops any emboli. This would have been a crazy idea, completely out of text; he would have asked, 'for what are you asking me that,' although he agreed that I should go and get the instrument. Again my phone call from Christ Hospital confirmed that there was an agreement between the two that this was our problem—embolism— and that we should stop it at any moment."

The chief surgeon said that he made several calls to Dr. Harris and Dr. Baba on Saturday afternoon and was told that Mrs. Shaw was improving. About 9 A.M. on Sunday, October 23, he phoned Dr. Harris and learned that Mrs. Shaw had just died.

"Why did you keep calling Dr. Harris about this specific patient?" Calissi asked.

"This is a very serious mortality; it is a case of great concern for me as director of the department. It's my duty to be after this . . ."

Dr. Jascalevich said that the death of Mrs. Shaw, which initially appeared to be a mystery, precipitated his request to the hospital's board of directors for a "mortality conference." The chief surgeon had an idea that Mrs. Shaw's liver, which he noticed to be large and tender when he visited her before her cesarean, had "something to do with her death," and he conveyed this opinion to Dr. Markley, the pathologist who was doing the autopsy.

Dr. Jascalevich told Calissi on November 11, 1966, that only yesterday he had asked Dr. Markley whether he had reached a conclusion and that the pathologist said, " 'Oh yes, finally I got it. There was multiple fat emboli, and I have the literature and this is not the first time; fatty, huge livers can seed the body with fatty emboli, little fat clots all over the kidneys.' He mentioned particularly kidneys and said that if she got it in the kidney, she got it all over. So this is the cause of death. I said, 'Wonderful, I'm glad that we did find a cause of death for this lady. Would you please transmit this finding to the surgeon?' "

Calissi tried to elicit Dr. Jascalevich's opinion about the handling of Mrs. Shaw, but he got an indefinite response. At one point the chief surgeon said that "most probably the manipulations of the surgery, or whichever were the maneuvers, had broken up pieces of fat tissue in this liver and seeded her body with it." At another juncture he said he knew "features about this case that are of alarm to me." But when Calissi asked whether prior to the operation anyone at Riverdell "should have diagnosed this case in such a way that would indicate that this woman had a fatty liver and should not have been operated on [because] she was going to die," Anderson advised his client not to answer.

"Do you find that any doctor did anything wrong with respect to this woman which caused her death?" the prosecutor persisted.

"Don't anwer that," Anderson said.

Calissi turned to the lawyer. "You mean . . . you are telling him not to answer this no matter whether the answer is yes or no?"

"I don't even know what the answer is," Anderson said. "I don't care to speculate."

"Suppose you discuss it with him."

"You want me to discuss it with him?"

"Yes, please."

"Come outside a minute, Mario."

Calissi and Galda sipped coffee and waited, and when Dr. Jascalevich and his lawyer returned, the question was reread by Edward Salbin, the stenographer. "Do you find that any doctor did anything wrong with respect to this woman which caused her death?"

"No, sir," the surgeon answered. "On the contrary, I should say that resuscitation maneuvers given to this lady were prompt and everybody did his best."

I was sorry that neither Calissi nor Galda had asked Dr. Jascalevich on November 11 about the call he supposedly received from Mooney, the lawyer/friend of the Shaw family. Had the chief surgeon told Dr. Harris and Dr. Lans about such a call and the threat of a malpractice suit, as they contended? The deposition didn't say. Why, when reading Mrs. Shaw's blood pressure levels to Calissi, did Dr. Jascalevich not mention the note at the same place on the chart—around 8:05 A.M. on Saturday, October 22—that said the patient was complaining of "pain in chest" and "shortness of breath"? Was it odd that Dr. Jascalevich didn't write on Mrs. Shaw's chart? What accounted for the disparity in his accounts of the clamp or clip—what was the business about the clip being "a crazy idea"? Why was Dr. Jascalevich not asked how—or if— he knew that Mrs. Shaw had "gone bad" again about 10 A.M. on Saturday? Did he see Dr. Harris rushing to her room then, and did he say something to the younger surgeon, as Dr. Harris had told Calissi? If so, why was Dr. Jascalevich going away from Mrs. Shaw's room at that critical moment? If he was. Was the AMA *Journal* article which Dr. Markley used to support his finding of death by fat emboli really applicable to Mrs. Shaw? I had read the article and had my doubts. The article summarized a study of 101 "sudden and unexpected" deaths in Baltimore in 1964 and 1965. "The definition of a sudden, unexpected death used in this study was death as a result of nontraumatic causes of a person who was not restricted to his home, a hospital or an institution . . . for more than twenty-four hours prior to death." But Mrs. Shaw had been in Riverdell for three days prior to her first "attack." Moreover the article, which said that "fat may escape from the large fatty cysts in the liver and cause fat emboli in the lungs and the brain," dealt mainly with persons who appeared to have been alcoholics. On autopsy, no fat emboli were found in the capillaries of Mrs. Shaw's lungs and her brain was not examined. A microscopist's report on her liver said, "There is no cirrhosis and there are no areas of necrosis." Moreover her family told me she drank very little. "You could put it all in one bottle, one fifth," her brother said.

Moving away from the deaths, Calissi showed Anderson an eight-page, "Return of the Search Warrant," containing a list of the seventy-one items removed from Dr. Jascalevich's locker number four on November 1.

"The items were read specifically to Dr. Jascalevich the last time that he was here, when I was advising him of his rights," the prosecutor said. "However I will be very happy to read them to you as his attorney unless you already have knowledge of what was in this particular locker."

"I have general knowledge," Anderson said. "I know that curare was found; some hypodermic needles, syringes were found . . . If I can look at it, I could possibly shorten the procedure and read it."

While Anderson studied the inventory, Dr. Jascalevich made an observation that lent more weight to the theory of his having been "framed" than any of his lawyer's musings. "As I was listening to the prosecutor reading to me this list [presumably on November 3], the one thing struck my mind, there is mention of a blue box, of a blue box containing a vial of tubocurarine. I never use this material myself. Now, first I want to see this rest . . ."

"Wait a minute," Calissi interrupted. "I don't understand this."

Dr. Jascalevich explained that the tubocurarine which he used, and which came from the General Surgical Supply, was ". . . a product of Lilly Laboratories and comes in a whitish box; but I may have misheard you, so I would like to see if there is a blue. Here it is, a blue box."

"Number five," Anderson interjected.

"I have never used a blue box containing it," Dr. Jascalevich went on, "but I may tell you this, and this comes out of observation, pardon me, a blue box contains tubocurarine made by another company. There is one called—one laboratory called Burroughs & Wellcome—and this laboratory supplies tubocurarine to Riverdell Hospital."

Anderson finished his review of the inventory of locker number four and Dr. Jascalevich was asked to officially identify it. The surgeon, who was given several opportunities to study the list, said that he recognized the items "as things that were in my locker" with the possible exception of a bottle of Ionosol, and the definite exception of any blue boxes that contained, or once contained, curare. There were five such boxes among the seventy-one items, and four of them were empty.

By matching a photostat of the inventory against the deposition, I saw what was happening. Eighteen vials of curare—most of them nearly empty, out of their boxes, and scattered about—had been found by Calissi in Dr. Jascalevich's locker. Half of them were manufactured by Lilly, were called tubocurarine, and came in white boxes. Half were made by Burroughs-Wellcome, were called Tubarine, and came in blue boxes. Although Dr. Jascalevich dwelled, in his deposition, on the boxes rather than the vials themselves, he appeared to be saying that someone had placed much of the curare in his locker without his knowledge. And the curare that he disowned, he linked to Riverdell.

"Did you ever get any Tubarine or tubocurarine of curare, to use the generic term, from the pharmacy at Riverdell at any time?" Calissi asked the surgeon.

"No, sir."

"You never took or requisitioned a bottle of curare—whether its trade name was tubocurarine or Tubarine—from Riverdell?"

"No, sir."

"You are positive of that?"

"I am absolutely sure of that, and this is the reason for my surprise to find, in your search list, a box described as blue. That doesn't go along with the kind of box that I get from my supplier."

Calissi let the matter rest. But the possibility of a frame-up arose again when Anderson asked to see one of the photographs that had been taken of Dr. Jascalevich's locker.

"Doctor," Anderson said, "are you able to tell us if this is your locker number four with the door open?"

"Well I—it's hard to recognize that this is my locker. Number one, I don't see the number."

"It could be?"

"Number two, it's such a disorder—the things that are contained in this locker—that it seems impossible it's mine."

"At—the last occasion on which you closed the door of this locker, if this is your locker . . ."

"Yes, sir."

". . . were the contents thereof in this condition?"

"No, sir, they were in an orderly place, you know. Each item."

Clearly something was wrong. On the morning of November 1, 1966, after all five Riverdell directors had seen the curare and the disarray in Dr. Jascalevich's locker, Dr. Lans told Calissi that he had watched Dr. Jascalevich open the locker and move things about. The surgeon, according to Dr. Lans, didn't register any surprise at the state of the locker or at the blue boxes of curare, or at anything. "He went back into his locker . . . with whatever he was putting in and out. Then he closed the locker and we went on into surgery."

To explain the presence of the Lilly-manufactured curare in his Riverdell locker, Dr. Jascalevich took Calissi back to 1963–64, when he had a $500 grant from the American Cancer Society to do experimental surgery on dogs at the Seton Hall Medical School in Jersey City. The grant was for the development of a tube by which patients could be fed directly through the skin and into the stomach. The $500 paid for a dozen dogs, chemicals, and other supplies. But not for curare.

"This was the experiment you conducted in 1963?" the prosecutor asked.

"1963 and part of 1964, yes, sir."

"Did you complete that experiment?"

"Yes, and it was reported to the American Cancer Society."

"And in the course of that particular experiment, what chemicals or drugs did you use?"

"Only Seconal, which is to put the dog asleep . . . I used iodine to paint the skin of the dog after shaving him. I used special soap to clean my instruments, but no other drugs."

"Now, you continued to conduct experiments after 1963–64, right?"

"Right, sir."

"Where did you conduct the experiments?"

"At the . . . Seton Hall School of Medicine laboratory . . . dog laboratory, I think is the name, which is up on the sixteenth floor of the building."

"Now, in order to obtain dogs for experiments, Doctor, what procedure must you go through?"

"Well, there are two ways. Of course, one is the official way. Let me put it this way . . . If you have a grant, if you have the money to obtain these dogs, there is no problem; the money is there. If the projects are out of your own pocket, out of your own enterprise, of course a less expensive way should be searched. My experiments in 1963 cost me nothing really because they were backed by the American Cancer

Society. A request on my part to the American Cancer Society for more money to continue with my studies was declined with a very cordial letter that I would like to show, a letter that precipitated my decision to carry then the experiments on my own."

"You haven't answered my question," Calissi said.

"Pardon me?"

"The two methods of obtaining the dogs," said Anderson.

"The other method," Dr. Jascalevich went on, "is well, to go after hours and to work on dying animals that have been worked [on] by previous investigators during the day, by giving a small tip to one of the several sweepers and animal care attendants."

* * *

"You conducted no experiments anywhere but at Seton Hall on dogs. Is that right?"

"Absolutely."

"The only place?"

"That's right."

Again Dr. Jascalevich noted that the dogs he obtained in 1963–64 at Seton Hall were "live" dogs, and the dogs in 1965–66 were "dying" dogs.

"Who said they were dying?" asked Calissi.

"Well, they are at the end of so many investigation procedures done on them . . . They have been already operated. They have been already cannulated. There have been different experiments that the previous investigators did."

"And in order to get dogs, and I just used your words, 'dying dogs,' how do you go about that?"

"Well, after 5 o'clock when the head of the—the man in charge is gone and the employees are still there sweeping and cleaning the place, it is rather easy to offer anyone a tip and, sometimes by simple request even without money, to do some work . . . on these animals."

"You mean you would see a fellow sweeping the floor or cleaning up and ask that person for a dog?"

"You could ask, right. Of course, you're not a newcomer."

"I understand that."

"You have been there already. You're recognized because they know that you have been working there for years. So you're not really a newcomer asking for a surprise, doing a surprising request. You are already a familiar face."

"You are familiar, you are a doctor, and these people are menials. Is that correct?"

"Exactly."

"After 5 o'clock?"

"Exactly."

"So why is it necessary for you to ask a janitor or a porter, or someone doing menial work, for a dog?"

"Because, sir, if I have to pay for a dog in the regular manner, it's very expensive. It cost me thirty dollars, which I paid to the animal attendant; that was in 1965, I believe, thirty dollars, to get just one animal to prove, to work on some instruments I had. The man that received the money is Mr. Riggi, the man in charge of the animal experiments, and I gave the money to him and he assisted me."

"How much did you have to give these people doing menial work to get the dying dogs?"

"Just one or two dollars," replied Dr. Jascalevich, who acknowledged, under further questioning, that he had made a "very handsome" income the previous year, including a net of $50,000 at Riverdell Hospital.

There was more discussion about the dying dogs, and Dr. Jascalevich told Calissi that while he had never witnessed it, the attendants were supposed to kill the animals ". . . and wrap them up in bags and dispose of them."

"The attendants are supposed to kill them?" Calissi repeated.

"Yes, yes," Dr. Jascalevich said, "and this I proved the other day when I left Pollak Hospital . . . I worked on a dog and my dog was still alive when I left."

Calissi passed over the reference to "proving" something at Pollak Hospital, a Hudson County-owned institution adjacent to Seton Hall. He asked Dr. Jascalevich if he was sure that the dogs he worked on after 1963–64 were left tied and dying on tables. Yes, said Dr. Jascalevich. Each live dog, he supposed, was assigned to a researcher and couldn't be given out.

"Who gives the orders to the attendants to dispose of the dogs, do you know this?" Calissi asked.

"I think there must be a departmental procedure that once the experiment is finished, the dog should be destroyed."

Dr. Jascalevich's lawyer, Anderson, interjected by asking his client if he had ever destroyed a dog when he was finished with it.

"Very few times." His own experiments rarely killed the animals, he said.

Calissi went on to ask whether, in 1965–66, the attendants were ever in the same room as Dr. Jascalevich while he was conducting his experiments.

"No, sir. They were cleaning the rest of the house and they would leave me alone. I will be able to do this." Nor were there other researchers in the lab, Dr. Jascalevich said.

"There weren't many times that I went there to have a chance to meet somebody. I don't recall exactly the number of dogs. In other words, dogs means visits because if I go I get one dog . . ." The doctor remembered that he probably "worked on something like six dogs in 1965, probably some nine dogs in 1966, so it makes a total of some fifteen dogs. That means fifteen trips." But later in the deposition, when pressed about the frequency of his visits to Seton Hall, the surgeon indicated that the number of "dying dogs" did not equal the number of his visits.

Dr. Jascalevich said he could only remember the first name of one of the "three or four colored fellows" whom he tipped in exchange for the dogs. The man's name, he told Calissi, was Lee.

Dr. Jascalevich's description of the experiments he was performing on dying dogs in 1965 and 1966 was no less complicated. The surgeon said he was trying out three or four ideas, all seemingly related to abdominal surgery. He explained that the only drugs used in this research —just as in 1963–64, when he was working on a stomach-feeding tube —were Seconal and Nembutal, to put the dogs to sleep. Then the surgeon mentioned an experiment that he called "the posterior liver biopsy." It was this experiment, he said, that required the use of curare. "This is especially important to you," he told Calissi, handing the prosecutor a piece of paper containing his "original drawings on the experiment that uses curare." The paper, about five inches square, showed an etching of the lung and the diaphragm and the kidney, done with a blue ball-point pen. In pencil were written the words "MOVE IT UP!! WITH CURARE!!!" and "1964/65 Research Series Posterior Liver Biopsy."

"When did you start the experiment involving the posterior liver biopsy?" Calissi asked.

"Throughout, sir, 1965 to 1966."

Calissi was confused. Was curare used on the dogs in 1965–66, or were Seconal and Nembutal the only drugs used? "Can you clear that up for me?"

"Certainly, certainly," Dr. Jascalevich replied. "Let's suppose Dog A is given to me, Dog A. Suppose I get a dog called X. I arrive that afternoon and I perform on that dog experience number one, two, three, four, five, and the experience number five is the one in which I need curare. That means that that dog, at the end, has gotten anesthesia, plain Seconal or Nembutal that I need for experience A.B.—for experience one, two, three, four, and now gets at the end the curare for experience number five. That means that the final product that dog has inside him [is] two drugs."

"Now, was the curare used first in these experiments or was it used second, or third, or fourth, or when was it used?" the prosecutor asked.

"I would say curare has been always used at the end, for one simple reason. Curare inhibits the respiration of the animal and so shortens the life of the animal so that it will be the end, the last experience I should do. First I use the animal for the other nonkilling experiences, and this is the one that carries the possibility that precipitates the death of the animal most probably."

"Excuse me, Doctor," Anderson said. "By experiences, you mean experiments?"

". . . Right, experiments."

"What you are saying to me, just so I have it clear in my mind," Calissi resumed, "is that in the six experiments that you indicate here that you conducted . . . one of the experiments being the posterior liver biopsy . . . you gave Seconal, Nembutal, anesthesia of some kind?"

"Anesthesia of some kind, right, sir."

"And then at the end you gave curare. Is that right?"

"Right, sir."

"And at the time you gave curare, the dogs were still alive, or were they dead?"

"Alive, alive, of course. If the dog would be dead, I wouldn't need the curare for the simple reason that what I'm trying to produce with the curare is the inhibition of the breathing. If the dog is dead, I have already what I want."

Dr. Jascalevich said the "idea of this experiment"—to perfect a means of reaching the liver with a needle without going through the belly or abdominal cavity, where "complications occur"—was "entirely original." Since doing his medical school thesis on the growth of the liver, the surgeon said, he had known that there was a very small area toward the back through which a needle could pass into the liver, but to "hit the spot . . . it's very important that the liver won't move." Curare, he told the prosecutor, "produces a stoppage of the breathing movement" that anesthesia alone cannot accomplish.

"The applications of this, if we carry this into the applications of the human being, it will be a great progress. At last we will be able to reach the liver without transversing the abdominal cavity, which has been a great deterrent point in pinching the liver with needles since the first time an experimenter thought [that] the liver could be pinched with a needle. Putting a needle in the liver means that I can put medicines, that I can put radio-opaque media for X rays, and there is no way up to now . . ."

Calissi, unaided by a medical advisor, was lost. He had just asked Dr. Jascalevich whether the needle would be going "into the liver without puncturing the liver itself," and the surgeon had said, "Yes, sir." Now he asked again.

"But you are not going to put the needle in the liver, are you?"

"Yes," Dr. Jascalevich said, "it goes straight into the liver substance . . . into the liver organ."

The prosecutor tried once more, asking the surgeon about the anatomical location of the liver and the direction the needle would take. Again Dr. Jascalevich recounted how the needle would go through the rear—through the small zone, the "peninsula" where the liver is attached to the posterior abdominal wall, and into the liver itself.

"So you don't put it in the liver?" Calissi repeated.

"You put it in the liver, right."

Calissi asked the surgeon's forbearance. "See, I'm a layman and I'm trying to find out what we are talking about here."

At this point Dr. Jascalevich showed Calissi two human anatomy books that he had brought with him; the two textbooks that, nine years later, I had found in the prosecutor's file. The Spanish book was *Anatomia III* by R. Gregoire y Oberlin. On page 161 was a printed sketch of the liver peritoneum and, next to it, a triangular hand drawing by Dr. Jascalevich of the peninsula through which the needle would pass on its way into the liver. Below the pictures were two columns with a dozen pencil notations of "H.T.," "missed," "poor," "Hit duodenum," or "?". The French book was *Schemas d'Anatomie* by C. L. Monod and B. Duhamel. As on the slip of paper that represented his original drawings of the posterior liver biopsy experiment, Dr. Jascalevich had written, on three pages of the French book, "MOVE IT UP WITH CURARE!!!" and here the words were underlined. From arrows the surgeon had drawn on the pages, it appeared that the purpose of the curare was to paralyze the diaphragm, thus keeping it "up" and hopefully away from the target of the peninsula.

In succeeding pages of the deposition, Dr. Jascalevich said that he did not recall having purchased any curare before 1965 because the drug was not needed for his 1963–64 research. He said that he would give each of the "dying dogs" at Seton Hall virtually an entire 10-cc vial of curare and "sometimes I would even need more because I missed the vein, I injected the 10 cc out of the vein. Then I would have to use another vial." The condition of the dogs, prior to his battery of experiments on any day in 1965–66, depended on what the previous researchers had done to the animals—some of the dogs, Dr. Jascalevich said, had their bellies open when he arrived and for "some of the others, I had to open the belly." Eventually the surgeon would return to Riverdell Hospital in Oradell and deposit the syringes—often with the needles still attached—"in a box properly labeled 'syringes, research at Seton Hall, used and reused' because I use and re-use the syringes. They are expensive."

"Now, you say these needles—pardon me, these syringes—are expensive?" Calissi said.

"I would say for a researcher that has to pay all by his own . . . The fact that it's disposable items of course may show you that it isn't so expensive, it's made in glass; but still there was no reason to throw it away and I could use and re-use it."

"So you put it in the box, and what did you do with the empty vial or ampule of curare?"

"The empty vial will go to a paper bag."

"In a paper bag?"

"A paper bag that will also contain the little carton boxes where the vial was taken from, all into this paper bag which was in my . . . locker number four."

Since Dr. Jascalevich had access to a "locker" at Seton Hall Medical School, Calissi asked why he took the empty curare vials back to Riverdell, fifteen or twenty miles away.

"It will be a pleasure to answer you that, sir," Dr. Jascalevich replied. "If you visit and see my locker at Seton Hall, I would label it unsafe. Curare is a drug that should not be left at the reach . . . of anybody, and I thought that the locker at Seton Hall—which is a glass enclosure without lock, actually . . . It was not safe. That's why I used my metal . . ."

"This is not a locker at all that you are describing to me, is that right? It's a cabinet with a glass front, it isn't a locker?"

Dr. Jascalevich agreed. It was a shared cabinet. Calissi again asked why Dr. Jascalevich took empty curare bottles to his Riverdell locker.

"Well," answered the doctor, "it's very important to keep for the researcher this material. The material will give you the batch number, the lot number of the drug, and the expiration date of the drug, any other question that may come up later in the research. It's very important to know what is the drug that you worked with, which was the expiration date, whether you worked with the right drug or not in the sense of whether it was active enough, any further question about the quality of the drug; it's important to keep the original vial."

Calissi tried, in the next ten or twelve pages of the deposition, to grasp the logic of the surgeon's research methods. But what emerged instead was a dizzying exchange—perhaps the most extraordinary in the document. It began with the prosecutor questioning whether there was anything so "mysterious" about the purpose or action of the curare to have warranted retention of the vials.

"I'll say this, something very interesting," Dr. Jascalevich replied. "Sometimes in my research, something that comes very apropos of this, I think it was in 1966, I noticed that I [was] getting . . . very poor respiratory inhibition with my drug." So, the surgeon said, he called his supplier and complained about the drug.

"And you told him the curare they sold you was no good?"

"I told them it wasn't working, right, it wasn't working, did they give me something different or what? 'No, Doctor, we did not.' And I think the matter was terminated there."

"Wait a minute," Calissi interjected. "As a result of this conversation you had with these people who were supplying you with the curare, did you take the lot-number bottle back to them and say . . ."

"No, I didn't."

"You didn't do that?"

"No, I didn't do that."

Obviously perplexed, Calissi again asked the doctor to bear with him. "I think I'm intelligent enough to understand if I can get it in maybe monosyllabic terms."

They re-covered the ground, with Dr. Jascalevich reaffirming that he saved the empty vials of curare so he would know their batch numbers if the drug appeared faulty.

"Now, my question to you is this," the prosecutor said. "When you injected or administered curare to these dogs, there was a reaction, you inhibited the respiration of these dogs?"

"Yes."

"Is that correct?"

"Right, sir."

"What more did you want the curare to do for you, at that stage of the proceedings in your experiment?"

"This was the purpose, to inhibit the breathing and perform this procedure, which takes just a few minutes because it is very fast to get through a needle through the back, and then open the belly and see where did you land."

"So the curare did its job. Is that correct?"

"The curare did its job." At this point Dr. Jascalevich apparently pointed to the two columns on page 161 of the human anatomy book in Spanish that he had given to Calissi. "As a matter of fact," the surgeon said, "I have here a picture of some of my dogs in which you can see 'hit target, hit target, no, hit target, hit target, question mark, hit target.' In here, 'miss, miss?' In other words, this was the purpose."

"But what I'm trying to find out, Doctor, is this. With regard to this experiment, the posterior liver biopsy, you gave curare to the dog and the dog then either died by reason of the 10 cc that you gave them . . . or they were moribund. Is that right?"

"Exactly."

"What else did you expect the curare to do?"

"Nothing more."

"Nothing more. Now, why was it necessary for you to then save the empty vial or ampule of curare that you used for that purpose?"

"My investigation is methodic, and I think it is one of every researcher that, if possible, every data should be kept. Nothing should be thrown away. And again I say the keeping of this permitted me some reflection on the effects of the drug—whether I missed the target, because actually I didn't get enough result with my drug; I didn't have enough respiratory inhibition or was missing the target because I was just in the wrong place."

"Where are your notes with respect to comparing the missing of the target or anything else in connection with this posterior liver biopsy and the type or quantity or the trademark of curare you used?" Calissi asked. "Where are your notes on this?"

Dr. Jascalevich referred the prosecutor to the Spanish and French anatomy books, neither of which contained any reference to the reasons for "missing" the target, or to the amount of curare used, or to the manufacturer of the drug.

"Now, when you didn't hit the target, which is indicated in the book at 161, did you believe that the curare that you used was the reason why you didn't hit the target?"

"Well, certainly it's very hard to answer that question. You can't hit the target just because you want. This is research that's going on. I still don't have the final answer to this. I may be completely wrong myself about all of this. It's very hard to say if I missed the target because the curare didn't inhibit breathing, but with 10 cc of curare I should be fairly sure there was a respiratory inhibition and consequently a fixation of the liver in position ready for the needle to come through."

It still didn't add up to Calissi, who asked the surgeon how often he had noticed a "failure" of the curare.

"I don't have those notes in which it shows that," Dr. Jascalevich said.

"You don't have any such notes?"

Anderson interrupted. "Did you make any?"

"I did, but I don't . . ."

"You don't have them?" Calissi reiterated.

"I don't."

"But you did make them?" the prosecutor asked.

"I did make them, sir."

Recalling Dr. Jascalevich's statements that some of the curare had, in fact, "worked," Calissi once more asked the surgeon why it was necessary for him to retain the empty vials.

"The empty bottles and carton boxes were kept so as to have a control on the lot number of the drug and expiration date of the drug."

"Well, did you note that in any of your notes and experiments, the lot number of the drug?"

"I didn't have need for that," Dr. Jascalevich said, "because I kept the empty vials. That's why I kept it."

"How would you know which empty vial you used on what dog?"

Dr. Jascalevich answered that ". . . it wasn't that kind of a detailed study . . . in these notations of mine, which I don't have, I had a control."

"Now you say you had a control?"

"Yes."

"What did the control say?"

"I had a list, a listing."

"Of what?"

"Of my dogs which I worked."

"What else?"

"And I have some notations about [the] reaction of the dog."

"What else?"

"And notes about the procedure itself, again if I missed or hit the target."

"What else?"

"I think that's all what I know of those."

Again Calissi asked the surgeon whether he had written down the lot or batch number of the curare vials. Dr. Jascalevich had said, only a moment earlier, that he did not need to do so because he had saved the vials themselves.

"Of course, that first, yes," the surgeon now responded.

"You put down the number of the batch of the particular bottle you used of curare?"

"Of the particular bottle, but I still—I kept the empty vial and the empty box as a control."

"No, I want to know whether you put on these experimental notes of yours the number of the lot and the number of cc's."

Dr. Jascalevich had another go. "The number of cc's I wrote down, sir."

"How about the number of the lot of the bottles?"

"The batch number?"

"The batch number—did you write that down in your experimental notes?"

"I don't know, sir. I didn't write them because I had the control."

I read these passages of the deposition so many times that the gray type seemed to be thinning out before my eyes. How I wished I could have been sitting on the lumpy leather couch in the prosecutor's office on that November day in 1966, when Calissi lost an opportunity to resolve so many of his questions and, now, so many of mine.

Dr. Jascalevich told Calissi that the only concern that supplied him with curare, and then only with the Lilly curare, was the General Surgical Supply Company, across the street from his home/office in West New York. And he said that he did not recall buying any curare there before 1965. But, I had previously discovered, the supply house's records showed that Dr. Jascalevich had paid $1.45 for a vial of curare on May 16, 1964. According to a detective's memo to Galda on November 14, 1966, Dr. Jascalevich informed the owners of the supply house that he was using curare "on dogs for experimental purposes, as he had a grant from the American Cancer Society." But that grant expired in 1964, and Dr. Jascalevich told Calissi that no curare had been used in the grant work. Moreover, the detective's memo said that Dr. Jascalevich had "never complained to any of the proprietors" of the supply house. I had read that memo when I first examined the Riverdell file. But only now, having read Dr. Jascalevich's deposition, did it mean something to me.

There were other discrepancies. Dr. Jascalevich said it was "very important" for a researcher to keep the empty vials—but had he, in fact, been faithful to this dictum? Between September 1965 and September 1966, according to the Riverdell file, the surgeon bought twenty-four vials of Lilly curare from the General Surgical Supply Company. But only nine of the eighteen vials taken from his Riverdell locker by Calissi were Lilly products. Where were the remaining fifteen Lilly vials? If they had been used, why weren't the empties in the Riverdell locker? If they hadn't been used, why did Dr. Jascalevich keep reordering the drug? And why didn't he house those full vials in the "safe" locker? Surely they were more dangerous than empties. When the surgeon found that some of his curare was "not working," he told Calissi, he didn't report the lot numbers of the vials to his supplier so the quality of the drug could be verified with Lilly. How, then, could he have "reflected" on whether he was hitting or missing his target because of the drug? And what was the point in continuing to use the faulty drug, as he said he had.

Dr. Jascalevich also said he was "methodic" and that "every data should be kept." But what did he mean when he said that "sometimes we use the same dog, same vial, so it wasn't that kind of detailed study"? And where were the notes he made on the posterior liver biopsy? Not the meager entries in the two anatomy books, which said "h.t." or "missed" and "MOVE IT UP WITH CURARE!!!" And not the one, undated slip of paper with his original drawings of the biopsy. But, rather, the notes that he said contained a "listing" of his dogs, the "approach I used," and the reactions of the dogs, and, again, whether he struck the target. Where were these notes? And how could Dr. Jascalevich say, at one stage of the deposition, that he didn't need to write down the lot numbers of the curare vials because he had saved the vials themselves; then say, a moment later, that the lot number was the first thing he recorded in his notes; and then say, in still another moment, "I don't know, sir—I didn't write them because I had the control." Surely he could have had little problem in remembering what he had done; the experiments, by his own account, were performed as recently as several months before his deposition.

The documents that Dr. Jascalevich submitted to Calissi on his other 1965–66 experiments were, in some instances, not notes at all. For one procedure, the surgeon turned in two illustrations, sketched on the pages of a pad advertising drugs. For another, he gave four sketches that seemed related to his 1963–64 research. With the sketches were two pages of notes, one of which outlined ten steps to be performed on each dog. The seventh and eighth steps involved "waking the dog" forty-eight hours after the gastrostomy, and the tenth step was to "finally de-intubate and observe dog for reactions." It would be difficult, I imagined, to wake up a dog forty-eight hours after it had been "destroyed" by curare or other means. Evidence of Dr. Jascalevich's work on another experiment, the gastric stapler, was contained in an article the surgeon had written and in several advertisements for the commercially manufactured stapler. I was drawn to the last sentence of the article, which said that the instrument had been in use as early as January 1964.

Dr. Jascalevich's gastroenterostomy tube, another of the "ideas" he told Calissi that he was testing in 1965–66, was also commercially manufactured. The surgeon showed the prosecutor a letter dated April 30, 1965, and said the date established "proof of the time" of these experiments. "This is the company that has fabricated this tube you see here [in] this photograph and the product [is] in the market today," he said. "Here it is, with my name on [it], the Jascalevich Gastroenterostomy Tube, sold throughout the country." The surgeon also submitted an article on the tube that he had written and that was published in the journal *Surgery,* in March 1966. Dr. Jascalevich specifically said, in the deposition, that the article was the result of his 1965–66, not his

1963–64, experiments. But on my third reading of the article, I noticed a footnote, in tiny print. The article had been "received for publication January 6, 1965."

The fourth element in Dr. Jascalevich's deposition dealt with the events of Wednesday, November 2, 1966, the day after Riverdell's directors had gone to Calissi. November 2 was a hectic day for Dr. Jascalevich and for others who figured in the Riverdell affair, and it was not easily reconstructed. Calissi had struggled, nine days later, to keep up with Dr. Jascalevich's account of November 2 as it moved from Oradell to Jersey City to West New York, with each place visited more than once. Nine years later I tried too. But as I examined Dr. Jascalevich's deposition and compared it to the statements of other doctors, medical researchers, and animal lab employees who had seen the surgeon on November 2, I was confronted only by a multitude of new questions.

The day began with a meeting at 11 A.M. between Dr. Jascalevich and Riverdell's directors at the home of Elliott J. Wiener, the hospital's administrator, in Oradell. Calissi had suggested on November 1 that the directors, who were anxious about Dr. Jascalevich's reaction when he discovered that his locker was empty, meet with the surgeon as soon as possible and get his explanation for the curare. Detective John Dunn of the prosecutor's office would monitor the meeting from a clothes closet in the Wiener home.

As Dr. Jascalevich recalled the session for Calissi more than a week later, he arrived thinking that the meeting would focus on the "explosive issue" of Eileen Shaw's death after cesarean surgery. Instead, he said, he found himself "surrounded" by the directors and Wiener and the hospital's lawyer, Andrew Emerson, and a tape recorder. Sarcastically, and in a "sort of triumphal" way, he went on, Dr. Sklar informed him that the prosecutor had executed a warrant "and searched all our lockers [in fact, only Dr. Jascalevich's locker had been entered] and in your locker medicines and drugs and syringes and things were found."

According to Riverdell's minutes, Dr. Jascalevich explained that the curare was for "gastrectomalogical surgery performed on animals at the Medical School of Seton Hall University; that he uses his locker at Riverdell Hospital as a convenient storage space between other hospitals where he practices and Seton Hall, where he goes for research only when animals are available; that the used syringes merely accumulated there; and that new, full syringes could be left exposed in an unantiseptic environment because there is no need to protect the objects of experimentation from infection." Dr. Jascalevich also said he had two lockers, not one, at Riverdell. Locker number four was his "dirty" locker—"dirty" in the sense that it was used to house the materials for his dog research. The other, larger locker, whose contents he now expressed great concern about, was his "clean" locker.

The deaths of some of Dr. Harris's patients were discussed at the November 2 meeting, and Dr. Jascalevich volunteered to supervise the younger surgeon's operations for three months at no extra charge to the patients. The chief surgeon, the minutes reflected, "had checked Dr. Harris's background and performance at Jewish Memorial Hospital [Dr. Harris was never on the staff of that hospital] and found that they were satisfactory. He felt that some of Dr. Harris's work seemed too slow and suggested that in the future he assist Dr. Harris in his more difficult operations. No other action concerning Dr. Harris was discussed, and no formal determination was made. Dr. Jascalevitch [*sic*] was then excused, and the curare matter discussed by the members of the board. None was of the opinion that suspension or other formal action was at this time required or warranted, on the basis of Dr. Jascalevitch's [*sic*] explanation. Accordingly, the matter was deferred pending the results of further investigation."

From Wiener's home, Dr. Jascalevich went to Riverdell "to see with my own eyes what happened to my locker." And from there, he told Calissi, he drove to Seton Hall Medical School in Jersey City, arriving about 1:30 or 2 P.M. Dr. Anthony Boccabella, the acting chairman of the anatomy department, gave Dr. Jascalevich a key to the glass-front cabinet on the fifteenth floor of the medical school building; and the surgeon, according to his deposition, went to the cabinet in a vain search for his "research bag" and certain surgical instruments for his experiments that he normally kept in locker number four. Dr. Jascalevich then saw Sal Riggi, the man in charge of the animal quarters on the sixteenth floor, and asked whether there were any dogs available for research. Riggi said that he could not provide any dogs and referred the surgeon to Dr. Timothy Regan, director of the cardiological department of medicine at Pollak Hospital, next door to the medical school. Dr. Jascalevich, who, by his own account, had never done any experiments at Pollak before November 2, immediately called on Dr. Regan.

"I introduced myself, I gave him my card, I told him I'm a clinical instructor in anatomy," Dr. Jascalevich said in his deposition. "I told him, 'Doctor, I'm in need. I'm testing some stapler.' He didn't know me."

"He didn't know you at the time?" Calissi asked.

"He didn't know me. He's in Pollak Hospital . . . I told him the kind of work I'm doing, that I was interested in testing this intestinal stapler and please I'll appreciate—because we don't have any more dogs at Seton Hall, they just gave me his name—please if he would let me work on his dogs. He told me, after some deliberation, he told me, yes, that I could, and he pointed me to the third floor . . . the place where I could get them."

With Dr. Regan's permission to experiment on two dogs that were to be disposed of that evening, Dr. Jascalevich went to the third floor at Pollak and introduced himself to Dr. William Burke, who was working on the dogs. Dr. Burke said he would finish his own experiments about 5 P.M. and suggested that Dr. Jascalevich return then.

Dr. Jascalevich drove to West New York, arriving about 3 P.M. At the General Surgical Supply Company, he bought three ounces of formaldehyde, and from his home, called Wiener at Riverdell Hospital.

"I told him, 'Sir, I went to Seton Hall today [and] there's not a trace of my instruments. There's not a trace of my research bag, and this is serious and I am going to the Oradell Police to make a deposition because I don't understand what's going on here; I don't want any part of this, and I'm going to contact my lawyer and I'm going to raise hell out of this situation.' And he said, 'No, don't do it, don't go to the police. Now wait, don't get excited, I could get it for you . . . I'll call you back.'"

Dr. Jascalevich hung up and, he later told Calissi, "took a rest." Meanwhile Wiener called Fred Galda, and the chief assistant prosecutor, for whatever reason, agreed to return some surgical instruments that had been seized under the warrant from locker number four.

At 5 P.M. on November 2, the surgeon was back at Pollak Hospital, where the two dogs were ready for him. Dr. Jascalevich, in his deposition, said that he wanted to test out a German-made stapler that he had —"this machine, very well known, all [such] machines since 1880s devised by a German surgeon, nothing new about it, one of the most common gastrointestinal machines. I'm interested in how much it bites the bowel, how much it destroys the bowel when it is applied . . . The animal sweeper . . . tied the legs in position so I could open the abdomen of this animal, and I performed my small procedure." The surgeon recalled that he put a piece of bowel in a plastic container with some formaldehyde and filled some test tubes with blood from the dog. He placed these items and the German stapler on the front seat of his 1965 Chevrolet Impala, and then "I went straight to Riverdell Hospital. Why? Because Mr. Wiener was about to get me these instruments and we had a concert at Lincoln Center at 8:30, so time was precious for me at that moment."

"Probably it will throw you," Dr. Jascalevich said toward the end of his deposition, "the idea why I am going to work on dogs on a day so crucial for me when an inquiry has been going on. How would I do some scientific work at a moment when I should be worried about this?"

But Dr. Jascalevich said it was not until 7 P.M. on November 2, when he received his instruments from Wiener in an envelope marked "County Prosecutor," that he realized law-enforcement authorities had carried out the search of his locker number four. Although the term "search warrant" had been used at his morning meeting with River- dell's directors, he was not given any official document to read or to see, and being "a layman in legal things," he did not appreciate the meaning of a search warrant. He had not heard anyone mention the county prosecutor or use the words "district attorney" before 7 P.M.— "because this," he said, "is something so serious that it would have shook me out of my shoes from the very first moment." Moreover, the ease with which Wiener assured him, at 3 P.M., that his instruments could be retrieved was "further reason for my idea that this was a purely internal matter at Riverdell Hospital." The directors of the hos- pital, he thought, may have seen the inside of locker number four— "because many times I leave the locker open"—and may have "mis- construed something," causing them to "sequester all these things as an internal investigation, as a domestic, purely domestic affair."

Calissi, it seemed, couldn't keep up with Dr. Jascalevich's account of November 2. Time—and perhaps will—ran out on November 11. An- derson reminded the prosecutor that he wanted to be out of his office by 3:30 P.M.; and Calissi, behind in his own schedule that afternoon, acceded to ending the deposition.

Too bad, I felt. The last part of Dr. Jascalevich's deposition was as unsettling as it was incomplete. For example, Calissi had asked the sur- geon whether he had inquired about the location of his research bag and surgical tools when he inspected locker number four between noon and 1 P.M. on November 2 and saw that it was empty.

Dr. Jascalevich said he hadn't, because an internal matter like this "is not something to be published or to be asking right or left, to nurses and everything, who took this or who took that."

"I didn't ask you to ask nurses," Calissi said. "I asked you, did you ask the administrator who took what out of your locker?"

"No, I didn't direct the question to him, no."

"You didn't ask anybody. Is that right?"

"Right. I thought it was the hospital took all these things."

That exchange appeared on page 191 of the transcript of the deposi- tion. On pages 192 and 193, the surgeon changed his account.

"Did you ask Mr. Wiener at that time who took the items out of your locker?" Calissi repeated.

"At 1 o'clock?"

"At 1 o'clock when you went from the meeting to the hospital, you opened up your locker, you looked in the locker, there is nothing in the locker."

"Yes."

"Did you ask anybody?"

"Yes, yes."

"In the hospital?"

"Yes, I asked Mr. Wiener," Dr. Jascalevich said. And the administrator, according to Dr. Jascalevich, advised him that his surgical instruments and research bag were probably in his second, larger Riverdell locker.

It was several pages more before Calissi asked the surgeon whether he then opened his second locker at the hospital. And the exchange that followed this question was even more confusing than Dr. Jascalevich's preceding about-face.

"No," the surgeon said, "because I was told, and this is another misleading thing, in the meeting that all lockers were opened, so I didn't even look in the second one."

"Why not?"

"All lockers were opened."

"You looked in the empty locker, did you not?"

"I didn't look."

"You didn't look in the empty locker?"

"No, I didn't."

"You saw the one locker, locker number four, was empty, did you not?"

"Pardon me, sir, this is—you will have to forgive me," Dr. Jascalevich begged. "When Mr. Wiener told me at 1 o'clock when I went back to the hospital and I saw my locker open, told me probably it's in the large locker, I told him probably it is . . . let's go, and we opened the locker. It wasn't there."

"Then you went to Seton Hall?"

"Because if it wasn't . . . in my locker, it must be some place."

Where did the truth lie? Was Dr. Jascalevich unaware until 7 P.M. on November 2 that it was Calissi who had searched his locker number four at Riverdell? Wiener later told Galda that he did not think Dr. Jascalevich knew of the prosecutor's involvement until perhaps 3 P.M. on November 2, when the administrator, in his telephone conversation with Dr. Jascalevich, may have indicated it to him. "I didn't want him to think that a burglar broke in and emptied the contents of his locker, although he had been told that there was a search warrant," Wiener recalled. But hadn't the prosecutor been explicitly mentioned at Dr.

Jascalevich's meeting with Riverdell's directors, and Wiener, at 11
A.M.? Whatever the surgeon said toward the end of his 208-page deposition, he earlier quoted Dr. Sklar as having said, "Mario, we have to
tell you that last night we were served with a warrant and that the prosecutor was here and searched all our lockers . . ." And the minutes of
the 11 A.M. meeting supported that recollection. Why would the surgeon go to Seton Hall to look for his "research bag" and instruments if
he believed that Riverdell's directors—"the hospital"—had taken the
articles? Dr. Jascalevich told Calissi that he sometimes left his surgical
tools for the dogs in the glass-front cabinet at Seton Hall, and "they are
difficult to locate sometimes, things that you see every day are so hard,
this is my bread and butter." Yet Dr. Jascalevich worried about the expense of research dogs and of disposable or quarter syringes. How
could he ever have thought the Seton Hall cabinet sufficiently secure
for his valuable instruments? And why would the "research bag," in
which the surgeon said he carried a "drug box" containing vials of
curare, be at the medical school? The Seton Hall cabinet wasn't "safe"
enough for the drug.

Eventually the "research bag," which was not in locker number four
when Calissi seized the contents, was found by Dr. Jascalevich. And
once more the circumstances were unusual.

When Wiener and Dr. Jascalevich opened the surgeon's larger,
"clean" locker—just before Dr. Jascalevich left for Seton Hall at 1
P.M. on November 2—they saw a number of surgical instruments other
than those that had been confiscated from locker number four. Dr.
Jascalevich, Wiener told Galda, said "'Oh, thank God' or words to
that effect" and closed the locker without taking the tools out or making an inventory. There was nothing in the Riverdell file to indicate
that anyone reopened the "clean" locker on November 2, although Dr.
Jascalevich was back at the hospital around 7 P.M. About 10 A.M. the
next day, November 3, the surgeon asked Wiener to revisit his "clean"
locker with him. But, just then, the phone rang and the administrator
had to take the call. So Dr. Sklar, who happened to be present, agreed
to go with Dr. Jascalevich.

"Did he give you a reason for requesting that someone or you go
with him to his locker?" Calissi asked Dr. Sklar later that day, after Dr.
Jascalevich and Riverdell's directors had been summoned to the prosecutor's office.

"I don't remember exactly, sir."

"You don't remember?"

"I just remember that he was interested in seeing his instruments
were all there, he wanted to make sure they were all there."

Calissi handed Dr. Sklar a cup of coffee, and the physician resumed his account. The second locker, he said, was also in the doctors' dressing room, a few feet from locker number four. Dr. Jascalevich glanced at some faint numbers that were written on the wall next to this larger locker and, dialing a combination, opened the chamber. "He said—well, I said something first. 'There's a lot of stuff in there,' and there was. There was a lot of instruments and things like that in there. And he said, 'I'm worried about a drug bag' . . . 'Drug bag' is, I believe, is the word he used, and 'I can't find it and some experimental things.' And at first he didn't seem able to find it because he pulled a lot of stuff out of the locker and laid them alongside the floor." Then, Dr. Sklar said, Dr. Jascalevich reached into the rear of the locker and came up with a blue and white Horn & Hardart shopping bag bearing the slogan, "The public appreciates quality." It was the surgeon's "research bag." Dr. Jascalevich closed the "clean" locker and carried the bag into the office of the nursing supervisor, Winifred Turrone. Blood was leaking from the bag, and Wiener, who had now joined Dr. Jascalevich and Dr. Sklar, dabbed it up from Miss Turrone's desk. As Dr. Jascalevich began to remove some items from the bag, the phone rang and "you people," Dr. Sklar said to Calissi, "wanted to see Dr. Jascalevich . . . 'What should I do with these?' " Dr. Sklar recalled the surgeon saying. "I said, 'I don't know what to do with them. Why don't you take them with you?' and he did."

Galda had a question for Dr. Sklar. "Of your own personal observation of the doctor and his general habits . . . would you consider him a neat man or a sloppy man?"

"Very neat," Dr. Sklar said. "The man does meticulous surgery . . . He is absolutely what appears to be a perfectionist. His cases turn out as if a perfectionist had handled them."

"And you say, as far as you know of his habits, he is meticulous?"

"Yes, sir, absolutely. He even dresses that way . . . The only other observation, and I would say it's a very candid one, this was some sloppy mess to have in anyone's locker, things in a Horn & Hardart bag with blood dripping and most unusual."

I, too, thought it was unusual. But even more absorbing was Dr. Jascalevich's explanation, as it was summarized in a report on November 4 by Detective Edward Kastner. "The second locker," Detective Kastner wrote, "allegedly contained the doctor's instruments that he used in performing human operations. Upon examining this locker, he found the items submitted . . . hidden in the rear, and he alleges that someone had removed this bag from the locker we were in [locker four] and placed it in his other locker. He further states that he is involved in research of a secretive nature using dogs and that these items would show conclusively that he has been working on dogs." But the detective wasn't taking Dr. Jascalevich's story at face value, because he went on to raise the question of whether the surgeon "could have put these items in this locker as a cover. It has been determined that on Tuesday, November 2, 1966, after discussing this matter with the [Riverdell] board of directors, he did try to obtain a dog."

But Dr. Jascalevich had done more than try to obtain a dog; he had actually gotten two and worked on at least one. I looked over the prosecutor's original list of the nineteen items, presumably all from the "research bag" that the surgeon had turned over to Calissi on November 3. Syringes. Tweezers. Scissors. An 11-inch "clamp." A pair of surgical gloves, inside of which was a 12-cc plastic syringe holding 2 cc of "a fluid that appears to contain curare." Four jars, labeled "Seton Hall Research ✕101," containing tubular pieces of tissue in formaldehyde. And one bottle, labeled "Formaldehyde," from the General Surgical Supply Company.

Two things surprised me. One was the labels on the jars—they appeared to be numbered and suggested that Dr. Jascalevich had worked on as many as forty-four dogs. But in his deposition the surgeon said that he had had a total of about fifteen dogs in 1965 and 1966. The other thing was the bottle of formaldehyde. In the Riverdell file was a roster of the materials that Dr. Jascalevich had purchased from the General Surgical Supply Company between January 4, 1965, and November 2, 1966. Only once during that period had he bought formaldehyde there—and that was on the afternoon of November 2, 1966, just before he returned to Pollak Hospital to work on the dog. How could this bottle of formaldehyde have gotten into Dr. Jascalevich's "research bag" sometime after he bought it on November 2 if someone other than the surgeon had the bag?

There were also Dr. Jascalevich's remarks about formaldehyde in his deposition. The surgeon said that before his experiment on a dog at Pollak Hospital at 5 P.M. on November 2, he had used formaldehyde only once in his research. The occasion, he said, was at the end of August or the beginning of September 1966, when he last did any work in the animal quarters on the sixteenth floor of the Seton Hall Medical School. An attendant there gave him some formaldehyde for the four jars that he submitted to the prosecutor on November 3, Dr. Jascalevich said.

Calissi wanted to know more. Why had Dr. Jascalevich bothered to buy preservative on November 2, "if it was so simple to get the formaldehyde by asking one of the colored boys over there at Seton Hall?"

"I think the reason is that I wanted to do a very large series of experiences and I couldn't depend on the material taken from the school. It's all right once, but certainly I wanted to have my own."

I fixed on the words ". . . I wanted to do a very large series of experiences . . ." When Dr. Jascalevich went so urgently to Dr. Regan at Pollak Hospital at 2 P.M. on November 2 and implored the cardiologist for a dog—he was "fairly pushy that afternoon," Dr. Regan later told detectives—the surgeon still didn't know the whereabouts of the "research bag" and instruments that were so important to him. Nor did he know their whereabouts when he bought the bottle of formaldehyde on his way home—before he called Wiener at Riverdell. Yet here he was telling Calissi that he had "a very large series" of experiments in mind. "Time," he said himself, "was precious for me."

So why should he fight the traffic that evening between his house in West New York, Pollak Hospital in Jersey City, and Riverdell in Oradell? According to a statement taken by detectives on November 4 from Robert DeSantis, the animal handler at Pollak Hospital, Dr. Jascalevich stayed only "fifteen or twenty minutes" at Pollak and worked on only one of the two dogs that had been made available to him. If Dr. Jascalevich planned "a very large series" of experiments, even without the research bag and instruments that were missing, why, having gone out of his way to obtain a dog, had he not performed at least his usual battery of a half-dozen experiments? And what was so pressing about the experiment with the common German stapler, an instrument with which Dr. Jascalevich seemed well acquainted and about which, he said, "nothing was new."

Something else baffled me. Dr. Jascalevich said he had gotten "dying dogs" at Seton Hall in 1965 and 1966 by tipping attendants who would sweep up after the evening departure of their boss, Sal Riggi, the man in charge of the animal quarters on the sixteenth floor of the medical school. Except for one instance in 1965, the surgeon did not approach Riggi for dogs because Riggi would either have charged him for a "live" dog or refused him, on the grounds that the dogs in the cages belonged to other researchers. In August or September 1966, Dr. Jascalevich told Calissi, he was informed by the attendants that "experimental surgery" on dogs was no longer being done on the sixteenth floor and that he would be unable to work there anymore. Still, the surgeon said, he expected "a change in policy" and continued to ask the attendants, from time to time, about the situation. "And the answer," he recalled, "was always, 'no dogs yet, no dogs yet.'"

This much I could follow. But I couldn't understand why, on November 2, Dr. Jascalevich had asked Riggi, rather than the attendants, about the availability of dogs. Reading Dr. Jascalevich's deposition, I got the impression that the surgeon merely asked Riggi "are we getting any dogs, any chance of working?" and the caretaker, before referring Dr. Jascalevich to Pollak said, "No, since September this is finished."

But looking over statements that were taken from Riggi at Seton Hall on November 4 and 5, I formed quite another impression.

Riggi said that he had met Dr. Jascalevich only once before November 2, 1966. It was in the summer of 1965, he recalled, and the surgeon "brought the new stapling machine" to the animal quarters on Seton Hall's sixteenth floor. The caretaker let Dr. Jascalevich use his instrument on a dog that Riggi said "I was told to get rid of because he was sick." Riggi anesthetized the dog with Nembutal and did not charge the doctor any money. On November 2, 1966, the caretaker continued, he met Dr. Jascalevich in the hallway, apparently on the sixteenth floor. "He asked me if I had any spare dogs because he wanted to try out a new instrument. Because most of these dogs belonged to different doctors, I told him he would have to ask the doctors if they could give him any," Riggi said. The caretaker specifically suggested that the surgeon contact Dr. Regan at Pollak because the cardiologist still had a dog out from the Seton Hall animal quarters and might lend it to Dr. Jascalevich.

The surgeon, according to Riggi, told the caretaker that he had "a cabinet that he kept his instruments in in one of the laboratories" and "asked me what we used to anesthetize. I said to my knowledge we used Nembutal, and he asked me the strength. I said 60 mm per cc—1 cc for every 10 lb of dog—and he wrote this down and mentioned curare and asked me if I ever used it. I told him we never had it."

Detective Vahe Garabedian asked Riggi whether Dr. Jascalevich "mentioned that he wanted to use it."

"Yes, he said that he had seen an animal under the influence of the drug and the animal was really relaxed and that during the operation the animal was awake but had no pain . . . The only thing he threw me was that he told me . . . he was getting about one dog a week from one of the guys for one dollar. And that was the first time I heard of that."

I was intrigued. Why was this experienced researcher suddenly asking Riggi about his method of anesthetizing dogs? Why was he bringing up curare? And why, to Riggi of all people, was he talking about the attendants who had given him "dying dogs"?

I hadn't been in Jersey City in many years, but on a fall night in 1975, I drove out to Beacon Street. I parked my car in front of number 118, the address listed by detectives on Riggi's statements nine years earlier. Finding no bell on the gray-shingle row house, I banged on the door. I got no answer and knocked again. On the second floor I could see lights behind the green brocaded curtains. I lifted the collar of my sport coat against the chill and hit the door once more. This time it opened, and standing there, in khaki workpants and a T-shirt, was a burly, balding man who looked to be in his midfifties. Sal Riggi invited me in, and we sat around his basement pool table while I laid out my purpose in coming.

Riggi, it turned out, had been a dog handler at Seton Hall from 1958 to 1962; from 1963 on, he had been in charge of the animal quarters. The medical school itself had subsequently been taken over by the state and was now located in Newark, where it was renamed the New Jersey College of Medicine and Dentistry. I had brought my copy of Dr. Jascalevich's deposition and, as Riggi listened to the surgeon's description of his activities on the sixteenth floor in 1965–66, he rubbed a big hand over the stubble of his cheek and shook his head.

"I'll tell you this much," Riggi said. "I don't know anything about this guy except what I told the detectives back then. But I'll swear on my father's grave that nobody did any experiments on the sixteenth floor, day or night. And I'll tell you why. Because there was no dogs to work on. Dying dogs? It's impossible. We used to send out the dogs in the morning to the labs where the doctors did their work, and that included Pollak. But at night the dogs came back to their cages, to be used on other days. Or they came back dead and wrapped in plastic bags, and were put in the refrigerator. What's this guy talking about dogs tied down on tables on the sixteenth floor? Never. It never happened. We only had one little table. We used it for shaving the dogs and anesthetizing them. But not for experiments. Like I say, it's impossible. I would have known about it. I was right there all day."

Riggi mashed a cigarette into the ash tray on the edge of the pool table. "I'll tell you something else. These guys who used to work for me—they used to get out of that place even before me at night. One of them was scared to death that he might see a mouse."

My talk with Riggi, who seemed so certain of his facts, added to my quandary. I left his house determined to learn more about the setup for dog research at Seton Hall around 1966 and more about Dr. Jascalevich, whom I was nearly ready to call. As a start I turned back to the deposition the surgeon had given to Guy Calissi on November 11, 1966. Calissi—who was known by his real first name, Gaetano, before an Irish classmate at his boyhood orphanage dubbed him "Guy"—had listened with interest as Mario Enrique Jascalevich noted that he, too, was of Italian ancestry.

"How did the French get into the middle, Enrique?" Calissi asked.

"Enrique is Spanish," Dr. Jascalevich explained. "Actually from my mother's side I'm Italian and from my father's side, Yugoslavic near the Italian border. So there is a very strong Latin-Italian ancestry, and having been brought up in the Italian pattern of education and customs and everything, I think that is how my Mario came in and even my Enrico." The surgeon said that he was born and raised in the Italian quarter of Buenos Aires, Argentina.

But Calissi asked little more, in 1966, about Dr. Jascalevich's life. So, in late 1975, I began to sketch it in from other sources, including, eventually, some in Argentina.

Mario Jascalevich's father, Enrique, was also a doctor, a graduate (as his son would be) of the University of Buenos Aires Medical School. Mario's mother, Anna Maria Gomez, was an Argentinian of Spanish and northern Italian extraction. The Jascaleviches were living in La Boca, an old section of Buenos Aires with many families of Italian origin, when Mario, their first child, was born on August 27, 1927. The family, soon increased by the birth of another boy, Oscar, continued to live in Buenos Aires until the mid-1930s when Enrique decided to move to Villa Alba, a village on the flat, grassy pampas about 100 miles west of the capital. Villa Alba, however, had only a grade school. So around 1940, as Mario approached the age for secondary school, the Jascaleviches settled in nearby Chivilcoy, a marketing center of 40,000 people.

Physically, Chivilcoy resembled a cow town of the American plains, with the roads more suited to horses than to cars and with few buildings more than two stories high. But the town had a good school and library, and the Jascaleviches seemed to like it. Enrique bought a house two blocks off the central plaza and resumed his medical practice. The doctor also received an appointment to the staff of the local hospital. Mrs. Jascalevich, whose domestic duties were lightened by a maid who helped to raise Mario and Oscar, was a calm woman and a faithful Catholic who had an altar at home and a cross over her bed.

"Mario was quiet and polite, oh, very polite, even with his own family," a friend of Enrique's recalled years later. "He was a smart boy, too; smarter than me and his father put together. In those days there wasn't much diversion for a boy in Chivilcoy. There was little going out for coffee or dancing or smoking, like now. Mario was a good swimmer, a good diver. And he liked the movies. He was interested not just in the subject, but in the quality of the acting. Mostly they were American films."

From 1940 to 1945 Mario attended the local high school. "Of us all," said a classmate, "Mario was the most dedicated to study. He was very delicate and refined, the kind to be at home while the rest of us were out playing ball. He was the person we went to see when an exam was coming because he knew the answers, and he would help." Mario did poorly in mathematics at the school. But he was adept at music— he played the piano at home—and at science and languages, including French, Italian, and English. His English, improved by Al Jolson records, back issues of *Life* magazine and a frequently consulted dictionary, was especially important to him because even then he was planning to become a doctor and emigrate to the United States. His uncle, Alexander Jascalevich, had gone to New York many years earlier, earning a graduate degree in philosophy at Columbia University. "Mario always wanted to go to the United States," his brother remembered. "He always had that idea. More than anything he dreamt about being good professionally and learning a lot in the U.S."

Mario entered the University of Buenos Aires in the summer of 1945 and completed its medical school curriculum in 1951. While writing his thesis on the development of the liver—citing, among other works, the two anatomy books that he turned in to Calissi in 1966—he assisted in the private clinic of his thesis adviser, Dr. Alfonso R. Albanese. Dr. Albanese, one of Argentina's most distinguished surgeons, would recall later that Mario went by the last name of Gomez, rather than

Jascalevich, in the early 1950s. He described Mario as "a brisk person, who agitated easily," but also "a very intelligent pupil. He knew very well his surgical anatomy."

The years that Mario spent at the university—he received his M.D. degree in 1953—coincided with Juan Perón's consolidation of power in Argentina. But politics held little interest for Mario, whose life was anchored in his classes and in the apartment that he shared with two other medical students, Daniel Pastorino and Rolbider Feola, in the Barrio del Once, a busy shopping district about ten minutes from the university. Mario's separate room was something of an American outpost. Copies of the English-language Buenos Aires *Herald* lay about, the songs of Bing Crosby and Frank Sinatra wafted out to Sarmiento Street, and from the wall over the night table, a photograph of Franklin D. Roosevelt looked benevolently on the young medical student. Mario's apartment mates would remember him as an amiable but essentially introverted person who "lived like a monk." "He worked very hard, and he wanted to make something of himself," Dr. Feola said. "He was in his own world." Mario made a similar impression on Javier Salzman, another student, and his wife. "He liked coming to see us, but he was always alone, he never had a girl friend," Mrs. Salzman reflected. "He was a very good person, bighearted, very kind to the children. He was distracted too, like a genius. Always in the clouds."

Javier Salzman admired Mario's skill in anatomy. As students, he said, they had worked together on dogs, mainly for lack of patients on whom to perfect their surgical techniques. The dogs would be anesthetized and given curare to relax their muscles, according to Dr. Salzman. A battery of surgical maneuvers, ending with a posterior liver biopsy, would then be tried. Dr. Salzman remembered it vividly. It was the way, he told me, that he and Mario routinely spent Wednesday afternoons in Buenos Aires.

Mario arrived in the United States in the spring of 1955. Then twenty-seven, he took an internship at Passaic General Hospital in Passaic, New Jersey, and in July 1956 he began a four-year residency at the New York Polyclinic Medical School and Hospital on Manhattan's West Side. Polyclinic, bankrupt and out of business by 1977, was not among the city's first-rank hospitals in the late 1950s. But it wasn't the worst, either, and Mario did well there. He was given a monthly stipend of $100 and a small room in the staff quarters, and he more than earned his keep. Industrious, efficient, reserved, deferential to his superiors—that was how he was remembered by senior physicians and fellow residents. "He learned quickly and had good hands," a resident at that time recalled. "He was always striving to do something better.

He didn't have much training in the basic sciences, but he wanted to be an inventor, a researcher. He had a tremendous ambition for this." While at Polyclinic, Mario developed a postoperative stomach-feeding tube, somewhat related to the experiments he would do at Seton Hall Medical School in 1963–64, and an apparatus for helping to clean intestinal openings in the skin after abdominal surgery. The devices were not seminal achievements. But like Mario's later modification on a standard stapler for suturing during surgery, they demonstrated the Argentinian's flair for improving on surgical appliances. To old ideas, Mario grafted new ones.

It was during his residency that Mario met his future wife. Nora Caperan was four years younger than Mario, but in the field in which her talents lay she was already more advanced. Under her mother's tutelage, Nora had begun her piano studies when she was four years old and living in Chivilcoy. She made her recital debut at the age of six, and when she was thirteen, she entered the National Conservatory of Music in Buenos Aires, soon winning first prize in the Hebrew Society Piano Competition. Nora graduated from the conservatory with highest distinction in 1948 and appeared in concert halls throughout Latin America in the early 1950s. In 1956 she joined the music department at the University of Iowa and a year later enrolled as a scholarship student at the Juilliard School of Music in Manhattan.

By 1957 both Mario and Nora were living in New York. But their introduction—they hadn't met in either Chivilcoy or Buenos Aires—came through Argentina. Like his son Mario, the elder Enrique Jascalevich had decided to emigrate to the United States, and he was taking English lessons in Chivilcoy from a Londoner named Vera Palumba. Miss Palumba also knew Nora's family, and she arranged for a letter from Mario's father to be sent to the pianist in New York. Enrique thought the young woman would be good company for his son. Mario, according to his fellow residents at Polyclinic, took quickly to the strong-minded pianist, and the two Argentinians spent much of their free time together. Occasionally Nora, who represented her country at the Brussels World Fair in 1958, gave a concert in the Chinese social lounge on the roof of the Polyclinic building.

Life was going less smoothly for Mario's parents. Just after his decision to emigrate, Enrique Jascalevich discovered that his wife had cancer of the breast, necessitating an operation. The surgery went well enough for Mario's parents to leave for the United States, and around 1958 the elder Dr. Jascalevich and his wife moved into an apartment in Weehawken, New Jersey. Weehawken, at the New Jersey mouth of the Lincoln Tunnel, was a frayed working-class town best known as the site where, in 1804, Aaron Burr shot Alexander Hamilton. But Mario showed his parents all over New York, and Enrique Jascalevich reported effusively on the city to his friends in Chivilcoy. The view from the top of the Empire State Building was "magnificent," he wrote; "one can see New York like a fantastic place full of skyscrapers and lights from everywhere . . . And it is wonderful to know the black neighborhood and the Chinese and the Latin neighborhood; all of them live with great comfort and with a car at the door."

A year after his arrival, Enrique Jascalevich suffered a stroke that left him partially paralyzed. And, in September 1960, his wife died of cancer. Mario's father moved back to Argentina, to the home of his son, Oscar, who had become a dentist. Enrique Jascalevich died in July 1966.

After Mario finished his residency at Polyclinic in June 1960, he became chief surgical resident at Christ Hospital in Jersey City. In 1961 he was naturalized and received his New Jersey medical license and, in early 1962, he and Nora were married by a magistrate in West New York, New Jersey. The couple promptly bought a two-story, white-brick row house across the street from the West New York Town Hall, and from one of the columns on the front porch, Dr. Jascalevich hung out his shingle. The house was at 435 Sixtieth Street, in the heart of West New York's commercial district.

But Sixtieth Street was also "doctor's row," and the practitioners there drew patients from a wide area. West New York overlooked the Hudson River and the West Side of Manhattan, and it had once been a genteel town of single-family homes and parks. By 1962, however, it had become the most densely populated community in New Jersey, with 40,000 people jammed into its square mile. The town had seen its waves of Irish, Germans, and Italians, but in the late 1950s and early 1960s, most of the newcomers were Cubans who had fled Batista's or Castro's Havana and had made their way north through Miami. Many of them spoke little English, and when their medical needs arose, they were inclined to favor a doctor who could converse easily with them. So the lines began to form at 435 Sixtieth Street, and Dr. Jascalevich, one of the first Spanish-speaking physicians in West New York, was kept busy. Then, as later, many of his patients could say nothing but the best about him.

In 1962 Dr. Jascalevich became a diplomate of the American Board of Surgery and broadened his hospital affiliations to include the Jersey City Medical Center, North Hudson Hospital, and in November of that year, Riverdell Hospital. He also joined the faculty of the Seton Hall Medical School as a nonsalaried, part-time clinical instructor in anatomy. The school was the first institution to grant medical degrees in New Jersey and was only six years old in 1962. For decades the power-

ful antivivisectionist movement in New Jersey had stood in the way of
a school in which animals would be subjected to experimentation.

In November 1966 Calissi's detectives determined that the "Lee"
who had supposedly given Dr. Jascalevich "dying dogs" at Seton Hall
in exchange for tips was Lee Henderson. Henderson, who had left
Seton Hall as early as January 31, 1966, was the only person named
Lee who had worked in the animal quarters in the 1960s. Although
Dr. Jascalevich told Calissi on November 11, 1966, that other attendants had also provided him with "dying dogs" in 1965–66, the detectives did not interview any of the attendants at the medical school. And
they didn't make much of an effort to find Lee Henderson. Seton Hall
gave the detectives his address—133 Randolph Avenue, Jersey City—
and his social security number. But the detectives soon discovered that
Henderson had moved away. And they found, too, that they were not
the only law enforcement officers looking for him. Henderson had split
up with his wife, and the Jersey City police wanted him on charges of
desertion and nonsupport. Calissi's detectives gave up. They asked the
Jersey City police to notify them if Henderson reappeared. But they
made no effort to find and question Henderson's wife, who was also
gone from Randolph Avenue, and they did not pursue a suggestion by
Riggi that Henderson might have returned to relatives who, Riggi
thought, were living in North Carolina.

I had to find Lee. I now asked Riggi where in North Carolina the
relatives might be. But the caretaker had no idea and hadn't heard
from Henderson for a decade. Moreover, Riggi pointed out, Lee might
have moved any number of times since 1966, even if he had gone
south then. I hoped that Henderson had given a relative's address—or
his birthplace—in his application for a job at Seton Hall. But the personnel office at the New Jersey College of Medicine and Dentistry said
that some of the files from 1960 had been destroyed and others couldn't
be located. I doubted that Henderson's old address held much promise,
but it was worth a try; somebody in the neighborhood might know the
man's whereabouts.

The area around Randolph Avenue was one of the toughest, most
crime-ridden in Jersey City in 1975. "Watch yourself," a cop cautioned
me when I stopped for directions. But, at 4 P.M., Randolph Avenue
seemed hospitable. It was a narrow, one-way street and the 100 block,
blighted by a few rubble-strewn lots, was a string of pleasant, if deteri-
orating, homes. Number 133 was just over a hill in the middle of the
block, a two-story frame structure obscured by the limbs of a tree that
soared to its peaked attic. I knocked on the door of the screened porch
and was received by a middle-aged black man. Henderson? The man

had never heard of him. The house, he believed, had changed hands several times since 1966. I thanked the man and started down the steep front steps. In the street a half-dozen kids, ten or twelve years old, were tossing a football, and I approached them, asking whether their parents knew anyone by the name of Henderson. One of the boys was about to say something when a woman popped out of a house across the street and yelled, "Don't talk to that man!" The woman shouted again and the kids moved away. I stood aside as they gathered around the woman. Maybe I look like a bill collector, I thought. It didn't matter, of course. This was her street, not mine. She had probably been watching me since I got out of the car. I wasn't going to learn much about Henderson on Randolph Avenue.

From the Jersey City tax rolls, I traced the ownership of Number 133 Randolph and discovered that Henderson had acquired the place in 1964 with the aid of a Veterans Administration–guaranteed mortgage loan. He had lost the house in late 1966, and it had passed into the hands of a bank in Newark. At the bank, officials told me that Henderson's name had a "Jr." attached to it and that his wife's name was Barbara Ann. But the bank did not have a more recent address for either of the Hendersons and neither, I found, did the VA.

There was another possibility: Henderson might have kept in touch with some of the other attendants who worked in the Seton Hall animal quarters. I wanted to talk to the other attendants anyway, especially to those who continued to work at Seton Hall after Henderson left in January 1966.

The New Jersey College of Medicine and Dentistry, still under construction in 1975, was housed in quonset huts opposite Martland Hospital in Newark. When I dropped by the animal quarters, Riggi was away from his office. I looked around for a few minutes, but the dogs began to yap. Two attendants who had been hosing down the cement floors came over and said that Riggi would be back in an hour. No, the attendants said, they had not worked at Seton Hall. I made use of the hour by talking to several people who had been questioned by Calissi's detectives in 1966. One was Robert DeSantis, the animal attendant who had seen Dr. Jascalevich experiment on a dog at Pollak Hospital on the afternoon of November 2, 1966.

While he cleaned up a lab, DeSantis told me that he had regularly picked up and returned dogs to the sixteenth floor at Seton Hall in 1965 and 1966, and he had never seen any experiments or dying dogs there. He remembered the names of some of the Seton Hall attendants of that era—Henderson, Logan Mongo, Roe Chambliss—but he didn't know where they were now. Except for Chambliss. Chambliss was dead.

DeSantis had run out of names when a researcher strolled into the lab and asked what I was doing. He introduced himself as Timothy Regan, and I recognized that name at once. He was the cardiologist who had given Dr. Jascalevich permission to work on the dog at Pollak on November 2, 1966. Dr. Regan asked me to step into his office, where he reprimanded me for conducting interviews without approval from the school. I could see that I wasn't going to get anywhere with Dr. Regan unless I went through channels. But, closing my briefcase, I hastily asked one or two questions. Only DeSantis, Regan said, took dogs back to Seton Hall from Pollak, "and they weren't dying dogs."

Figuring that Dr. Regan would notify officials of my presence, I hurried on to the office of Anthony Boccabella, who was still chairman of the anatomy department. Dr. Boccabella gave me a polite welcome. He said that apart from the dogs which were sent over to Pollak from the sixteenth-floor animal quarters at Seton Hall, dogs were distributed by Riggi to laboratories in the Seton Hall building itself. "I used mice on the fifteenth floor, so I wasn't too involved in that, but physiology, maybe on the eleventh floor, used dogs quite a lot. Why don't you ask them? I know Jascalevich once showed me a dog up on the sixteenth floor, when he had a grant in 1963 or 1964. I vaguely remember him working up there then."

Mindful of Riggi's claim that no experiments had been done on the sixteenth floor, I pumped Dr. Boccabella for details. "Think about it," I said. "Are you sure it was on the sixteenth floor?"

"Yes, I think so. Our office, the anatomy office, was on the ninth floor, and this was upstairs."

"Could it have been in 1965 or 1966, not earlier?"

"No," the anatomist said, "it was when he had that grant. I'm positive of that, and it was only that one time."

"Well, did you ever see anyone else, any other doctor or researcher, up on the sixteenth floor?"

"No, I don't think I ever did. But, as I said, my work wasn't done up there."

"How about the dog Jascalevich showed you?" I asked. "Could it have been tied down on a table? Perhaps in a dying condition?"

"Oh, no. Definitely not. He was walking it around. It had tubes in it."

I unzipped my briefcase, took out Dr. Jascalevich's deposition and read Dr. Boccabella a few passages regarding the "dying dogs" in 1955–66. He was incredulous.

"I just don't believe that anybody left dying dogs—that's out," he said. "They were damn careful with animals. They were so frightened of adverse publicity from antivivisectionists. I know the physiologists used to kill off the dogs right when they were finished with them. I mean, right down on that floor where they were being used. I was here many nights in '65 and '66, and I never saw Jascalevich come in. Dogs left dying on tables?" Dr. Boccabella stifled a laugh. "That's out," he repeated. "Have you asked Riggi about this; he's the one to ask."

"Yes, I have; and Riggi says there wasn't any research at all in the animal quarters. What do you make of that?"

"I don't know. Riggi ran the place. He was damn good."

"Would you trust Riggi's word?"

"Yes, I think I would," the professor said. "We've never had cause not to."

"Dr. Jascalevich was well thought of too, wasn't he?"

"He was quite good as a teacher and certainly pleasant enough with his colleagues . . . He was all business. A serious individual."

"Did he stay at Seton Hall after '66?"

"He left the department about 1968. I think he said he could no longer afford the time."

"Why did you think the detectives had been around in '66?" I asked.

"I was never sure what they were after," Dr. Boccabella said. "I never knew."

Riggi was in when I got back to his office. Again he insisted that Dr. Jascalevich could not have worked on "dying dogs" on the sixteenth floor at Seton Hall and that no research of any kind was carried on there. Despite Dr. Boccabella's recollection of a dog with "tubes in it," Riggi had no idea where the surgeon had done his experiments in 1963–64. The caretaker added one name, Dewey Mincey, to the DeSantis list of former Seton Hall attendants. But, like DeSantis, he didn't know where any of the men could be found now. Dewey Mincey, he said, had left not long ago and might still be living in Jersey City.

Riggi showed me to the door. "What are you going to do with all this?"

"I'm not certain yet."

"Well, whatever I've told you is the truth."

"I hope so, Sal. Because I wouldn't be here if it wasn't important. Nobody is going to get in any trouble today for having given some dogs ten years ago. If it happened, just say so."

"Mr. Farber, the man's wrong."

"Well, Sal, when you saw Jascalevich on November 2, 1966, and he told you that he was getting dogs for a dollar or two from the attendants, did you ask them about it?"

"No, I don't think I did."

"Why not?"

"Why should I? I didn't know what the guy was talking about."

I didn't believe that Riggi was lying about research on the sixteenth floor. But could he be mistaken? Could Dr. Boccabella be wrong about the floor on which Dr. Jascalevich showed him the intubated dog? Or could it have been a one-time occurrence that escaped Riggi's attention? In the Riverdell file was the report of a detective's interview with Joseph Salerno, the Seton Hall administrator in 1966. Salerno, according to the report, said that Dr. Jascalevich was "only authorized to use the lab on the fifteenth floor, which is the anatomy lab." I took up Dr. Boccabella's suggestion to ask the physiologists. The one I spoke to had held a prominent position at Seton Hall in the mid-1960s and was said to be thoroughly acquainted with the research procedures there. He assured me that animal experiments at the school had been conducted "in absolute conformity with the rules." "Haven't you ever heard of the Helsinki Convention?" he asked testily. "You sound like an antivivisectionist." Well, I said, how about the research on the sixteenth floor at Seton Hall? "The sixteenth floor?" the physiologist asked. "There were no facilities for experimenting on the sixteenth floor."

Monticello Avenue in Jersey City, only a mile from Henderson's old neighborhood, was dreary and deserted at 9 P.M. At the corner of Brinkerhoff, I slowed my step and tried, in the glare of an arc streetlamp, to read the address of a grocery with iron window gates that were pulled down and bolted. I couldn't make it out and passed on to the next door. There I was presented with a 1 and a 9, and the light was just bright enough for me to see, between the numbers, the imprint left by a missing 0. I held up a piece of paper and checked the 109 against the address I had been given. Then, slipping the paper into the pocket of my raincoat, I reached for the door. It was ajar, and as I gently pushed it open, I was greeted by three children who were playing in the hallway of the small, shingled building.

"Excuse me, kids. Do any of you know Dewey Mincey?"

"Dewey's upstairs," one of the youngsters shot back. "You want me to get him?"

"Mind if I come up?"

"C'mon."

I mounted the uneven stairs, preceded by three scrambling children. And at the top I was rewarded by the beefy figure of the former Seton Hall dog attendant. Mincey ushered me to the kitchen table while ordering his kids to turn down the television in the bedroom. I told Mincey who I was but not what I was doing. I said that I would explain all of that if Mincey would agree to answer a few questions first. Mincey said he couldn't imagine why a reporter for *The New York Times* would want to ask him anything, but he was willing to cooperate. Disguising my real interest, I eventually brought Mincey around to his Seton Hall years.

Mincey said he had gotten his job in the animal quarters in the winter of 1965–66, replacing Lee Henderson, and had worked there and subsequently in Newark, until he developed leg trouble. On no occasion, he said, had he seen experiments or dying dogs on tables on the sixteenth floor of Seton Hall. And never, he said, had anyone offered him a tip in exchange for the opportunity to work on a dog in the animal quarters. With that, I read Mincey the relevant parts of Dr. Jascalevich's deposition. But like Riggi, Mincey stuck to his story. He had never heard of Dr. Jascalevich. Mincey also said that he and Roe Chambliss, with whom he worked at Seton Hall, left before Riggi in the evening. "I remember we used to see Riggi coming out when we were waiting for the bus," he said. Chambliss, Mincey confirmed, was dead.

"Do you think that if Chambliss were providing the dogs for tips, he would have told you about it?" I asked.

"He never said anything to me about it, and I think he would have if he was doing it. Why don't you ask Odessa, his wife. She works over at one of the hospitals here."

"Which one, do you know?"

Mincey swung his head and bellowed toward the bedroom. "Honey, where does Odessa Chambliss work?"

"Greenville," a woman's voice called out.

"Greenville Hospital," Mincey said. "Down on the boulevard."

I got up. "Tell me, Mr. Mincey, if someone had indeed asked you to get them a dog to work on, for a tip of a dollar or two, what would you have said?"

Mincey snorted. "Mr. Farber, I wouldn't have done it. I had nine little babies, and I had to hold a job somewhere. What would a dollar have done for me?"

At Greenville Hospital the receptionist paged Mrs. Chambliss while I moved restlessly from one chair in the lobby to another. I was thinking how much I must look like an expectant father when an attractive, uniformed black woman came over. "I'm Odessa Chambliss and who are you?" "I wonder if we could talk in that little room?" I said, nodding toward an administrative office near the cashier. The conversation was over in minutes. Roe Chambliss had never said anything to his wife about "dying dogs" or tips at Seton Hall. "If it happened, he would have mentioned it," Mrs. Chambliss said. "We were very close."

My meeting with Dewey Mincey only made me more determined to find Henderson. I didn't expect any favors from the Social Security Administration—with good reason. Social Security is among the most tight-lipped of the federal agencies when it comes to information on individuals. But I asked the agency to bend a little and provide me with the most recent address it had for Henderson. Nothing more—not his income, not the names of his dependents. Just his address. As usual, Social Security said it couldn't comply.

Mike Naver, the press relations official to whom I spoke, said he sympathized; after all, he had been a reporter himself. For whom? I asked, making conversation. When he said the *Bergen Record,* I shut my eyes and sighed. Of all the newspapers in the country, Naver had worked for the *Record!* For weeks I had worried that the *Record* would get wind of my inquiries in New Jersey and start meddling in the case. It hadn't happened. But now what? Naver wanted to know what was so important about Henderson. Why did I want to reach him? I couldn't bring myself to tell him. Naver would, I thought, have some old friend on the *Record,* and he'd be on the phone with him as soon as I hung up. Immediately I took another tack, asking Naver just to check whether, in fact, he had an address for Henderson. Just to satisfy my curiosity. I read out Henderson's social security number, the number taken down by the detectives in 1966, and got off the phone. When Naver called back, he had an address for Henderson. Was it in North Carolina, I asked, assuring Naver that he wouldn't be giving up much by identifying the state. "Close," he said, "but that's not it." And except for verifying that the state wasn't New Jersey, Naver wouldn't say more.

I was drained. I now had no idea at all where Henderson was living. The only consolation was that he was still alive. In desperation I went back to Naver. Would Social Security consider sending a letter to Henderson at the address Naver had? Possibly, said Naver, but the letter couldn't be sealed; Social Security would want to see it. And only one letter would be forwarded. I sat down at my typewriter. In the letter to Henderson, I tried to be both enticing and vague. I didn't want either Henderson or Social Security to know the exact nature of my inquiry. Not yet anyway. In a covering letter to the Social Security Administration, I wrote that I was making this request "with full belief that the interests of justice will be served by my having an opportunity to contact Mr. Henderson . . . May I add that Mr. Henderson is under no suspicion of any kind. I am deeply grateful for your cooperation."

During my search for Henderson, I was also trying to pull together other threads of the Riverdell case. And there, too, I encountered frustrations. Irving Hall, the nurse who had sat with Nancy Savino during the last night of her life, was dead now. Dr. Gillson, the pathologist who had done some of the autopsies in 1966, was also dead. So, too, was Dr. Weiss, the physician at Holy Name Hospital in Teaneck who supposedly knew about the "sponge" story involving Dr. Harris.

I was able to find Dr. Markley, the physician who had autopsied Eileen Shaw after her sudden demise. Dr. Markley had retired, but I got his phone number in Quincy, Illinois. The physician, who had been Dr. Gillson's assistant, said he didn't recall any controversy or investigation regarding unusual deaths at Riverdell. Only "vaguely" did he remember the death of a woman who had just given birth by cesarean delivery. And the name Jascalevich didn't register with him.

Even less productive was my attempt to reach Jorge Ortega, the intern who had rushed to Nancy Savino's bedside when she couldn't be awakened. Dr. Ortega had been gone from Riverdell for years, and neither the American Medical Association nor the American Osteopathic Association had a listing for him. But using the address on a detective's interview with the intern in 1966, I drove out to Sheppard Avenue in Brooklyn. If the intern had moved, I might still be able to pick up the trail. But where Dr. Ortega had once lived, there was only the shell of a brick building—its door a slab of sheet metal, its windows blown out. The entire neighborhood was now a wasteland.

Meanwhile, I went back to Joe Woodcock, the Bergen County prosecutor, to ask him why Dr. Jascalevich's deposition was not in the Riverdell file. I wondered whether Woodcock or his chief of detectives had kept it aside and were holding out other materials. But neither of them knew anything about the deposition. Woodcock asked me where I had gotten my copy, and I declined to say. But I did agree to photostat a copy for the prosecutor, who was chagrined at having an incomplete file.

I also asked him about some strips—three or four translucent strips resembling heavy cellophane—that I had seen in the file. The strips, Woodcock said, were actually untranscribed tapes of several conversations that Calissi or Galda had had with Dr. Jascalevich at the start of their investigation in 1966. I asked to hear the tapes, but Woodcock said his office no longer had the machine—a Walkie Recordall—on which to play them. It took me more than a week, and more than a dozen calls to manufacturers and outlets, as well as to court stenographers, to locate the makers of the little-known Recordall. The company was Miles Reproducer, and its office was at 598 Broadway in Lower Manhattan, on the seventh floor of a grime-stained building whose windows looked as if they had never been washed. The office was a workshop-warehouse, with long, dark aisles of spare parts and equipment and with yellowing advertisements and tributes from Recordall users who, by now, were probably deaf or dead. There were only two employees—a man in his eighties, himself hard of hearing, and a wiry, genial character maybe twenty-five years younger who identified himself as the actual builder of the Recordall. The latter fellow, John Fischer, spoke as if the machine was still in use everywhere and by the biggest clients, but it was soon apparent that Miles had only one aging Recordall to loan and it was considered too precious for a journey to Hackensack. Prying the machine loose took an hour of flattery and twenty-five dollars. That night I wrapped the Recordall in a soft blanket, and the next morning I drove out to the prosecutor's office, one hand on the wheel and the other on Miles's baby. It was wasted effort. Something was amiss with the Recordall, the tapes, or both.

At *The Times* I commandeered an office off the third-floor newsroom. It was perfect: near my desk, yet out of the way, no windows, a door that locked. Spreading out my notes and documents, I began to outline what I knew of the Riverdell case and what—besides Lee Henderson's address—I lacked. There was some urgency to all this, because Artie Gelb and Mike Levitas wanted a progress report. Just the other day I had crossed Gelb's path in the newsroom, and the metropolitan editor, breaking his loping stride, had collared me. "Hey, stranger, what's happening in that hospital case?" But I wasn't ready to talk yet. "Soon, Artie, soon," I said. I had already consulted one of the country's leading authorities on curare and had been told that the muscle relaxant, normally excreted through the urine, might still be present in a nine- or ten-year-old body. But I wanted the advice of a qualified forensic pathologist. I also wanted to know more about the end of the investigation in 1966 and why it had aborted. And, finally, I wanted to talk to Dr. Jascalevich. The time had come.

Antonia Miranda, the secretary who took my call, said that Dr. Jascalevich would be in later that afternoon, and I asked her to have him phone me. After several hours and no call from the surgeon, I tried again. Miss Miranda said that she had given the message to Dr. Jascalevich "when he walked in, and he said you should write him a letter." Wondering whether Dr. Jascalevich had already learned my name and what I was doing, I asked to be put through to the surgeon, but Miss Miranda wouldn't consider it without knowing who I was and the purpose of the call. I didn't want to tell her. I didn't know how long she had worked for Dr. Jascalevich, and if she were unaware of Calissi's investigation, it seemed only fair for her to hear about it from Dr. Jascalevich. If the surgeon didn't want to tell her, that was his business.

"Look, Miss Miranda, it's a personal matter, something the doctor might want to keep confidential. I'm sure he'll understand if you present it that way." The reply sounded well rehearsed. "I take all his personal as well as medical calls, Mr. Farber." I could see that the only alternative was to drive out to West New York and barge in on the surgeon, or to stop him on the street. But as much as I wanted to sit down with Dr. Jascalevich, I wasn't going to force myself on him. The surgeon could agree to an interview or not. But he couldn't say that *The Times* had harassed him or been anything but reasonable.

"O.K., Miss Miranda, tell Dr. Jascalevich that I'm a reporter for *The New York Times* and that it's about the episode at Riverdell Hospital in 1966 regarding the curare." The secretary said she would deliver the message, with my phone number: the doctor couldn't be disturbed just now. When Dr. Jascalevich failed to call that evening or the next day, I phoned him again. This time I got his answering service, and I left a fuller message. But still there was no call in return. So, using *Times* stationery, I gave the surgeon the courtesy of a letter.

"As you undoubtedly know from the messages I have left with your answering service and with your secretary, I have been trying to reach you regarding the Bergen County prosecutor's investigation of the deaths at Riverdell Hospital in 1966. I am a reporter for *The Times,* and I am looking into this whole affair, including the discovery of curare in your locker at Riverdell at that time. I would appreciate an opportunity to interview you on this subject. Please call me at *The Times,* 212-556-7553. If I am not available at that number, please call the city desk, 212-556-1534, and ask that I be notified." As an afterthought, I self-addressed a green Postal Service card and sent the letter registered, return receipt requested.

For a week, I kept a close watch on my mailbox and on the message center in the *Times* newsroom. I jumped when the phone rang. Then the card came back. And, as one week ran into the next, I realized that the signature on the card was all I was going to get.

Once, my desire to talk to Dr. Jascalevich became so urgent that I drove out to West New York, parking in front of the Town Hall. It was a numbingly cold afternoon, and for hours I huddled in my car. Across the street the voile curtains were drawn on the surgeon's office. If Dr. Jascalevich came out, I had decided, I would approach him; alone and face to face, maybe we could come to terms on an interview. But no one entered, or left, the surgeon's office, and eventually I grew tired of waiting. Dr. Jascalevich knew where to find me.

Judge Galda, when I dropped by his home in Saddle River, could recall few details of the Riverdell case. But Calissi's former assistant, who was named to the bench in 1967, was sure of this much: the hospital's directors had said "contradictory things," particularly about the use of curare at Riverdell, and there was a possibility that Dr. Jascalevich had been "framed." It was a "fantastic" case, Galda said; he had planned years ago to write a book about it and, in fact, had kept something that might interest me. I couldn't have been more surprised when Galda trotted out a copy of Dr. Jascalevich's deposition, on onionskin paper and bound in plastic. It looked just like the "originals" of the other depositions that I had seen in the Riverdell file. Galda had also saved a sixty-two-page digest of the Riverdell investigation that had been prepared for him in 1966 by two detectives. The judge was willing to make a copy for me.

At *The Times* I removed my loafers and hoisted my feet onto the table of my inner sanctum. I scoured each of the sixty-two ruled, handwritten pages, but most of the report to Galda was a summary of depositions I had already read. Still, there were some indications of what had been said on the tapes that I had been unable to hear. And there were useful references to events that occurred after the morning of November 3, 1966, when Dr. Jascalevich turned in to Calissi the bloodstained Horn & Hardart "research bag" that the surgeon said had been removed from locker number four at Riverdell and shoved into his "clean" second locker. Most striking, I thought, was a strange story about a Chevrolet Impala.

On November 4—a week before Dr. Jascalevich's deposition—James Anderson called Galda and said that his client had information regarding the case. Taking the Walkie Recordall with them, Galda and a detective drove over to Anderson's law office in Union City, where Dr. Jascalevich was waiting. At the meeting, according to the Galda report, Dr. Jascalevich "stated that locker number four was kept orderly, and that curare derivatives in the locker were his and purchased from General Surgical Supply, and that he used the drug in experiments on dogs at Seton Hall. He again indicated items had been taken from locker number four and were recovered in his second locker." The report did not show whether, at that session, Dr. Jascalevich had disowned the "blue box" Burroughs-Wellcome curare found in locker number four or whether he had been asked who might have disarrayed his locker on or before October 31.

On November 7, Anderson called Galda again. This time it was about Dr. Jascalevich's car, a brown 1965 Chevrolet Impala. Detective Ernest Frahm and another officer went to Anderson's office and, as related in the sixty-two-page report, they were told the following story.

Dr. Jascalevich said that, when he had gone to Riverdell about 6:30 P.M. on November 2 to retrieve his surgical instruments from

Wiener, a folder containing Riverdell surgical policies and a "purse-string" bag were in his car. In that bag, he said, was the bottle of formaldehyde he had bought earlier in the day, a plastic vial containing dog tissue, three or four test tubes containing dog blood, and his German-made stapler. Dr. Jascalevich explained that the dog tissue in his car was "fresh," unlike the tissue in the four jars in the Horn & Hardart "research bag." The formaldehyde-soaked tissue in those jars, he repeated, was from his earlier experiments in 1966.

Dr. Jascalevich said that when he arrived home about midnight on November 2—apparently after going to the concert at Lincoln Center —he parked his car on Sixtieth Street in West New York and brought his surgical instruments and German stapler into his house, leaving the other articles behind. He did not use his car again until 7 A.M. on November 7, he said, when he noticed that it had been broken into. The "purse-string" bag was there, he said, but its contents, including the "fresh" dog tissue and the bottle of formaldehyde, had been stolen. And someone had put into the car a "Hy-pak" syringe box containing a vial of Lilly-manufactured curare, a vial of heparin, and several glass syringes. Dr. Jascalevich said that the items in the syringe box were his, but that they should have been in either locker number four or his Horn & Hardart "research bag." At this point, Detective Frahm appears to have "advised" Dr. Jascalevich that the bottle of formaldehyde was among the items the surgeon himself had given to Calissi with the Horn & Hardart bag on November 3. Dr. Jascalevich "indicated some surprise," according to the sixty-two-page report, "and said, 'Oh, so that's where it went.'"

After the November 7 meeting at Anderson's office, the contents of the syringe box were dusted for latent fingerprints. None, other than those of Dr. Jascalevich, were found.

Any way I looked at it, the implications of this account seemed sinister. If Dr. Jascalevich was telling the truth about the car—and about the transfer of the Horn & Hardart "research bag" from one locker to another, and about the planting of the Burroughs-Wellcome curare vials in his locker number four, and about the messing up of that locker— then someone was indeed going after him in 1966. But why at this stage, with detectives all over the place? Assuming the culprit was aware that Dr. Jascalevich had been keeping curare vials in his "dirty" locker, what was the point of adding an equal number of curare vials the surgeon would know weren't his? Assuming the culprit knew that Dr. Jascalevich might have a difficult time establishing that he had used the drug on dogs in 1965–66, what was the point of switching the Horn & Hardart bag, with its four jars of tissue, to the "clean" second locker —where the surgeon would almost certainly find it? Why not destroy the "research bag" and its contents? What purpose did the culprit have in mind when he broke into Dr. Jascalevich's car after midnight on November 2 and made off with the bottle of formaldehyde, only to put it in the Horn & Hardart bag by 10 A.M. the next morning? And what about the other articles missing from the car? Were the blood-filled test tubes taken from the Impala the source of the blood leaking from the Horn & Hardart bag the following morning? Where were the "fresh" tissue from the November 2 experiment at Pollak Hospital and the folder on Riverdell's surgical policies? I couldn't understand the culprit's logic. What was the sense in planting the syringe box and its contents in the car? Compared to the contents of locker number four, the box seemed innocuous. If the object was to return the box to the surgeon, why wasn't it tossed in the Horn & Hardart bag?

On November 8, Anderson was back on the phone with Galda, relaying information from Dr. Jascalevich. In retrospect, this call may have been the most important service Anderson provided his client. For what the attorney said, on November 8, created an issue that profoundly, and perhaps decisively, influenced Galda's view of the case.

Two days after Riverdell's board of directors had initiated the investigation, Dr. Frieman had been asked by Calissi or Galda whether he "would be in a position to know" whether anyone connected to Riverdell, at any time, "ever used curare for any medical purposes whatsoever?"

"Absolutely not," the Riverdell director had replied on November 3. "We have no purpose for curare in our hospital. We try to run a pretty close hospital and know what goes on. We use Anectine, or succinylcholine chloride, for a muscle relaxant, which is the only thing curare could possibly be used for in a hospital. So we have no use for this drug at the hospital."

Dr. Frieman was wrong, as Galda learned from Anderson on November 8. Dr. Jascalevich, Anderson said, had just been to Riverdell and had seen vials of curare in the operating room and elsewhere. As soon as he hung up, Galda dispatched several detectives to the hospital. Riverdell's pharmacist, Anthony Cocco, said he hadn't ordered any curare since he came to the hospital in April 1965, and he didn't think the hospital had any leftovers of the drug. But a check of the pharmacy stock uncovered four vials of Burroughs-Wellcome curare. Another vial was found in a drug closet in the operating room, and still another vial in a refrigerator there. Bottles of Tensilon, an antidote for curare, were present as well.

On November 9, a deposition was taken from Dr. DeMarco, the hospital's chief anesthesiologist. Dr. DeMarco said that curare had been kept at Riverdell since he joined the staff several years earlier, but that he had used the drug during only one operation, around 1965. He also said that the anesthesiologist who preceded him and Dr. Baba—Dr. James Costello—had favored curare. While Dr. DeMarco was giving his statement, the detectives paid a visit to a Burroughs-Wellcome regional office in Tuckahoe, New York. They found that between 1960 and 1963, when Dr. Costello left Riverdell, there were six shipments of curare to Riverdell. None was sent thereafter. And the batch numbers in these six shipments corresponded with the numbers on the vials in Riverdell's pharmacy and operating room. Similarly, the numbers matched the Burroughs-Wellcome vials seized from Dr. Jascalevich's locker number four.

On November 10, Dr. Frieman was asked to give another deposition at the prosecutor's office. Calissi, noting that "we have this problem with our investigation," reminded Dr. Frieman of his previous statement regarding the use of curare at Riverdell. The prosecutor said he wasn't "trying to badger" the physician. "It's in the thoroughness of the investigation, and I'm satisfied that when you leave here you will appreciate how much the prosecution does."

By now Dr. Frieman was aware that curare had been found in the operating room and in the pharmacy. He raised the possibility that Dr. Costello might have used curare, "but it has been several years . . . As far as I know . . . the routine procedure of the hospital is not to use any curare . . . The other thing . . . is that a hospital pharmacy is like any pharmacy, any drugstore, that you will find anywhere else. We must have everything, not only what we use, but if a doctor or consultant comes in and says he needs a particular drug at a particular time, or if we happen to need an emergency anesthetist or something of that sort, we must be supplied . . . We have gas gangrene there. I doubt if we use one vial in two years, but we have it."

* * *

Galda then informed Dr. Frieman that Riverdell had bought curare from Burroughs-Wellcome "starting back in 1961, regularly, for periods of time . . . Is there anything unusual about that?"

"No. Could I have the dates when they were purchased?"

"Show it to him," Calissi said, and Galda handed the physician a list. After studying it a moment, Dr. Frieman pointed out that the last bill was from 1963. "I think, there is no question, sir, that back in 1963, 1962, and 1961, we may have used curare. I don't recall what Dr. Costello used. What I was getting to is the fact that it is not a drug in common usage at the hospital in volume at this time."

Calissi resumed. "What we are trying to ascertain, the information given to us in each stenographic statement: 'Absolutely not, no reason for it in the hospital, it wasn't in the hospital,' et cetera. These are what the statements say, Doctor."

"I think a lot of times, you are carried away with the importance and the circumstances," Dr. Frieman replied. "It would certainly have been more judicious and correct to say that the hospital right now—that any drug could appear in a hospital pharmacy. No member of the board, not even the pharmacist himself, knows every item that is present."

Under further questioning Dr. Frieman said he did not think it was "unusual" for the hospital to be stocking the antidote for curare, or for it to have a vial of curare in the operating-room refrigerator. And he suddenly remembered that "long before this came up," Dr. DeMarco had given a medical "dissertation" in which the anesthesiologist had noted the advantages of Anectine over curare.

Galda broke in. "The inquiry is: Five doctors, reputable men, come before a prosecutor and initiate an investigation to the extent that they have eliminated the use of curare at the hospital, any place in the hospital, and therefore it is unusual to turn up in a locker. This is where we start off with the first problem."

"I think, sir, that it is not quite so," Dr. Frieman responded. "It was —the reason we came was not the fact of the hospital using Tubarine. Even if the hospital had used Tubarine—let's just say we had used it regularly—it would still be most unusual for a surgeon—not an anesthetist, but a surgeon—to have in his possession and in his locker all of these empty and full [vials of] tubocurarine, or whatever you want to call it. Certainly, if we found this in Dr. DeMarco's locker, I would have said, 'Well, certainly, it's a drug in use.' But a surgeon is a surgeon, not an anesthetist. The thing is, it's where you found it and the quantity in which we found it. If we found one or two vials, we would have said, 'Well, this is logical or possible.' But we found all of this, and we came to you with the idea that we didn't know; we felt that this deserved an investigation. We did not come with the idea of accusation or anything else."

Five hours after Dr. Frieman offered this explanation, Dr. Lans gave his second deposition in Hackensack. His first statement, in which he was not asked about the presence of curare at Riverdell, had also been taken on November 3.

"Would it surprise you," Calissi asked on November 10, "if you knew that the pharmacy at Riverdell stocked curare and that there was curare in the operating-room closet and in the refrigerator?"

"I don't think it would surprise me," Dr. Lans said. "I think there would be curare in any hospital, any hospital anywhere."

"Can you explain why the same stock number or batch number of curare on a bottle in the pharmacy would be also on the bottle of curare in Dr. Jascalevich's locker?"

". . . I wouldn't know. I don't know what that means."

On November 15, Elliott Wiener, Riverdell's administrator, was called back to the prosecutor's office for another deposition. Andrew Emerson, Riverdell's lawyer, accompanied him. At the close of this meeting—in which Wiener, who had been at Riverdell for only four months, was questioned extensively about the hospital's ordering practices—Galda said that a "sharp cleavage" had developed in the investigation. And for the first time, he suggested that the investigation was winding down. "We start off with an investigation that says that there is never any curare used in the hospital, and frankly our approach to the problem is that any number of the doctors indicated it had been there for some time now. It seems rather inconceivable that five doctors come in and say never . . . When the anesthetist, Dr. DeMarco, himself acknowledges that his name appears on one of the boxes of Tensilon, the curare antidote, as having ordered it."

"I think it is quite clear, first of all, that not all of them denied curare has been used," Emerson interjected.

But Galda didn't agree. "I can refer to the first meeting, such statements as 'absolutely not, absolutely never' . . . We are not dealing now with one person; we are dealing with any number who have access to this particular problem, if there is a problem."

"Yes," said Emerson.

"Thank you again," Galda finished. "I think we have all—we like your company, Mr. Wiener, we like you to stop down any time you wish, but I think we are about concluding your need to come any longer. But we will evaluate everything."

The next day a deposition was taken from Dr. Baba, the junior of Riverdell's two anesthesiologists in 1966. It was the last deposition given in the case. Calissi was absent, and Galda handled the questioning. The chief assistant prosecutor began with a statement of his own—a rambling statement that when I read it nine years later, begged for explanation.

"I don't know whether you heard or not, but we are conducting a general investigation relative to some of the functions, operations, and personnel of the Riverdell Hospital in Oradell," Galda informed Dr. Baba. "And in substance, as it originated from the board of governors, their inquiry by the way of information which had to deal with the unexplained number of deaths in the hospital. I think that is a good way to start off as any, and that was the initial approach to this entire investigation, instigated by the five [board] members of the hospital.

No one, I want to impress on you, is under any suspicion . . . In addition to that, we being a group have to be complete and have to be thorough . . . We need corroboration and we need proof and we need sufficient information by way of evidence before we take any firm conclusion. And I might say, notwithstanding that they sent down some twelve or thirteen files"—here Galda turned to two detectives who were sitting in on the deposition in Galda's office and said, "you stop me, gentlemen, if I'm wrong"—"to be investigated, that number has been greatly diminished to nothing based on experts, not members of law enforcement, experts . . ."

Dr. Baba's deposition took forty-five minutes. The anesthesiologist said he had seen Burroughs-Wellcome and other brands of curare in the drug closet and the refrigerator of the operating room at Riverdell "for some period of time." While he thought that curare was still used occasionally at Riverdell by Dr. DeMarco, he himself had used only Anectine as a muscle relaxant there. And he doubted that a surgeon, without consulting the anesthesia record, would know what muscle relaxant was being used during any operation.

Dr. DeMarco, Galda remarked, "says substantially the same thing as you said" about the use of curare at Riverdell.

"I would think so, sure," Dr. Baba replied.

"That doesn't throw a different light on the problem," Galda continued, "because originally we were conducting an inquiry where they said it was never used in the hospital. Maybe that may sound ridiculous, but this is the original information."

"I think it is used in every hospital in the country probably," the anesthesiologist said.

In addition to being asked about the death of Eileen Shaw—Dr. Baba commended Dr. Jascalevich's efforts to help the woman—the doctor was questioned briefly about the operations on Margaret Henderson and Nancy Savino and about the relations between Riverdell's surgeons. "Would you say there is animosity?" Galda inquired. "I want you to be perfectly candid."

"There is some animosity, certainly there is, which is common with most hospitals between surgeons or specialists," the anesthesiologist replied.

"Which gentlemen are you specifically thinking about in your opinion at this moment?"

"I will say primarily Jascalevich and Briski."

"It was Briski who was assigned, relegated to somewhat of an inferior category, was he not?" Galda asked.

"That's right."

"From privileges?"

"That's where the animosity lies, in that problem," Dr. Baba said.

"How about Dr. Harris and Dr. Jascalevich?"

"As far as I know, there is none."

"Would you care to render an opinion as to any suggestion you may have thought of relative to what has been referred to as a high mortality rate at the hospital?"

"Well, of course I'm only aware of the ones that I was involved in," the anesthesiologist remarked. "I was involved in three that were, as far as I know, unexplainable, and those are the three patients you brought to my attention. The others I know nothing about."

When Dr. Baba walked out of the prosecutor's office at 3:30 P.M. on November 16, 1966, the Riverdell investigation was all but over. "There doesn't appear quite any reason why we will have to call you again," Galda told the anesthesiologist.

Galda seemed obsessed, in 1966, with Dr. Frieman's initial mistake about the availability of curare at Riverdell. But why? Had he detected a conspiracy among Riverdell's five directors and Dr. Harris to hide the fact that curare was commonly used at the hospital between 1960 and 1963, and that some vials from those years were still around? I didn't see the evidence for such a conspiracy. Dr. Harris wasn't even asked whether curare was used at Riverdell. When Galda put the question to Dr. Lans, the director said he didn't think it was "generally used," but he wouldn't be surprised if it was stocked at the hospital. This was hardly the stuff of a cover-up. And Dr. Frieman, who was so skeptical of Dr. Harris's inferences about Dr. Jascalevich when they were first made, seemed an unlikely candidate for conspiracy in this case. "Don't call me, I don't want to know from you," he had told Dr. Harris after the surgeon met with the directors in October 1966. "I don't want you to, in any way, color or tint my mind."

Nearly a decade later Andrew Emerson recalled an exchange he had had with Galda midway in the 1966 investigation. "We were in Calissi's office," Emerson told me. "Everyone was milling about, and I walked over to the side of the room to see the bag of stuff that had been taken from Jascalevich's locker. I touched something and, quickly realizing that I might be leaving fingerprints, I drew away. Galda saw it and told me not to worry. And that is when he said this whole thing might be a 'frame-up' by Harris or members of the hospital's board.

"I looked at him," Emerson remembered. "I'm sure my surprise showed. 'Oh, no, no, no,' I said. But he said 'Yes, it could be. It could be.'"

I was also intrigued by Galda's statements to Dr. Baba on November 16, 1966, that "no one . . . is under any suspicion" and that the thirteen deaths have been "greatly diminished to nothing" by medical experts. Whatever existed in the way of "proof from an investigative standpoint," there was no medical testimony in the Riverdell file—with the possible exception of Dr. Jascalevich's—that countered the "unusual or unexplained" nature of many of the deaths.

I called both Galda and Calissi to ask the basis for Galda's statements. Galda said he had been "puffing" when he made those remarks, trying to put Dr. Baba at ease. It was absurd to say that no one was under suspicion then, Galda added. "You're taking what I said out of context." But Galda stuck by his statement that medical authorities— he couldn't recall who—had studied the deaths by November 16 and found them "plausible." "Somebody reviewed the cases," he said.

Calissi disposed rather quickly of Galda's assertion that the deaths had been accounted for medically by the middle of November 1966. "That's horseshit," the judge said. Reminding me of our meeting in August 1975 and what he had said about a "diversity of opinion" in the prosecutor's office in 1966, Calissi repeated that his own suspicions of Dr. Jascalevich had never been allayed. "You won't find anything in that goddamn file to say I wasn't suspicious. You read my questions and decide if I wasn't suspicious. There was something to that goddamn case, I'll tell you that." In later interviews in Jersey City, where he was serving on the bench, Calissi said the Riverdell affair was complicated by "hatred" between Dr. Jascalevich and Dr. Harris:—"they had a vendetta going; I don't know why." And whereas Dr. Jascalevich was "cultivated," he said, the Riverdell directors who raised the issue of murder were not "impressive people, not polished. They didn't look like what you would expect of doctors." After learning that Riverdell had its own stock of curare and that some of the vials from that supply were in locker number four, Galda came to feel that someone other than Dr. Jascalevich was up to no good, Calissi said.

But Galda's position, the former prosecutor added, wasn't the reason the case was dropped. The main thing, he said, was "the advice I got from medical authorities that it was impossible to find curare in dead bodies. Who was I to question them with their years of experience? Without some way of finding curare in the bodies, there was no point in going on. That's why we didn't exhume any bodies. If I was stupid, call me that; but my reputation was not for being stupid." Calissi leaned forward in the high-backed chair in his judicial chambers, a hurt look on his face. "I wasn't venal," he said. "A reputation in this world is it. From a glass of water to a trillion dollars, you couldn't buy me. I'd spit in your eye. In this case I followed my medical advisers and trusted them. It was a question of proof. Without that, you don't go to a grand jury. You don't indict on suspicion. I came to the wall, and I couldn't penetrate the wall."

The only "medical authority" whom Calissi could recall by name as having advised him about curare was Dr. Denson, although the former prosecutor thought there was someone else as well. Dr. Denson, who had become the chief medical examiner of Bergen County in 1967, told me that except for Rohrbeck, he hadn't rendered an opinion on the Riverdell deaths and didn't know why bodies hadn't been exhumed. His feeling in 1966, he said, was that "the only way to prove" the suspicions about the drug was to disinter bodies "and see what we could do." But he also believed at that time that "there was little chance of finding curare, considering the small amounts." And, he said, he probably conveyed that impression to Calissi.

Each night in the late fall of 1975, as I fitted together the last known pieces of Calissi's investigation, I was moving my stack of materials from the office I had appropriated off the newsroom to my five-foot-high coat locker in another part of the *Times*'s newsroom. I had begun worrying about the security of my little room when I came in to do some work one night and found several *Times* janitors lounging in the office, their mops and brooms in a corner. It had never occurred to me that the janitors had keys and might use the room for a break. The men were smoking and joking, and seemed oblivious to the mound of documents on the table. But the incident unnerved me, and thereafter I resorted to the use of my locker. Each time I opened the locker, I half-expected to find a cache of curare vials. But the only peculiar sight was myself—whisking through the newsroom at night and in the morning with my precious papers piled high on the seat of a rolling armchair. Unfortunately, I discovered one morning that I had competition for the use of the office. The door to the room was ajar when I arrived that day and there, at the table, was John Corry, another *Times* reporter. Corry, alas, had spread out his own materials like he was hunkering down on a long project.

"What are you doing?" I asked gingerly.

"Oh, just pulling together a piece," Corry said.

"Oh? What's it about?"

Corry smiled. "It's about a murder. Arthur Miller was in to see Artie Gelb about it. It's about a kid in Connecticut who's accused of killing his mother. Miller thinks he's innocent."

"Miller the playwright?"

"None other."

"How many murders did you say figured in the case?"

Corry smiled again. "How many murders? Just one. Isn't that enough?"

I wheeled my loaded armchair into Corry's view. "John, let's see if you can make space for me. Because I've got about a dozen deaths on my hands."

I settled down to complete my review of the 1966 investigation. What else had the prosecutor's office accomplished?

The most important thing, it seemed to me, was the discovery of dog hairs on five items, including syringes, that had been seized from Dr. Jascalevich's locker number four. Here was something that at first blush, appeared to corroborate Dr. Jascalevich's story about his experiments in 1965–66. But the more I thought about the hairs, the less certain I was of their significance. And equally vexing was another matter: the mineral oil in the syringe.

The Riverdell file showed that on the night of November 1, Calissi and Dr. Denson met in the prosecutor's office with Dr. Robert L. Strickman, a chemist who operated, out of his house in Hillsdale, New Jersey, a laboratory called Allied Testing and Research. A half year after his meeting with Calissi, Dr. Strickman would be widely publicized as the inventor of a "revolutionary new cigarette filter" endorsed by Columbia University. Eventually the filter project would go sour, and an embarrassed Columbia would withdraw, saying it had made a "well-intentioned mistake." But in November 1966, all of that lay ahead for Dr. Strickman. Then he was simply the head of the Allied laboratory, eager to pick up jobs from New Jersey prosecutors who lacked their own crime laboratories and who, in the interest of time, occasionally bypassed the FBI or the state lab in Trenton and hired private concerns. With Dr. Strickman on the night of November 1 was Dr. Umberger, who was then "moonlighting" as a consultant to Allied. In addition to Eileen Shaw's tissue, Allied was given eighteen of the seventy-one items taken from locker number four and asked to perform chemical, microscopic, and serological (blood) tests on them. On November 4, Allied was given the nineteen items turned in to the prosecutor by Dr. Jascalevich on November 3. These were the items—syringes, four jars of tissue soaking in formaldehyde, three vials of "red material," and so forth—that Dr. Jascalevich said would prove that he had been working on dogs earlier in 1966. They were the same items he had found in his Horn & Hardart "research bag" on the morning of November 3, after the bag was allegedly transferred by someone from locker number four to his second, "clean" locker at Riverdell.

Detective Kastner, who questioned whether Dr. Jascalevich might have gotten some of these items from a dog on November 2 and placed them in his second locker "as a cover," asked Allied on November 4 to run some special tests. Kastner wanted to know the following: whether any of the syringes taken by Calissi from locker number four had ever been in the "research bag"; the contents of the syringes from both locker number four and the bag; whether the "red material" in the three vials was actually dog or human blood and, if so, was it all from the same body and how recently had it been taken from the body; whether the pieces of tissue in the four jars were really "sections of dog bowels" and, if so, were they all from the same dog and how long had they been resting in formaldehyde; whether the adhesive-tape labels that said "Seton Hall Research ⌗101" had been recently written and affixed to the jars, and whether all the labels had been written at the same time. The veteran detective seemed determined to cover all bases. He instructed Allied to "conduct any tests possible" that might determine whether there was a link between the items from locker number four and those in the "research bag."

On November 8, according to Galda's sixty-two-page digest, a "preliminary report [received] via telephone from Allied stated that in the syringes and the vials removed from locker number four, tests showed positive for curare. It was also reported that one syringe showed mineral oil. Syringes also showed blood." On November 11—the day that Dr. Jascalevich gave his deposition—"there was also a verbal report received by Mr. Galda from Allied Testing Co. that the items submitted on November 1, taken from locker number four, and on November 4, turned in by Dr. Jascalevich on November 3, both had dog hairs on them."

It was not until several months later that Allied filed its final reports on the items from the bag and from locker number four.

Among the eighteen items from locker number four that Allied examined were four of the eighteen curare vials, three evidently put out by Burroughs-Wellcome and one by Lilly, and ten syringes, ranging in capacity from 2 cc to 20 cc. The four vials contained various amounts of fluid, but Allied confirmed that the fluid in each was "consistent with curare." Most of the ten syringes, according to the laboratory, were "relatively clean"; a few were coated or smeared—whether on the inside or out wasn't clear from the lab's report—with a thin, colorless fluid consistent with mineral oil. The fluid in one of the 10-cc syringes, to which a hypodermic needle was attached, was said to "provide crystals consistent with" curare. In addition, "some crystalline material observed in the tips" of two plastic hypodermic needle covers appeared to be "dried" curare. A test for blood on one hypodermic needle was negative; on another it was positive, but since the "trace amounts on which the chemical test was performed were microscopically invisible, no attempt was made to carry out serological tests." A test on "minute particles of dried blood" on yet another hypodermic needle gave "a negative reaction with antihuman serum. This," the lab report concluded, "indicates that the blood is nonhuman."

Then there were the hairs. Cotton or synthetic "hair fibers" were found on most of the ten syringes from locker number four. One "dog-hair fiber" was isolated on each of three syringes. Several "dog-hair fibers" were identified on a fourth syringe, and an unspecified number of them were found on another syringe and on a "screw tip" that may have been a needle protector but whose function was not explained.

From Allied's companion report on the "research bag" items, it was obvious that none of the more complicated tests requested by Detective Kastner had been done. The report presented no analysis of the pieces of tissue in the four jars—whether or not they were "dog bowel" or how long they had been soaking in formaldehyde—or of the adhesive-tape labels on the jars. And it made no attempt to correlate the items taken from locker number four with those submitted by Dr. Jascalevich two days later. Of the six syringes in the "research bag," only one contained a fluid that appeared to be curare. It was the 12-cc syringe with about 2 cc of liquid, the one that was found inside a pair of surgical gloves. The "red material" in the three vials—not curare vials—was identified as "dog's blood," although the question of whether the blood had all come from the same dog, and how recently, was unanswered. Many of the nineteen items from the bag were spotted with "dried bloodstains"—perhaps, I thought, as a result of the leakage when the bag was removed by Dr. Jascalevich from his second locker at Riverdell. Besides synthetic or cotton fibers on a variety of the items, several "dog-hair fibers" were found in the pair of surgical gloves.

After studying them closely, I wasn't sure what the Allied reports added up to. Without answers to Kastner's questions, it was impossible to tell whether the tissues or vials of blood in the "research bag" had come from the dog that Dr. Jascalevich worked on at Pollak Hospital on November 2, 1966. Despite Allied's apparent generalization to Galda on November 8, curare had ultimately been indicated in only one of the ten syringes from locker number four and in only one of the six syringes in the "research bag." Whether the muscle relaxant had been injected into the veins of "dying dogs" or the intravenous feeding tubes of patients, wouldn't some trace of it have been left in more than two syringes? I wondered, too, why there were as many as sixteen syringes. Hadn't Dr. Jascalevich said that he "used and re-used" the syringes because the syringes were "expensive." Wouldn't, then, a few syringes have sufficed for the fifteen dogs that he said he experimented with in 1965 and 1966?

Especially ironic was the identification of a fluid "consistent with mineral oil"—not curare—in the one syringe in locker number four that appeared to be "full." This instrument—a 10-cc syringe with 9 cc of fluid—must have been the "rather large-size syringe" that Dr. Harris noticed among the curare vials when he opened the locker, the syringe that Dr. Harris later described as "loaded, ready to go." The prosecutor's office knew as early as November 8, 1966, that one of the syringes from locker number four contained mineral oil. But when Dr. Jascalevich gave his deposition three days later, he was not asked about mineral oil, even though a pint bottle of the substance had also been found in locker number four. Calissi seemed to have assumed, during the deposition, that the fluid in the "full" syringe was curare. "One [syringe] was completely full of fluid," he said to Dr. Jascalevich on November 11. "Now, what is the purpose of having that?" "If a syringe is not used . . . I would just return with the material . . . but I would use it on the next dog, so that I would return with the syringe full." However plausible that explanation, it shed no light on the mineral oil. Why would Dr. Jascalevich have mineral oil, a laxative, in a syringe? One possibility I entertained was that Dr. Jascalevich didn't put the mineral oil in the syringe, that this—like the placement of curare vials from Riverdell's stock in locker number four, and the disarray of that locker, and the secreting of the research bag in Dr. Jascalevich's locker, and the breaking into the surgeon's car—was another part of a "frame-up" against Dr. Jascalevich. But then again, what was the logic of it? Certainly someone bent on framing the surgeon as a curare-wielding murderer might plant a loaded syringe in his locker. But what was the sense in filling up the syringe with mineral oil?

The hairs and the blood were another matter. Although I was initially impressed by the discovery of the "dog-hair fibers," the more I examined Allied's reports, the more I was struck by the lack of such fibers on most of the syringes from locker number four. Indeed, on three of the six items from the locker that showed dog—as well as cotton or synthetic—fibers, only one dog hair was found. Was it possible that these dog hairs dated back to 1963–64, when Dr. Jascalevich had unquestionably worked on dogs at Seton Hall Medical School? And had he used syringes in those experiments? The surgeon's deposition didn't say. But if he had, what had he done with those "expensive" items later? I had no reason to doubt Allied's findings of "dog's blood" in the three vials submitted by Dr. Jascalevich on November 3; surely that volume of "red material" was adequate for testing. But I wondered about the reliability of the blood results on the items from locker number four, where only minute amounts were examined.

Hoping that Kastner might know something more about Allied's work, I placed a call to the county detectives bureau in Hackensack.

But, again, too much time had elapsed. Kastner was dead. Then I went back to Dr. Umberger, whose name was typed at the bottom of the Allied reports. But the toxicologist said he had worked only on Mrs. Shaw's tissues, not on the items from locker number four or the "research bag." He didn't recall who had examined those items for curare or blood, but he remembered that Alfred P. Stoholski, a "provisional chemist" who was in charge of "criminalistics" for the New York City medical examiner's office, had done the work on fibers. "Try Stoholski," he said. But, unfortunately, Stoholski had been "phased out" of the medical examiner's office in early 1975, and he wasn't easily reached. Meanwhile I tried Dr. Strickman, who still had a lab in New Jersey. Dr. Strickman, who said that Stoholski, like Dr. Umberger, had been a consultant to Allied in 1966, had little to contribute. "I myself didn't do any of the work on that case, and I never met the doctor in question," he explained. "If you've already talked to Umberger, try Stoholski." Eventually I located Stoholski, whose job as a criminalist had been to identify "trace evidence"—small objects like fibers or nail scrappings—under the microscope, sometimes for use in trials. The conversation wasn't very productive. Stoholski recalled having found dog hairs in the Riverdell case, but he didn't know who had done the blood or curare analyses or why many of Kastner's questions had not been answered. "There was so much running around in this case," he remarked. The discovery of the dog hairs was "consistent" with Dr. Jascalevich's story of having conducted experiments, Stoholski felt. But at the same time, the microscopist said, he was never certain of where the hairs had originated or how long they had been on the syringes or other items.

"How could I know this?" he asked.

As far as I could tell, there wasn't much more to Calissi's investigation. From the Bergen County Medical Society and from the New Jersey Board of Medical Examiners, which said that Dr. Jascalevich had "no previous record of an offense or violation," the detectives compiled biographical data on Dr. Jascalevich. They also asked administrators at Christ and North Hudson hospitals and nurses at Riverdell, about the surgeon's professional reputation, and were told that it was "very good" or "excellent."

One Riverdell nurse was questioned about Nancy Savino's death, although she was apparently not on duty when the child died. But neither of the two nurses who rushed to the child's bed appeared to have been interviewed. The nurse who took care of Margaret Henderson, and who found the twenty-six-year-old woman dead, was not questioned. Nor was the nurse who was on duty when Eileen Shaw died asked whether she heard the patient complain about a strong injection or medicine prior to her respiratory arrest. Pasquale Benvenuto, the elderly patient of Dr. Harris who had recovered from a respiratory arrest a week before Mrs. Shaw died, was not troubled for a statement. Depositions were not taken from Dr. Gillson or Dr. Markley. No one on Calissi's staff called Dr. Harris's former chief at Jacobi Hospital in New York to ask whether Dr. Jascalevich had inquired in October 1966 about Dr. Harris's surgical skill. No one from the prosecutor's office checked the story about Dr. Harris's having left a sponge in the body of a Riverdell patient who was subsequently admitted to the Holy Name Hospital in Teaneck and treated by a Dr. Weiss. There was a note in the Riverdell file that Galda would contact Mooney—the alleged lawyer and friend of Eileen Shaw's family. But if the chief assistant prosecutor had followed through, there was no evidence of it. There was a note that Calissi would write a letter to Argentina to see whether Dr. Jascalevich had "a background for mental disorder." But there was no such correspondence in the file.

Galda had remarked to a doctor on November 9, 1966, that "we have been working round the clock . . . because of the magnitude this investigation has developed into." But within a week of that statement, the prosecutor's men were no longer working around the clock, and with the passage of a few more days, they had all but ceased working on the Riverdell case. This was clear from the concluding sentences of the sixty-two-page digest, which was written soon after Dr. Baba's deposition on November 16. "It was decided that no further investigation would be conducted in this matter pending lab reports on the tissues submitted. We were advised on November 1 by Dr. Umberger that the tests [for curare] to be conducted on the tissue would take at least six weeks."

Dr. Umberger took well over six weeks to examine the tissues from Eileen Shaw's body. But his report on February 19, 1967, stating that "chemical findings in this case should be considered suspicious without sufficient confirmation for definite positive or negative results," did nothing to reactivate Calissi's investigation. Nor did the two other Allied lab reports of the same date. If the three reports were read by anyone in the prosecutor's office, there was no sign of it in the Riverdell file. No notes in the margins of the reports. No memos attached to them. Nothing.

The investigation ended without any of the publicity that Dr. Jascalevich's lawyer had feared. Dr. Jascalevich resigned from Riverdell's staff on February 6, 1967. And shortly thereafter, the Lans-Harris-Lifflander efforts sputtered to a halt. I asked Dr. Lans, in 1975, why he hadn't turned to the attorney general of New Jersey or the state Board of Medical Examiners. The physician blinked. "What are you talking about?" he said wearily. "Here we'd gone to the county prosecutor and to a private investigator and a newspaper and to the chief medical examiner of New York. Now you ask why we didn't go elsewhere. Because it wouldn't have done any good, that's why. Because no one would have listened, that's why. And for another reason, too—because we were very young. Do you understand? We were young. Now, it's simple to say we should have done this, or we should have done that. Back then. But back then, my man, we were very young."

Dr. Jascalevich, it appeared, also kept the Riverdell affair under wraps after his resignation. "It was all a mistake," Dr. Boccabella, the Seton Hall anatomist, recalled him saying. Some Riverdell physicians, including at least one director of the hospital, still referred patients to Dr. Jascalevich. And his practice in West New York and Jersey City continued to thrive. Dr. Jascalevich did not publish anything on the posterior liver biopsy, the experiment for which he used curare. But in the years after 1967, he indulged his bent for creating, or improving upon, surgical devices. The surgeon also began investing in Florida real estate, and by the early 1970s, he and his wife had moved from the row house they had bought as newlyweds to a more luxurious home in Englewood Cliffs, New Jersey, keeping the place in West New York as Dr. Jascalevich's office. The Jascaleviches adopted two children, and in December 1975, a month when I was still trying to reach her husband, Mrs. Jascalevich wrote to a friend in Argentina that all was fine. The children were well, she had a girl to help her with the house, and Dr. Jascalevich, she said, was very busy with his surgery and research and professional meetings.

Although Dr. Jascalevich had left the anatomy department at Seton Hall in 1968, in 1970 he became a part-time, unsalaried instructor in surgery at Seton Hall's successor institution. And in 1972 his rank was upgraded to clinical assistant professor. In 1973 he was named chief of one of four surgical divisions of Christ Hospital in Jersey City. The same year he was elected a fellow of the New York Academy of Medicine, on the recommendation of several doctors whom he had known at New York Polyclinic. In an Academy questionnaire Dr. Jascalevich was asked to list his hospital affiliations, and he did so for the period from 1961 to 1973. Riverdell Hospital was not included.

More and more, in 1975, I was focusing on Dr. Umberger's report on Eileen Shaw's tissue. Calissi didn't recall ever having seen the report, or talking to Dr. Umberger after the first night of the Riverdell investigation. Nor had he spoken to Dr. Helpern, although he gave

Matthew Lifflander a copy of Dr. Jascalevich's deposition and other materials in the hope that the New York medical examiner could be of some help. But I wondered, now, whether it could have made a difference if Dr. Umberger had tested tissue that, unlike Mrs. Shaw's, wasn't soaking in a jar of formalin. Dr. Umberger had concluded in 1967 that it was "impossible to detect curare in therapeutic levels in formalin-fixed tissue." But did that include the tissue from bodies that had merely been embalmed? No, Dr. Umberger told me. "If we had exhumed one or two bodies that had only been embalmed—where the tissues had not been lying in formalin—we might have come up with something. But, like I told you when you first called, nobody wanted to exhume any bodies. So I said the hell with it."

I couldn't say the hell with it. Was it possible that curare might still be traced in bodies that had lain in the ground for nine years? What did a nine-year-old body look like? Was the flesh gone and perhaps the bones as well? Was there more than dust? I didn't have any idea; and Larry Altman, the *Times*'s medical writer, didn't have any firm answers either. But Dr. Altman suggested that I call Michael Baden, the deputy chief medical examiner of New York City. "He's the best forensic pathologist around here," Altman said.

I had been introduced to Dr. Baden and his seventy-one-year-old boss Milton Helpern, in the summer of 1973. I was then starting to write about drug abuse, and both pathologists were recommended to me by Jim Markham, my predecessor on the *Times*'s drug beat. Dr. Helpern, who had been chief medical examiner since 1954, was widely admired for his technical skill and for his efforts to professionalize a field that is still dominated by part-time lay coroners whose real work may be barbering or undertaking. Dr. Baden, at thirty-eight, was Dr. Helpern's heir apparent, and he was one of the most talented and versatile pathologists working at the confluence of medical science and the law. He advanced the concept of the medical examiner as an "ombudsman of death," dispassionately detecting "what happened" rather than "who done it." The forensic pathologist, in his view, had to be deaf to the special pleadings of insurance companies or prosecutors or defense attorneys—or even to relatives of the deceased: "You better not compromise yourself. It's all you got," said the Janis Joplin quotation on his office wall.

Dr. Baden was cordial, but he couldn't provide me with any definitive answers. He said there was no telling what remained of a nine-year-old body, or a body of any age, unless one looked in the grave. There were a lot of popular misconceptions about this kind of thing, he said. For example, worms were almost never found in corpses.

How about curare? I asked him. Could it be found in a body that had been buried for a decade?

Dr. Baden said he'd have to read up on that. Offhand, it was his impression that the tissues would be worse now than they were nine years ago, but the technology for tracing a drug like curare would be much improved.

I asked whether he had ever heard of a series of deaths in New Jersey that might have been connected to curare. But all he could think of was the case of Dr. Carl Coppolino. That case, he pointed out correctly, involved not curare, but succinylcholine chloride. And it wasn't in New Jersey; it was in Florida.

Clearly Dr. Baden knew nothing about the Riverdell affair. And I decided, at least at this stage, not to tell him.

When I next saw Joe Woodcock, the prosecutor's interest in the Riverdell case had increased substantially. Woodcock's manner was stiff, and his conversation spare. He said he hadn't wanted to "step off into the dark" on such an old case, but Chief Kikkert had studied Dr. Jascalevich's deposition and had found a number of "inconsistencies." The Riverdell file, Woodcock said, had now been "roped off," and he was going to have the patients' medical records reviewed by an "independent" expert, whom he hadn't chosen. I left the prosecutor's office thinking about my own plans. I had nearly decided to ask Dr. Cyril Wecht, a prominent forensic pathologist in Pittsburgh, to evaluate the medical information I had gathered. Now I wasn't so sure about rushing off to Dr. Wecht. Maybe it was better to wait and see what Woodcock's expert came up with. Still, that could mean the loss of time. And I might never learn whom Woodcock went to, or what the expert said.

The expert on whom Woodcock settled was Mike Baden. Woodcock didn't know Dr. Baden and hadn't sought him out directly. But when he called the New York medical examiner's office, it was to Dr. Baden that he was referred. Dr. Baden hadn't expected to hear about the New Jersey deaths again, but after my inquiry, he had reviewed some of the literature on the stability and detection of curare. And now he was responsive to Woodcock's request for aid. "In accordance with recent conversations which we have had," Woodcock wrote to him on December 10, 1975, "will you kindly arrange the services of your good offices to assist the Bergen County prosecutor's office in the investigation we are presently conducting into some suspicious deaths which occurred in 1966 in Riverdell Hospital, Oradell, N.J. During the original investigation, the then prosecutor was led to believe that scientific tests to detect certain drugs were not available. It is my understanding after talking to you that these techniques have now been refined, and the possibility exists that specific drugs can be detected in embalmed and buried tissue even at this late stage."

Dr. Baden got to work on thirteen Riverdell hospital charts and other documents.

The message was wedged between the other items in my mailbox. It was from Gil Haggerty, a news assistant on the *Times*'s metropolitan desk, and it said that "Mr. Gelb wants to see you *NOW*." There was no misreading it.

The meeting with Gelb and his deputy, Mike Levitas, took place late in the afternoon, after the daily conference at which the *Times*'s news editors discuss the stories that will go into the paper that night. Arthur Gelb had a small, sedately furnished private office off the newsroom, and inside its corked walls, it was possible to escape entirely the bustle just beyond the door. What was not possible to escape was Gelb. The metropolitan editor sank into a couch underneath some Hirshfeld sketches of theatrical figures and gave me a look that was anything but sympathetic. "What in the world are you doing on that hospital story?" he asked. "In case you've forgotten, I'm still the metropolitan editor and I want to know if there's a story there."

With Gelb and Levitas interrupting, it took me an hour or two to outline what I had learned. But, when I was finished, Gelb had lost his testiness. "Now I want you to write this story, and I want you to start now. You can continue your research, but I want at least a draft of that story on my desk within a week." I started to protest, but Gelb got up. The metropolitan editor towered over me. "A week. No more. Anybody in this building can do a draft in a week."

"One more thing, Artie. I've just found out that Mike Baden is reviewing the deaths for Woodcock."

"O.K. You've met Baden, haven't you? Find out what he tells the prosecutor."

"I'm not sure . . ."

"Well, ask Woodcock then. And, by the way, what's the chance that Woodcock will blow all this to the *Bergen Record*? They'd love it."

"Art, I don't think that's going to happen. I really don't know Woodcock, but if he's clammed up to us, like I said, I don't think he's going to run to the *Record*."

Gelb started to go. "Remember what I said. A week. And you'd better keep an eye on the *Record*."

Each afternoon in late December, I walked the few blocks from *The Times* to the Port Authority bus terminal on Eighth Avenue to buy the *Record*. Relieved to find nothing on Riverdell, I hurried back to the locked room at *The Times* where, day and night, I was pounding the typewriter keys. That week I ate most of my meals in the *Times*'s cafeteria, supplementing them with coffee and juice and cookies from food machines. When I was too tired to go home, let alone to think or to write, I napped on the carpet next to my typewriter.

It took the full week that Gelb had allotted me to complete the first draft of the Riverdell story. The draft needed "better shape" and "smoother continuity," Gelb quickly decided, and it was too long for a single article. It had to be broken into two parts. With Marv Siegel, Gelb's assistant in charge of special projects, I went over the draft repeatedly. Like most reporters, I was more enthusiastic about adding than pruning material; and, because Siegel was a willing listener, I won some arguments. But I lost some, too, because Siegel was a smart editor with confidence in his own judgment.

The second draft that Gelb received, divided into two articles, totaled about 6,700 words, or about nine columns of *Times* newsprint. Gelb liked it and took it to Abe Rosenthal. Rosenthal also approved. But when Gelb left the managing editor's office, another important decision had been made: Dr. Jascalevich's name would be deleted from the piece. "He hasn't been charged with a crime, so we're leaving his name out," Gelb explained to Siegel and me. "What else can we use?" Our first thought was to substitute a name, but there was the risk of coincidentally using the name of another doctor in New Jersey. "How about an initial?" I suggested. "X," Gelb said. "That's what we'll use. Call Jascalevich Dr. X."

Carefully, because one slipup would defeat our purpose, Siegel and I exorcised Dr. Jascalevich's name from the copy. Still, I worried. Again I read over the copy. And again. But Dr. Jascalevich was gone. In his stead, in every instance, was Dr. X.

The remaining adjustments to the Riverdell story were relatively minor, and while I was making them, I placed yet another call to Woodcock. The prosecutor wouldn't say what, if anything, Dr. Baden had found in his review of the hospital deaths or whether the analysis had been concluded. But he did say that his office was in the process of drawing up some "papers"—and that was enough to set me on edge. If there were "papers," and they were going to be made public, I wanted them for my story. For that I would wait.

On January 6, 1976, Bergen County assistant prosecutor Sybil Moses filed an affidavit from Dr. Baden with the county's assignment judge, Theodore W. Trautwein. The three-page affidavit was one of those legal documents that contain a lot of words like "duly" and "pursuant to" and "abovementioned," but its meaning was plain. Dr. Baden swore that, taking into consideration "clinical findings, hospital course, circumstances surrounding the deaths, including the clustering of the deaths, and autopsy examinations where performed, it is my professional opinion that the majority of the cases reviewed are not explainable on the basis of natural causes and are consistent with having been caused by a respiratory depressant.

"I am aware," the pathologist continued, "that prominence of unexplainable respiratory arrests having been involved in many of these deaths, the possibility of poisoning by a curarelike drug (specifically *d*-tubocurarine) was considered and investigated at the time of the initial inquiry in 1966. The ability to identify *d*-tubocurarine, often referred to as curare, in human tissue, was limited at the time of the initial investigation. It is my professional opinion that recent technological advances now permit the detection of very minute amounts of *d*-tubocurarine in tissues from dead bodies. This is because *d*-tubocurarine is a chemically stable compound that can exist unaltered for many years . . . In addition, because the majority of these deaths could not be explained by natural causes which would produce respiratory arrests, it is my professional opinion that exhumation, autopsy, and re-examination is warranted to determine the validity of the original causes of death as attributed at that time."

Mrs. Moses also submitted an affidavit of her own on January 6. She said the prosecutor's office had "re-opened the investigation into the aforementioned deaths as a result of (*a*) newspaper articles indicating a series of similar deaths at a veteran's hospital in Michigan, occurring during the summer of 1975 and (*b*) questioning and investigation by a reporter for *The New York Times,* the result of which indicated that this office should continue and increase its investigation." Citing Dr. Baden's opinion, she asked the court to authorize the exhumation of Carl Rohrbeck, Frank Biggs, Margaret Henderson, Emma Arzt, and Nancy Savino. The order was signed by Judge Trautwein, and that night the first installment of the Riverdell story rolled off the huge steel presses in the basement of *The Times.*

7

By the next afternoon the Associated Press and United Press International were churning out copy from Hackensack and Oradell. Woodcock met with the reporters and said that the first of the five bodies marked for exhumation would be disinterred within a week. Of the thirteen deaths that Dr. Baden had reviewed, four appeared to the pathologist to be due to natural causes. Dr. Baden categorized six of the deaths—including those of Savino, Henderson, Biggs, and Rohrbeck—as "highly suspicious"; three, including that of Arzt, as "suspicious." For most of the nine, the original cause of death had been speculative; and none of the nine, according to their hospital charts, had received curare as part of their treatment at Riverdell.

"Given the background and knowing what the patients suffered from, the causes of death attributed on the death certificates [are] a medical impossibility," Woodcock said. "All nine of these deaths exhibited conditions exactly like a respiratory arrest that could be consistent with curare poisoning. Each of these patients had gone in for a simple operative procedure. All died swiftly." Woodcock told reporters that he had gone outside the county for expert advice because there were "people in the Bergen medical examiner's office who were involved in the investigation ten years ago. We want a purely objective investigation."

The prosecutor declined to identify Dr. X, saying "we have no right to take such a position until we investigate the case fully." But a few reporters in New Jersey had already learned Dr. X's name, and others were soon to find out. Some of these reporters approached Dr. Jascalevich for comment. The surgeon was polite, but unedifying. He had nothing to say about the Riverdell affair.

All day on January 7 my phone rang. I was occupied with the second part of my opening article on Riverdell, making sure that it was "clean" for publication that night, and I let the message desk take most of my calls. But toward afternoon I went through the slips and was surprised to see that many of the calls were from book publishers and literary agents. I had no plans to write a book, but more out of curiosity than anything else, I returned Lucy Kroll's calls. She turned out to be the literary representative of Harold Schonberg, the Pulitzer Prize–winning music critic of *The Times*. Mrs. Kroll said she had read every word of my story that morning and was "hanging on a cliff" in anticipation of the second installment. Would I have lunch with her soon? she asked. I didn't see much point in it, but being a music buff and an ardent admirer of Schonberg, I agreed.

"Thirteen, Artie," I said the next day. "Count 'em. Thirteen."

I spread a copy of the January 8 *Bergen Record* across Gelb's desk and pointed to a special box with the *Record*'s lead story. "The *Record*'s assigned thirteen reporters to this story. How am I going to keep up with them?"

Gelb smiled and turned to Mike Levitas. "Look at him, will you? He's got a little competition for once and he's panicking."

"Oh no, Art. Not panicking," I said. "All I ask is that you quadruple my salary while I'm up against this pack. I'm not asking for thirteen times the salary. Just multiply it by four."

"Fine," said Levitas. "You can have it. As long as you show today that you are four times the reporter you were yesterday, and as long as the thirteen aren't splitting one reporter's salary. Will you please take this *Record* with you as you go? And read it; you might learn something."

Now that the Riverdell story was in its second day—no one in the news media was printing or broadcasting Dr. Jascalevich's name—many of the papers were carrying reaction pieces. And it was clear from those, and subsequent, articles that the Riverdell affair was no less divisive a matter in 1976 than it had been a decade earlier.

Dr. Lans told the *Record* that "there was no question in my mind where the guilt lay" and that there had been a "terrible miscarriage of justice" in 1966. Dr. Harris was also tough on Calissi, saying that a "proper" conclusion to the case was "long overdue" and that the bodies should have been exhumed when the case first arose. But Edwin Frieman, who, like Dr. Lans, was still a director and a part owner of Riverdell Hospital, chafed at the revival of the case. He told the *Passaic Herald-News* that he didn't think Calissi was "shielding anyone" in 1966 and that "Dr. X" had given "some logical explanations" for having curare in his locker. "We have a great deal of insinuations and allegations but no facts," Dr. Frieman said. "The time for investigation was ten years ago."

Judge Galda didn't comment publicly on the case, but Judge Calissi was quoted repeatedly, particularly after Woodcock suggested that the attorney general of New Jersey might review the handling of the case in 1966 for any indication of prosecutorial misconduct. Repeating what he had said earlier to me, Calissi told reporters that he had "deep and strong suspicions" in 1966 and that his investigation had been "intensive and serious."

"This was a medical problem," he said on January 8. "What the hell do I know about curare? I relied on the medical profession . . . If curare couldn't be detected in 1966, why dig up the bodies—to sit them in a chair?" Lawrence Denson told the *Record* that he was "quite peripheral to the whole thing" in 1966. "I was assistant medical examiner, and I was only involved for the first five hours of the investigation," Dr. Denson said. The *Record* also reached Dr. Umberger and Dr. Helpern, who had retired in early 1974 and was succeeded as chief medical examiner of New York City by Dr. Dominick DiMaio. "This will turn out to be the most bungled case ever to hit the Eastern seaboard," said Dr. Umberger, apparently referring to Calissi's investigation. But Dr. Helpern, who had had a falling out with Dr. Baden before retiring and never spoke to the younger man again, took another view. "We had suspicions back then [in 1966], but suspicion is not enough," he said. "You have to have proof." Given the probable conditions of the bodies now, he went on, Dr. Baden and Woodcock were engaged in a "grandstand play . . . a waste of taxpayers' money." "How the devil," he asked, "can they pick things up [from] that putrid mess of stuff?"

On January 11, the story focus shifted. Woodcock disclosed that he was asking the New Jersey Board of Medical Examiners to consider suspending the doctor's license pending the outcome of his own investigation. Like the reporters, Woodcock continued to refer to Dr. Jascalevich as Dr. X. The prosecutor, whose office had received a number of calls from patients asking whether their doctors might be Dr. X, said he had a "responsibility to the public" to determine whether Dr. Jascalevich's license should be lifted temporarily. "I'm not asking that his name be pinned to any courthouse door," Woodcock said. "But it's important that public confidence in the physicians in New Jersey isn't shaken while our investigation goes forward."

In going to the Board of Medical Examiners, Woodcock was, in effect, going to a man who was already upset with him: Edwin Albano. Dr. Albano was both chief medical examiner of New Jersey, a position that gave him responsibility for the investigation of suspicious deaths in the state, and president of the Board of Medical Examiners, an official agency that controlled the licensing of 12,000 doctors in New Jersey. The elderly physician resented the prosecutor's decision to go out of state for a medical analysis of the Riverdell deaths. But now Woodcock was coming to him as head of the Board of Medical Examiners, and Dr. Albano said the board was more than willing to consider whether Dr. X's license should remain in force.

The board, most of whose fifteen unsalaried members were medical doctors, was much changed since 1966; it was now in the forefront of national efforts to discipline malpractitioners. Most of its cases involved physicians who were charged with prescribing or selling drugs where there was no medical justification. Medicaid fraud, deviant behavior, sexual abuse, or professional incompetence were other cases the board dealt with. But in accepting Woodcock's request, the board was taking on a case for which it had no real precedent. Certainly the board could suspend a doctor's license if there was "an immediate threat to public health." But the Riverdell affair was ten years old, and Dr. Jascalevich had solid standing as a physician and surgeon. "This particular case," remarked a spokesman for the board, "is really up in the air."

On the morning of January 13, 1976, Maryrest Cemetery was covered with snow. From the window of his office, George Borkes could see the reporters shivering out there on Darlington Avenue, beyond the stone wall that enclosed the New Jersey cemetery. One of them, the cemetery superintendent noticed, held a television camera, and Borkes wished the reporters would go away. This was no place for commotion. He thumbed the card he needed that morning. Nancy Savino. Born: October 27, 1961. Died: March 21, 1966. Buried: March 24, 1966. Block B, Section B, Plot 91, Grave No. 2. Tombstone: "Best Dark Rock of Ages," Vermont granite. Good stone, Borkes thought. Keeps its shape and color.

Frank Tomaino got out to the cemetery at 7:30 A.M., just ahead of Woodcock's investigator and the sheriff's photographer. As an aide to Dr. Albano, Tomaino was accustomed to supervising exhumations. But never in a case like this; this case, he knew, had to be handled perfectly. As the backhoe ripped into the earth above Nancy Savino's grave, Tomaino glanced around at the rows on rows of graves, many bearing Christmas wreaths with crimson ribbons and fake gold bells that glistened, then dimmed, in the fitful sun. Two verdant pines stood near the foot of the Savino grave. Here and there, fist-sized pockets of snow had accumulated between the pine needles, looking like white blossoms.

The backhoe grunted, jerked, and swung away from the grave, now open to a depth of five or six feet. Using shovels, Tomaino and the others carefully cleared the earth from the top and sides of the cement vault in which the coffin rested. Two experts on vault construction, manipulating a tripod with a chain block and wire tackle, opened the casing and gently retrieved the wooden casket. The coffin was intact and that comforted Tomaino. As the casket was draped with straps and lifted into an unmarked van, Tomaino bottled a little of the liquid that lay in one end of the vault. Also for testing, he scooped up two containers of dirt from the gravesite. The exhumation had not taken long, an hour and a half. But Tomaino was cold. Trudging across the cemetery to Borkes's office, he reproached himself for not wearing boots. Borkes made coffee while Tomaino called Dr. Baden to say that he was on his way. Moments later, the van eased through the gates of Maryrest Cemetery, past the reporters and past the statuette of the Virgin Mary with its worn inscription from the litany of the rosary: "Pray for Us Now and at the Hour of Death."

In fifteen years Dr. Baden had autopsied 10,000 bodies at the morgue at First Avenue and Thirtieth Street. But apart from the remains of a 1,900-year-old American Indian, the pathologist had never autopsied a body that had been buried for more than five years. As far as he knew, no one in the United States had examined a corpse of that age for purposes of a homicide investigation. To witness the Savino autopsy—actually it was a reautopsy—Dr. Baden invited Dr. DiMaio, now his boss, and Dr. Albano. With Dr. Albano came New Jersey's chief toxicologist, Richard Coumbis. To assure privacy, Dr. Baden chose the morgue's special autopsy room, a subterranean chamber where "KEEP CLOSED" was painted in heavy black letters on the door. The walls were tiled in an ivory hue, and a thick odor of decomposition and disinfectant clung to the two stainless-steel autopsy tables in the center of the room. At 11:30 A.M., Tomaino unfastened the latches and removed the lid from Nancy Savino's coffin.

A gasp broke the silence. Dr. Albano's eyes bulged. Dr. Baden, riveted like everyone else to the sight of the child ten years after death, thought fleetingly of Dr. Helpern's prediction of a "putrid mess." "My God," he muttered, "she almost looks like she could step out of there."

Later the experts would say that it had been a combination of things: good soil, the location above the waterline in the cemetery, superior embalming, and tight sealing of the casket and the vault around it. Whatever the reasons, Nancy Savino's body was in extraordinary condition on the morning of January 13, 1976, as well preserved as some bodies that had been buried for merely a week or two. Her lips, on which cosmetic was still apparent, had been pressed together by the mortician, giving her a stern expression. The globes of her eyes had been covered with small fragments of cotton and were now sunken. Her well-combed hair was a rich brown tinged with red. A small satin pillow supported her head, which was bent forward, and around her neck was the thin chain of a gold-plated cross that rested, askew, on her chest. The child's dress was light pink, with short sleeves, white lace trim, and a pink bow on the left side at the waist. Although the petticoat underneath was slightly damp, the dress itself was dry and clean. Between her ankles was a bouquet of white flowers. It, too, had been preserved.

Dr. Baden placed the child's body on an autopsy table three times her length. He saw the cut-down incision on the left ankle where the intravenous feeding tube had been implanted after surgery in 1966. There was also a Y-shaped chest incision from the original autopsy. The skin was intact, for the most part, although adipocere—a hardening of the fat of the skin—gave a waxy touch to areas of the back, arms, and legs. Transferred to a metal stretcher and wheeled into the morgue's X-ray room, the entire body was screened.

The real work began after the X rays. Dr. Lowell Levine, a forensic ontologist, examined the teeth, and pronounced them those of a four-year-old. They were then extracted. Dr. Baden, clad in a belted white uniform, moved in, positioning himself between the two autopsy tables. On the table behind him were containers and plastic bags for the organs he would remove. Seated beyond, on stools, were Dr. Albano and a half-dozen other officials from New Jersey and New York. Dr. Baden hunched over the body, took up his scalpel, and began cutting and dictating simultaneously. "The initial Y-shaped autopsy incision is reopened. Hardening compound is present within the thoracoabdominal cavity, a portion of which is saved. The sternum overlies the viscera . . ."

At 4:28 P.M. Dr. Baden laid down his scalpel. As he lifted his head, he could feel the stiffness in his neck muscles and in his back and legs. The average autopsy takes an hour; this one had taken five. All of the organs had been held up for Dr. Albano and the others to see. Neck. Head (the brain had not been returned to the body after the first autopsy, but it was said then to have been "normal"). Lungs. Heart. Liver. Gallbladder. Spleen. Pancreas. Gastrointestinal Tract. "Not remarkable," "unremarkable"—Dr. Baden had uttered those words repeatedly since noon. The pathologist dressed the corpse, laboring to make it appear that the body still had the organs he was keeping for microscopic and toxicological analysis. Tomaino was anxious to get going; he wanted to reinter the corpse that night. Dr. Coumbis, the toxiocologist from New Jersey, took Dr. Baden aside. Could he have some of the tissues to work on? How about the eyes? Eye fluids had been used before to detect poisons.

Dr. Baden had already arranged for the basic chemical tests to be performed by Dr. Leo A. Dal Cortivo, the chief toxicologist of Suffolk County, New York. But knowing Dr. Albano's pique at New York's entry into the case, he gave Dr. Coumbis Nancy Savino's left eye. Dr. Baden showed the New Jersey officials to the front door of the medical examiner's building, while the corpse was whisked out the side. Turning back, the pathologist passed the Latin inscription in the lobby—*"Taceant colloquia. Effugiat risus. Hic locus est ubi mors gaudet succurrere vitae."* ("Let conversation cease. Let laughter flee. This is the place where death delights to help the living.") Dr. Baden pushed through the waist-high swinging gate that led to his office and called Sybil Moses in Hackensack.

"Sybil," he said to the prosecutor, "I didn't see anything in that body that could have caused her death."

Richard Coumbis had very definite plans for the eye. On the morning of January 14, he called Dr. Sydney Spector, head of the pharmacological section at the Roche Institute of Molecular Biology in Nutley, New Jersey. The toxicologist asked whether the Roche laboratory would perform a radioimmunoassay test on an eye. Bring it over, Dr. Spector said.

Enlisting Dr. Spector's aid was a logical move for Dr. Coumbis. In 1973 Dr. Spector and Dr. Peter E. Horowitz were the first scientists to adapt the radioimmunoassay (RIA) technique for the measurement of curare in body fluids. The scientists at Roche, a research institute associated with the Hoffmann-LaRoche pharmaceutical company, hadn't used RIA to detect curare in other tissue extracts, but their work on blood and urine, part of an effort to determine how various concentrations of curare act on the body, had been well received. The RIA test itself, discovered in the late 1950s by Dr. Rosalyn S. Yalow and Dr. Solomon A. Berson at the Bronx Veterans Administration Hospital, was generally acknowledged as one of the century's most significant applications of basic research to clinical medicine. Originally used to quantify the hormone insulin in the blood of adult diabetics, the technique was now employed in thousands of laboratories for the measurement of hundreds of hormones, vitamins, viruses, enzymes, drugs, and other substances in the body, many of which had previously eluded measurement because they were present in quantities that were too minute or diluted, or because their chemical properties were too similar to those of other substances.

The RIA test, for which Dr. Yalow was to share the 1977 Nobel Prize in Medicine and Physiology, was likened, in sensitivity, to the ability to detect an object the size of a lump of sugar in a lake sixty-two miles wide and long and thirty feet deep. In the RIA adaptation for curare, which was based on an immunologic principle known as the antibody-antigen response, rabbits were innoculated in their foot pads with a combination of curare and bovine serum albumin. This procedure produced antibodies—later collected in blood drawn from the rabbits' ears—that were capable of coupling or binding with tiny amounts of curare. A certain amount of antibody would then be mixed in a conical centrifuge tube with an identical amount of curare that had been made radioactive or "hot" (the antigen). Added to this solution would be the urine or blood specimen being examined for curare. If no curare was present in the specimen, all the "hot" curare in the tube would bind with the antibody. If curare was present in the specimen, a competitive reaction would occur between the "hot" curare and the nonradioactive, or "cold," curare—with each of the curares seeking to attach themselves to the limited number of binding sites on the antibody. As a result, some of the "hot curare," which can be seen because it is radioactive, would lose out and be left floating free in the solution.

At Roche, Dr. Coumbis was given a sterile syringe and needle and, with it, he plunged about one milliliter of phosphate-buffered saline into Nancy Savino's eye, to dissolve and flush out any chemical deposits. The solution caused the walls of the eye to bulge spherically, and Dr. Coumbis noticed that the walls remained intact. Aspirating the syringe, the toxicologist transferred the solution to a centrifuge tube, ready for use by Dr. Spector's colleagues. Within a few hours the RIA was completed and Dr. Coumbis had the result. The test was "positive." It indicated the presence of curare in Nancy Savino's eye.

Dr. Dal Cortivo, in his laboratory in Hauppauge, Long Island, was working independently of Dr. Coumbis. Before examining Nancy Savino's tissues, the Suffolk County toxicologist added curare to tissues removed during other autopsies. Then, modifying a method developed in 1963 by Dr. Ellis Cohen of Stanford University, he plotted the chemical extraction of that curare. In some instances he waited a couple of days; in others, a couple of weeks. But he was always able to detect the curare that he had introduced. Nancy Savino's tissues, of course, posed more difficult problems. Here were tissues that had lain in the ground for almost a decade, and despite the findings on the eye at Roche, it was still uncertain whether curare could be traced in other parts of the child's body. If, indeed, the drug had ever been there.

Dr. Dal Cortivo began with portions of Nancy Savino's liver—the liver being the organ that breaks down most drugs in the body. The toxicologist added water to slices of tissue about the size of a grape and weighing less than five grams, homogenized the mixture in a blender, and put the macerated tissue through a series of reactions with ether, menthanol, dichloroethane, and a stream of nitrogen gas. In a cleaning or refining process intended to reduce "interference" and the chance of misleading test results, he extracted entire classes of acidic or basic drugs that did not represent curare. As an initial test for curare, Dr. Dal Cortivo chose one of the most common analytic tools of the toxicologist—thin-layer chromatography, or TLC. Chromatography relies on physical and chemical characteristics of individual drugs in a solvent so that mixtures can be separated into their components as they flow along a thin layer of silica gel. On the base line of a silica-gel plate, Dr. Dal Cortivo put three drops: a drop of solvent, a drop of known curare, and a drop of extract from Nancy Savino's liver tissue. He watched as the drops started to move up the plate by capillary action—much as water does when it climbs up tissue paper in a glass— with each drop leaving a streak. Eventually he sprayed the plate with platinic iodide and, as expected, this made the known curare turn violet at a certain point on the plate. But something more, he saw, had happened. A violet spot, indicating curare, had also appeared in the streak made by Nancy Savino's liver tissue.

Using a standard bleaching technique, Dr. Dal Cortivo eluted from the plate the violet spot in the Savino tissue. He assigned the spot a code number, and he did the same thing with some crude extract from the Savino liver. Both of these specimens were then taken to New York for RIA testing by Dr. Richard S. Matteo, whose assistance had been arranged by Dr. Baden. Dr. Matteo, an anesthesiologist at Columbia University's College of Physicians and Surgeons, had worked with Sydney Spector at the Roche Institute and had considerable experience using the RIA to measure curare in body fluids. In his own research at Columbia on the safety of curare for children undergoing surgery, Dr. Matteo was just about to apply the RIA for tracing curare in body tissue. On February 12, 1976, Dr. Matteo performed the RIA on the specimens from Dr. Dal Cortivo—the eluted spot and the crude extract from Nancy Savino's liver. Both specimens, he reported, were "positive" for curare.

Even as Dr. Matteo ran his tests, other portions of Nancy Savino's liver—and others of her organs—were being segmented and parceled out for examination. Dr. Coumbis, in New Jersey, reported that he, too, had found curare in the child's liver—and in her lung as well. Dr. Dal Cortivo packaged additional extract from Nancy Savino's liver and air-freighted it to the Finnigan Corporation in Sunnyvale, California, for analysis by mass spectrometry. The mass spectrometer is an instrument that, by electron bombardment, cracks or fragments a compound into particles that can be identified as they pass through a magnetic field. The machine, which Finnigan manufactures, creates for a specimen a set of chemical fingerprints—each compound cracks in its own distinctive manner—that can be matched, by computer, against the prints of 40,000 known compounds. On March 12, 1976, the Finnigan Corporation notified Dr. Dal Cortivo that the extract from the Savino liver exhibited a mass spectrometric pattern consistent with the presence of curare.

"It's a textbook case," Dr. Dal Cortivo told Mike Baden. But still the toxicologist was taking precautions. As a "control," he would have liked to have exhumed another body that had been buried for ten years, one in which there was no suggestion of curare. Then he could have tested its liver and other tissues. But lacking that opportunity, Dr. Dal Cortivo did what else he could. He made extracts from tissues that did not contain curare—fresh liver tissue, partially decomposed liver tissue, and liver tissue from an embalmed body that had been exhumed on Long Island after nearly four years in the ground—and had all these extracts tested by thin-layer chromatography, RIA, and mass spectrometry. The toxicologist wanted to see whether the tests would show any of these tissues to be positive for curare, a finding which would cast doubts on the validity of the Savino results. But in these tests no curare was found.

The second body exhumed was Margaret Henderson, the twenty-six-year-old factory machine operator who died at Riverdell on April 23, 1966, less than a day after Stanley Harris and Robert Livingston did an exploratory pelvic laparotomy on her. Margaret Henderson was extensively decomposed. Her clothing was friable and disintegrated on touch. Many of the woman's organs—including her heart, liver, and brain—had been discarded after her autopsy in 1966. For microscopic analysis, Dr. Baden took tissues from the trachea, diaphragm, intestines, and dura mater, or lining of the brain. And for use by the toxicologists, the pathologist removed a portion of the spinal cord, the left eye, the urinary bladder, muscle tissues, and the right-knee tissues and cartilage.

Emma Arzt was the next to be disinterred, on February 3. The seventy-year-old retired librarian had died on September 23, 1966, a day after Dr. Harris had removed her diseased gallbladder. She had not been autopsied in 1966. Mrs. Arzt's body was well preserved, although somewhat shrunken, and the jewelry and eyeglasses she had worn to the grave were all neatly in place. Again Dr. Baden took a variety of tissues.

Three weeks had passed since the exhumation of Nancy Savino, and still nothing was known publicly about the curare results. Dr. Baden said only that the tests were "continuing," and Woodcock said little more. "We're doing a full, fair, and impartial investigation, and we're doing it in a very orderly fashion," the prosecutor told me on February 8. His office, he said, was "not drawing any conclusions until we've seen the results of the tests." Woodcock declined to comment on a report that Dr. Jascalevich was giving a new deposition, so I called James Anderson, who was still Dr. Jascalevich's lawyer.

No, said Anderson, the surgeon had not been in to see Woodcock. "We will go in if he's asked." The lawyer wouldn't let me interview Dr. Jascalevich. "He does not wish to be disturbed by this nonsense," Anderson said. "This whole thing is a silly Frankenstein-monster movie. I'll be amazed if all those chemists with their test tubes find anything. If they find what they should find, they won't find anything."

In fact, Dr. Jascalevich had already visited Woodcock. On February 4, a day after the exhumation of Emma Arzt, the surgeon went to Hackensack to give a deposition, and Anderson was with him. The lawyer had not only requested the session, but he had also asked Woodcock to find a meeting place free of any reporters who might recognize and pursue his client. The session was held in the building that housed the county's narcotics task force, the same building where, a half year earlier, I had first seen the Riverdell file. When the deposition ended that day, one aspect of it seemed particularly strange to Woodcock. Dr. Jascalevich had told Calissi on November 11, 1966, that he conducted all his dog experiments in 1965 and 1966 in the sixteenth-floor animal quarters at Seton Hall Medical School in Jersey City. The only exception, he had said, was his one visit to the third-floor laboratory at Pollak Hospital, adjacent to the medical school, several hours after he met with Riverdell's directors on November 2, 1966.

In that same deposition in 1966, Anderson asked Dr. Jascalevich whether he had ever done any work at Pollak Hospital before November 2, 1966.

"No," Dr. Jascalevich replied.

Now, a decade later, Woodcock had again raised the question of where Dr. Jascalevich performed his dog experiments with curare in 1965 and 1966. But this time, the answer was different. The surgeon said he did the work in 1965 and 1966 in the third-floor laboratory at

Pollak. He said nothing about any experiments at Seton Hall in those years.

The fourth body to be exhumed, on February 9, was that of Carl Rohrbeck. The seventy-three-year-old retired public works employee had died on December 13, 1965, shortly after Dr. Jascalevich postponed his operation for repair of a ventral hernia. After ten years in the ground, Rohrbeck's hands, feet, and head were considerably decomposed, but his chest and abdominal areas, Dr. Baden found, were relatively intact. As with Margaret Henderson, several major organs, including the heart, had not been returned to the body after the initial autopsy in 1965. However, the brain, which had not been examined in 1965, was available, and tissues were taken from it and other organs.

The last of the five to be exhumed was Frank Biggs, who was reautopsied by Dr. Baden on February 10. Biggs, a fifty-nine-year-old accountant, had died on August 28, 1966, eight days after Robert Briski had operated on him for a bleeding peptic ulcer. On exhumation Biggs was not in much better shape than Rohrbeck, with partial skeletonization of the head and other areas. The heart and the lungs, examined during the first autopsy, were missing from the body, but the other internal organs were intact and provided tissues.

I had yet to hear from Lee Henderson, and as I was unaware of Dr. Jascalevich's new and contradictory deposition, I revived my search for the former Seton Hall dog attendant. A spokesman for the New Jersey College of Medicine and Dentistry was quoted as saying that the school had "no records that any curare experiments ever took place" at Seton Hall. "We do not leave dying dogs around," he added. I had already heard that version; I wanted Lee Henderson's.

Toward February 1976 the Social Security Administration advised me that it had forwarded my letter to Henderson in care of an employer who listed earnings for him, though it couldn't guarantee that the letter would be delivered to Henderson "or that you will receive a reply. In any event, we are unable to forward a second letter." The news wasn't very encouraging, but it gave me an idea. I knew that Henderson couldn't have earned very much at Seton Hall in the mid-1960s, and I wondered whether Lee or Barbara Ann—I had gotten Mrs. Henderson's name from the bank that had acquired the Henderson house in Jersey City—might have received welfare payments after the couple split up.

I called the welfare agencies for both Jersey City and Hudson County. A first call produced nothing. But on the second call, to the county agency, I repeated my request. Though adamant about the impropriety of giving information to the press, a woman agreed to check the records. I waited, confident that if either of the Hendersons had been on welfare, the records would contain biographical data, including addresses. The woman came back on the line; yes, she had a file on Mrs. Henderson; no, she wouldn't discuss it. I drew closer to the phone, fearful she would hang up. Quietly I explained that I was only trying to reach Lee Henderson; I believed Henderson had returned to relatives in the South, but I didn't have the exact address. Well, the woman confided, it was probably South Carolina because Henderson's father, who was also named Lee, was from South Carolina. Whitmire, South Carolina. Immediately I remembered what Mike Naver of the Social Security Administration had told me—that North Carolina was "close" to the state in which Henderson lived. Good God, I thought, this is it! I started to thank the woman; but she said not to bother, she wasn't going to tell a reporter anything.

Information for Whitmire had a listing for Lee Henderson on Maybington Road, but I couldn't tell whether it was Lee, Jr.—the man I wanted—or his father. And the number didn't answer. I called Naver in Baltimore, and he said the letter to Henderson must have gotten through; at least it had not come back as undeliverable. I hung up without mentioning Whitmire. Why hadn't Henderson answered me? It was already February 11.

My plane landed at Columbia, South Carolina, at 10:28 the next morning. I rented a car at the airport and checked my map. Whitmire was only a dot on the map, barely visible along the Enoree River in the heart of Sumter National Forest. An hour later I turned off Interstate 26 and began the slow climb north into the forest. Even in the noon sunshine, Whitmire looked deserted. There was no hotel, no movie theater, no restaurant, and the liveliest outpost on the short Main Street seemed to be Roche's pharmacy. From there I called the Henderson number on Maybington Road. Again, no answer. A customer at Roche's told me that Maybington Road was way out of town. But some of the Henderson folks, he said, lived on Duckett Street, just a few blocks away. I found Helen Henderson's place shut tight and silent. Across the street, however, a man was leisurely washing his car and watching me. Lee Henderson, the younger? Why yes, the man knew him. He didn't know where Lee lived, but Helen Henderson was Lee's momma, and old Mr. Henderson, who wasn't well, lived out on Maybington Road. Come to think of it, he was pretty sure that Lee Jr. worked at the J. P. Stevens textile mill on the other side of town. As a matter of fact, he wouldn't be surprised if Lee worked the 8 A.M. to 4 P.M. shift. I glanced at my watch. It was close to 1 P.M.

The personnel director at the Stevens plant was friendly but uncooperative. Lee Henderson did indeed work at the mill, and on that shift, but I couldn't see him in the plant and the director would neither identify Henderson nor give him a note from me. The director didn't recall any letter for Henderson from the Social Security Administration. Outside, I stationed myself on a bench near the main gate of the mill, a square, artless brick building that looked like a throwback to the Industrial Revolution. All I knew about Henderson's appearance was that he was black. But when the employees surged out at 4 P.M., many of them were black and none, among those I was able to stop, was Henderson. None so much as said he knew Henderson.

Then, as luck would have it, I met the Rev. Thomas Jackson Crisp, Jr., a loomfixer and pastor of God's Healing Springs Baptist Church. Reverend Crisp, who was white, didn't know Henderson either, but he did know Duckett Street, and when he offered to accompany me back there, I quickly accepted. Jack Crisp had lived in Whitmire for forty-five years, and even without his collar, this sweet-tempered man of the cloth seemed to be just what I needed.

Unfortunately, the atmosphere on Duckett Street had changed. Shouting above the din of a CB radio, the woman who answered Helen Henderson's door demanded to know what I wanted with Lee. Before I could say anything, another, more elderly black woman appeared on the porch and began wheezing and clutching her heart. Neighbors quickly gathered on the lawn of the little clapboard house. Amid the squabbling—"Let *him* take you where you want to go," someone screamed, pointing at Reverend Crisp—the clergyman looked rather anxious. "I think we should go now," he whispered.

The reception was warmer at Shorty's Market. Over sodas, Reverend Crisp plied each of the customers for suggestions on finding Henderson. Finally a black policeman suggested that I look in "Subertown," on the grounds of an abandoned plantation, and keep an eye out for a green pickup truck. That, he said, would be Lee Henderson's place. Reverend Crisp and I bumped around the dirt roads of Subertown for some time before we caught sight of the pickup truck next to a well-kept house on a knoll. At the top of the winding driveway, we found a middle-aged black woman rocking herself by the screen door on the back porch. Lee, she said, had come home from the mill but had "stepped off. He might be here in a little while," she said, "and, then again, he might not. What is it you want?" I was certain that if I didn't open up, Lee would be gone for quite some time. Emphasizing that Henderson was not in any trouble, I explained my purpose in coming to Whitmire. I was well into a monologue when a sturdily built black man in a blue denim outfit and checked shirt came around the side of the house. After these many months, I was pleased to shake hands with Lee Henderson, Jr.

The living room of the Henderson house was spotless. Reverend Crisp drew up an armchair, next to a framed photograph of Rev. Martin Luther King, Jr. I sat down on the edge of the bed, across from a wood-burning potbelly stove and an antique pendulum clock. Henderson, who said he'd never received the letter I had sent through Social Security, was unaware of either the current investigation by Woodcock or the investigation, in 1966, by Guy Calissi. I showed him the portion of Dr. Jascalevich's 1966 deposition dealing with the "dying dogs" in the sixteenth-floor animal quarters at Seton Hall Medical School. Dr. Jascalevich had told Calissi there were "three or four colored" attendants whom he tipped in exchange for the dogs in 1965 and 1966, but "Lee is the only name" he could remember. "I recall one of them," the surgeon had said; "we used to call him Lee."

After Henderson responded, I asked if he would write out a statement of what he had told me. He had no objection, but unsure of his writing, asked me to draw it up. Using a borrowed typewriter and a piece of loose-leaf paper, I prepared a summary. I asked whether Henderson would mind having the statement notarized, and again he was willing. Henderson's companion offered the services of a notary public and lawyer she knew, State Senator Robert C. Lake, Jr. And at about 8 P.M. Senator Lake ushered us into the kitchen of his ranch house across town. The senator asked Lee if he definitely wanted to sign the paper, and Henderson said he did. I reminded Henderson of the importance of what he had said and urged him to back off now if there was anything untruthful in the statement. But Henderson was firm. Then Senator Lake read the statement aloud:

I, Lee Henderson, Jr., of Whitmire, South Carolina, was employed in the animal quarters of Seton Hall Medical School in Jersey City, New Jersey in the early to mid nineteen-sixties. At the time of my employment there, I, to the best of my knowledge, was the only person named Lee working in the animal quarters. At no time during my employment at Seton Hall did I solicit or receive any tip or money or goods in return for providing Dr. Mario Jascalevich, or any other person, a dog or other animal, in any condition. The only money I received, in payment for my regular work, was from my employer. To the best of my knowledge, I do not know and have never met Dr. Mario Jascalevich. During my employment in the animal quarters at Seton Hall, I never observed, or engaged in, any experiments on the sixteenth floor of the medical school, where the dog quarters were located. I have never seen a "dying dog" strapped to a table in the animal quarters at Seton Hall.

With that, the statement was sworn to and signed.

Two weeks later a detective from the Bergen County prosecutor's office, which was also on Henderson's trail, showed up in Whitmire. The detective, Edward Schiro, was introduced to the textile worker by officials of the Stevens mill. Henderson, according to a Schiro memorandum that was later made public, said he "never" accepted "gratuities" at Seton Hall, "knew nothing" of any experiments in the animal quarters, and "never assisted any doctor, technician, or students on any such experiments." After "eight hours of smelling the dogs," Henderson said, he wouldn't have stayed past 5 P.M. "for anything in the world." Before leaving Whitmire, Schiro drafted a formal statement for Henderson to sign. Lee consulted Senator Lake, who was "suspicious" of the need for another statement and "suspicious of anything going on from Jersey." But Henderson signed the statement prepared by Schiro, and the senator notarized it. On March 1, 1976, it arrived in the prosecutor's mail at Hackensack.

On March 3 Dr. Jascalevich returned to the prosecutor's office to continue the deposition that had begun a month earlier. By now Woodcock had received a report indicating that curare was present in the corpse of Nancy Savino, the first of the five bodies to be tested for the drug, and he informed the surgeon that he had become the "target" of the Riverdell investigation. Although Dr. Jascalevich was not in custody and was again accompanied by his lawyer, James Anderson, he was given the "Miranda warning" of his constitutional rights to have an attorney and to remain silent. Woodcock asked Dr. Jascalevich whether he still wanted to go ahead with the deposition, and after a brief huddle with Anderson, the surgeon said he did.

The discovery of curare in Nancy Savino's tissues, disclosed publicly on March 7, was a turning point for both Woodcock and Dr. Jascalevich. Woodcock convened a grand jury on the Riverdell affair, with the first witnesses, Dr. Harris and Dr. Baden, appearing on March 15. And Dr. Jascalevich approved Anderson's idea of a press conference. On March 16 some fifty reporters crowded into a meeting room at the Sheraton Motor Lodge in Hasbrouck Heights, near Hackensack; but those who had come to question Dr. X, as the surgeon was still being called, were quickly disappointed. Dr. Jascalevich was not there.

Referring to his client only as "the doctor," Anderson began by accusing the press of creating a "Roman circus spectacle" by publishing "details of scientific tests" in the Riverdell investigation. The press, he said, had given the impression that such test results were "always absolutely correct, valid, and reliable. This is simply not so. The results . . . rely almost completely upon the knowledge, skill, and competence of those performing them, and the techniques used to guard against error. This is particularly so when the tests are so complex and, in some cases, apparently untried and unproved as those involved in this investigation."

Anderson went on to say that his client "was not the only man" at Riverdell who had access to curare—it was "in common use . . . as a muscle relaxant in surgery. All technically trained hospital personnel are aware of the nature of curare, its properties, and its potentialities. It follows, therefore, that if indeed any of these patients expired of curare poisoning, anyone could have done it." And why, the lawyer asked, would a man of his client's "intellectual capabilities, using any substance in a hospital for unlawful purposes, have his own supply when there were ample supplies in the hospital's stock? Even more so, keeping it in his own locker would be amazingly stupid under such circumstances. Nowhere has there appeared any motive for anyone to have done anything wrong here, any more than there is any valid proof that anything wrong has been done."

Anderson disclosed that in addition to his 1966 deposition, "the doctor" had spent about eight hours with Woodcock, "again being examined without any objection to any question and without the raising of any privilege, immunity, or constitutional right . . . Common experience is that any man who has anything to hide will not co-operate with the authorities." The lawyer said that were he publicly to identify his client, "the doctor" would be beset by "the curious and the morbid" and "would be obliged to go into seclusion."

The reporters' interest was stirred. "Why are you standing here?" one newsman asked the attorney. "What you are saying is that you are here to dispel allegations that haven't been made about someone you won't name," another remarked. "Why not let him tell his story?" said a third reporter.

Leaning against a wall on the side of the room, I waited my turn. Having talked to Lee Henderson and written about his statement in Whitmire, South Carolina, I now wanted to question Anderson about Dr. Jascalevich's dog experiments.

"Mr. Anderson," I began, "you said something a while ago about keeping curare—correct me where I go wrong here—about keeping curare in his own locker would be amazingly stupid under the circumstances."

"Yeah."

"You said something before that about an ample supply at the hospital. What was the point you were making?"

"The point I was making, Mr. Farber, was that there was curare already in the hospital."

"Right, right."

"Why go out and grab something of your own when what you want, if that's what you want, is there. It's perfectly silly."

"He had curare in his locker, though," I said.

"Certainly."

"Why?"

"He was performing experiments. You know that better than I do, Mr. Farber. At least as well, judging by your column."

"Where was he performing them?"

"Mr. Farber, I believe that in some manner, you have obtained at least a portion, if not all, of his testimony in 1966. You have shown an amazing amount of knowledge about what happened ten years ago, and I don't think really there's anything I can do to enlighten you. You, perhaps, have more knowledge of this case than I do."

"Well, counselor, why don't you try? I mean, where was he performing these experiments?"

"Mr. Farber, I repeat what I have said. You have a copy, or you have access to that information, with reference to the information he gave Mr. Calissi in 1966, sir. And I am not going to elaborate upon it."

"You won't answer the question?"

"I will not answer the question."

The next morning *The Times* identified Dr. X as Mario Jascalevich, and much of the other news media immediately followed suit. Even before the *Times*'s action, the surgeon's identity appeared to be well known in New Jersey medical circles and among reporters assigned to the Riverdell story. At Anderson's press conference, one reporter said he had already interviewed some of Dr. X's patients outside the surgeon's office. Moreover Dr. Jascalevich's name had now emerged in the grand jury proceedings and in legal documents that were publicly available. His name was on subpoenas that had been served by the prosecutor on Christ Hospital, the Jersey City Medical Center, and North Hudson Hospital. On a visit to the Jersey City Medical Center, I had even been given a copy of a subpoena requiring the institution to provide Woodcock with a list of the gastrectomies performed there by Dr. Jascalevich between 1962 and 1970. Evidently the prosecutor was broadening his investigation, as was the state Board of Medical Examiners, which was still considering Woodcock's request about the possible suspension of Dr. Jascalevich's license.

"The disclosure of his name is nonsense," Anderson told the UPI after *The Times* came out on March 17. "It's a little bit premature. Does it seem fair to disclose the name of a man who has not been indicted or charged with any crime?" Dr. Jascalevich, the lawyer said, "won't talk to the press" and "is in a state of shock."

On March 23 Christ Hospital in Jersey City informed Dr. Jascalevich that his clinical privileges—his right to operate—had been suspended "in the best interest of patient care." Dr. Jascalevich, who performed 90 percent of his surgery at Christ Hospital and had operated there as recently as March 19, responded by contesting the hospital's move in Hudson County Superior Court in Jersey City.

Dr. Jascalevich did not come to court for the hearing on March 26. Anderson was there to represent the surgeon. And so, I noticed, was another attorney—a tall, thin, elderly man in a rumpled blue suit. I edged along the press bench and asked a local reporter if he knew the name of the second lawyer.

"That's Ray Brown. A big gun. The best criminal defense lawyer in the state."

I took another look at Brown. There was nothing flamboyant in his appearance to suggest a kinship with the melodramatic heroes of the criminal defense bar. His shoulders, as if bearing the weight of many cases over many years, were markedly stooped, one more so than the other. His face was distinguished by a high, smooth forehead and a mustache that matched the fringe of gray hair around the back of his head. As he leaned against a railing, waiting for the hearing to start, Brown might have been a banker or a professor or a senior civil servant and, next to the stout figure of his co-counsel, he seemed quite ascetic. But when he rose to address the court, Brown was in full command of himself and his arguments. His voice was laced with derision and outrage as he pleaded with Judge Frederick C. Kentz, Jr., to overturn a suspension "so broad and so vague as to be incredible. If they have charges, let them file them," Brown demanded, attributing Christ Hospital's action to the news stories, "designed for one thing—to destroy this man. Here is a surgeon. That's all he is. That's all he does."

Francis X. Kennelly, a lawyer for the hospital, conceded that Christ Hospital hadn't lodged charges against Dr. Jascalevich and didn't intend to. The suspension meant that Dr. Jascalevich couldn't admit patients to Christ, Kennelly explained, but he was still a member of the medical staff and "the hospital is very proud to have him as a member in good standing. No one has ever said that he, in any way, is held in less esteem than any other surgeon in the hospital."

Kennelly's description brought Brown to his feet, his long arms flailing. "Yes, they say he's a great guy, we love him, and they cut off his livelihood."

During a recess I moved closer to the attorneys' tables. Kennelly was telling Brown that Dr. Jascalevich was "a great guy," and Brown was saying "there's a bastard in this case." "I'd just like to slap the shit out of him," Anderson joined in, glancing at me.

Judge Kentz ruled in Dr. Jascalevich's favor. He set another hearing for April 9, but meanwhile, he ordered the hospital to restore the surgeon's clinical privileges. The summary suspension, the judge held, violated Dr. Jascalevich's constitutional due-process rights and could cause him professional embarrassment and loss of income.

Kennelly didn't wait until April 9. On March 30 he was back in court, urging Judge Kentz to dissolve the temporary restraining order. Kennelly said the hospital's only concern was Dr. Jascalevich's "ability to perform serious and delicate operations" at a time when "he was being hammered by the press to the degree that he had to hire bodyguards to keep people away from him." A number of physicians at the hospital, Kennelly said, thought it would be "better for Dr. Jascalevich, the hospital, and his patients that he be suspended until some of his problems die down."

Brown would have none of this argument. Noting that Dr. Jascalevich had performed scores of successful operations since the start of the year—including one that morning—Brown submitted affidavits from a nursing room supervisor and a urologist who had seen the surgeon operate at Christ since his identification as Dr. X. The supervisor said that Dr. Jascalevich was his "usual calm, polite, efficient, and undisturbed self"; and the urologist said he showed "no signs of hesitation, fatigue, or incompetence, and no signs of pressure." To cap things off, Brown offered an affidavit from Dr. Jascalevich himself. "I know I am innocent of any wrongdoing," the surgeon wrote, "and therefore none of the publicity engendered by newspapers, TV, or radio has interfered with my ability to perform my duties in the practice of surgery at the highest levels."

Again the judge ruled for Dr. Jascalevich. Leaving the courthouse with his law partner, Irving Vogelman, Brown, who is black, observed that "a nigger, a Jew, and an Argentine immigrant beat the shit" out of the "old Irish" firm representing Christ Hospital.

On April 1, 1976, the executive committee of the hospital's medical staff voted to reinstate Dr. Jascalevich's clinical privileges. The matter ended there.

James Anderson had not been in court on March 30, and I never saw him again. Brown had taken over as Dr. Jascalevich's lawyer. Brown's reputation, I discovered, was every bit as formidable elsewhere in New Jersey as it was in Hudson County. Brown loved the courtroom, loved the intensity. And while he often cast himself as the

defense experts, including Dr. Henry Siegel, the chief medical examiner
of Westchester County. Dr. Siegel, who was serving as a private consultant, said there was no substitute for studying the tissues in their "virgin state." Dr. Jascalevich provided an affidavit, too. "In 1966," he
wrote, "I satisfied the prosecutor of Bergen County that I was in no
wise involved in the deaths." Before Judge Trautwein could rule on the
request, Brown expanded it to include re-exhumation of the five bodies
that had been disinterred in January and February. Save Dr. Jascalevich from "this lynching," Brown exhorted the judge. "Give this man a
chance to fight back."

Woodcock's office opposed all aspects of the motion. Dr. Jascalevich, Sybil Moses said, had no legal right to violate the secrecy of the
grand jury and obtain evidence being presented to it. Moreover, re-
exhumations would be an "exercise in futility" because all available tissues had been removed from the bodies by Dr. Baden. She assured
Judge Trautwein that if Dr. Jascalevich were indicted, he would have
access to all the state's evidence to which he was entitled. In a supporting affidavit, Dr. Baden said that tissues were being preserved
for any defendant in a locked deep freezer, where they "will not
significantly change or deteriorate toxicologically until needed." Other
materials, including pictures of body organs, autopsy reports, and records of the curare tests, were being "carefully documented" in writing
and in photographs.

Judge Trautwein reserved decision on Brown's motion. Not having
heard of a case in which a potential defendant was given access to the
state's evidence, he wanted to think this one through.

Events overtook Judge Trautwein. On May 18, 1976, Dr. Baden
completed his grand jury testimony. The pathologist had told the grand
jury in March and April that curare had been detected in the tissues of
Frank Biggs and Emma Arzt, as well as in the corpse of Nancy Savino.
In each instance, he had said, the "manner of death" was homicidal because curare only took effect when it reached the bloodstream, and the
patients couldn't have injected themselves or received the drug inadvertently. Now Dr. Baden came to the bodies of Margaret Henderson and
Carl Rohrbeck. Neither of the bodies had been well preserved in the
ground, and the curare tests were "still in progress." Dr. Baden said the
tests so far "do not prove the absence of curare" and that taking the
autopsy findings and other information into consideration, the "most
reasonable" cause of death for Henderson and Rohrbeck was curare
poisoning. Only the previous day, he said, curare had been indicated
by RIA in Rohrbeck's kidney.

On the afternoon of May 18, having heard thirty-three witnesses
over a period of two months, the grand jury of twenty-three Bergen

County residents handed up a five-count indictment. It charged that "against the peace of this state, the government, and dignity of the same," Mario E. Jascalevich "did willfully, feloniously, and of his malice aforethought, kill and murder" each of the persons whose bodies had been exhumed in the Riverdell investigation. Judge Trautwein sealed the indictment.

Dr. Jascalevich, whose patients had remained as loyal as ever in recent months, was up by dawn on May 19, a rainy Wednesday morning. He had three hysterectomies to perform at the Jersey City Medical Center, and the patients were waiting. Also waiting, in the gray silence outside the surgeon's home in Englewood Cliffs, were two detectives. As Dr. Jascalevich left his house, he was placed under arrest.

From the county courthouse, the surgeon called Jersey City to cancel his operations. Woodcock called Ray Brown. And by the time Judge Trautwein came in to unseal the indictment, word was filtering out about the arrest. Dr. Jascalevich's composure appeared shaken only once during the arraignment, when Moses noted that the indictment charged multiple murders. "I don't think there is a more serious crime in the history of jurisprudence or in common law," said the assistant prosecutor, who asked that bail be set at $250,000.

Brown, entering a plea of not guilty for Dr. Jascalevich, objected to Moses's "vicious presentation" on bail. His client was presumed innocent, Brown said; he had roots in New Jersey, had shown no "tendency to flee," and needed his freedom to help prepare his defense. Judge Trautwein ordered Dr. Jascalevich released on execution of a $150,000 personal recognizance bond, including $15,000 cash and $45,000 equity in his home. The defendant had to surrender his passport and could not travel outside the New York–New Jersey metropolitan area without permission of the Court. At 1:55 P.M. Dr. Jascalevich hurried out a courthouse door in the company of several men and was driven away.

The next morning I noticed an interview in the *Daily News* with Nancy Savino's father. The reporter had asked Michael Savino whether he was relieved by the grand jury's action.

"Am I relieved? No. Is it going to bring my daughter back?"

Dr. Jascalevich resumed his surgery on May 21, smoothly performing the hysterectomies he had canceled two days earlier. A senior staff surgeon at the Jersey City Medical Center observed the operations with Dr. Jascalevich's consent.

That afternoon, however, Dr. Jascalevich ran into new trouble. The state Board of Medical Examiners charged the surgeon with five counts of malpractice relating to the deaths for which he was indicted. And in a matter entirely unrelated to Riverdell Hospital, it also charged him with additional counts stemming from his behavior as a surgeon in a Jersey City case in 1974 and 1975. The board ordered Dr. Jascalevich to show cause the following week why his license should not be suspended pending the outcome of a hearing on these charges.

Only sketchy information was made public concerning the Jersey City case. Dr. Jascalevich was accused of fraud and neglect that endangered a patient identified simply by his initials, J.E. The board alleged that:

—On August 2, 1974, during an operation on J.E., Dr. Jascalevich falsely represented that the patient had a "mass in the pancreatic region."

—On August 15, 1974, Dr. Jascalevich submitted tissue for pathologic analysis that he represented was from the gallbladder bed of J.E. "when he knew full well that the tissue had not been obtained" from the patient.

—On August 16, 1974, Dr. Jascalevich received the results of the tissue analysis and "knew or should have known" that the results "did not represent accurate findings" concerning J.E.

—After August 16, 1974, "as a result of false information placed in the hospital report by him and/or as a result of his conduct concerning patient J.E.," Dr. Jascalevich failed to treat J.E. properly, causing the patient "injury, unnecessary suffering, and mental anguish."

—On or after April 5, 1975, Dr. Jascalevich again operated on J.E. and diagnosed his condition as "carcinoma of the bile channels" when he "full well knew that such diagnosis was false and therefore entered false information in the operative records and falsely advised the hospital staff," again subjecting the patient to injury.

Ray Brown made it clear that he would resist suspension of Dr. Jascalevich's license. "There's only one way to fight this whole matter, and that's to fight it everywhere," he said. But on May 25, a day before the board was to decide on the suspension, Dr. Jascalevich voluntarily agreed to halt his medical practice until his hearing on the charges. Anthony F. LaBue, a state deputy attorney general and counsel to the board, said the surgeon's action was "without prejudice" and did not constitute "any admission of guilt." Dr. Jascalevich performed his last operations the following afternoon, and on June 1, 1976, he turned in his medical registration certificate to the board. A message left on the front door of his office in West New York said the office was closed because of vacation. Surgical emergencies were referred to another physician.

The hearing on Dr. Jascalevich's license was scheduled to start in the middle of July 1976, but after a delay requested by Brown, it began on

September 1. By then two things had happened. The board had selected Sidney Goldmann, a retired presiding judge of New Jersey's second highest tribunal, the Appellate Division of Superior Court, as the hearing officer, and the board had brought an additional charge against Dr. Jascalevich. It now alleged that, in 1973, Dr. Jascalevich had altered or caused to be altered the operative record of a Jersey City patient and had caused the "fraudulently prepared" record, containing the forged signature of a supervising nurse, to become part of the patient's hospital file. The patient, who had sued Dr. Jascalevich for malpractice, was identified only by the initials T.R.

The hearing was convened in a conference room at the state office building in Newark. Judge Goldmann sat at one end of a long table; Brown, at the other. Flanking Brown were LaBue, who was going to prosecute the charges, and Dr. Albano, the president of the Board of Medical Examiners. Off to the side, on a folding chair, was Dr. Jascalevich. The surgeon, occasionally squinting or frowning as he rested his head against his hand, had bags under his eyes, and his hair —which had been brown in May—was now gray with a silver tinge. A dozen reporters stood by an open doorway while Brown demanded that the hearing be closed to the press to avoid "sensationalism of the worst kind." The lawyer said he had been assured that the hearing would be conducted in private, and threatened to "withdraw" if the reporters remained. Judge Goldmann, gently puffing on a cigar, took it all in and ruled in Brown's favor.

The hearing took longer than anyone expected. There were fifteen sessions before it was recessed in January 1978, and it didn't resume until 1979, three years after Dr. Jascalevich had stopped practicing in New Jersey.

Meanwhile, Brown was doing his best to have the murder charges dismissed in Hackensack. In July 1976, he filed a motion asking that Dr. Jascalevich's indictment be thrown out on the grounds that it had come too late. Since 1953, Brown pointed out, the New Jersey statute governing the time in which indictments could be brought said that "no person shall be prosecuted, tried, or punished for any offense not punishable with death unless the indictment shall be found within five years from the time of committing the offense . . ." And in 1972 the New Jersey Supreme Court had invalidated the state's death penalty, leaving life imprisonment as the maximum penalty. Since Dr. Jascalevich could not be put to death if convicted, Brown asserted, he could no longer be tried for alleged crimes that occurred in 1965 and 1966. Coupled with the failure of the legislature to change the wording of the 1953 law after the court's decision in 1972, he said, "the plain meaning of the statute bars any prosecution for murder brought more than five years after the commission of the alleged offense."

Brown was not the first to raise this argument. In February 1975 Robert Zarinsky was indicted for the murder of a New Jersey teenager on a summer evening in 1969. After Zarinsky was convicted in April 1975, his lawyer asked that the verdict be set aside because of the five-year time limitation on prosecutions. On July 20, 1976, only six days after Brown filed his motion in Hackensack, the Appellate Division handed down its decision in the Zarinsky case, and it didn't bode well for Brown. The court held that the legislature had always "intended to insure that crimes of the most serious class, including first-degree murder, would not escape prosecution by the mere passage of time . . . The unenforceability of the death penalty has not wiped the statute off the books . . . It is one thing to suspend the imposition of the death penalty for constitutional reasons, but this affords no reason for frustrating the legislative will by staying its additional sanction against murder—namely, the relentless prosecution of that crime without limitation in time." Zarinsky's lawyer appealed to the state Supreme Court while Brown tried to persuade Judge Trautwein that the Appellate Division's holding was wrong.

On November 5, 1976, Judge Trautwein said he was in "substantial agreement" with the Zarinsky opinion and denied Brown's motion for dismissal. The judge also rejected a request that the trial be transferred to Trenton because of what Brown called "adverse publicity." Brown could renew his motion as the trial approached, but as of now, the judge said, "the general overall tenor of the coverage has been neither so vitriolic nor so adverse" as to have precluded a fair trial in Bergen County. "The news media, although not always as circumspect as it might have been, has not convicted this defendant in the court of popular opinion."

Brown sought leave to appeal Judge Trautwein's ruling on the time limit for prosecutions. The New Jersey Supreme Court, having already agreed to hear the Zarinsky appeal, turned him down. But it instructed Judge Trautwein to postpone the Jascalevich trial until its decision in the Zarinsky case. There was no point in conducting a trial that might be invalid.

By the end of 1976 Woodcock had decided to return to elective politics. On February 1, 1977, the former state senator announced that he was resigning as prosecutor, probably to seek the Republican nomination for governor. Woodcock was succeeded by his thirty-nine-year-old chief assistant, Roger W. Breslin, Jr., a Democrat whose family had been active in Bergen County's legal and political affairs for generations. As his chief assistant, Breslin chose another young prosecutor, Raymond Flood. But one of the candidates for that post—in fact, she had been a marginal candidate for Woodcock's job—was Sybil Moses.

Sybil Rappoport was born in Newark in 1939. Her father, one of eleven children, had emigrated from Poland as a teenager before World War One; her mother, one of twelve children, had come as a girl from Hungary. In 1937 William Rappoport went into the furniture business with relatives in Newark, and by the time Sybil was ready for school, the family had a secure, pleasant life in the Newark suburb of Livingston. In 1956, when Sybil was a junior in high school, her father bought a grocery store/delicatessen from a cousin in Capitol Heights, Maryland, and the Rappoports moved to that Washington suburb. Sybil entered the University of Maryland in 1957 and, during the next four years, accumulated a near-perfect academic record. In 1960 she married Stephen Moses, then a first-year law student at the University of Pennsylvania, and upon her graduation from Maryland, she won a Woodrow Wilson Fellowship to study international relations at Penn. The couple lived on a tight budget in a basement apartment near the campus in Philadelphia until 1962, when Stephen finished law school and Sybil received a master's degree, *magna cum laude*. The Moses family moved to East Orange, New Jersey, where Stephen had signed on as a clerk in a law firm. Sybil took a series of part-time teaching jobs. In 1971, when the younger of her two children was three and Stephen was established as a lawyer in Hackensack, Sybil decided that she wanted to do more, and she jumped at her husband's suggestion that she try law school. In 1974 Mrs. Moses graduated with honors from Rutgers Law School. And that September, a month after being admitted to the bar, she became an assistant prosecutor of Bergen County.

The office that Sybil Moses joined was much changed from Calissi's time. Not only were Woodcock and his assistants full-time prosecutors —and newly subject to the supervision of the state attorney general —but the number of assistants had tripled to twenty-two, and the investigative force had grown commensurately. Whether the county's increased crime rate reflected the commission of more crimes or merely the reporting of more of them, many more cases were pursued by the prosecutor's office, there were more grand juries, more criminal courts, and more trials.

In 1974 Mrs. Moses was assigned to the office's trial section, where she was responsible, at any one time, for as many as sixty cases involving drugs, armed robbery, assault, fraud, weapons possession, and other offenses. The two murder cases that came her way prior to the Riverdell case were settled by pleas before trial. When Woodcock decided to reopen the Riverdell matter in the fall of 1975, he and Breslin felt there were only four or five assistant prosecutors with the ability or experience to handle so complex a case. But two of them were tied up with an extensive organized crime investigation, and another two were about to return to private practice. So Sybil Moses, not suspecting that she was to become embroiled in the broadest murder investigation in the county's history, was given the nod. She presented the evidence to the grand jury. And if the case went to trial, she would try it for the state.

Preparations went ahead in 1977, despite the state Supreme Court's order delaying the trial. Under New Jersey's liberal "discovery" rules, which grant a defendant access to virtually all of the state's evidence, Brown received thousands of pages of material, including Calissi's 1966 Riverdell file, hospital records and correspondence, autopsy reports, patients' files, reports of interviews with potential witnesses, grand jury proceedings, and curare test data. Judge Trautwein finally refused Brown's request to re-exhume the five bodies disinterred by the prosecution, although Brown contended that Dr. Baden had done an inadequate job of collecting, photographing, and saving the tissues. The judge also rejected a defense motion to exhume bodies of other persons whose deaths at Riverdell had been discussed during Calissi's investigation. Before being amended, the motion even included the "disinterment" of two former Riverdell patients who were still alive. Ida Trujillo read about her proposed fate in the newspaper. "They can't exhume me," she protested.

The prosecution's tests for curare—refining earlier procedures and adding another one, high-pressure liquid chromatography—continued until August 1977, when Judge Trautwein cut them off. Meanwhile the defense undertook its own tests. And the defense team of experts was expanded to include Dr. Frederic Rieders, a former chief toxicologist of Philadelphia who was now a private consultant; Dr. Henry Fales of Bethesda, Maryland, a mass spectrometrist; and Dr. Valentino Mazzia, an anesthesiologist at the University of Colorado. Henry Siegel, the defense pathologist, went as far as Sweden to enlist the aid of Dr. Bo Holmstedt, chief toxicologist at the Karolinska Institut in Stockholm.

From time to time I went out to Hackensack for the arguments on Brown's motions. I still wanted to interview Dr. Jascalevich, who never attended the court sessions, and I repeatedly asked Brown and his associates for the opportunity. "You must be kidding," said Henry Furst, a young lawyer who worked for Brown. "We're never going to talk to you."

The Times expected me to keep up with developments in the

Jascalevich case. But after the Board of Medical Examiners hearing was closed to the press, there wasn't much news, and I moved on to other assignments. I also agreed to write a book about the Riverdell affair. Lucy Kroll, the literary agent whom I had met after my first Riverdell articles appeared, negotiated a contract with Doubleday & Company, Inc. and I signed it in July 1976. In 1977 I began drafting a manuscript.

On the night of November 16, 1977, Jonathan Friendly, an assistant metropolitan editor, walked back to my desk at *The Times*. "Get on this," he said, handing me a piece of UPI copy.

"In a precedent-setting decision," I read, "the New Jersey Supreme Court will rule Thursday that the state's five-year statute of limitations applies to murder, a justice of the high court said Wednesday. In a copyrighted story, the *Bergen Record* said Justice Morris Pashman outlined the upcoming decision at a Chamber of Commerce luncheon in Paramus. The ruling would apparently make New Jersey the first state in the nation to set a time limit on murder prosecutions. Pashman said the decision in the case of Robert Zarinsky will prevent the prosecution of Dr. Mario E. Jascalevich . . ."

I couldn't believe what I was reading. There was something wildly improbable about Justice Pashman's indiscretion. I picked up the phone and called Woodcock, figuring the former prosecutor might have heard something. The line was busy. I called Sybil Moses. The line was busy. Then I called Justice Pashman. It was only 10 P.M., but the justice had to be roused from a deep sleep. I read him the UPI dispatch, but the only response I got was a growl, and "This is ludicrous." That wasn't enough. The *Times*'s second edition was coming up in minutes, and with radio and television starting to carry the court decision, Jon Friendly had to make his own ruling. I called another justice of the New Jersey Supreme Court. The justice said he couldn't comment for publication, but if he were running *The New York Times,* he wouldn't publish the story. And *The Times* didn't.

The next morning the state Supreme Court announced that it had decided 6 to 0 against Zarinsky. Justice Pashman, speaking only in hypothetical terms the previous day, had not disclosed the court's ruling, and he had been badly misunderstood.

Dr. Jascalevich's trial was put off several times in the following months, and during that period, Riverdell Hospital declared bankruptcy. The hospital had been "hurt as a result of the publicity surrounding the so-called Dr. X affair," according to a receiver's report, but its major cash-flow problems predated 1976. Riverdell faced other difficulties, too. The families of several of the patients who died in

1966 now lodged civil suits against the hospital and, in some instances, against Dr. Jascalevich as well. Some of Riverdell's staff thought it was only a matter of time before the institution was reduced to "a parking lot."

In February 1978 Brown revived his motion to have Dr. Jascalevich's trial moved out of Bergen County, where he said the press coverage of the case had been "vicious and inaccurate." A $10,000 telephone poll commissioned by the lawyer showed that 311 of 478 respondents were familiar, to some degree, with a recent case "involving a doctor." Of the 311, about 9 percent believed the doctor was definitely guilty; 36 percent, probably guilty; 9 percent, probably not guilty; and 1 percent, definitely not guilty. Forty-five percent of the 311 had no opinion.

In an opinion on February 15, 1978, Judge Trautwein denied Brown's motion. He said the reporting on the case had been "orderly, even-handed, and factual" and that Brown had failed to show clear proof that a "fair and impartial" jury could not be selected from among Bergen's registered voters.

That night it appeared that the Jascalevich trial might be postponed again: a judge whom Brown was defending on a case-fixing charge was shot to death in an Atlantic City motel. But on the morning of February 27, 1978, Brown and his retinue, and Moses and hers, filed into a windowless courtroom on the fourth floor of the Bergen County Courthouse. Lying ahead was the longest criminal trial for a single defendant in American history. And a "trial" within a trial.

9

In his chambers behind Courtroom 407, Bergen County Court Judge William J. Arnold carefully donned his black robe. This was a big day for him, eclipsing all else in a judicial career that was nearing a close. Judge Arnold would retire next year at age sixty-five. But now, for whatever time it took, he was in the limelight. Even as he prepared for the first day of the Jascalevich trial, reporters were filling up the press rows in the courtroom and law professors, predicting a battle of experts over the curare findings, were describing the case as "mind boggling." Judge Arnold liked the idea that he would be presiding. One way or another he had been part of this courthouse for a quarter of a century. And while there would be ends to tie up afterward, he would say good-bye with this case, a case that was being watched throughout the country.

In contrast to the case, there was nothing exceptional about Judge Arnold or his career. Billy Arnold was born and raised in Woodsfield, Ohio, in the Allegheny foothills. After graduating from Ohio Northern University Law School in 1940, he worked as an insurance company investigator and adjuster. In 1948 Arnold passed the New Jersey bar and became associated with law firms in Newark and Hackensack, where most of his practice—negligence cases, contracts, divorces, tax appeals—was on the civil, rather than criminal, side. He bought a house in Englewood, New Jersey and was soon president of the local Democratic Club.

In 1953, when Guy Calissi was Bergen County manager of Robert Meyner's successful run for governor, Arnold worked hard in the campaign. And the following year, when Calissi was named county prosecutor by Meyner, Arnold became one of his three part-time assistants, as did Fred Galda and another lawyer. (By the time of the Jascalevich trial, all four of the former prosecutors were judges in the Bergen County Courthouse.)

Arnold tired of being an assistant prosecutor by 1960. But only a few months after he returned to full-time law practice, he was offered a seat on the county's lowest court, or District Court. By 1967 he had moved up a step, to become a County Court judge. Judge Arnold approached retirement with some satisfaction. When he had first arrived in New Jersey, with the down-home informality and slow manner of speech that were still his traits, he had often been ill at ease. In rural southeastern Ohio, he had been used to people who "mean what they say," as he put it, and he felt such candor was lacking in many of the people he encountered as a young lawyer in New Jersey. But over the years, he had come to appreciate Bergen County and he had made a mark, however modest, there. If he wasn't fussed over or written about or talked about for promotion, he was still regarded as a fair judge. And he was liked personally—an unpretentious, open-faced man, a high school athlete who remained a "frustrated football coach," a gardener proud of his prize dahlias. "Arnold," a colleague remarked, "is so low-keyed you could meet and have dinner with him and not even know he was there."

There were varying stories of how Judge Arnold came to preside over the Jascalevich trial. He was assigned to the case well before 1978 and had ruled on some of the pretrial motions. By one account, Judge Arnold went to Judge Trautwein and specifically asked for the case: it would be his swan song. But that wasn't Judge Trautwein's version. "I had concluded that it would be an emotionally charged trial," he said, "and I wanted a person who would remain calm and not get caught up in the maelstrom. Bill always impressed me as a calm person. In fact, we called him 'Steady Billy,' and I thought he was ideally suited."

"All rise!" the bailiff barked as Judge Arnold shuffled through the door from his chambers on the morning of February 27, 1978. From his raised bench the judge had an unobstructed view of the walnut-veneered courtroom. The combatants were directly in front of him, at a table in the pit of the court: Sybil Moses, in a forest-green wool suit, her black hair neatly set in a page boy; Ed Schiro, the red-bearded detective who was helping her; Ray Brown, twirling his Ben Franklin eyeglasses; Henry Furst, Brown's young assistant; and, at the edge of the defense side of the table, Dr. Jascalevich. He was expressionless as Brown argued that the lawyers, rather than Judge Arnold, should conduct the *voir dire* examination of prospective jurors. The judge rejected the motion but allowed Brown to use an opinion-research expert in profiling candidates for the jury.

Ninety-six people, picked from a central pool of Bergen County voters, were led into the courtroom and seated in the rows that would later be occupied by scores of spectators. Moses and Furst read out a list of some 200 potential witnesses for the trial. A dozen of the prospective jurors were then called to the jury box, and Judge Arnold, relying in part on fifty or sixty questions submitted by Moses and Brown, launched his interrogation. "Are you an antivivisectionist?" "Will you give more weight to a police officer's testimony?" "Do you think a doctor should be held to a different standard of conduct?" "Have you or any member of your family ever instituted a malpractice suit?" One candidate was excused by the judge because he had been treated by a physician at Riverdell. Another noted that her husband "distributes arms." "Arms?" Judge Arnold echoed. "Guns," explained the woman, drawing the first laughter of the trial. She, too, was excused.

By the end of the day, Brown had exercised four of his twenty peremptory, or automatic, challenges to jurors; Moses had used none of her twelve. To much groaning, Judge Arnold told the prospective jurors that he expected the trial to last as long as eight to twelve weeks. But he said the jury would not be sequestered. Court was adjourned, with the judge advising the jury candidates to "talk about football tonight, or basketball, or baseball. Don't talk about this case or read about it. Remember, newspaper articles are not the basis for evidence."

The reporters who trailed Dr. Jascalevich from the courtroom were turned away with a "no comment." The defendant had spent most of the day leafing through a thick law book and inspecting the roster of jury candidates. Rarely did he look toward the jury box, and only once did he pause by the press rows several feet behind his chair. Remarking that he painted in his spare time, he asked a television artist if he could acquire the sketch she had done of him.

As jury selection went on, Brown made a strenuous effort to have Judge Arnold expand the number of defense challenges to fifty—ten for each of the five counts of murder. According to Brown, this was the scheme intended by the state legislature. "I refuse," he said, "to call our legislature illiterate." The judge, without characterizing the lawmakers, denied the request.

On Wednesday morning, while Judge Arnold droned on with another batch of ninety-six potential jurors, Henry Furst beckoned to me in the courtroom. I followed him into the corridor, where the portly defense lawyer, who always looked as if he had just shaved, slapped a folded piece of paper against my chest.

"Mr. Farber, you are served," he said, as I instinctively reached for the paper. It was a subpoena to testify at the Jascalevich trial as a defense witness.

I wasn't entirely surprised. Two days earlier I had heard Furst read off my name as a possible defense witness. I didn't know why Brown would want to put me on the stand. He and his associates had been interviewing, or trying to interview, prospective witnesses for more than a year. Yet Brown had never tried to discuss the case with me.

I told Furst that I would let *The Times* know about the subpoena. I had been subpoenaed, as a reporter, a few times in the past, and had been threatened with other subpoenas. And the cardinal rule was: don't do anything before calling the paper. I had never actually testified.

I left Brown's assistant and called Alex Greenfeld of the *Times*'s legal staff. Alex told me to sit tight and continue covering the jury selection. Meanwhile he would try to reach Floyd Abrams, the *Times*'s "outside" legal counsel at the law firm of Cahill, Gordon & Reindel. I went back to Judge Arnold's courtroom, but everyone had gone to lunch. I was hungry myself, so I grabbed a sandwich in the courthouse coffee shop before placing another call to Alex. He was out, and I decided to get some fresh air. As I was returning to the courthouse about 1:30 P.M., I noticed Dr. Jascalevich in the lobby. It was the first time I had seen him without Brown or Furst. I sped up and managed to squeeze into a crowded elevator with the surgeon just as the doors were closing. For more than two years, I had wanted to talk to Dr. Jascalevich and now, perhaps, I had my opportunity.

When the doors clanked open on the fourth floor, I stepped into the hallway and turned to Dr. Jascalevich. We had never met, but I was sure that Brown or Furst had pointed me out to him in the courtroom.

"Doctor, I'm Myron Farber of *The New York Times*. I want you to know that *The Times* has always tried to be fair to you."

"Who are you?"

"I'm Myron Farber, of *The Times*. I wrote the stories about you."

"Are you from the hospital?"

"The hospital?" I echoed weakly. "Doctor, I'm Myron Farber. Myron Farber, of *The Times*. You know, the reporter you just subpoenaed." I felt completely foolish. How could he not know who I was? I had written of him, had called his office, and his lawyers had been talking about my stories for two years now.

"Jeez," Dr. Jascalevich said, "are you Wiener?"

"Wiener?"

"We had an administrator named Wiener at the hospital. Jeez, you look just like him. Do you know—you look just like him."

I had met Elliott Wiener, and I didn't think I resembled him at all. I studied Dr. Jascalevich's face. He was wearing large rectangular glasses, and I couldn't make out anything in his faint eyes. We began strolling down the corridor toward the courtroom, and I couldn't resist taking him by the arm. I put my hand on his elbow and stopped him.

"Doctor, for God's sake, I'm Myron Farber. The reporter, Doctor. The reporter." I was almost shouting.

"Are you a reporter? Oh, I'm sorry," he shrugged, "I can't speak to reporters." And then he was gone.

The next day a jury of eleven men and seven women was impaneled for the Jascalevich trial. Only twelve jurors would eventually render a verdict, but the alternates would not be chosen until lots were cast at the end of the trial. Most of the jurors were young or middle-aged, and all but one—a black nurse—were white. Only a few had attended college, and none had advanced training in chemistry or biology. Apart from the nurse, the jurors' occupations included plant worker, stock clerk, phone cable splicer, advertising copywriter, secretary, electrical engineer, payroll clerk, bank teller, girl Friday, plant manager, and sales representative. Two of the jurors were housewives and two were accountants. One was a retired postal employee and another was a college student.

Judge Arnold gave the jurors a long weekend and reminded them to avoid news accounts of the trial. "In the end," he said, "you people will be the most informed about the case. It's a serious case, and I'm counting on you."

That afternoon I was summoned to Judge Arnold's chambers with Moses and Brown. The judge, chewing on an unlit cigarillo, explained the court's "sequestration" rule, excluding witnesses from the courtroom until after they have testified. Unless the prosecutor and the defense attorney agreed to waive the rule for me, he said, *The Times* would have to substitute another reporter. Moses had no objection to my presence in the courtroom. And neither did Brown—as long as Moses didn't object to the presence of Nora Jascalevich, whom the prosecution had listed as a witness. "Let them all in, Judge," said Brown. "Let everybody in." But Moses didn't want Mrs. Jascalevich tugging at jurors' heartstrings from the front row, and neither she nor Brown would budge.

Floyd Abrams, the *Times*'s lawyer, came out to Hackensack to protest my exclusion and to let Judge Arnold and Brown know that *The Times* would fight any subpoena for unrestricted testimony by me. I thought very highly of Abrams, who had represented me before. Only forty-one years old, he was already dubbed "a paladin of the First

Amendment." After graduating from Cornell and Yale Law School, where he now taught part-time, Abrams had developed an interest in the relationship between the press and the courts just as those institutions were beginning to collide in the early 1960s. By 1978 he was a leading expert in this field, having represented the three major television networks as well as other news organizations, having argued a number of key cases before the U. S. Supreme Court, and having served as co-counsel to *The Times* in the Pentagon Papers case. He was a personally charming intellectual who worried over the literary quality as well as the legal validity of his briefs; a man who seldom raised his voice, but who loved a joke with an ironic twist.

Certainly, Abrams told Judge Arnold, *The Times* could assign another reporter to the Jascalevich trial, but that reporter "will know less, have less background, and the public will be less served." The free press clause of the First Amendment, Abrams argued, required Brown to show that my presence would pose a "substantial and immediate and direct" threat to a fair trial. Otherwise, attorneys "in good faith as well as bad faith" could affect the coverage of the courts. Not only had Brown failed to make such a showing, Abrams said, he had actually taken the position that all the witnesses, including Mrs. Jascalevich, "should be permitted to attend the trial."

Brown said that if I really felt the need to cover the trial, I should see a psychiatrist. Offering as evidence my original stories on the case, he told Judge Arnold that I had "worked with the prosecution since 1976" and had perhaps "worked as a detective." Rather cryptically, he also indicated that the defense had information linking me to the case even before 1975. Brown said it was hard for him to "follow sophisticated arguments." But it seemed to him there was "nothing at stake here but one thing, nothing to do with *The New York Times* or with the First Amendment. Mr. Myron Farber, will you be subject to the same rule of law as it is applied to literally well over 150 citizens who are being kept out of this courtroom? . . . Now, if he is above the law, then there is nothing we could do about it."

Judge Arnold asked whether Brown would be satisfied to have me excluded from the courtroom during the testimony of "certain particular witnesses." No, said the defense attorney. "As far as we are concerned, we think if only because of his special and encyclopedic covering of the matter, his investigation, that all witnesses are pertinent. We ask that he be excluded from them all." Brown generalized, inaccurately, that I had been "privy to all these people, their thoughts and actions. He interrogated all of them."

Having gotten nowhere with this approach, the judge tried another.

Would Brown tell him, in private, the kind of admissible testimony that I could give?

"I will not do it," Brown said. "I stand here as a lawyer defending this man. If Your Honor sends me to jail tomorrow, I will not tell you or any living man anything about his defense, and I say that most respectfully . . . I stand here fighting in a corner under such conditions that I am supposed to violate my client's rights for *The New York Times*. Judge, I will go to jail first and whenever you are ready—"

Abrams smiled and offered to defend Brown from a jail sentence.

ARNOLD: Let me ask you, Mr. Abrams. Mr. Brown states you are violating his rights to a fair trial here. Let us assume for the moment no doubt the press has certain rights, but can the rights of the press ever exceed the rights of a defendant to a fair trial?

ABRAMS: Your Honor, as so phrased, I can tell you that that is a question the Supreme Court of the United States and the Supreme Court of your own state have said they hope they never have to reach. I don't think that you or I have to reach that totally complete collision course.

ARNOLD: It looks like a pretty good collision course to me.

ABRAMS: It is not, Your Honor, because what it is we are asking of Mr. Brown, we want to know what this is all about.

The issue, Abrams underscored, was not whether *The Times* or I were "above the law," because the press rights guaranteed by the First Amendment coexist with the fair trial rights assured a defendant by the Sixth Amendment. When Judge Arnold replied that I was a "mere witness," Abrams objected. "I don't have a mere witness here . . . not just, as Mr. Brown would have it, Myron Farber, citizen."

In a fifteen-page opinion, Judge Arnold said that he had examined my stories on the Riverdell matter, "and they demonstrate exceptional quality, a grasp of intricate scientific knowledge, and the style of a fine journalist. The Court can understand why Mr. Farber received a nomination for the Pulitzer Prize. They also demonstrate considerable knowledge of the case before the Court and deep involvement by Mr. Farber showing his attributes as a first-rate investigative reporter. However, if a newspaper reporter assumes the duties of an investigator, he also assumes the responsibility of an investigator and must be treated equally under the law, unless he comes under some exception." Abrams, the judge said, had sought to "carve out of these proceedings a First Amendment privilege which provides the exception," but ". . . it is this Court's opinion that the rights of the press under the First Amendment can never exceed the rights of a defendant to a fair and impartial trial."

We decided not to appeal. Brown and Judge Arnold had said some pretty misleading things about my work on the Riverdell affair and about my role as a reporter. The judge appeared to be equating me, in legal terms, with a private investigator. But Floyd and I, and the *Times*'s own staff of lawyers, thought it was best now to concentrate our attention on the subpoena for oral testimony that I had received. While Artie Gelb and I were discussing the matter in his office, he took from his shelf a book by James V. Bennett, a former director of the Federal Bureau of Prisons. "Be brave," Gelb scrawled on the flyleaf, tossing the book to me. The title was *I Chose Prison,* and because neither Gelb nor I knew what was in store, we had a good laugh.

The courtroom was jammed Monday morning, March 6, with journalists—including David Bird in my place for *The Times*—trial buffs, law clerks, supporters of Riverdell Hospital, relatives of prospective witnesses, and nearly a dozen of Dr. Jascalevich's patients, the latter deploring the "injustice" being done the defendant. The fifty-year-old surgeon hurriedly kissed several of the women before Judge Arnold called the court to order. The judge's first move was to drop from the eighteen-member jury a juror who had said he might need a hernia operation during the course of the trial. Judge Arnold didn't want any comparisons drawn between the juror's hernia problems and those of Carl Rohrbeck. The judge also disposed of two last-minute motions. Brown wanted to prevent Moses from describing the prosecution's curare tests as "scientific," rather than "experimental," and Moses wanted the jury to be able to take notes of the testimony. Judge Arnold rejected both motions. At 11:10 A.M. Moses rose, turned to her left to face seventeen solemn citizens, and opened the state's case.

It was, of course, a circumstantial case, and the thirty-eight-year-old prosecutor owned up to it right away. There were no eyewitnesses who would implicate Dr. Jascalevich in the five deaths at Riverdell in 1965 and 1966, she said, but "the sum total of all the evidence" would prove the grand jury's charge that he had "willfully"—she repeated the word five times—"willfully" murdered the patients. "One name, one person was there before and after the deaths of these people," Moses said, pacing before the jury. "He's there. This defendant." The prosecutor looked over at Dr. Jascalevich. The surgeon was alternately gazing at the jury and jotting notes on a legal pad.

Moses promised the jury that it would hear of the treatment given the five patients, of the patients' "unexpected" deaths at the hospital, of the feeling among some Riverdell doctors that "something was wrong," of the discovery of syringes and of eighteen vials of curare—some full, others empty or nearly so—"crammed" into Dr. Jascalevich's fourteen-square-inch hospital locker, and of the decision, within twelve hours, to go to the county's prosecutor. When Moses characterized Calissi's en-

suing investigation as "inconclusive," Brown was on his feet, demanding a mistrial. No one, the defense attorney said, had asked that the patients' bodies be exhumed in 1966. Judge Arnold refused the move for
a mistrial, and the prosecutor finished up. Curare, she told the jury, is a
drug that can kill "if not administered in the appropriate way, at the
appropriate time, with the appropriate safeguards." There was no
reason, save one, for Dr. Jascalevich "to have that curare in that
locker," Moses said, "and that reason resulted in these deaths. We will
prove to you that these people died as a direct result of the injection of
this poison, this muscle relaxant."

Motive? As a matter of law, the state was not required to prove motive, and Moses really skirted the issue. But she noted that Dr.
Jascalevich had been the only "active" general surgeon at Riverdell in
1963 and 1964, before Stanley Harris and Robert Briski were added to
the staff. And she said that witnesses would tell of what happened to
Dr. Jascalevich's power, practice, and income after the new surgeons
arrived in 1965 and 1966.

Brown, holding a sheet of handwritten notes, offered the jury several
defense themes. Curare is no more dangerous "than aspirin" unless it is
misused—and it wasn't misused by the defendant. The state's tests on
the exhumed bodies were worthless, based—as was the prosecution's
entire case—on "speculation and concepts which you will find have no
factual bearing." Naturally Dr. Jascalevich was "always around Riverdell Hospital"; it was a principal means of his livelihood. Not only was
Dr. Jascalevich a good doctor and a good man, he was a responsible
chief surgeon at Riverdell who wouldn't countenance his colleagues'
ineptness. And as a result, he was framed in 1966 by doctors who were
fearful of his criticism.

Brown denied Moses's suggestion that the deaths had something to
do with Dr. Jascalevich's income—"not true, not true," he said. Disturbed by the deaths of Dr. Harris's and Dr. Briski's patients, Brown
said, Dr. Jascalevich sought a meeting with the hospital's board of directors in late 1966. But when Dr. Harris learned that the deaths were
to be reviewed, he "moved to make sure" that the meeting never took
place, and he has never answered for these deaths, Brown said, "not to
this day, never." Brown portrayed Dr. Harris and Dr. Lans as cowards
who by "guise, stealth, and deception" opened Dr. Jascalevich's locker
and conferred "in the middle of the night" with Jay Sklar. These doctors, Brown said, "knew precisely what would happen" if Dr. Jascalevich appeared before the board of directors.

"The writing was on the wall," the defense attorney continued. "Dr.
Jascalevich was not satisfied with the way surgery was going in that
hospital. He did not approve of the methods and the high mortality

rate which resulted. Ergo, go in his locker, find curare, the poison." Referring specifically to the death of Nancy Savino, the defense attorney asked, "Why should Jascalevich pay this horrible price because Harris and others knew he was too well trained to allow a mortality by any other doctor and he would not stand for it?"

Flourishing his glasses, Brown told the jury that "the whole score here is the settling of a score" against Dr. Jascalevich, who was victimized again in 1975. Only this time, Brown said, the Riverdell doctors were joined by "the deputy medical examiner of the city of New York, where *The New York Times* is published," by prosecution experts for whom the defendant was "mere opportunity . . . to advance their concepts of what science can do" and by an "enterprising" reporter for *The Times* who "brought certain items to the prosecutor that apparently had never been in the hands of the prosecutor—depositions, other matters—and therein hangs the tale . . . Ladies and gentlemen, this case will prove once and for all whether the prosecutors, the newspapers, and politicians can use their freedom and risk the lives of people for the sake of their careers, whether medicine, politics, or legal. I trust you won't let that happen."

So that was it, I thought Monday night. Two conspiracies against Dr. Jascalevich, separated by a decade; and I was a prime mover in the second. Perhaps that explained Brown's remark in 1976 that "there's a bastard in this case." That seemed to be the role Brown had assigned to me. Other "bastards" included Woodcock and Moses and independent medical scientists in four states, all of us so ambitious and so morally corrupt and so dumb that we would aid some strangers at a New Jersey hospital to frame a surgeon we didn't know for the murder of five people none of us had ever met. But, from what I knew of Woodcock and Moses and Dr. Baden, there was nothing to suggest a conspiracy, nothing to suggest that they had done anything other than what they thought was necessary and proper.

As for myself, I knew what I had done and why I had done it—and I suspected that Ray Brown really knew, too. If I had conspired with anyone, it had been with my editors at *The Times*, and our objective had been nothing other than the telling of an important story as faithfully as we could. And once Woodcock stepped in, the story was destined to be told—if not first by *The Times*, then by the *Record* or some other publication. If one accepted the prosecution's thesis that the patients had been murdered, the importance of the story was obvious. But even if one rejected the notion of murder and embraced the defense theory of a frame-up in 1966 by frightened and incompetent doctors whose "methods" were responsible for the deaths, the story was still well worth the telling. Did it need saying that the Riverdell victims—and in either event, they were victims—were entitled to their lives?

Perhaps, as Brown said, there had been a conspiracy against Dr. Jascalevich in 1966; perhaps he could show that Dr. Harris and Dr. Lans, who hadn't known each other before Dr. Harris came to Riverdell that year, had combined to "get" the chief surgeon by running to a prosecutor over whom they had no control. But I had no evidence they had framed Dr. Jascalevich. All I had were a lot of questions and a belief that somebody had done something to somebody else. And hadn't told the truth.

Allan Lans was waiting in the corridor outside Judge Arnold's courtroom, waiting for Brown to finish his opening statement. It had been twelve years to the month since Nancy Savino had died and nearly as long since he and Riverdell's other directors had burst in on Calissi in this very courthouse. And for nearly all of that time, Dr. Lans was sure he knew what had happened to his patient. Now he was going to be the prosecution's first witness against Mario Jascalevich, and the waiting was nearly over. Inside the courtroom, Brown was reminding the jury that the state must prove guilt "beyond a reasonable doubt"; outside, as he paced the hallway, Dr. Lans was long past doubting. Once the courtroom doors opened, and two departing spectators brushed by the physician, marveling at the "brilliance" of Brown's presentation. Dr. Lans swallowed hard and kept walking, concentrating in his mind on Sybil Moses's list of "suggestions" for prosecution witnesses. Listen carefully. Speak loudly and clearly. Do not volunteer information not actually asked for. Avoid distracting mannerisms. Never argue with the defense attorney . . . "Any lawyer who can make a witness mad will probably cause the witness to exaggerate, appear unobjective and emotionally unstable. *Keep your cool.* You are sworn to tell the truth. Tell it. Every material truth should be readily admitted, even if it is not to the advantage of the prosecution. Do not stop to figure out whether your answer will help or hurt your side . . . All we want you to do is just to tell the truth as clearly as possible."

Allan Lans was as ready as he would ever be.

PART II
Two Trials

10

For days Moses questioned Dr. Lans. The board minutes and other papers piled higher and higher as the prosecutor first attempted to show that Dr. Jascalevich discouraged the appointment of other active general surgeons who would have the full operating privileges that he enjoyed. Dr. Lans said that when Robert Briski was given temporary surgical privileges in April 1965 by the Riverdell board, his application for a permanent staff position was referred to Dr. Jascalevich for review. When "nothing happened," the witness said, he himself spoke to the chief surgeon. Finally in July Briski was permitted to do at least two major, or A-type, operations, with Dr. Jascalevich as the assistant surgeon.

MOSES: What happened in July of 1965?

LANS: The first patient, a Mrs. Mary Allen, in the immediate postoperative course—

"Hearsay," Brown interrupted.

Moses withdrew the question and handed the witness a letter he had written to Dr. Jascalevich on July 21, 1965. "As a result of a meeting last evening," the letter said, "the board of directors have given Dr. Briski Class B surgical privileges. It is to be your responsibility and at your discretion to clearly define the scope of Dr. Briski's privileges."

As Dr. Lans read the letter to himself, Brown asked for a "sidebar" conference of the lawyers at the judge's bench, beyond earshot of the jurors. The defense attorney was miffed at the reference to Mrs. Allen, whose death wasn't part of the indictment. "Somebody ought to straighten out this witness, you better straighten him out," Brown whispered.

In open court Brown objected to admission of the letter and to the introduction of similar correspondence. Judge Arnold sent the jury out, and for hours the lawyers argued. It would prove to be typical of the days to come.

Brown began by accusing Moses and Dr. Lans of "insinuating" to Dr. Jascalevich the actions taken with respect to Dr. Briski when in fact, he said, the board determined Dr. Briski's surgical privileges in 1965 and Dr. Jascalevich had "no authority."

MOSES: Now, Judge, that's just not so. Judge, that's just not so.

ARNOLD: Now, please, Mrs. Moses, I'm talking to him. Stay out of it.

MOSES: No sir, I won't stay out of it.

ARNOLD: Yes, you will.

MOSES: I'll wait my turn.

ARNOLD: Will you sit down? Sit down. I'm listening to Mr. Brown.

MOSES: I certainly appreciate that.

* * *

ARNOLD: Are you saying that way back in [1965], Mr. Brown, they conspired to write these letters then? . . . Before anything happened, they were making a conspiracy?

BROWN: No question about it, that Dr. Lans and others wanted their eighty-bed profit-making hospital to do well, and they wanted more surgeons because Dr. Lans then got 25 percent.

* * *

In support of the view that Dr. Jascalevich was "helpless," Brown read the judge a memorandum sent to his client in June 1964 by John Kelly, then Riverdell's administrator. "In order to conform with the requirements of the American Osteopathic Association Committee on Hospitals, it is necessary that your medical status be changed from regular staff member to courtesy staff. This change does not affect your position in the hospital other than to deprive you of voting rights within the medical staff."

Moses countered by saying there was "no question" that Dr. Jascalevich "controlled the privileges" at Riverdell and "didn't want to give [Dr. Briski] his credentials." Brown, she said, had "slurred over" the last sentence of the Kelly memo in 1964. Dr. Jascalevich's change of status to courtesy staff "had nothing to do with his position as chairman of the department of surgery," but related to "medical staff matters which concern osteopathic procedures, et cetera."

Brown was incensed. "Anyway you go, she said I slurred. I guess it's either my bad speech or I was trying to deceive you, Judge. I often do that. I try to deceive judges. I would not be here if I did . . ."

Brown also advanced another reason for excluding the letters, relating to the claim in his opening statement that Dr. Jascalevich was unhappy with the quality of surgery at Riverdell in 1965 and 1966. In April 1965, Brown told Judge Arnold, Dr. Jascalevich submitted a written resignation as Riverdell's chief surgeon over "the issue of whether or not the hospital was going to follow the doctor's directions as to improving the staff." But the prosecution, Brown said, doesn't have Dr. Jascalevich's letter and if "they can't produce that letter, Judge, I say the whole series has to fall."

Moses replied that Dr. Jascalevich's resignation as chief surgeon in 1965 was "never consummated" and apparently withdrawn, "and the State would say that an equal inference to be drawn from the testimony that will be presented to the jury is that Jascalevich threatened to resign in order to force the board of directors to give Briski 'B' privileges and not to allow him to do major surgery." As soon as Dr. Briski was allowed to perform some major cases in July 1965, "he had problems," Moses stressed. " 'B' privileges again. Up and down. The man was up and down."

ARNOLD: What does it prove?

MOSES: It proves a great deal of relevance to motive, which we do not have to prove, but which counsel has injected into this case. He accused these doctors; I think he called it a scheme, conspiracy, guise, stealth, used words of this type; and the State has suggested, to the contrary, they were doing whatever the defendant wanted in regard to the new surgeons on staff, especially Briski . . . Briski has been accused of causing the mortalities, as well as others.

Judge Arnold admitted certain of the letters temporarily, and on March 8, 1978, Moses continued her questioning of Dr. Lans. The witness said that Dr. Briski's surgical privileges were under discussion throughout the late summer and early fall of 1965. In November of that year, they were the subject of a special board meeting, apparently requested by Dr. Briski himself. Dr. Jascalevich attended the meeting and, according to Dr. Lans, made "a full explanation."

Q: What did he say?

A: Dr. Jascalevich said that he felt that Dr. Briski was inexperienced and had not had enough time operating to continue with privileges more than he was willing to grant him at that time.

When the board decided to retain "B" privileges for Dr. Briski for at least a year, Dr. Lans said that he re-examined the application of Stanley Harris.

Q: After reviewing the application, what happened to it?

A: The application was then given to Dr. Jascalevich for his review and recommendation.

Q: Did he do anything, to your knowledge?

A: Not to my knowledge.

Dr. Lans said that in late December 1965, he asked Dr. Jascalevich "what the problem" was and why he had not "taken action" on Dr. Harris's application. The chief surgeon said he was "reviewing the credentials." But two months later, Dr. Lans said, the board went ahead and granted Dr. Harris full surgical privileges.

Q: Who did you use as a referring physician?

A: I used Dr. Jascalevich.

Q: Did you have occasion in 1966 to use Dr. Harris?

A: Yes, I did . . . in March 1966 . . . The first case I referred to Dr. Harris for surgery was Nancy Savino.

Stopping repeatedly to define medical terms, Dr. Lans gave a long and detailed account of the four-year-old's treatment and operation on March 19, 1966. Late that night, Dr. Lans recalled, he had visited Nancy in Room 211. "I saw a little girl waking up from anesthesia after having surgery. There was a nurse with her. She had an I.V. on . . . My opinion was that she was going to recover just fine from surgery and she was well."

Holding Nancy's chart, the witness continued in a soft but hoarse voice to go over the patient's treatment, hour by hour, on Sunday, March 20, 1966.

On Sunday night, Dr. Lans visited Nancy again. "She was more wakeful, her abdomen was soft, her color was good, her cry was alert, she was getting better . . . she was complaining about the Levine tube in her nose, which is quite uncomfortable. She still had the I.V. running in her leg . . . My opinion was that she was recovering nicely and was in excellent condition."

Q: On Monday, March 21, 1966, did you receive a telephone call at home?

A: Yes.

Q: Who was that phone call from?

A: The phone call was from Irene Nelson.

Q: Who was Irene Nelson?

A: She was the charge nurse on the floor that morning.

Q: What time did you receive the call?

A: It was approximately 8 o'clock in the morning.

Q: As a result of that phone call, Dr. Lans, what did you do?

A: I went to the hospital.

Q: What happened when you got to the hospital? Where did you go?

The questions were coming faster and faster now—and closer, too. Tears welled in the witness's eyes, and his voice cracked as he said, "I went to Nancy's room." A court attendant hurried to the stand with a glass of water, but Moses pressed on.

Q: What did you see?

Dr. Lans felt his hands trembling and tightened them around Nancy Savino's chart. "Nancy was dead."

Over Brown's objection that it was incomplete, the child's death certificate from the state was admitted into evidence.

Q: Is that the death certificate you signed for Nancy Savino?

A: Yes.

Q: What does it say?

A: Under cause of death it lists, "causes undetermined pending autopsy report."

Moses asked the witness whether he had subsequently seen the autopsy report attributing Nancy's death to an "undetermined physiologic reaction."

Dr. Lans answered, "Yes I did."

Q: Did you ever send in another death certificate?

A: No, I did not.

Q: Why not?

BROWN: I object—irrelevant and immaterial.

ARNOLD: I will allow it.

A: I never had a satisfactory cause of death.

Q: In March of 1966 did Dr. Jascalevich ever speak to you about the death of Nancy Savino?

A: No.

Q: Did you ever speak to him about the death of Nancy Savino?

A: No.

Q: Did you ever apologize to him for not sending him the surgery?

BROWN: I object.

The lawyers moved up to the bench, and Moses repeated her question for Judge Arnold: "Did you ever apologize to Dr. Jascalevich for not sending him the Savino surgery?" The prosecutor said the question was "extremely relevant" because, in his sworn deposition to Woodcock in 1976, "this defendant says—"

Brown cut her off, saying that the 1976 statements were not yet in evidence and that he intended to object to their admission on the grounds that Dr. Jascalevich had been deprived of his constitutional rights against self-incrimination.

Without addressing the latter issue, Judge Arnold said the time for Moses's question regarding the apology was on "rebuttal," after the defendant testified. When Moses persisted, Brown ridiculed her. "She is so enervating, and what she is saying is either through ignorance or zeal." A minute later the defense attorney warned her not to "shush" him. "You are not the judge in this courtroom," he scolded.

The apology question went unanswered.

At the end of the first week's testimony—with all the time spent on legal arguments, Dr. Lans had testified for only five hours in five days —a beaming Dr. Jascalevich rallied outside the courthouse with some thirty of his supporters and former patients, most of them Spanish-speaking women. The defendant, who had earlier tried to avoid news photographers as well as reporters, joined his cheering well-wishers in flashing "V" signs for the cameras. "He's very good-looking, much better than his picture," one of the women remarked as the surgeon accepted a bouquet of red and white flowers. "He saved my life," a patient said. "God is in the sky and Dr. Mario Jascalevich is on earth," marveled a North Bergen woman.

Dr. Lans's direct testimony lasted another day and a half.

The witness said that in April 1966 Dr. Jascalevich was upset about a proposal to change the hospital's fee and billing system. Since its inception, Riverdell had been handling the billing for its staff physicians and, as a means of reducing the hospital's mortgage and providing general support, had been charging the doctors 25 percent of the amount of the patients' bills as a "service fee." But in April 1966 the board decided to impose thirty-five-dollars-a-month dues on its staff members and to dispense with the billing service. The assessment would continue only for surgeons and anesthesiologists, who would not pay the dues; and the highest assessment in 1966, apparently based on income from the hospital during the previous year, was to be paid by Dr. Jascalevich. The figure was $9,600. Describing it as "crucial" to her case, Moses offered a letter of complaint by Dr. Jascalevich to John Kelly, Riverdell's administrator, on April 16, 1966. Brown objected, saying that "none of this suggests that he would kill people [over] the addition of other doctors," but Judge Arnold ruled in Moses's favor.

In the letter, the chief surgeon expressed his "displeasure and discouragement" at the proposed change. "I find its amount unrealistic and cosequently [sic] unfair to me. My income at Riverdell Hospital in 1966 should be significantly *lower* than in 1965 as the theoretical possibility of new arrivals to the G.P. staff will be surely outbalanced by the *increase in the number of surgeons available* for the daily schedule in the year ahead. Consequently, my work in 1965, *when I was the sole available surgeon in the house,* cannot be taken as a fair guideline for the establishment of a fair and equitable assesment [sic]" [Jascalevich's emphasis throughout]. The board, Dr. Jascalevich wrote, should be careful not to injure the hospital's "highly skilled professionals." In an apparent allusion to the fight several years earlier between Dr.

Elting and other Riverdell directors, Dr. Jascalevich noted that "Riverdell Hospital had in the few years of its existence moments of crisis, some of them in the public eye, and cannot afford now another institutional convulsion. Restlessness, insecurity, and unhappiness in the general staff will inevitably follow, as it was in the past experience, with only lost ground per balance."

On April 21, 1966—before the board dropped its proposal—Kelly and Dr. Frieman replied to Dr. Jascalevich's letter. "Your conjecture that your volume of work will be reduced this year, over last year, was considered and may or may not be so," they wrote. "The hospital experienced an exceptionally slow first quarter this year. This is a factor in making this change in policy. We anticipate that conditions will improve as a result of this change. Your reference to past problems within the medical staff is considered to be unnecessary and is not appreciated. The purpose of this policy change, as we clearly explained to you, is to improve the relationship between the medical staff and the board of directors. The board of directors does not intend to permit a situation similar to the one you refer to, to develop within Riverdell Hospital. Physicians who are not content with the policies will be requested to resign. We trust that you will accept this policy change in the spirit in which it is proposed. We believe that if you give it a sufficient time period and do what you can to promote harmony within the staff, you will find that you and the hospital will benefit."

Resuming his testimony about the deaths, Dr. Lans said that on April 22, 1966, he concurred in the decision by Robert Livingston to perform an exploratory laparotomy on Margaret Henderson. When Miss Henderson suddenly died the following morning—"I could find no reasonable explanation for why she died," Dr. Lans told the jury—the hospital's board asked a staff committee to investigate both her mortality and that of Nancy Savino. The committee, headed by Dr. Bernard Topfer, president of Riverdell's medical staff, recommended the following month that all new surgeons or other doctors at Riverdell serve a six-month probationary period before final approval by their department chairmen. The committee also recommended that for six months, Dr. Livingston be required to obtain the consultation of another surgeon with full privileges before doing major operations. Neither Nancy Savino nor Margaret Henderson was mentioned by name in the two-page report, which contained no analysis of the patients' deaths.

During the spring of 1966 Dr. Briski pushed for increased surgical privileges, and Dr. Jascalevich, asserting that Dr. Briski's record up to March of that year had been "excellent," advised the board to add several kinds of surgery to the list of operations his younger colleague could perform under the supervision of an A-rated surgeon. The board agreed, and in early August, Dr. Briski was also allowed to do gastrointestinal surgery, under supervision. On August 23, 1966, with the assistance of Dr. Jascalevich, he performed stomach surgery on Frank Biggs, who died at Riverdell five days later.

Dr. Lans testified that when he returned from vacation at the end of August 1966, he asked Dr. Jascalevich why Dr. Briski's patients were dying postoperatively. "He said that he was somewhat mystified. He was at a loss to explain it. He said that perhaps Dr. Briski was jinxed."

Two days after Biggs's death, Dr. Lans said, the board accepted a recommendation by Dr. Jascalevich that Dr. Briski be restricted to minor surgery. On September 12, 1966, the subject of Dr. Briski's privileges arose again, this time at a meeting of Riverdell's joint conference committee, which included the hospital's administrator, officers of the medical staff, and representatives of the board. "It was decided," according to the minutes of the meeting, "that the chairman of a service is within his province to upgrade or downgrade any member of his staff without asking for approval or criticism by either the board of directors or members of the medical staff."

Dr. Lans told the jury that in September 1966 he reviewed the hospital charts of Nancy Savino and Margaret Henderson, "looking for some common denominator." He also recalled meeting in late October 1966 with Stanley Harris and examining a number of patient charts.

"What was your opinion?" Moses asked.

A: My opinion was that, in fact, these patients had been tampered with and, in fact, they had been murdered.

Q: Did you form any other opinions?

A: Yes. My opinion was also that Dr. Jascalevich was responsible for these deaths.

Instantly, Brown was on his feet, calling for a mistrial. Judge Arnold denied the motion but cautioned both the witness and the prosecutor. "The jury will disregard that. We are not interested in opinions [on guilt or innocence]. Please, Mrs. Moses, none of your witnesses shall give opinions. The jury will decide."

Dr. Lans continued his chronology—the call from Dr. Jascalevich hours after Eileen Shaw died on October 23, 1966, saying that a lawyer and friend of the Shaw family named Mooney was threatening a malpractice suit against Dr. Harris and the hospital; the meetings between Dr. Harris and the board on October 25 and 27; the furtive opening of Dr. Jascalevich's locker number four on October 31 and the discovery of curare vials, first by Dr. Harris and then by board members; the photographing of the locker that night; the observation of Dr. Jascalevich in the Riverdell locker room the next morning; and the decision by the board that day—November 1, 1966—to go to Prosecutor Calissi.

Brown, seeing where the witness was headed, objected to any testimony about the board's confrontation of Dr. Jascalevich on November 2 at the home of Elliott Wiener. The defense attorney argued—as he had already done in connection with Dr. Jascalevich's 1976 deposition to Woodcock—that his client had not been informed of his constitutional rights against self-incrimination. The board, he said, was acting on November 2 as an "agent" of the prosecutor, who had arranged to have a detective hiding in Wiener's home, secretly taping the session. Moreover, both that tape and another tape recording of the meeting that was made by the board in full view of Dr. Jascalevich were missing—thus denying the defense the opportunity to effectively cross-examine Dr. Lans. The minutes of the session, which had been preserved, were insufficient and inaccurate, Brown said.

Judge Arnold ruled that since Dr. Jascalevich was not in custody on November 2, he had not been deprived of his rights.

Dr. Lans testified that Dr. Jascalevich seemed "shocked" and momentarily "at a loss for words" when he was told on November 2 that the prosecutor had been into his locker and found curare. The surgeon "sat up and his eyes opened widely." But Dr. Lans said that Dr. Jascalevich seemed unconcerned about the drug. " 'My instruments,' " the witness recalled the surgeon saying. " 'What about my instruments?' "

Brown, as he liked to do, opened his cross-examination by trying to throw the witness off balance. First he had Dr. Lans recall his statement to Calissi that Dr. Jascalevich was a "brilliant" surgeon. Then Brown brought out that Dr. Jascalevich performed many operations at Riverdell—perhaps thirty-six—from the time that curare was discovered in his locker until his resignation from the hospital three months later. And in some of those operations, he was assisted by none other than Dr. Lans, a man who thought the chief surgeon was a murderer.

From that point, Brown launched an unremitting, four-day attack on both Dr. Lans and Riverdell Hospital. Constantly reviving a remark by Dr. Lans that he was "intimate" with Riverdell's affairs, Brown sought to prove that in reality the witness either didn't know what was happening at the hospital or had misrepresented the facts to the jury. All the while, Moses and Brown continued to go at each other. Once when their bickering had subsided for a few hours, Judge Arnold complimented them, with the jury absent, for not giving him "a hard time this morning."

"If this keeps up," he joked in open court, "I may even be able to take a nap during this case."

Brown spent hours attempting to show that Dr. Jascalevich had not held up Dr. Briski's appointment or been responsible for any reduction in his privileges, but Dr. Lans wouldn't agree. The more he and Brown sparred over the subject, the more confusing it became. Even Brown seemed occasionally lost in the thicket. At one point Dr. Lans asserted that Dr. Briski "became half A and half B and part A and part B." "My God, Doctor," Brown moaned, "do you know what you are saying?"

Dr. Lans conceded that Dr. Jascalevich had acted quickly to grant Robert Livingston full surgical privileges in obstetrics and gynecology in March 1966, a month before Margaret Henderson died. But the witness was unyielding in his testimony that Dr. Jascalevich had been slow to act on Stanley Harris's application for privileges in general surgery. Brown dwelled on hospital records showing that the board first referred Dr. Harris's application to Dr. Jascalevich on January 18, 1966, and that Dr. Harris was given full surgical privileges by the board less than a month later, on February 15. "So that's expeditious, isn't it?" the defense attorney asked. But Dr. Lans stressed that the same records had the board acting without a "final decision" by Dr. Jascalevich.

Brown also pressed his assertion that Dr. Jascalevich was unhappy with the way Riverdell was run.

In October 1963 Dr. Lans had written to the chief surgeon, requesting that he comply with hospital policy by arranging for monthly meetings of the surgical department staff. Apparently the matter was unresolved because in November 1965 John Kelly reprimanded Dr. Jascalevich for his failure to convene such meetings. In a caustic memo, Kelly said that Dr. Leonard Shedler, then the president of Riverdell's medical staff, "has informed me that in spite of the fact that he has urged you to conduct regular meetings of your department, and has impressed upon you the importance of such meetings, you have not yet done so . . . I have been warned that if this practice continues, the accreditation of Riverdell Hospital is in jeopardy. I personally feel that it is unfair to many other people who go to great lengths to see that this hospital is accredited if as chairman of a major department, you fail to meet your obligations." Kelly ended by saying that if the meetings were not held, he would take the matter to the hospital's board.

Now Brown had Dr. Lans read Dr. Jascalevich's reply to Kelly; the reply was dated December 20, 1965.

"One, your memo of November 15, 1965, just arrived in my hands, being lost for almost a month in my mailbox amid reports and odd pieces. My answer to you, with apologies for being so late on it, is that my reasons for not starting the surgical meetings at the hospital are out of my discouragement at the lack of a vigorous action on the part of the institution to insure a consistent participation of our pathologists in these meetings . . . Repeated conversations with you along the last two years, I have presented my request in this direction without positive results up to the moment." Nonetheless, Dr. Jascalevich agreed to convene meetings between January and June 1966—"with my reservations about its continuance beyond June, if point one persists unresolved at that time."

Was it true, Brown asked Dr. Lans, that "you hadn't been providing the pathologists to discuss the tissues of the morbidity and the mortality?"

"That is not the purpose of the surgical meeting," Lans replied; it was the responsibility of the tissue committee. But the witness didn't know if the hospital's pathologist ever met with that committee. And a few minutes later Brown brought out that in January 1966 Riverdell's policy was changed to require only four meetings a year of "major" departments like surgery.

As another means of illustrating his client's discontent at Riverdell, Brown returned to the subject of Dr. Jascalevich's threatened resignation as chief surgeon in April 1965. Dr. Lans said he had never seen Dr. Jascalevich's letter of resignation and was unaware of the move until a half year later.

"Are you aware of the fact," Brown went on, "that that letter was a letter of resignation unless the hospital upgraded its facilities in terms of the pathology department, the nurses around the clock in the recovery room, and so forth? Did you ever come to know that?"

Moses objected: the letter could not be produced, so testimony regarding its contents was hearsay. Judge Arnold allowed Brown to continue.

Q: Did you ever come to know that Dr. Jascalevich was saying that unless the pathology is upgraded, unless the recovery room has nurses around the clock, unless it's open on weekends, that I think this is something dangerous, and I won't stay here? Were you aware of that?

A: No, I was not aware that that was in the letter.

Q: Well, you are aware of the fact, are you not, that your recovery room closed at 3 P.M. every day, aren't you?

A: Well, it didn't close at 3 P.M. It closed at the end of the day's surgery.

Q: Well, were there nurses on duty after 3 P.M.?

A: Only if there were operations and continuing scheduled surgery.

Brown used the recovery room issue as a wedge for cross-examining Dr. Lans about the treatment of Margaret Henderson and, to a lesser extent, Nancy Savino. The Savino child was operated upon on a Saturday night; Miss Henderson, late on a Friday afternoon. Neither patient was taken to the recovery room after surgery. Miss Henderson's chart showed that when she was admitted to Riverdell at 5:05 A.M. on April 22, 1966, she was put in a bed in the operating suite hallway, where she was examined. At some point following her "emergency" operation that afternoon, she was transferred to a room, but the chart had not been changed. It only said "hall." From the materials that Brown received before the trial, he must have known that Miss Henderson had been placed in a room where Dr. Jascalevich visited her about a half hour before she was found dead the following morning. But now the defense attorney saw an opportunity to corner Dr. Lans and to give the impression that either Miss Henderson had been kept in a hall bed throughout her treatment at Riverdell or that patient records at the hospital were inaccurate.

Brown found other reasons, as well, to fault the treatment of Miss Henderson. On the morning that Miss Henderson was admitted with severe abdominal pain, Dr. Livingston diagnosed her condition as "degenerative myomata"—tumors, or masses—of the wall of the uterus. The gynecologist then asked Dr. Jascalevich for a consultation, and the chief surgeon recommended further tests and observation before any operation. Later that day, however, Dr. Livingston asked Dr. Lans for a consultation. Dr. Lans detected a mass and advised a "D and C"—dilation and curettage or scraping of the uterus—and a possible laparotomy. With the assistance of Dr. Harris, Dr. Livingston operated on Miss Henderson, but no mass was found in the eighty-minute exploratory procedure.

Dr. Lans admitted now that he was "mistaken" about the mass. Still, he said, the operation was justified "to determine what was going on." But Brown, noting that when Dr. Lans examined her, the patient's temperature and respirations were normal and her blood count was "about normal," wanted to know why Dr. Lans had not called the chief surgeon, if only as a courtesy, and said, 'Doctor, I disagree with you. There is a mass here. We don't think your recommendation that there shouldn't be an operation at the time should stand.' Did you call him?"

"I did not call Dr. Jascalevich," Dr. Lans replied, "but I had been speaking to Dr. Livingston and to Dr. Harris, and Dr. Livingston said her condition had changed considerably since early in the day."

Brown also questioned the doctor about the wisdom of examining the patient under sedation, and the fact that the examination took place in a corridor in the operating room suite. Lans conceded that it "was not the most perfect setting."

The lawyer went on to contend that since Dr. Livingston had "found nothing wrong" with Miss Henderson during the operation, "whatever it was that was causing her to go downhill" still existed after the surgery and might have caused her death. But Dr. Lans refused to go that far, saying he didn't believe that Dr. Livingston thought "her life was in danger." Brown then brought up the autopsy report signed by Dr. Raphael Gilady, Bergen County's chief medical examiner in 1966, which concluded that Miss Henderson had died of "acute hepatic necrosis," a diseased liver. Dr. Lans said he disagreed then and now with the finding.

BROWN: What you mean is, is it not, that you disagreed because the pathologist who did the autopsy found a cause of death, and you didn't want to accept a cause of death because you and Harris had to save the hospital and blame it on somebody—is that right?

MOSES: I object.

Judge Arnold sustained the objection.

* * *

Brown also threw doubt on the hospital's intentions in having Dr. Topfer and his committee investigate the Henderson and Savino deaths. Did the Riverdell board really want to uncover what—and who—was responsible for the mortalities? Brown had Dr. Lans read to the jury a letter to Dr. Topfer, written a few days after Miss Henderson's death by Dr. Sklar, then chairman of the hospital's board.

BROWN: It says, "It will be fact-finding, but it won't cast any reflection on the hospital," is that right?

LANS: It will be fact-finding.

BROWN: But—go ahead. I'm sorry.

LANS (*reading*): "I'm convinced that in your hands this will be a purely fact-finding survey and that these unfortunate incidents will not cast a poor light on the level of practice in our hospital."

Q: How could it not cast conceivably a light on the level of practice at the hospital, if it were fact-finding? It ruled out the fact that it might cast a level of criticism at the hospital, is that right?

Dr. Lans said that despite Dr. Sklar's words, the board had not intended to "qualify" the investigation.

BROWN: The letter does.

Brown's interrogation regarding Nancy Savino was relatively short, and mild. The defense attorney rebuked Dr. Lans for failing to record his visits to Nancy on the day before her death and for, much later, giving her surgical tissue slides to his friend Matthew Lifflander, even at Calissi's behest. The slides were now missing and, according to Brown, would have gone a long way toward helping the defense establish "the true cause" of the child's death. But Dr. Lans wasn't nearly so bothered by Brown's questions about Nancy Savino as he was by a question from Judge Arnold.

For several hours on March 10, the fourth day he was on the stand, Dr. Lans had described in great detail the last days of Nancy Savino and his deep involvement in her case. And he had answered questions about her death on subsequent days. But on the afternoon of March 16, only a couple of hours after Brown had last raised the subject and perhaps an hour after Judge Arnold said he was looking forward to napping in court, the judge turned to Dr. Lans and asked: "Did you have anything to do with Nancy Savino?"

Astonished, Lans looked on as Brown reminded the judge that "he was her primary physician."

Nearing a finish, Brown trained himself on the "larcenous . . . raid" on Dr. Jascalevich's locker on October 31, 1966, and on other events leading up to Calissi's investigation the following month.

Hadn't Dr. Lans and his "fellow conspirator," Stanley Harris, made up their minds about Dr. Jascalevich's guilt a week before the locker was entered? Yes, said Dr. Lans. Hadn't Dr. Lans agreed with Dr. Harris to break into the locker, even though Dr. Harris got there first? Yes. After curare was found in the locker, wasn't Calissi brought in "just to make it look good?" No. Hadn't Dr. Lans and Dr. Harris, by going into the locker on October 31, prevented Dr. Jascalevich from discussing Dr. Harris's mortalities with the board that night—even if that meeting had been called by the board, as Dr. Lans maintained, rather than by the chief surgeon? "You weren't going to let that happen, were you? . . . It was Harris and Briski who had been killing people, wasn't it?" Brown asked, striding between his seat and the jury box. "And wasn't it 'perfectly legal,'" he demanded of the witness, "to have curare in a locker?"

"It's legal, but it's mighty unusual," Lans said.

Q: That's your opinion. Why does he have to explain it to you?

A: He has to explain it to me because there was an extraordinary number of surgical mortalities at the hospital, and the mortalities were consistent with a respiratory death caused by an overdose of curare, and he had that curare in his locker.

Brown asked Dr. Lans why he hadn't told Dr. Jascalevich that he had gone into his locker when he saw the chief surgeon in the locker room about 7:45 A.M. on November 1, 1966. "Why didn't you tell him man to man?"

A: Because I thought it was a matter for the prosecutor and because what was in that locker was the very thing that substantiated all my fears.

Q: Is that right? Right then and there you needed no further proof? You knew right then?

A: I wasn't going to say anything until I had seen the prosecutor.

Q: Because you knew all along that you and Harris had now found your pigeon.

MOSES: Objection.

ARNOLD: Sustain the objection.

Q: Well, you and Harris had decided the issue already as to who had been responsible for his excessive mortalities, and it was Jascalevich at the moment at 7:45 A.M. on November 1—is that right?

A: I know what my feeling was and what my decision was and what I had to do.

Q: And you knew that you and Harris had discussed it and you reached a conclusion, hadn't you, by 7:45 on that morning?

A: By 7:45 that morning I knew what had happened.

Q: You had reached a conclusion, is that correct?

A: I knew the truth.

Q: Oh, you knew at that moment the truth? Had you seen Dr. Jascalevich do anything to any one of those patients?

A: I hadn't seen that, but I had seen the truth of what was in that locker.

Q: And that was all you needed?

A: And what happened to those patients, and I knew I had to go to the prosecutor.

Q: And you knew that you had to defend your poorly run hospital because of what would have been destructive suits because of the high mortalities of your companion in crime, Harris?

MOSES: Objection.

ARNOLD: Sustained.

BROWN: The 18 percent [Dr. Lans's financial interest in Riverdell] was above any sense of justice you had.

ARNOLD: I didn't hear that.

BROWN: I said, "The 18 percent was above any sense of justice that you had."

MOSES: Objection.

Again Judge Arnold hadn't heard the question, and the court reporter read it back to him.

ARNOLD: I don't know what you're talking about.

BROWN: He makes 18 percent and he faces high mortalities and he has to find a sacrificial lamb.

ARNOLD: I'll allow it.

A: I have not spent my life in the pursuit of Dr. Jascalevich. I have spent my life in many ways, and when this jury came back and when the prosecutor reopened the file, I was here willing and able to tell my version of what had happened.

Later in the day—March 17, 1978—Brown challenged Dr. Lans's description of the chief surgeon as "aloof and distant."

Q: Did he bother anybody?

A: No.

Q: Was he a gentle person?

A: Yes.

Q: Kind to people?

A: Most people.

Q: Who was he unkind to, you?

A: No.

Q: Who was he unkind to?

Dr. Lans paused and considered the question. "Nancy Savino, Margaret Henderson," he said.

Q: That's been your life and your bias for a long time, Doctor. Other than those dear people, who else did you see him unkind to, including Savino, including Margaret Henderson? Did you see him unkind to those people?

A: No.

Q: Did you see him unkind to any living soul in that hospital?

A: No.

Q: But he was cold, and you wouldn't have a cup of coffee, but you had a buddy named Harris, right, whose mortality rate was what for that year?

Dr. Lans said he was uncertain of the mortality rate for 1966, and Brown went on to allege that in 1967 there were twenty deaths at Riverdell "and twelve of them were Harris's. Did you know that?" No, Dr. Lans said, he didn't believe that Dr. Harris had any "surgical mortalities"—deaths after operations—in 1967.

Q: Have you checked it out?

A: Yes, I have.

On March 20, as the trial entered its fourth week, Dr. Lans read out Riverdell's postsurgical mortality statistics for the years 1963 through 1966. Brown complained that the statistics reflected "assumptions" by Dr. Lans regarding a few of the deaths and didn't distinguish between deaths that resulted from surgery and those that merely occurred at the hospital after surgery. But these were the statistics the witness had prepared, and Judge Arnold admitted them into evidence. In 1963 the proportion of total deaths at Riverdell that were postsurgical was 2.4 percent; in 1964, 1.9 percent; in 1965, 7.4 percent; and in 1966, 20.0 percent. Of the fifteen postsurgical deaths in 1966, ten had been patients of Dr. Harris. Three others had been operated on by Dr. Briski.

At a "sidebar," Judge Arnold told the lawyers that he "wished to hell" they had not gotten into the figures because it was "doubling the length" of the trial without necessarily proving anything. But over Moses's objection, the judge granted Brown's request that Dr. Lans compute statistics for 1967. For that year, which took in eleven months after Dr. Jascalevich's resignation from Riverdell in February 1967, the proportion of postsurgical deaths—not, necessarily, patients of Dr. Harris—was 12.5 percent, Dr. Lans testified.

Why, Brown asked, had Dr. Lans permitted Dr. Jascalevich to operate on his patients when he suspected him of such "terrible deeds . . . Would you give your people on a table under a knife of a murderer?" Dr. Lans said the chief surgeon had operated on only two or three of his patients after November 1, 1966. Surgery had already been set for those patients, he added, and Calissi told him "to proceed as scheduled and not to change."

Dr. Lans couldn't confirm, offhand, that Dr. Jascalevich's net income at Riverdell had actually increased after other general surgeons were added to the staff. Brown said the figure in 1965 was $44,791; in 1966, $48,000. But the witness did allow that other staff physicians were upset about Riverdell's billing and assessment system well before Dr. Jascalevich complained in April 1966 and that the board ultimately agreed, in part, with the surgeon.

Brown closed by resurrecting the issue that in 1966 had so concerned Fred Galda.

Q: Do you know as a fact that your officials of the hospital at first said there was no curare in the hospital? You know that to be a fact, don't you?

A: I know that statement was made by some members of the board.

BROWN: I have no further questions.

Dr. Lans—the first of the witnesses for the prosecution—peeled himself off the stand.

11

In mid-March, when the trial was only several weeks old, the Bergen County Bar Association held a meeting at which its president, Michael Breslin, made some introductions. Breslin, a cousin of Woodcock's successor as county prosecutor, noticed a familiar jurist among the guests and announced: "We're proud to have Dr. Jascalevich's defense lawyer with us tonight: Judge Arnold." The judge smiled as laughter swept the room.

In court, however, the judge wasn't smiling. As the trial continued through March, with testimony from another Riverdell director, an anesthesiologist, and a nurse, the judge seemed irritable and fatigued. Occasionally his eyes closed and he appeared to be dozing. He was having difficulty remembering Moses's name, reading patients' charts, distinguishing medical from lay terms, and hearing questions and answers. At one point, for example, Brown was questioning the anesthesiologist about an "airway" tube that was used to facilitate Nancy Savino's breathing during her operation. The word "airway" had been used nine times before Judge Arnold interrupted to ask: ". . . weighed?" Brown spelled it out for him: "A-I-R-W-A-Y." At another stage, in front of the jury, Judge Arnold observed that he didn't "know anything about medicine." But it was said wistfully, innocently; not at all the way Brown would say such a thing.

Brown could be self-deprecating, but he knew a lot about medicine. He was surrounded by defense experts, and he was ready to challenge the most confident of doctors who were called by the prosecution. Just as his client's arena was the operating room, the pit of the court was his turf. He had been prowling courtrooms for nearly half of his sixty-two years. They were all familiar terrain, and no path was as secure to him as that which led from the defense table to the witness stand. He trod it over and over, in crepe-soled ankle boots, accusing, repeating, shouting and whispering, eliciting the answers that helped and mocking those that hurt, all the while hunting for the contradictions that could undermine the credibility of any witness. A grand jury could indict on "probable cause," but a jury could not convict if even one of its members had "reasonable doubt" of the defendant's guilt. Create doubt. Take the offensive. Put Riverdell Hospital in the dock.

"Dr. Jascalevich is on trial," Judge Arnold reminded Brown after Dr. Lans's testimony.

"So is the hospital," Brown shot back.

"Oh no it isn't," Moses chimed in unison with the judge.

But Brown went his way, accusing witnesses of casting "inferences" before the jury and of hiding behind Moses. When a witness asked Brown for a clarification, the defense attorney ridiculed him. "We'll change places, I'll come up there," he said. When a witness asked to see a document that Brown was questioning him about, Brown said he could request it until he "turns blue." Catching a witness in a discrepancy between his grand jury testimony in 1976 and his testimony on the stand, Brown snarled, "When are you lying? Under that oath or this today? That's the question." When Brown charged Moses with "testifying" through her objections, Judge Arnold remarked, "Both of you do a pretty good job." "I don't testify, Judge," Brown replied. "I take documents and shove them down their throats."

Brown was as tough on Moses as on her witnesses. He seldom referred to her by name or title. Moses was "she" or "that lady" or "the school teacher." Moses pirouetted before the jurors, winking at them, Brown complained. She was "always trying to get an edge," whereas he couldn't "get a word in." Give her "a little gavel," Brown suggested to the judge. We have "a more brilliant mind among us." Once during the first month of the trial, Brown stood behind Moses in court and wiggled his hips in an effeminate manner. "Judge," Brown would say, "would you ask the school teacher to object in the appropriate form, please." Just before Dr. Lans left the stand, Brown derided Moses in a voice heavy with sarcasm. "Is school in session?" he asked. Moses blew up. "Your Honor, I think the record will reflect that I am an attorney in the state of New Jersey. I certainly will refuse to be a circus performer."

In court, Brown lamented Moses's "claptrap"; in Judge Arnold's chambers, he despaired of the "utter, utter, utter rot" coming from the prosecutor. When Moses asked the judge to clamp down on "staged demonstrations" for the defendant and on out-of-court statements by witnesses, including Dr. Jascalevich, the judge said he was "reluctant to enter an order because some damn fool reporter will make an issue, and we will have another *New York Times* issue." Well, Moses said, the judge could always deal with that problem after regular court business.

BROWN: Judge, she's asking for trouble. The lady is asking for trouble.

MOSES: Who?

BROWN: This lady. You're a lady.

MOSES: Who are you talking about, the prosecutor?

BROWN: Yes.

MOSES: Talk about the prosecutor, and I think that's the way we have to handle this.

BROWN: If you don't want to be described as a lady, that's fine . . . I'm sorry if I offended."

Judge Arnold's failure to intercede during this exchange in his chambers was not unlike his behavior in court. When the barbs flew, often in front of the jury, the judge generally waved his hand and reproved the lawyers with a mild "all right" or "let's proceed." Sometimes he struck Brown's or Moses's remarks from the record, but other times he did nothing. When Brown warned a witness that the "wrong answers" could lead to his indictment, Moses asked the judge for an "instruction" to the jury. "The jury heard it," the judge said resignedly.

By the end of March 1978, "Steady Billy" Arnold wasn't so steady. The ruddy-cheeked judge was worrying aloud about the length of the trial and snapping at both lawyers: "I know what I'm doing. I don't know whether you two do sometimes. I've had just about enough of it." But the person he snapped at most often and most harshly was Moses. When Brown took to repeating the answers of a prosecution witness, Moses asked whether he was entitled to do it.

ARNOLD: If I say so. In this case I'm letting him.

MOSES: I see you're letting him, sir, and I ask that you not. I ask that you not, sir.

ARNOLD: You heard me, Mrs. Moses.

On the morning of March 28, Judge Arnold advised the jury to disregard the fighting between Brown and Moses. "During the heat of the trial," he said, "any attorney may, without being aware of it, make a remark concerning another attorney." But no sooner had the judge cautioned the jury than Moses was faulting Brown's cross-examination of the nurse on the stand; Brown was saying he could establish that the nurse was "an absolute liar in every respect." Moses was objecting anew, and Brown was nearly beside himself. "What the hell is this?" he raged. "Is this some kind of amateurish moot court from some horoscope?"

Judge Arnold, too, seemed to detect amateurism. At one point during the day, he explained a court rule to Moses, "in case you didn't know it, Mrs. Moses." At another he said he was "getting tired of laying out elementary law to either of you." And then, in a head-on clash with Moses over Brown's request that a witness "leave out the dramatics," the judge told Moses in front of the jury that she wasn't "doing a very good job."

"I'm sorry you feel this way about the Bergen County prosecutor and the person who is trying this case," Moses said. "It's obvious."

The strife continued the next day, March 29. When Brown included a comment in a question, Judge Arnold told him to "save it for summation." When Moses asked that the witness be given time to examine a patient's chart, the judge said, "I don't want to hear from you." And when Moses objected to a question by Brown because it "assumed facts not in evidence," the defense attorney slugged back.

BROWN: She constantly objects, not for the law. Why doesn't she testify?

MOSES: I am entitled to object.

ARNOLD: Just object.

BROWN: She is not supposed to—

But it was all too much for the judge. "Let's take lunch," he said.

MOSES: I want to make my objection without being interrupted. I want you to rule on my objection, sir.

ARNOLD: I'm going to dinner. I don't know about you two.

MOSES: I ask that you rule on that objection.

ARNOLD: I am not ruling on it. You interrupted when I told you not to, and he interrupted. You both interrupted. You're both wrong. We'll start over.

And Judge Arnold went to lunch. But it was really too late to start over, because the trial had already become what the *Miami Herald* called "a debating society gone berserk." Certainly the proceeding went berserk the following day, March 30.

The morning began with two hours of testimony. At 10:57 A.M. the witness and the jury were excused, and Brown moved to bar display of the items seized by Calissi from Dr. Jascalevich's locker in 1966. Perhaps Brown didn't realize that I had never seen these items, because now the defense attorney argued that the "chain" of possession had been broken when Woodcock allowed me to examine the old Riverdell file in 1975. Before the items could be shown to the jury, Brown said,

Moses had to prove that they had not been "tampered with" or "substituted," presumably by me. Moses wanted to introduce the locker's contents in the usual fashion—by calling the prosecutor's property clerk or detectives who would identify the items in court and attest to their whereabouts since 1966. Soon the lawyers were engaged in another melee. With both of them talking at once, Judge Arnold couldn't hear either. He stood up, instructed the court stenographer to stop taking notes, and said that he was going to lunch. Moses and Brown could argue all they wanted, he said. But he was leaving.

After lunch, Moses complained to Judge Arnold about his order to the court stenographer. The state, she said, wanted "everything that goes on in the courtroom . . . in the record," especially objections. But the judge disagreed. The quarreling between the attorneys was too confusing for him and for the stenographer, he said, and "we're not going to put [it] on the record . . . I have a right to recess at any time . . . If you make comments that are prejudicial to this trial, either one of you, you can be subject to contempt."

Moses said that Brown's argument "boiled down to one thing . . . that there's been tampering with the evidence. Well, Judge, he has the burden of proof in this matter. There's been no evidence whatsoever before this Court that there's been any tampering with it." She challenged Brown to call "his witness, Mr. Farber," to testify "that there's been tampering." The prosecutor began to refer Judge Arnold to several court rulings, but the judge cut her off. "Don't bother," he said, "I don't want to hear it. I don't want to hear your cases. If I want to hear them, I'll ask you." Moments later he urged Moses to finish her argument. Then he stopped her altogether.

ARNOLD: You may sit down. Now, Mr. Brown, I'll hear you.

MOSES: Do I get two chances?

ARNOLD: I don't think so.

MOSES: Why not?

ARNOLD: I can dispose of it after I hear from Mr. Brown.

MOSES: He already had a chance.

Brown went on for five times the length of Moses's argument, and charged that "there is a pervasive air of, what shall I say, chicanery, fraud, and, at the very least, negligence on the part of the authorities of this county" with regard to the items from Dr. Jascalevich's locker.

When the defense attorney finished, Moses rose to say that there were "a few things I have to address myself to."

ARNOLD: I don't want to hear you.

MOSES: I appreciate that.

ARNOLD: I'm not hearing you, so sit down.

MOSES: No, Judge.

ARNOLD: If it's related to this matter, I am not hearing you.

MOSES: He brought up certain items which were not true.

ARNOLD: I told you, you would each have your turn.

MOSES: He had two turns.

ARNOLD: Do you want to be held in contempt?

MOSES: If you feel that I am being contemptuous of this Court—

ARNOLD: You are. You are acting in that manner.

MOSES: I'm trying to do my duty as a prosecutor.

ARNOLD: You are not doing your duty.

MOSES: I am doing my duty.

ARNOLD: I do not want to hear you.

MOSES: I have relevant information for the Court. The Court does not want to hear relevant information?

ARNOLD: I don't want to hear it.

The judge was seething. He put a question to Brown, and after the defense attorney's answer, Moses offered to clarify that specific point.

ARNOLD: I'll hear you on this question . . . You will not be heard unless I give you permission to be heard, and I want you to understand that, and I'm not hearing you until I'm ready to hear you on this matter. I'm not going to let you and Mr. Brown talk at will, either one of you. When I've heard enough evidence on your argument on an issue, I'm not going to let you stand here all afternoon and take the jury's time, which is what you're doing.

MOSES: I haven't been taking the jury's time.

ARNOLD: I don't know if it's because you can't get witnesses or what. I'm telling you.

MOSES: Don't yell at me.

ARNOLD: I'm yelling at you.

MOSES: No, sir. I have had a witness out in the hall since 11 o'clock . . . and Your Honor is well aware of it.

ARNOLD: I'm not going to be—

MOSES: If Mr. Brown is going to accuse the prosecutor's office—

The spectators in Courtroom 407 shifted uneasily as Judge Arnold roared at Moses, "Just sit down."

MOSES: I think there are certain things that must be said.

ARNOLD: Will you please obey my order.

Moses appeared livid. "I cannot in good conscience."

ARNOLD: I'll have to advise you, Mrs. Moses, that you're being held in contempt as of right now, if you refuse to obey my order not to talk and sit down. I'm advising you that you're being held in contempt—

MOSES: I will obey your order if you will allow me time to respond to the charges of chicanery and fraud that Mr. Brown made against the office of the Bergen County prosecutor.

ARNOLD: When it's appropriate, I will let you do that.

MOSES: I think it's appropriate. I ask that you give me that time. Mr. Brown has spoken for forty-five minutes on this issue, and I have spoken for nine.

ARNOLD: Are you refusing to obey my order?

MOSES: Give me time to respond.

ARNOLD: I'm not giving you any conditions.

MOSES: If you feel that I have been contemptuous, then hold me in contempt.

ARNOLD: I'm holding you in contempt . . . We'll hear it after this trial is over.

Minutes later, when the judge called a recess to consider Brown's motion, Moses stalked angrily from the courtroom. She was headed downstairs to her boss's office.

David Bird, the *Times* reporter, compared Moses to an actress "who has memorized her role but hasn't quite worked herself into it fully." It was a characterization that wouldn't fit Moses's boss. At forty, prosecutor Roger Breslin was only two years older than Sybil Moses, but he had been practicing law for a decade before she was admitted to the bar. Being a Breslin in Bergen County meant being a lawyer—nine were practicing in 1978—and it also meant being a leader. Roger's uncle, John J. Breslin, had been county prosecutor some years back. His father, Roger, Sr., had been a Superior Court Judge in Hackensack until his recent retirement. And both Roger, Sr., and three of his brothers had been president of the Bergen County Bar Association. Breslins had been Democratic county chairmen, mayors, and municipal attorneys longer than could be remembered, and they were uniformly respected.

For weeks Roger Breslin had listened to Moses's tales of abuse and harassment. He had read the newspapers, and he had heard his cousin's joke about Judge Arnold at the bar association meeting earlier that month. The joke had discomforted Breslin, a serious, quiet-spoken model of rectitude. But now that one of his assistants had been cited for contempt—even though Judge Arnold later rejected Brown's motion on the locker items—Breslin felt it was time to reassess the situation in Courtroom 407. He talked things over with Moses, and thought some more, and then decided on a course of action for the next day. What he had in mind was something that perhaps only a Breslin, in Bergen County, dared do.

On Friday, March 31, Breslin accompanied Moses to court. With the jury out, Moses rose and formally requested Judge Arnold to step down as the judge in the Jascalevich trial because of his "inability to conduct . . . a fair and unbiased" trial. Moses also demanded an immediate hearing by another judge on her contempt citation. It was as if a bomb had exploded in the courthouse. Scores of courthouse employees and others dropped what they were doing and descended on Room 407, cramming the galleries and creating long lines outside the double doors. Moses made it clear that she was not asking for a mistrial, but only that Judge Arnold be replaced by another jurist who could familiarize himself with the trial to date by reviewing the transcript. Ticking off twenty-nine categories, Moses accused Judge Arnold of "inattentiveness," favoring the defense, tolerating "provocative" and "insulting" comments to her by Brown, refusing to rule on her objections, and a host of other "prejudicial" actions. She fleshed out her categories with extensive references to pages and lines in the transcript, and wound up by emphasizing the "cumulative" impact of the judge's conduct. Then Breslin took the floor.

"Your Honor," he said, "apart from all of the specific grounds which Mrs. Moses has referred to, and on which the State bases its application, the bottom line with respect to the State's position is this: over the course of the last five weeks, it's become more and more evident that Your Honor does not have the personality, the temperament, the intellectual intensity, and stamina which is necessary both to cope with the issues in this case and to control the attorneys in the case."

Judge Arnold was somber as the lean, boyish-looking prosecutor continued. "I don't envy you in regard to that last responsibility. Mr. Brown, I don't have to comment on his reputation. He is—and I say it affectionately as one lawyer to another—a 'buster,' and well he should be where he's representing a defendant in this kind of a case. On this side of the table, I will acknowledge that Mrs. Moses is no 'pussycat' either. So that it's a most difficult task. But what this case needs if it's going to proceed to a just verdict is a judge who's going to take hold of the case, and figuratively speaking take these attorneys by the scruff of the neck and make them adhere to the rules of court and procedure . . ."

Brown was on his feet, indignant. "I want to say, if there is any lack of intellectual knowledge in the courtroom, it may be in the pit, and it may be on the defense-counsel side. I can't sit here and listen to this. In the first place, by the grace of God, no one is going to take me by the scruff of the neck. His name, why the name of Breslin, and he bears a name that is revered to me, and I'm shocked to hear that any

Court in the state is supposed to take counsel by the scruff of the neck. I speak for myself. It's not going to happen to me from anybody. But the fact that the prosecutor is held in contempt and now is turning to the Court and defense counsel as the malefactors is incredible indeed. Now, there has never been a time where the Court has shown any lack of intellectual or any other capacity that I've been aware of, and I've been here every minute, and Mr. Breslin in pursuance of his duties has been here when he found it necessary, but certainly not as much as anybody else."

The accusations against Judge Arnold were "unfair," Brown went on. "The fact of the matter is that this is a highly touted and much publicized case, which has been the bedrock of much of the interest in this county, and the prosecutor's case is beginning to fall apart because the substance is not there, and now there's a tactic to take the position where defense counsel has to be taken by the scruff of the neck. Whether it would be Mrs. Moses—it's the first time that I would speak for her. I don't want anybody to take her by the scruff of the neck, either . . . I happen to hold Mr. Breslin, and particularly the Breslins before him, that made him what he is today, in the highest esteem. But to suggest to the Court because a case is not going well for the prosecutor means—and this is my opinion and no one else's—that . . . the judge must be removed so that the State can have whatever atmosphere it perceives, [is] contrary to everything that the state of the law stands for. If the prosecutor can pick the judge because it doesn't like the way the case is going," Brown rumbled, "it's all over, and that flag to your right is no longer standing for what it stands for."

The defense attorney paused as applause broke out in the spectators' section. "It is rotten to the core," he said.

Judge Arnold adjourned court for the weekend.

On Monday, the judge announced that he would continue to preside over the Jascalevich trial. "The Court favors no one, despite what may be the impression of imbalance," he said firmly. "I see nothing in the record to convince me that justice was not being done and that the defense and the State are not receiving a fair trial." Moses took issue with the judge's ruling, but to no avail. And Brown, noting that he had "stopped crying" when he was three years old, was no more successful with a new motion to dismiss the case. "This has been prosecutorial misconduct of the worst and most serious kind," he shouted, beating his fists together. "They didn't stop with bias, they didn't stop with bias, Judge. They said incompetence. If something isn't rotten in Denmark, it certainly is in Bergen County."

Late in the afternoon Judge Arnold called each of the seventeen jurors into his chambers individually. When the last of them departed, he was satisfied that none of the jurors knew of this latest battle in the drawn-out war over five old corpses from Riverdell Hospital.

On the day that Moses asked Judge Arnold to disqualify himself, Dr. Frederic Rieders, the defense's chief toxicology expert, wrote a letter to Ray Brown from his office at Toxicon Associates, Ltd., a consulting firm in the Philadelphia suburb of Willow Grove. The letter, accompanied by some photographs of thin-layer chromatograms, contained the results of experiments Dr. Rieders had undertaken for Brown between November 1977 and March 1978.

The prosecutor's office had provided Dr. Rieders with tissue samples from the five bodies, and he had performed his own TLC and mass spectrometric tests. By January 1978 he had concluded that there was no identifiable curare in the tissues of Arzt, Biggs, Rohrbeck, and Henderson. Nancy Savino was another matter. There he did find the drug—in "substantial amount" and "essentially clean"—in a sample of her liver.

When Brown received this preliminary report a month before the trial, he posed another question: had the curare in the Savino liver been there from the time of the child's death? Dr. Rieders decided to look for any interaction between curare and the kind of embalming fluids that had been used on the bodies of the five Riverdell patients. He gave his answer to Brown in the letter of March 31, 1978.

"The experiments," he wrote, "show that these embalming materials . . . destroyed *d*-tubocurarine within a couple of days of incubation. Thus they would even more certainly and extensively do so over the many years during which these embalmed bodies were buried . . . It is my scientifically reasonably certain opinion that any *d*-tubocurarine which may have been found and confirmed analytically in any of the specimens after exhumation was in fact *not* present in these specimens up until the time of exhumation but got into the specimens either during or after the exhumations."

Before calling any of her scientific or medical experts, Moses wanted to establish that the five deaths at Riverdell had been sudden and unexpected, that Dr. Jascalevich had curare, and that he was at the hospital around the time of the patients' respiratory failures. She also wanted to challenge the defendant's story about dog experiments in 1965 and 1966. The prosecutor was saving Stanley Harris as her final witness from Riverdell Hospital. So Dr. Lans was followed to the stand by twenty other witnesses from Riverdell, Seton Hall Medical School, and Pollak Hospital, as well as by detectives and county employees. Some of the Riverdell witnesses had been involved in the treatment of more than one of the five patients, but Moses tried, in the interest of coherence, to deal with one patient's death at a time. The witnesses from Riverdell relied mainly on the charts of the five patients, which Moses introduced into evidence, and on their memories of twelve years ago. Brown's cross-examination was extensive, and even before Dr. Harris took the stand, the tulips and the flowering plum trees were in bloom on the Hackensack Green.

NANCY SAVINO

To dispute Dr. Jascalevich's 1966 deposition, Moses called two Riverdell nurses who were in Nancy's room when Dr. Jascalevich was first summoned. They testified that the surgeon was wearing street clothes, not a scrub suit. Irene Nelson and Irene Kling—whose last name in 1966 was Price—also said that Dr. Jascalevich had been across the hall from Nancy Savino's room, 211. Mrs. Nelson, who was now the chief nurse at Riverdell, said she had personally called to the surgeon from the hallway and he had come out of Room 212 or 214. It had occurred to her that Dr. Jascalevich was in the vicinity because she had noticed him pass the open nurses' station and go down that corridor to see his patients at about 7 A.M. She had not seen him return, she said, and "when it seemed that we weren't getting anywhere" in reviving Nancy, "I got panicky and turned around because I knew that Dr. Jascalevich was someplace in the immediate area."

Further, the nurses questioned the timing of the emergency.

Mrs. Nelson herself had written the final entries on Nancy's chart, about two or three hours after the child was found dead. She wrote then that at 8 A.M. the "technician [was] unable to awaken child . . . Pronounced dead at 8:15 . . ."

But now, Mrs. Nelson put the time at about 7:30 A.M.—considerably earlier than the 8 A.M. she later recorded. And Mrs. Kling said it was about 7:45 when the emergency arose.

After Dr. Jascalevich pronounced Nancy dead, Mrs. Nelson testified, she and the surgeon left the room together, and she called Dr. Lans and Dr. Harris. She did not see Dr. Jascalevich near Room 211 again that morning. Mrs. Kling testified that she stayed behind with Dr. Ortega and "straightened up little Nancy"; then she left to take blood pressures in other rooms along the floor. She did not see Dr. Jascalevich make a second visit to the child.

Dr. Jorge Ortega, the intern, was not called as a witness. Father Joseph Doyle, who was also present that morning, testified that he could not remember the time of his visit to Nancy's room or what Dr. Jascalevich was wearing. Herman Fuhr, an operating room technician who had "babysat" with Nancy for twenty minutes after her surgery on March 19, 1966, and who brought her a teddy bear the following day, testified that he stopped in Room 211 to see the child as soon as he arrived for work on the morning of her death. The time, he said, was 6:40 A.M. Nancy was alive and alone. Fuhr stayed a few minutes, and on his way to the operating room, he noticed Irving Hall, the child's private duty nurse, giving a report at the nurses' station. Fuhr said he did not see Nancy again.

Fuhr testified that he first saw Dr. Jascalevich that morning when the surgeon began scrubbing in the operating room suite. The time, he said, was "two minutes after eight." Within a minute, Fuhr said, Dr. Jascalevich was called away from the scrub sink and left the operating room—wearing his green scrub suit, not street clothes. The surgeon was gone for twenty to twenty-five minutes, and when he returned, about 8:30, he began operating, Fuhr said. Moses did not ask the witness whether Dr. Jascalevich had been summoned twice from the operating room. Nor did Brown ask that question on cross-examination.

Brown dealt with the "street clothes" issue by suggesting that the nurses were, at best, confused. Fuhr's testimony that Dr. Jascalevich was in the operating room when he was called, wearing scrub clothes, had helped Brown. It would fit nicely with testimony from the technician Barbara Spadaro, whom Brown had listed as a defense witness.

Mrs. Nelson, the desk nurse at the time, insisted on cross-examination that Dr. Jascalevich was across from Nancy's room when she herself fetched him. But what about the chart? Brown asked. Hadn't Mrs. Nelson written "child sleeping" at 7:40 A.M. and that Miss Spadaro was "unable to awaken child" at 8 A.M.? Times were often inexact on charts at all hospitals, especially in those years, Mrs. Nelson said, "and you can imagine the fuss that was going on" at Riverdell that morning. All the times after 7 A.M. could be off—ahead or behind, she admitted —by as much as twenty minutes.

It was a curious turnabout. Here was Riverdell's chief nurse vouching for the accuracy of a chart's "content," but not for the very times she wrote. And here was Riverdell's chief critic, who frequently attacked the reliability of the hospital's records, laboring to confirm the chart.

Brown's effort to place Dr. Jascalevich in the vicinity of the operating room well before the Savino emergency continued with Arthur DeMarco, the anesthesiologist. Before the trial Dr. DeMarco had signed a statement for the prosecution saying that he normally arrived at Riverdell before the surgeons. He would prepare the patients for anesthesia while the surgeons engaged in their ten-minute scrub, which he was able to view from his station in the operating room. Dr. DeMarco said he would not begin anesthesia until he knew that the surgeon had entered the hospital, and he usually waited until the surgeon was visible in the O.R. area.

On the morning of Nancy Savino's death, Dr. DeMarco had assisted in Dr. Jascalevich's first operation, with anesthesia beginning at 8:05 A.M., according to that patient's chart, and surgery starting at 8:25. Now, on the stand, Dr. DeMarco said he had "no recollection either way" of seeing Dr. Jascalevich at the scrub sink that morning. Nine times in a row he said that it was sufficient for him to know that the surgeon was "in the building" for him to initiate anesthesia. "It's a very small hospital." But Brown struggled on, emphasizing the anesthesiologist's earlier statement of what he "usually" did. "No one is trying to trick you," Brown assured the witness. Eventually Dr. DeMarco agreed that if he had followed his "usual course," he would have seen Dr. Jascalevich scrubbing at 7:55 A.M. on March 21, 1966. "Thank you, Doctor," Brown said. "I appreciate that very much."

Brown's cross-examination of Father Doyle, who was Riverdell's "unofficial chaplain," was as brief as the priest's direct testimony. The defense attorney finished by asking Father Doyle to describe Dr. Jascalevich's attitude toward patients. "This is probably the only man alive who can be objective and let this jury know what kind of a man [Dr. Jascalevich] is, Your Honor, probably the only objective man alive," Brown said. Moses objected to the question, but Judge Arnold allowed it. And Father Doyle went on to depict the defendant as "kind, gentle, thorough, a gentleman at all times."

On redirect examination, Moses asked Father Doyle who would be his first choice as a surgeon now. "Dr. Harris," Father Doyle answered.

Brown rose with a question.

Q: Would you consider Dr. Jascalevich to operate on you?

A: If Dr. Harris weren't available.

MARGARET HENDERSON

By 1978 Robert Livingston was one of Bergen County's best-known physicians. In 1971 the gynecologist had forced a test of New Jersey's antiabortion law by publicly announcing that he had performed an abortion on a mother of eleven children. Dr. Livingston was indicted by a Bergen County grand jury, but the indictment was dismissed after the U. S. Supreme Court's ruling in 1973. In 1975 the

physician was back in the news. This time he was indicted for chal-
lenging a state law that prohibited anyone but a relative or a state-
approved agency from arranging an adoption. Dr. Livingston had arranged a number of adoptions between pregnant patients and couples
whom he was treating for infertility at his Englewood clinic. The gynecologist was still awaiting trial on the adoption charges when he was
called by the prosecution to testify about Margaret Henderson.

Ordinarily Dr. Livingston's indictment would have had no bearing
on the Jascalevich trial. But at a meeting to discuss his prospective testimony, the physician had told Moses that he would not be as coopera-
tive as possible with his time unless the prosecutor's office considered
reducing the charges in his indictment "or something like that." Moses
said she couldn't do anything for him, and reported the overture to
Judge Arnold and Brown.

Dr. Livingston's testimony echoed the old depositions as he went
through the events of April 22, 1966, when Miss Henderson was in
such "excruciating" abdominal pain that she "could not really
straighten up." But, now, the witness said that he ordered the barium
enema that Dr. Jascalevich had recommended, and after seeing the results, he had phoned the doctor around 3:45 P.M. "I told him that the
patient was having increased pain . . . was definitely getting worse, and
he then asked me what the X-ray findings were, and I told him the results . . . I asked him if he had any other suggestions as to what we
could do for this patient . . . and he had no other suggestions. I asked
what he thought about operating on the patient, and he said that he did
not feel there was anything else we could offer except to do a laparotomy and then to explore the patient to find out what the cause was."

Dr. Livingston had touched a nerve, and Dr. Jascalevich, seated
some ten feet away from the witness, was reacting. The defendant had
always said that he was unaware of the operation on Miss Henderson
until after it had occurred—in fact, he had been disappointed that no
one had shown the courtesy of calling him in advance. Now, as he listened to Dr. Livingston's testimony, the usually placid Dr. Jascalevich
was vigorously shaking his head, as if to dissent.

"7:30 [A.M.] bath [on April 23]. 8:00, 1000 cc of G & W [an intravenous infusion of glucose and water] started by Dr. Jascalevich. Com-
pazine, 10 milligrams intramuscular. Patient very apprehensive. Complaining of inability to swallow and pain in legs and chest. Dr.
Jascalevich visited. Dr. Del Valle [an intern] visited. Dr. Livingston
called. Patient apparently ceased to breathe at 8:45 A.M."

Those were the final nurse's notes on Miss Henderson's chart, and
they were written by Irene Nelson about an hour after the death. Al-

though Irene Nelson testified that she had "very little recollection of this case" and that the notes were based on what others told her, Irene Kling said she would never forget Miss Henderson because the patient said "a very peculiar thing" to her before she died. "I'll remember it as long as I live," the nurse said.

Mrs. Kling testified that shortly after she came on duty, around 7 A.M. on April 23, she stopped in Room 206 and saw Dr. Jascalevich visiting a patient of his, Helen Connolly, in the bed next to Margaret Henderson. Dr. Jascalevich soon finished with Mrs. Connolly and left, Mrs. Kling said, and after a few minutes, she herself moved on to care for patients in the next room. She did not see Dr. Jascalevich in Room 206 or in the corridor again that morning. At 7:30 A.M., the nurse said, she returned to Room 206 and, drawing the bed curtains around Miss Henderson, proceeded to bathe the patient, who appeared quite weak and upset.

Mrs. Kling said that Miss Henderson sat in a chair while being bathed, with her intravenous infusion still running. A little after 8 A.M., when she was put back to bed, she again told the nurse that she was very weak. "She felt weak all over, and she told me that she was going to meet her Maker."

BROWN: That she was going to meet her Maker?

KLING: Yes.

MOSES: What did you say to her when she said that?

A: I told her not to be ridiculous, that she was only a young girl, and I tried to calm her down.

Several minutes later, Mrs. Kling recalled, she reopened the curtains around Miss Henderson's bed and left the room to see other patients.

Q: What happened then?

A: I came back into the room about a half hour later, and Miss Henderson was dead.

The sequence of events was picked up through Dr. Livingston's testimony. The gynecologist said that around 7:30 or 8 that morning, he was awakened at home by a call from Dr. Jascalevich, who said Miss Henderson wasn't "doing very well" and "looks kind of dry, so I started an I.V. for you." The surgeon suggested that Dr. Livingston "better come to the hospital." By the time the gynecologist got there, Miss Henderson was covered with a sheet.

Dr. Jascalevich had not written any notes in Miss Henderson's chart that morning. But Dr. Livingston testified that he called the surgeon about 9 A.M. "to ask him what he found when he checked my patient."

MOSES: What did he say?

A: He said that she had some chest pains . . . And that she looked dry and, therefore, that was why he started an intravenous.

Dr. Livingston testified that a nurse's decision to remove the intravenous infusion on Miss Henderson at 5 A.M. that morning had been "consistent with" his orders, although "A.M. usually means around 7 A.M." in the hospital. Judging from the chart, and the amount of fluid Miss Henderson had received postoperatively, the gynecologist said he didn't see how the woman could have been dehydrated on the morning of her death. "My opinion," he testified, "is that she was not dehydrated."

The witness said he hadn't really agreed with Raphael Gilady's autopsy finding that Miss Henderson had died of "acute hepatic necrosis," or disintegration of the liver. "This patient," he testified, "did not have elevation of her liver-function tests; she did not have clinical jaundice; there was no coma or loss of consciousness for a period of time; she had no elevation of her white blood count; she had no fever." Moreover, the witness said, her liver felt normal during the laparotomy and looked "normal to me" at the autopsy.

Anticipating Brown's cross-examination, Moses had the gynecologist admit that he was under indictment on adoption charges.

Q: Did the office of the Bergen County prosecutor, myself or anyone else, promise you anything, inducement, favor, or anything, in return for your testimony in this case, *State* vs. *Jascalevich?*

"Absolutely nothing," said Dr. Livingston.

Brown opened his cross-examination of the gynecologist by roasting him for seeking a "deal" with Moses. Dr. Livingston denied that he would have altered the truth in the Jascalevich case "one bit" in exchange for a reduction in the charges against him, and Brown said, yes, he understood. But over the next three days, the defense attorney tried to show that the witness was indeed manipulating the truth.

Nothing in Margaret Henderson's chart substantiated Dr. Livingston's call to Dr. Jascalevich on the afternoon of April 22—the one in which the surgeon allegedly concurred in the laparotomy on the patient. And Brown brought out that when Dr. Livingston appeared before the grand jury in 1976, he said only that he was "fairly sure" that he had talked to Dr. Jascalevich between the time of the barium-enema test and the operation. What about it? Brown asked now. Wasn't it true that Dr. Jascalevich told him not to operate?

"That's a lie," the witness shot back. The surgeon "absolutely and positively" approved the laparotomy.

Well, said Brown, how about the fact that Miss Henderson was given Fluothane anesthesia, which is considered harmful to patients with pre-existing liver disease. "This patient did not have pre-existing liver disease under any circumstances," the gynecologist said. Still, Brown continued, didn't Dr. Livingston tell Dr. Jascalevich during Calissi's investigation in November 1966 that Miss Henderson's death had been caused by a liver disease brought on by Fluothane? Yes, said the witness, he had lied to Dr. Jascalevich then because he was startled by his call and "wanted to have as little conversation with him as possible, and since that was the official legal thing on the death certificate, that was what I gave to him." But wasn't it the witness himself who wrote on the death certificate, "acute hepatic necrosis, probably toxic." Dr. Livingston said he hadn't wanted to sign the certificate that way in 1966 and had only done so on the orders of Dr. Gilady. "He had the legal authority to tell me what to do . . . I didn't want to get into a big hassle with him." But, Brown noted, Dr. Livingston told the grand jury in 1976 that Dr. Gilady had been a "medical examiner at Bergen County for forty years, and I had been in practice for about six months, and if he said that she died of liver failure, that was good enough for me."

Q: Isn't that what you said?

A: The legal concept of it, not the medical concept . . . I accepted his authority to tell me what to put down.

Q: Please, Doctor. Is there any way—you'll be all right, Doctor. You are not indicted yet.

ARNOLD: The jury will disregard that.

MOSES: Counsel is very—

BROWN: You don't have a second indictment—

MOSES: Judge, counsel is very excited this morning and is doing things which are so unethical, Judge, that—

ARNOLD: I am going to excuse the jury. Now, ladies and gentlemen—

BROWN: Let me read this to you, Doctor.

ARNOLD: Now, stop. We are going to lunch. I am not going to listen to this from either of you.

No less than with Nancy Savino, Brown brought out inconsistencies in times on the Henderson chart. Irene Nelson said the times might be off by as much as a half hour. But even that factor couldn't resolve some conflicts. For example, Irene Kling adamantly denied that she was in Miss Henderson's room when the patient died.

But Brown laid before the witness a statement taken by Calissi's detectives in November 1966 from Alice Cook, one of three patients who had shared Room 206 with Miss Henderson. The statement said a nurse fitting Mrs. Kling's description—"tall, blonde, and good-looking" —had finished washing Miss Henderson and was "preparing for an I.V." when the patient died. Mrs. Cook, who was now dead herself, "felt that the I.V. had not been inserted prior to [Miss Henderson's] death. Just before Miss Henderson died, she gasped. There was no physician present when she passed away or prior to her death that morning."

All Mrs. Kling could say was that Mrs. Cook was wrong. And, in fact, she was wrong about "no physician" being present that morning. Dr. Jascalevich, in his deposition to Prosecutor Woodcock in March 1976, said that when he was making rounds on the morning of April 23, 1966, he was summoned by a nurse to Miss Henderson's bedside. Only then, he said, did he realize that the patient had been operated on on the previous evening. Miss Henderson was "very sick," unable to speak clearly, but complaining of "tingling sensations and spasms" in her chest and legs, Dr. Jascalevich had said. Her lungs appeared to be clear, he recalled, but her pulse was fast and she was "somewhat pale." Concerned that the patient might go into shock, Dr. Jascalevich said, he started an intravenous infusion "as a generally supportive measure on somebody that appears critical" and to keep a vein open for any "urgent medication" that Dr. Livingston might dictate to a nurse who was trying to reach him by phone.

Dr. Jascalevich also thought the microscopic analysis of Miss Henderson's tissues ruled out acute hepatic necrosis as a cause of death. "I cannot agree with it, sir," he told Woodcock, "because the examination of the liver—again I'm not a pathologist—but there is no description here of the severe changes that you would expect in an acute hepatic necrosis . . . it would show destruction of cells of the liver." Perhaps, Dr. Jascalevich suggested, Miss Henderson had had a viral disease all along, and it had been worsened by the "stress" of a "totally unnecessary" operation.

FRANK BIGGS

The testimony regarding Frank Biggs began with the operation on August 23, 1966, for relief of a peptic ulcer. Robert Briski, who was now practicing in Phoenix, was a nervous witness, breathing and speaking unevenly. "Relax, Doctor," Moses would say with little effect.

Dr. Briski testified that Dr. Jascalevich had assisted him in the operation and, at the outset, had suggested the use of a surgical stapling "gun" that Dr. Briski considered "clumsy." The operation went forward with the stomach clamps that Dr. Briski preferred, but around noon, two thirds through the surgery, the patient's blood pressure dropped sharply and Dr. DeMarco, the anesthesiologist, "piggybacked" two pints of blood into Biggs. Dr. Briski remembered Dr. Jascalevich placing his hand in Biggs's abdomen and saying there was a "bleeder," a ruptured vessel, present. "I got a little upset. I wanted to see where the bleeding was," Dr. Briski testified, adding that he removed Dr. Jascalevich's hand from the abdomen. With Dr. Jascalevich's help, the vessel was tied off and the operation continued. But shortly thereafter, Dr. Briski said, Dr. Jascalevich "abruptly" left the operating table without a comment. The surgery was finished, leaving Biggs in a "completely stable" condition. According to Dr. Briski, the patient's life was never in danger.

The bleeder incident also arose in the testimony of Hubert Stavrand, Biggs's personal physician, and Herman Fuhr, the operating room technician. Dr. Stavrand said that he was standing next to Dr. Jascalevich during the difficulty, holding retractors and sucking with an aspirator to clear the field of vision. He also testified that after the vessel was clamped off, "Dr. Jascalevich turned away from the table, very forcefully took off his gloves, threw them on the floor, and walked in a very hurried manner out of that room." Fuhr said that Dr. Briski and Dr. Jascalevich had both worked "feverishly" to stop Biggs's bleeding. At one stage, he recalled, Dr. Briski said to Dr. Jascalevich, "Stop, you're ruining the whole thing." Dr. Jascalevich didn't reply. About five minutes before the operation closed, Fuhr said, Dr. Jascalevich left the operating room, and when Fuhr came out, the surgeon "raised his hands" in a gesture but, again, said nothing.

Dr. Briski and Dr. Stavrand testified that despite some vomiting and nauseousness, the fifty-nine-year-old accountant was recovering very well from the gastrectomy over the next five days. Dr. Stavrand, who said that he saw Biggs every day after his operation, remembered that the patient was in "good spirits" on the morning of August 28. "He had been started on a diet early, liquids by mouth; and he was able to walk about his room, and he was able to walk into the bathroom wheeling his I.V. stand with him."

MOSES: . . . Did you subsequently return to Riverdell Hospital?

A: Yes ma'am . . . I received a phone call between 9 and 9:30 in the evening from Riverdell Hospital. I believe Dr. Ortega, the resident doctor, called me. The telephone call was very cryptic and brief.

Dr. Stavrand said that he rushed to the hospital, arriving within ten minutes. As he hurried down the corridor, he met Dr. Jascalevich, who, he said, was leaving.

Q: When you saw Dr. Jascalevich, did he say anything to you or did you say anything to him?

A: He looked at me and very quickly said, "Too bad about your patient."

Q: What happened?

A: Nothing. He just kept on going, and I kept on going in the other direction.

Biggs was lying nude on his bed, covered by sheets, when Dr. Stavrand entered the room about 9:30 P.M. Nurse Gertrude Bradley was there, as were patients who shared Room 210 with Biggs. Biggs had no vital signs, Dr. Stavrand recalled. "His face was a purplish blue. I pulled the sheets back and there was—his body was a blue color . . . in its entirety was blue."

Q: And was an I.V. running at that time?

A: There was an I.V. still hanging there.

By this time Dr. Briski had arrived at Riverdell and he, too, examined the body. "I couldn't believe what had happened," the surgeon recalled.

The final notes on Biggs's chart were written minutes after his death by Mrs. Bradley, who was the head nurse that Sunday night. Mrs. Bradley testified that while she was making rounds, she saw Dr. Jascalevich in Room 210, talking to a patient of his in the bed next to Biggs. "It was after visiting hours, so it was 8:30, 9 o'clock," she estimated. She didn't go into the room then, or see Biggs, and she had no exchange with Dr. Jascalevich before returning to the nurses' station some twenty feet away.

A little after 9 P.M., Mrs. Bradley went on, she was summoned to Room 210 by a nurse's aide or "someone" who said that Biggs "didn't look well." Mrs. Bradley found Biggs "cyanotic, having difficulty in breathing. He had been put in bed; he was lying flat in bed. And I picked up his phone and called the house doctor." The hospital operator then paged Dr. Jascalevich, who arrived within "a few minutes." But the effort to save the patient, later described by Mrs. Bradley on Biggs's chart, was unavailing; after twenty minutes he was pronounced dead. Dr. Jascalevich left the room "right after" that, Mrs. Bradley said, and Dr. Ortega called Dr. Stavrand from the phone near the body.

Mrs. Bradley, who assisted with medications for the dying patient, testified that when she answered the emergency in Room 210, Biggs had an intravenous infusion running and his face was "kind of bluish."

Like Dr. Stavrand and Dr. Briski, Mrs. Bradley said she had observed Biggs's abdomen that night and hadn't noticed any "distention."

MOSES: After [Biggs] was pronounced dead, before Dr. Jascalevich left, did he do anything else other than the resuscitative measures you just described?

A: No.

Q: Did he do anything in regard to catheterization of the bladder of the dead man?

"No," said Mrs. Bradley, as Brown jumped to his feet, objecting. The defense attorney knew where Moses was going, and he wanted to put a stop to it. In his deposition to Woodcock in March 1976, Dr. Jascalevich said that on his death bed, Biggs had a "gigantic bladder distention . . . like a four-month pregnancy." Once Biggs was dead, he said, he and Dr. Ortega passed a catheter into the body and removed "probably" 1,000 cc of urine, "and the man deflated and considerably so." Although Dr. Jascalevich did not record the catheterization on Biggs's chart, "the nurse was with us most surely," he told Woodcock. "So she was actually a witness."

Now Moses wanted Mrs. Bradley to describe the procedure at Riverdell for catheterizing a patient, but Judge Arnold agreed with Brown that it was irrelevant. The prosecutor resumed.

Q: Mrs. Bradley, before Dr. Jascalevich left the room, after the patient was pronounced dead, was there anything that he did?

A: No.

At Dr. Stavrand's request, an autopsy was performed the next day at a funeral home in Closter, New Jersey. The gross, or naked-eye, examination was done by Luther Markley, Dr. Gillson's assistant. There was "no anatomic lesion that points directly to a cause of death," Dr. Markley wrote. But the pathologist noted that the bladder was "greatly distended and contains up to 2,000 cc of clear urine." This appeared to be the basis for Dr. Markley's conclusion that Biggs had died of "ventricular fibrillation . . . due to vesicle (urinary bladder) reflex, due to distention"—the bloated bladder had caused the heart to beat too fast, resulting in death. Dr. Markley also noted that Biggs had a fatty liver.

On cross-examination, Brown sought to establish that Dr. Jascalevich had saved Biggs's life during the operation and that there was no real conflict that day between the defendant and Dr. Briski. Herman Fuhr had told the prosecutor in 1976 that Dr. Jascalevich located and tied off the bleeding vessel, and "thank God he finally got to it." Shown the statement now, the technician affirmed that Dr. Jascalevich's quick work had prevented Biggs from "bleeding to death." At least that was his impression from the foot of the operating table. Dr. Stavrand and Dr. Briski agreed, under Brown's questioning, that Dr. Jascalevich had been "helpful" during the operation and was acting properly as the supervisor of Dr. Briski's "first subtotal gastrectomy."

Brown moved on to Biggs's postoperative treatment. If Dr. Stavrand had visited Biggs every day at Riverdell, as he had testified, why was his name on the patient's chart only once between surgery on August 23 and death on August 28? Dr. Stavrand said the nurse would record only the visits she was aware of, and that he hadn't made notes because he hadn't done anything special for Biggs, who was then in the care of

Dr. Briski. If Biggs's blood pressure was taken every day, a supposedly standard procedure at Riverdell, why hadn't the results been recorded on Biggs's chart after August 25? Dr. Briski couldn't say, but he was sure that the test had been done daily. But how well was Biggs really doing? Brown asked. On August 24, he was draining "green-colored mucus, with red particles" through his Levine tube; on August 25, he was occasionally "apprehensive"; on August 26, he was, at one point, "confused, plucking at bedclothes, seeing things on the ceiling." Dr. Stavrand explained that the blood-stained mucus from the intestinal tract and the apprehensiveness were normal reactions to that type of surgery, especially for a man of Biggs's age, and the confusion and hallucinations were most likely related to the use of Phenergan, a sedative that can "disorient your normal sensibility." Also, said Dr. Briski, an intravenous infusion had stopped running on August 26, and Biggs apparently needed more fluids.

Brown saved most of his questions about Biggs's last hours for Mrs. Bradley, the nurse. Mrs. Bradley acknowledged that everything she saw Dr. Jascalevich do on the night of August 28 was "normal and according to practice"; that Dr. Jascalevich and the intern "did the best" they could to save Biggs's life; and that contrary to what a Riverdell director had told Calissi in 1966, Dr. Jascalevich was often at the hospital at night to see patients who were scheduled for surgery. She believed that the patient whom Dr. Jascalevich was visiting in the bed next to Biggs before 9 P.M. was due for surgery soon. Brown also tried to prove that apart from the four patients in Room 210, Dr. Jascalevich was not alone in that room before Biggs's respiratory failure. Evening care—back rubs, bed straightening, emptying of bedpans—was given after 8 P.M. and would last about ten minutes for each patient, Mrs. Bradley testified. So between 8 and 9 P.M., she conceded, a nurse or nurse's aide would have been in and out of Room 210 and certainly "in the area."

Hours of testimony were devoted to Biggs's urine and to the amount of fluids the patient was known to have taken in and discharged during his hospitalization. If Dr. Jascalevich had removed as much as 1,000 cc of urine from Biggs's bladder after death—something that Brown didn't mention in front of the jury—and Dr. Markley had found "up to 2,000 cc" at the autopsy—something that Brown mentioned often—then Biggs's bladder on the night of August 28 may have contained four to six times the 500 cc, or one pint, normally found in a moderately full bladder. But why? Dr. Stavrand said that Biggs's balance of fluids was normal until the morning of August 28, when Dr. Briski ordered bathroom privileges for the patient. Because he had never heard of anyone dying from a distended bladder, Dr. Stavrand said, he raised the issue in 1966 with Dr. Markley and with Dr. Gillson, who was not present at the autopsy but who did the microscopic work on Biggs's tissues. They "said there was no other explanation that they could find and put their signatures to," the witness recalled.

Dr. Stavrand rejected a suggestion by Brown that Biggs might have died of a liver disease associated with fluid retention in the lungs. He said that preoperative examinations by him and by Dr. Briski, as well as a chest X ray, showed Biggs's lungs to be clear. But Brown stressed that Biggs had a fatty liver and that at some stage—on a photocopy of the "authority for autopsy" sheet—Dr. Markley had written "massive pulmonary congestion and edema," excess fluid in the lungs. Dr. Stavrand couldn't account for Dr. Markley's note. "At the time that I reviewed [Biggs's] chart," he said, "this was not on the chart, nor did it appear in the official autopsy that I had benefit of, nor was it mentioned to me by Dr. Gillson or Dr. Markley." The witness said he was relying on the anatomic and microscopic analyses in the autopsy report. And there, he emphasized, Biggs's lungs were described as normal, with the exception of what, in his opinion, were postmortem changes. The liver, too, was normal except for the fat, which Dr. Stavrand attributed to the "high fat intake" of Biggs's ulcer therapy diet. A fatty liver, the physician contended, would not have precipitated Biggs's respiratory collapse.

With Dr. Briski on the stand, Brown returned to Dr. Markley's finding of ventricular fibrillation. Wasn't it true that several months after Biggs's death, Dr. Briski adopted Dr. Markley's conclusion by inscribing it on Biggs's chart? Yes, the surgeon said, but he only did so because the hospital's medical records department instructed him to complete the chart at that time and to insert the pathologist's cause of death. He himself regarded Dr. Markley's finding as theoretical. Well, said Brown, hadn't he told a Bergen County detective on March 31, 1976, that Biggs's death was "sudden, unexplained except that he could have experienced . . . acute cardiac arythmia"? Yes, he had said that, Dr. Briski replied. And wasn't acute cardiac arythmia akin to ventricular fibrillation? Yes. And hadn't he told the detective in 1976 that it was not until he had read a *Newsweek* article the previous week that he had any knowledge to indicate that Biggs's death or the deaths of other patients at Riverdell were not attributable to reasonable medical causes? Yes.

Q: All right. Now, Doctor, have you also read *The New York Times,* and has that affected your thinking on the subject?

A: I never read it.

Q: You never read *The Times?*

A: I have read *The New York Times* newspaper, but you should clarify the statement.

Q: Have you read anything in *The New York Times* newspaper about these—about Dr. Jascalevich and any charges?

A: No, sir, never.

Q: You didn't get it out in Traverse City—but *Newsweek*—I have no further questions, Doctor.

EMMA ARZT

Theresa Cassell, a head day nurse, testified that Emma Arzt looked "good" and her vital signs were stable on the early morning of September 23, 1966, a day after Dr. Harris removed the woman's gallbladder. At 10:10 A.M., however, two other patients from Room 201 came down the hall and reported that something had happened to Mrs. Arzt. Mrs. Cassell hurried to the room and found that the seventy-year-old former librarian had stopped breathing and was cyanotic. Her intravenous infusion was functioning. The nurse said she ran outside and "grabbed" Dr. Jascalevich, who was by Room 204. She also called for more help. Dr. Harris, who was in the hospital, responded. Another doctor, Frank Grosso, arrived too. According to the nurse's notes, Dr. Jascalevich gave artificial respiration and heart massage to Mrs. Arzt; Dr. Harris inserted an endotracheal tube into the patient's windpipe to secure an air passage, and Dr. Grosso hooked up a mechanical respirator. Dr. Jascalevich, having done all he could to help, left the room when Dr. Harris "took over his case," Mrs. Cassell said. Mrs. Arzt was alive.

Dr. Grosso remembered the circumstances somewhat differently. He testified that he was passing Room 201 between 10 A.M. and noon when he saw Dr. Jascalevich trying to resuscitate the "blue and motionless" patient by lightly drumming on her chest with the tips of his fingers, "which I thought was quite unusual." Demonstrating on the rail of the witness stand, Dr. Grosso said the "appropriate" method of cardiac resuscitation involved pressing on the chest with the heel of one hand, with the other hand on top for added force. "You compress the heart to push blood into the circulatory system. By using the tips of your fingers, it's impossible to do this." Dr. Grosso said he watched Dr. Jascalevich's effort for two minutes, and then "I told him, 'Let me do it.'"

Q: Did he respond?

A: He just walked away and left the room. I called for help, and a nurse and Dr. DeMarco came. Dr. Jascalevich never came back.

Dr. DeMarco testified that it was about 11:15 A.M. when he was summoned from the operating room. There was "confusion" at Mrs. Arzt's bedside, he recalled, with a number of doctors—whom he did not name—laboring over the patient. Mrs. Arzt's personal physician, Bernard Topfer, testified that he first learned of Mrs. Arzt's difficulties shortly before 11 A.M. After seeing the patient, he called in an internist, Herbert Pardell, who concluded that Mrs. Arzt had had "acute left ventricular failure following cardiac arrest, probably due to acute myocardial infarction." Dr. Topfer testified that a preoperative electrocardiogram had shown Mrs. Arzt's heart to be normal. A second electrocardiogram, taken several hours after her difficulties were noticed, showed the heart to be healthy but beating too rapidly, he said.

At 1:15 P.M. Mrs. Arzt was given medication for her heart, prescribed by Dr. Pardell and Dr. Topfer. At 1:30 P.M., according to Dr. DeMarco, Mrs. Arzt was "bucking and reacting" to the tube in her windpipe, and he removed it. The patient, described by the anesthesiologist as "alert but apprehensive," was breathing on her own. At 2 P.M., however, Mrs. Arzt was perspiring heavily. Once again her breathing stopped. Dr. Pardell attached a respirator, but ten minutes later, the patient was pronounced dead by Dr. Topfer.

On cross-examination, Brown was all over Dr. Grosso. First the defense attorney pointed out that nowhere on Mrs. Arzt's chart did it say that Dr. Grosso had massaged the patient's heart; the chart said only that he had hooked up a respirator. Then Brown attacked Dr. Grosso for "jumping on the patient full force," particularly if she had aspirated and vomited, as the chart indicated. Brown also brought out that in 1976 Dr. Grosso had described Mrs. Arzt to the grand jury as "slightly obese" and between the ages of fifty and sixty. "Check her weight, Doc, check her weight," Brown demanded, handing Dr. Grosso the patient's chart. The witness conceded her weight to have been 107 but said that "when a patient is in distress, she may have . . . a full face and I may feel that she was slightly obese." The physician acknowledged now that Mrs. Arzt was seventy, not younger—"I'm not very good at ages," he said. Dr. Grosso didn't recall seeing Dr. Harris in Mrs. Arzt's room on the day of her death and couldn't remember why he himself was in the vicinity of Room 201 that morning. He hadn't answered an emergency call from Mrs. Cassell, the nurse.

Q: Did you have patients down at the end of that hall?

A: I may have had patients.

Q: No. I'm asking you if you had any patients there.

A: I may have.

Q: Well, now, please—

A: It's twelve years ago. It's quite difficult to recall.

Q: But you remember details like the little fingers. You remember that. How about your own patients?

A: I can't forget that.

Q: Of course you can't, but you forgot your own patients.

The more Brown pursued the subject of the heart massage—once suggesting that Dr. Jascalevich might have been tapping Mrs. Arzt's chest for a spot in which to inject a heart stimulant—the more the witness grew restive.

"You want me to repeat it?" Dr. Grosso asked the defense attorney. "You want me to repeat it again?"

Cross-examining Dr. DeMarco, Brown tried to show that the removal of the endotracheal tube from Mrs. Arzt's windpipe at 1:30 P.M. might have prompted a fatal heart arrest. Wasn't it a fact that insertion or removal of such tubes was a "critical" procedure that "frequently" led to cardiac arrests? Yes, the anesthesiologist concurred, it was a "critical time," but "if it frequently led to cardiac arrest, there would be a lot more cardiac arrests reported." Moreover, the witness said, if Mrs. Arzt had suffered a heart arrest due to his removal of the tube, "it would have been immediate, not a half hour later." Despite the notes on the chart, Dr. DeMarco seemed unconvinced that Mrs. Arzt had had a cardiac arrest at any time on the day of her death. Her original problem that morning, he said, was a "respiratory arrest," and her heart—which normally would give out within a "matter of minutes" after a respiratory arrest—might still have been beating when it was first massaged and she was attached to a respirator. Brown was chagrined. "What are we fighting the chart for?" the attorney asked.

Brown also sought to demonstrate that Mrs. Arzt couldn't have died of curare poisoning because the effect of the drug—even if it had been injected in her body around 10 A.M. on September 23—would have worn off long before her demise four hours later. Dr. DeMarco testified that curare takes effect in two or three minutes and that without artificial respiration, a recipient would die within another three to five minutes. With assisted breathing, a man of average weight who received a 10-cc dose of curare—"that's a lot," he said—would have muscle flaccidity or paralysis for up to an hour and perhaps longer, with the "peak action" during the first twenty-five minutes. The fact that Mrs. Arzt was "bucking" on the tube in her windpipe at 1:30 P.M., Dr. DeMarco said, would indicate that the effect of any curare had dissipated by then. And was there anything in Mrs. Arzt's chart, Brown asked, showing that Dr. Jascalevich had been "anywhere around that lady" between 1:30 and her demise at 2 P.M.? No, said

Dr. DeMarco. Was there anything showing that the defendant had "anything to do" with Mrs. Arzt after the note at 10:10 A.M.? Again the answer was no.

In questioning Dr. Topfer, Brown suggested that Mrs. Arzt's medical history—her hypertension, her "hardening of the arteries"—provided significant "signs" of heart disease well before her gallbladder operation. But the witness disagreed. Mrs. Arzt, Dr. Topfer said, was "mildly" hypertensive and "she had normal sclerosing [of the arteries] that would occur in a patient this age . . . You can live with sclerosing for an indefinite time and have no effect on your outcome." Trying another approach Brown asked Dr. Topfer whether he still believed, when Moses talked to him in early 1976, that Mrs. Arzt had died of "acute circulatory failure," the cause he had written on her death certificate.

A: That's correct.

Q: O.K. And still do, don't you, really?

A: That's correct.

Q: O.K. Well, I don't know why I should ask any more questions.

CARL ROHRBECK

Annette O'Brien, a nurse who came on duty at 7 A.M. on December 13, 1965, testified that she saw Rohrbeck about 7:20, while she was making her first rounds. She had returned to the nurses' station, adjacent to Rohrbeck's room, and was arranging her medications when Dr. Jascalevich stopped by and said he wanted to see the patient. Together they went into Room 207, and with Mrs. O'Brien at the foot of the bed and Dr. Jascalevich at the head, the surgeon engaged Rohrbeck in conversation and "motioned around the patient's neck," loosening his nightshirt. Dr. Jascalevich remarked that Rohrbeck's neck veins looked somewhat distended, the witness recalled. "He came down to the end of the bed . . . and said to me that he didn't like the way Mr. Rohrbeck looked, and he felt that we should postpone the surgery until he had been further evaluated, and he asked me to get him an I.V." The nurse said she left the room for fifteen to twenty seconds.

Q: Did he do anything other than look at his neck?

A: Not in my presence, no.

Mrs. O'Brien said she wheeled the intravenous equipment cart into Rohrbeck's room and prepared the intravenous infusion, attaching the tubing, at one end, to a 22-gauge needle and, at the other, to a bottle of dextrose in water. Mrs. O'Brien gave the intravenous apparatus to

Dr. Jascalevich, along with an alcohol wipe sponge, an arm board, a tourniquet, and tape. She then went back to the nurses' station and wrote on Rohrbeck's chart: "7:30, Dr. Jascalevich visiting. 7:40, Mrs. McKeon notified of postponement in surgery until further medical evaluation can be obtained. 7:45, I.V. of 5% dextrose and water, 1000 cc, started by Dr. Jascalevich in right arm."

Mrs. O'Brien said she continued with her morning duties and noticed Dr. Jascalevich "leave the floor within a few minutes." But a minute or two later, she testified, the surgeon was back, "walking briskly" in the direction of Rohrbeck's room. In another minute or two, he appeared by the nurses' station. "He said to me, all he said to me was, 'Mrs. O'Brien,' and I said, 'Yes.' He said, 'Your patient is dead.'"

Mrs. O'Brien said that Dr. Jascalevich then walked away, and she rushed into Rohrbeck's room and "the first thing that I did was run to the side of the bed, to the right side of the patient, and I spun around the I.V. bottle."

Q: Was the I.V. running?

A: Yes. It was.

Q: What happened then?

A: I was concerned that there may have been a mistake . . . I spun around the I.V. bottle to check that the label was correct.

Q: Was it correct?

A: Yes, ma'am, it was.

Dr. Sklar, who had been Rohrbeck's personal physician for three years, had discussed the patient's case at some length with Calissi in 1966. And his direct testimony now—including his recollection of Dr. Jascalevich's having "a premonition about doing Mr. Rohrbeck"— covered much of the same ground.

Over Brown's objection, the witness said he had accepted Lawrence Denson's autopsy report at the time of Rohrbeck's death and "felt that Dr. Jascalevich had greater insight than I did into the situation and that I was wrong and he was right." Dr. Sklar said he had continued to send patients to Dr. Jascalevich. He hadn't referred any patients to Dr. Harris until 1967, after the chief surgeon's resignation. And he never sent a patient to Dr. Briski.

Dr. Denson told the jury there was no question that Rohrbeck had heart disease—"he had significant arteriosclerosis. He had had, apparently, heart attacks, so-called myocardial infarctions with fibrosis, in the past, and it was significant." But the medical examiner said he did not form an opinion immediately as to the cause of Rohrbeck's death —"the nature of the death occurring preoperatively did make me wonder a bit on a person who presumably had no complaints." To satisfy himself, Dr. Denson recalled, he asked a toxicology lab to examine Rohrbeck's liver and kidney for any evidence of drugs, particularly opiates and belladonna alkaloids. "I questioned whether or not there might be some type of overdose of preanesthetic medication," and "I signed the case 'pending.'"

* * *

MOSES: Did you request, on December 13, 1965, a toxicological examination for the drug, *d*-tubocurarine?

A: No.

Q: Do you know, in your experience as a medical examiner and as a physician in the state of New Jersey, whether *d*-tubocurarine can be found without a specific request?

A: I would doubt it, is the best answer.

Moses did not mention, during Dr. Denson's testimony, Dr. Jascalevich's note saying he had canceled the surgery "on the basis of minimal clinical signs of heart failure that I would like to have further evaluated before proceeding with the operation." While the note on the chart lacked both a time and a date—Judge Arnold observed that "we don't know when it was written; it may have been written two days later"—it gave a medical reason for cancellation of Rohrbeck's surgery, and that reason was consistent with Dr. Denson's ultimate finding. So the note was a problem for Moses, and she dealt with it indirectly, trying to turn it to her advantage. She described the symptoms which presumably led Dr. Jascalevich to suspect heart trouble, and she asked Dr. Denson a hypothetical question, based on testimony about Rohrbeck.

Q: Would you, Dr. Denson, start an intravenous solution of 5 percent dextrose and water as the first response to the signs I've just described?

A: No . . . I would not feel it was indicated. A mild congestive failure would seem to me at least no reason to put fluid into a system.

Rising to cross-examine Dr. Denson, Ray Brown reached among the medical textbooks that were piled high on the defense table. The book he selected was written by several former medical examiners of New York City and by Charles Umberger, the toxicologist.

Brown read: ". . . In approximately 75 percent of sudden deaths from coronary artery disease, the lesion is a gradually progressive coronary arteriosclerosis without thrombosis but with marked lumenal narrowing or complete occlusion of segments of one or both coronary arteries."

Q: Is that correct?

A: I agree with that.

Dr. Denson conceded that it was "quite common to find nothing in the myocardium [at autopsy] and the only finding to be in the coronary artery system . . . You will not see acutely dead heart muscle, no," the medical examiner said. "You will not see it. I think that's what you mean, sir."

* * *

Moving along, Brown read to the witness Dr. Jascalevich's note regarding cancellation of Rohrbeck's surgery. The defense attorney also pointed out that by 7:45 A.M. on December 13, 1965, Rohrbeck had been "without food or drink for twelve hours or more."

Q: Is it totally inconsistent that the type of I.V. [started by Dr. Jascalevich] would be used to sustain the individual before all these other tests that you were talking about would be entered into?

A: No, it is not inconsistent.

With Dr. DeMarco, Brown suggested another theory regarding the I.V.—actually a theory of Dr. DeMarco's. The anesthesiologist, apparently in an interview with Moses, had speculated that the intravenous infusion was set up to counter any grogginess or faintness from the Demerol that Rohrbeck had received forty-five minutes earlier. Now Brown asked Dr. DeMarco about that. Couldn't Rohrbeck have been affected that way by the Demerol? Yes, it was possible. And wouldn't it be "realistic and practical" to start the intravenous infusion to offset the Demerol? Wasn't that so? "Yes," said Dr. DeMarco. "I stated that."

Dr. Sklar had told the jury, as he had told Calissi, that he visited Rohrbeck twice on the morning of December 13, 1965, while the patient was still alive. The visits were between 7:15 and 7:55 A.M., when Dr. Sklar returned for a third time and pronounced Rohrbeck dead. But on cross-examination, Brown brought out that neither of Dr. Sklar's first two visits was charted in the nurse's notes, even though Dr. Sklar said that, on one of the visits, he was accompanied by a nurse.

Relying on the chart, Brown tried to counter Dr. Sklar's "inference" that Dr. Jascalevich was unconcerned about Rohrbeck's death and "just stood there when the nurse called" the operating room. Wasn't it true, according to Mrs. O'Brien's notes, that Dr. Jascalevich visited the patient at 7:50 and "found him deceased?"

A: Yes, sir.

Q: So that Dr. Jascalevich was there and found him dead before you got there [at 7:55], isn't that right?

A: Yes, sir.

Q: So he did, on the occasion of [Rohrbeck's] death, attend the patient? He found him dead?

A: Yes, sir; but he didn't tell that to me.

Q: I didn't ask you that, did I?

Brown also questioned the accuracy of Mrs. O'Brien's memory. The nurse, who remembered Rohrbeck as "calm, composed, no worry" shortly before his death, couldn't describe, on cross-examination, the other patients who were in Rohrbeck's room on December 13. Nor could she recall the names of the other nurses on duty that morning. Mrs. O'Brien said that she was at the nurses' station or in Room 207 for at least a half hour after 7:20 A.M. and she did not see Dr. Sklar in that area then. It was possible that he could have passed unnoticed, she said, and his note at 8 A.M. stated that he, as well as Dr. Jascalevich, had examined Rohrbeck during the hour before his death. But she still thought it was "unlikely."

Mrs. O'Brien explained that she hadn't attempted to resuscitate Rohrbeck because she accepted Dr. Jascalevich's word that the patient had expired.

Q: You know that that's the first order of a nurse's priority, isn't it, to do that?

A: Not when a doctor tells me a patient is dead.

"Haven't you said that you should have done it?" asked Brown, referring to a statement the witness gave to Moses in 1976.

A: I said, in retrospect, now I suppose I might have. Yes. But I concluded that Dr. Jascalevich was correct in his assessment of the patient's condition.

Q: As a matter of fact, until you read *The New York Times* . . . it was your feeling, which you expressed, that his diagnostic skill had prevented the patient from dying in the operating room. Isn't that true?

A: That's true.

Q: Until you read *The New York Times*—

A: I concluded that he had made a tremendous observation, and I thought it was remarkable that he observed neck distention and the patient subsequently died five minutes later. I thought that was amazing.

In fact, Mrs. O'Brien testified, she later told Dr. DeMarco that he "ought to give Dr. Jascalevich a big kiss because he saved you from a possible anesthesia death."

12

"The State calls Dr. Stanley Harris."

It was May 16, 1978, and Sybil Moses was bringing to the stand her star witness from Riverdell Hospital, the man who had opened the defendant's locker twelve years earlier and accused him of "performing" deaths, the man whom Ray Brown labeled "the architect of this entire travesty." Judge Arnold had predicted a trial of eight to twelve weeks; this was the twelfth, and the end of the trial was nowhere in sight. The prosecution had yet to call any of its curare or other experts, and the defense, of course, hadn't put on any witnesses. The proceeding had begun on a chill winter's day; now the Hackensack Green was fully thawed, and the temperature in the courtroom, where the air-conditioning worked erratically when it worked at all, hovered around 80 degrees.

Stanley Harris was eager to testify. For three months he had read news accounts of the trial, and he was sickened by Brown's portrayal of him as incompetent and malicious. Now it was his turn—his chance to explain, in his own words, what he had done and why. And he welcomed the opportunity. Let the jury see what kind of a person, what kind of a doctor, he was. That's what he wanted.

The forty-six-year-old surgeon, in a vested blue-gray suit, walked briskly to the witness stand and, as he was sworn in, looked over at Dr. Jascalevich. The defendant was smiling, and Dr. Harris wondered what he could possibly be smiling about.

Q: Dr. Harris, what is your profession?

A: I'm a Doctor of Medicine and a surgeon.

Q: What education did you receive, sir, prior to becoming a doctor?

A: I received a New York scholarship which I applied to the University of Rochester.

BROWN: I object, his education has nothing to do with that. Lots of us went to school on scholarships.

ARNOLD: I will allow it.

Brown continued to object as Moses elicited Dr. Harris's background, including his honors at Rochester and at Yale Medical School and his "very intensive and tough" residency in the Bronx, where he had "experience with all age groups, from infancy to the very old." The witness was a "smart aleck" intent on "lecturing" the jury, Brown complained, and, unless he was controlled, "we will be here forever."

Dr. Harris went on to say that, after he joined the Riverdell staff in February 1966, he was not supervised "at all." Dr. Jascalevich did not watch him operate at that time, or discuss his surgery, and there were no meetings of the surgery department, the witness said.

Although more detailed in some areas, much of Dr. Harris's testimony regarding Nancy Savino was a repetition of what the jury had already heard, particularly from Allan Lans. But Moses took Dr. Harris through his experience with the patient, step by step, even asking him to draw a diagram of how he had resected her bowel during the hour-and-a-half surgery on that Saturday night, March 19, 1966. "All of this is unnecessary," protested Brown. "It is a very simple business [but] it is becoming a drama."

Dr. Harris recounted two of his visits to the child's room on March 20; both times he found her condition to be stable. Moses then asked the witness if he had seen Nancy again that day.

A: Yes, you can see I was concerned about this baby.

BROWN: I object to this. He either saw her or he didn't.

ARNOLD: Strike it.

BROWN: He'll get his Oscar in other ways, Judge.

MOSES: That comment is outrageous for the Court and jury.

ARNOLD: The jury will disregard Mr. Brown's remark and disregard the witness's remark.

Dr. Harris said he came back to see Nancy at 10 P.M. Sunday night. "At that time," he testified, "the baby looked quite good. She had no fever; [her] abdomen was quite soft, very stable. The cutdown which I had put in was running very well, and she looked quite nice. She was voiding, looked very good, alert. She looked terrific."

When Nancy was found dead the next morning, Dr. Harris said, he insisted on an autopsy, which Dr. Gillson performed later that afternoon at nearby Pascack Valley Hospital. The witness said he did not see anything about the body, during the autopsy, that was "not normal."

Dr. Harris also testified, but not at length, about the death of Margaret Henderson a month later. The witness, who had assisted Dr. Livingston in the exploratory laparotomy, was stunned the next morning to learn that Miss Henderson had died. "I felt it was important to find out what this patient died of, and I went to the postmortem" conducted by Drs. Gilady and Gillson.

Moses asked Dr. Harris whether he had formed an opinion at that time about the cause of death.

A: My opinion was that there was nothing at the autopsy to suggest a cause of death in this patient.

Dr. Harris said he continued to do "all kinds of surgery" throughout the spring and summer of 1966—like Dr. Lans, he too said that Dr. Briski did very little surgery.

Q: Now, in September of 1966, did there come a time when you had a case by the name of Emma Arzt?

A: Yes, I did.

Dr. Harris testified that, before operating on Mrs. Arzt for an inflamed gallbladder on September 22, he had checked to see whether the patient had any "underlying" stomach or colon disease. While Mrs. Arzt's loss of thirty-two pounds over the previous year or two was consistent with her gallbladder ailment, he said, he wanted to exclude the possibility of other serious disease. Except for the gallbladder, he said, the tests revealed "no evidence of other gastrointestinal pathology," and the preoperative electrocardiogram was "normal." After the eighty-five-minute operation, Dr. Harris continued, he visited Mrs. Arzt in the recovery room.

Q: How did she, in your opinion, sustain the surgery?

A: She did very well, she was stable throughout.

The witness said he saw Mrs. Arzt between 9:30 and 9:45 A.M. the morning following her surgery when he changed her dressing. "The patient looked quite alert and quite stable. We conversed . . . Her blood pressure, pulse, respirations were normal, and so was her temperature." About twenty minutes later, Dr. Harris said, he was called back to Room 201 because Mrs. Arzt had suddenly gone "bad." Dr. Grosso was massaging the patient's heart, Dr. Harris said. Dr. Jascalevich was there "for a brief period and then left quickly thereafter."

Q: Did you speak to Dr. Jascalevich?

A: He told me that the patient had vomited and aspirated.

Q: What is that, "aspirated"?

A: If a patient vomits and aspirates, it means the stomach contents are then entered into the trachea, into the lungs, as it were.

Q: What else did he say?

A: That the patient had a cardiac arrest.

Q: Now, did Dr. Jascalevich do anything in regard to this patient when you got there?

A: No, he was on his way out.

Dr. Harris, who saw no evidence that Mrs. Arzt had vomited or aspirated, said the patient's heart was beating but she looked blue, "markedly cyanotic." She was "lying completely unresponsive . . . completely flaccid and relaxed. She was not breathing." After "mouth-to-mouth-breathing her," Dr. Harris said, he inserted an endotracheal tube that (with help from Dr. Grosso and Dr. DeMarco, who had also arrived) was attached to a mechanical respirator. "The patient gradually improved," the witness remembered. "She started breathing on her own; blood pressure, pulse, and respirations became more normal and she looked better." But she was "still critical," Dr. Harris said.

Q: What was your impression at the time?

A: My impression from all the things that had happened at the time was she may have suffered a heart attack and this was more a medical problem than a surgical problem, and the further care of the patient was turned over to Dr. Pardell and Dr. Topfer.

About 11:30 A.M. Dr. Harris wrote a progress note on Mrs. Arzt's chart and left Room 201. He never saw the patient again.

After Dr. Harris testified that he rejected Dr. Jascalevich's proposal for an "emergency coverage" arrangement in early October 1966, Moses was ready to finish up with the witness. Brown had charged, during Dr. Lans's testimony, that Dr. Harris had a dozen or so postsurgical deaths in 1967, after Dr. Jascalevich was gone from Riverdell. Now, Moses put the question to Dr. Harris himself. Dr. Harris said he performed over 400 operations in 1967. And not once, he said, did he have an unexplained death after surgery.

Several Riverdell directors had already recounted the events leading up to Calissi's entry into the case on November 1, 1966, and Dr. Harris's testimony on that score was largely anticlimactic. But the courtroom was as crowded as it had been on the day that Moses asked Judge Arnold to disqualify himself; nurses and doctors from Riverdell, some accompanied by their spouses, were wedged between Dr. Jascalevich's ever-present supporters; retired lawyers, businessmen, housewives, and other trial buffs; and a class of high school students who were doing a "law project" on the case. Allan Lans's wife, Joan, sat in the middle, her hands clenched so tight that her knuckles were white. At the defense table, Dr. Jascalevich craned his neck forward, a faint smile on his lips.

Dr. Harris recalled that when he became convinced in late October

1966 that the sudden deaths at Riverdell ran a pattern, he took his suspicions to Dr. Lans and to the hospital's board. By the afternoon of October 31—unaware, he said, that the board intended to meet with the chief surgeon that night to review the mortalities—he "felt compelled" to open Dr. Jascalevich's locker, believing it might contain succinylcholine chloride. When he saw the curare vials in the "completely disarrayed" locker and a loaded syringe and needle, "that was enough." Dr. Harris said he touched one or two of the vials "to make sure what I was seeing." Then he phoned Dr. Lans and told him it was not succinylcholine, "it was curare . . . and this was the curare that Dr. Jascalevich had used to kill these patients."

Brown, opening his cross-examination, instantly attacked the witness's credibility.

Waving a copy of Dr. Harris's 1976 grand jury testimony—testimony in which Dr. Harris said he didn't recall being at Margaret Henderson's autopsy—the defense attorney asked, "Why did you lie, to the grand jury, or here?"

"All I can say to that, Mr. Brown, is that I was at the postmortem examination even if I didn't remember it" in 1976. "I didn't lie," said Dr. Harris. "There is no question I was at the postmortem."

Dr. Harris had also told the grand jury, contrary to his testimony now, that he didn't remember seeing Dr. Jascalevich on the day of Emma Arzt's death. Brown hit hard on the discrepancy. But Dr. Harris explained that after his grand jury appearance, he had read his 1966 statement to Calissi and his memory had been jogged. "I am sure I told the prosecutor in 1966, when I was closer to the event, that [Dr. Jascalevich] was present, and I think, perhaps, if we can review the 1966—"

Both Brown and Judge Arnold interrupted. "The witness isn't going to tell the attorneys what to do," the judge said, "Don't let the witness tell us what we are going to do."

Q: According to your new memory, Doc, what did you see [Dr. Jascalevich] doing, where did you see him, and what were the circumstances with respect to Mrs. Arzt?

Dr. Harris said that when he was called back to Mrs. Arzt's room about 10 A.M. on September 23, Dr. Jascalevich was there, but "I didn't see him doing very much in terms of the patient . . . Nothing specifically." Mrs. Cassell, the nurse, was also there with Dr. Grosso, but "I don't recall exactly what she was doing."

Q: Are you aware that Nurse Cassell summoned Dr. Jascalevich and went into that room with him?

A: No, I am not aware of that.

Q: Are you aware—by the way, was there an I.V. running at that time with respect to Mrs. Arzt?

A: Yes, there was.

Q: Who started it?

A: I can't remember who specifically had started the I.V., but this patient had an intravenous going during surgery. There were I.V.'s running postoperatively and I.V. orders that were written for her.

Q: Isn't it generally true that I.V.'s are running postoperatively for most patients?

A: It depends on the patient.

Q: Is it true in most instances the I.V.'s are running or not?

A: No, it depends strictly upon the operation, Mr. Brown.

Q: It is not then usual to have an I.V. running?

A: I didn't say that, either. I said it depends upon the operation.

Again, Brown pointed to Mrs. Cassell's note saying that Dr. Jascalevich had massaged Mrs. Arzt's heart and given her artificial respiration about 10 A.M. There was no evidence, Brown reiterated, that the defendant had been in Room 201 either before 10 A.M. or in the four hours preceding Mrs. Arzt's death at 2:10 P.M. Dr. Harris himself had written notes saying that Mrs. Arzt had vomited and aspirated and suffered a cardiac arrest around 10 A.M., Brown stressed. Even Dr. Pardell, the heart specialist who replaced Dr. Harris at Mrs. Arzt's bedside about 11:30 A.M., made reference to "acute left ventricular failure following cardiac arrest."

But Dr. Harris refused to concede that Mrs. Arzt's problem that morning stemmed from a heart attack. He based his notes, he said, on what Dr. Jascalevich had told him. As for Dr. Pardell, he, too, "indicated what was told him . . . He didn't see [Mrs. Arzt] when she had an acute episode" around 10 A.M. "He came much later."

Like Moses, Brown spent relatively little time with Dr. Harris on the treatment and death of Margaret Henderson. The witness said he was aware, from Miss Henderson's chart, that Dr. Jascalevich had advised against surgery on the morning of April 22, 1966. But he didn't know whether Dr. Livingston had spoken to Dr. Jascalevich that afternoon after the barium-enema X ray. He himself had not talked to the chief surgeon.

Brown was more persistent with regard to Nancy Savino. Why hadn't Dr. Harris diagnosed her mesenteric cysts before surgery, as a "competent" doctor would have? Wouldn't X rays have helped? Would the witness accept as an authority Wallace Dennison's textbook on pediatric surgery?

Dr. Harris replied that a preoperative diagnosis of ruptured mesentric cysts was rarely made and wouldn't have been aided by radiography. He would accept "a report by Handonsman and Ravage from Johns Hopkins and Mount Sinai, who reported their experience and reviewed the literature; and if you will read their report, they had a three-year-old child who had almost the precise clinical course as the patient in this case, Nancy Savino, in which they obtained no barium enemas or any other X-ray studies, in which they had a preoperative diagnosis of acute appendicitis—which is what is usually made in these cases and which most authors would agree—and they went ahead and operated."

Q: I didn't ask you for all that. I asked you did you accept . . .

A: You asked me who I accepted.

The sparring continued when Brown, observing that the child's preoperative temperature was 102, drew the witness's attention to a manual prepared by the American College of Surgeons, "of which you are a member." Wasn't it true, the defense attorney asked, that the manual "absolutely commanded" that a child with a temperature greater than 101 needed to be rehydrated and given antibiotics and ice bags before any operation?

A: I definitely would not want to give any child who had a fever preoperatively, antibiotics . . . When a child reaches 103 and 104, you get very concerned, cool the patient down, give the patient aspirin, as necessary, before we take the child into an operation.

Q: So you disagree with the *Manual of Pre-Operative and Post-Operative Care* published by the American College of Surgeons?

A: As a general rule that can be applied to every patient in every situation, absolutely . . . Each child is an individual, and the care has to be so assessed.

* * *

Q: Well, Doctor, you didn't follow those guidelines, that's for sure.

A: I didn't feel in this case—

Q: I did not ask you that. You didn't follow those guidelines, right?

A: That's right.

Q: And the child died, right?

A: The child died.

Brown, thinking ahead to the case he would present for the defense, repeatedly tried to establish that Nancy Savino might have had a deadly infection, not an inflammation, in her peritoneal cavity. But Dr. Harris, who had written "acute chylous peritonitis" as well as "mesenteric cyst of ileum" on Nancy's chart, was making no such concession. He had only meant "peritoneal irritation."

Brown also focused on the fact that Nancy Savino had cried from time to time, postsurgically, had complained periodically that her leg or belly or throat hurt, and had been given five 20-milligram doses of Demerol for pain. He asked Dr. Harris if all that was "consistent with a stable child whose well-being is self-evident, as you indicated?"

A: Yes, absolutely, it is.

Probing into other areas, Brown implied that Dr. Harris was greedy and inconsiderate of Dr. Jascalevich's gesture toward a partnership. The defense attorney brought out that Dr. Jascalevich's proposed order of call for emergencies—Dr. Harris, first; Dr. Jascalevich, second— was not "obligatory." And he emphasized that not only had Dr. Harris become chief surgeon at Riverdell in November 1967, but he had also done four times more operations that year than in 1966.

Dr. Harris said his relationship with Dr. Jascalevich in 1966 was "very impersonal"—neither "good or bad," he agreed with Brown. But the defense attorney emphasized that Dr. Harris had never taken his concerns about his patients' deaths to the chief surgeon. And the witness admitted, as he had to Calissi, that apart from his own "analysis" of the situation, there was nothing about Dr. Jascalevich to suggest that the chief surgeon was "doing something that wasn't proper" with patients.

Wasn't it true, Brown asked, that the witness and Dr. Lans had "zeroed in" on Dr. Jascalevich?

BROWN: It is only after you, by stealth and guise, obtained the key and went to the locker that they [the directors] went to the prosecutor?

HARRIS: They went to the prosecutor after they saw what was in the locker. They didn't need me to tell them.

Q: Who led them to the locker?

A: I opened the locker, no question about that.

Q: Who then spread the word that brought them to the locker?

A: I told them, absolutely. I told them.

Q: I'm sure you did.

A: No question about that.

Q: I'm sure you did, Doctor.

A: I wouldn't have kept that quiet for the world.

"Of course you wouldn't," said Brown, wheeling around and shouting, "because after that you became chief of surgery and made a lot of money, is that right?"

Moses was on her feet, asking that "counsel be restrained." It was the witness who needed restraining, Brown replied. "Don't worry about counsel."

Q: Doctor, there was a syringe that you mentioned, is that right?

A: Yes.

Q: Have you come to know that that syringe was filled with mineral oil?

Moses objected, arguing that the question was not based on any evidence before the jury. But Judge Arnold overruled her, and Dr. Harris said that he "wasn't familiar with that."

Although he went through them one by one, Brown dealt only sketchily with Dr. Harris's mortalities in 1967. He finished his cross-examination by making a point of Dr. Harris's suspicions in October 1966 that Dr. Jascalevich might have had succinylcholine in his locker. Hadn't Dr. Harris thought that succinylcholine—rapidly metabolized and hard to find in tissues—was the "ideal" drug "if somebody was going to do a hideous thing" like murdering patients? Yes, said the witness, that's what he had thought. Succinylcholine, Brown underlined. Not curare.

On redirect examination, which was usually a rehash, Moses had Dr. Harris explain that he had fixed on succinylcholine because of the allegations at that time against Carl Coppolino. The prosecutor also took Dr. Harris through a more detailed accounting of his mortalities in 1967. Not only could the deaths be explained, Dr. Harris said, but none of them was what he would classify as a "surgical mortality." In one case cited by Brown, he had only assisted at surgery. In three cases, there had been no surgery at all, only rectal examinations—performed, for lack of other space, in the operating room. One of the patients, an eighty-year-old woman, died in a nursing home a month after the amputation of her second leg because of gangrene. Five of the patients, some of whom were only biopsied by Dr. Harris, died of cancer; another, of diffuse peritonitis.

Dr. Harris also testified, on redirect examination, that Nancy Savino's temperature, 102 several hours before her operation, dropped to 100.8 at midnight. "Thereafter," he said, "starting at 4 A.M., this baby had no fever whatever; it was under 100, all within normal range." He said, too, that cultures taken of the chylous fluid in her peritoneal cavity were studied for two days postoperatively and showed "absolutely no" signs of infection.

In a final effort to blunt Brown's cross-examination, Moses showed Dr. Harris his statement to Calissi in 1966. At that time Dr. Harris had told the prosecutor that he personally knew that Dr. Jascalevich was present in Mrs. Arzt's room on the morning of the day she died. Dr. Harris had also told Calissi that he was at Margaret Henderson's autopsy the previous April.

On recross-examination, Brown brought out that Dr. Harris had performed two operations within fifteen days in 1967 on an elderly woman who had terminal cancer. "When you operated on this lady who was sure to die, did you tell the daughters, particularly, or any member of that family, that this lady was going to die anyway, when you did these two operations?"

A: I don't recall what I said to the family, but if I had to speak to the family, I would have told them that she had a far advanced tumor, but that at the second operation, she had an obstruction which was an acute process, and how much longer would she last if we relieved her obstruction—nobody could answer that question. So the only human thing to do at that time was to do what you had to do for the acute episode, the obstruction, and then the lady did go on. We tried in every way—tube feedings, protein supplements, intravenous fluids—to maintain her, but she died over one month from the last operation.

Q: You were paid for both operations, weren't you?

Judge Arnold sustained Moses's objection.

Brown rarely missed an opportunity with prosecution witnesses to accent the time lapse between the events in question and the trial. And more than a few witnesses obliged him: "It's twelve years." . . . "It's twelve years ago. It's quite difficult to recall." . . . "Again, sir, it was twelve years ago." . . . "I don't remember, sir. What's there is there. It's twelve years." The defense attorney brought out that Dr. Jascalevich was not the only staff physician to start intravenous infusions at Riverdell, even if the job customarily fell to the house doctors; that the hospital's stock of curare was not always kept under lock; that Dr. Jascalevich was concerned about Dr. Briski's qualifications as a surgeon from the time the younger man applied to Riverdell; and that, no matter what Dr. Briski's understanding, no document existed to show that Dr. Briski was ever granted the "A" privileges held by Dr. Jascalevich and Dr. Harris. Brown also underscored the inexact nature of medicine and the frequency with which physicians differed among themselves.

"There are no absolutes in medicine," Dr. Denson conceded under cross-examination.

Of major concern to Moses and Brown were Dr. Jascalevich's prior statements—two taped conversations with Fred Galda, the chief assistant prosecutor, on November 3 and 4, 1966; the written deposition of November 11, 1966; and the two-part written deposition taken by Woodcock on February 4 and March 3, 1976. A tape of the November 2, 1966, meeting between Dr. Jascalevich and the Riverdell board had apparently been lost by the prosecutor's office years ago, but over Brown's objection, the board minutes of that session were admitted into evidence early in the trial. The conversations with Galda, taped on the Walkie Recordall, had eventually been re-recorded for clarity by Woodcock's detectives—well after my unsuccessful attempt to have one of them played on the Recordall I had obtained in New York. But the new tapes, which I was unaware of until the trial, were barely more audible than the originals.

Moses considered it critical to get Dr. Jascalevich's 1966 and 1976 depositions before the jury. But as soon as she moved to introduce the first of them, Brown insisted that it be accompanied by the tapes Galda had made in early November 1966. The tapes and the defendant's 1966 deposition were two parts of a whole, Brown argued; and if either of the parts was inadmissible, then the other part had to be ruled out as well. To introduce the 1966 deposition without the tapes was to give the jury "only a fragment of this man's response" because the tapes included some questions not asked by Calissi the following week, Brown said. The tapes were "crucial and favorable to the defense case."

Moses charged that Brown's focus on the tapes was only a maneuver to keep out the 1966 deposition. But she had no objection to admitting "every audible portion" of the tapes with Galda.

After listening to their often scratchy, distorted sounds, Judge Arnold ruled that the tapes "could lead to erroneous impressions" and were too unintelligible to be heard by the jury. The 1966 deposition, he held, "can stand on its own two feet" and was admissible. The judge rejected a motion by Brown to delete from the statement Dr. Jascalevich's opinions about the deaths of three of his alleged victims. But he agreed to strike out the part dealing with Eileen Shaw, whose death was not part of the indictment.

The question of admitting Dr. Jascalevich's 1976 deposition was put off, while Moses tried to introduce the detectives' report of Dr. Jascalevich's complaint that his car had been broken into in November 1966, and that certain items relating to his dog research had been stolen, while other items, which belonged in his Riverdell locker number four or in his "research bag," had been placed in the car. Now, Moses wanted to show that the complaint was "another piece of the cover-up, another piece of the story he is concocting." Ray Brown didn't want the report admitted, even though the car incident, if true, was consistent with the defense theory of a "frame-up." The incident was "irrelevant," and the surgeon's rights against self-incrimination had not been protected during his interview by detectives, Brown said. Judge Arnold kept the report out. "I'm not convinced that it adds anything to the case at this time," he said, observing that he might "wind up trying a breaking-and-entering case in the middle of a murder trial."

Brown also won on another issue: exclusion of the prosecution list showing that Dr. Jascalevich had bought twenty-four vials of curare between September 1965 and September 1966. Judge Arnold barred the list, which had been prepared for Calissi's detectives in November 1966, on the grounds that the original invoices on which it was based had not been preserved.

To persuade the jury that Dr. Jascalevich was not doing dog experiments in the sixteenth-floor quarters of Seton Hall Medical School in 1965–66, Moses called three witnesses. All three—Joseph Salerno, Dr. Anthony Boccabella, and Sal Riggi—had been interviewed by Calissi's detectives in 1966, and their testimony generally conformed with their earlier statements and with what Dr. Boccabella and Riggi had told me in 1975.

On May 22, Moses again moved to introduce the two-part deposition that Woodcock had taken from Dr. Jascalevich on February 4 and March 3, 1976. She considered the first part of the deposition essential to her case, because it was in that part that the defendant said he did his 1965–66 dog experiments in the third-floor cardiology laboratory at Pollak Hospital, adjacent to Seton Hall Medical School. Moses planned to stress the disparity between this statement and the surgeon's statement to Calissi in 1966. In 1966 Dr. Jascalevich said he did all his experiments in 1965–66 in the sixteenth-floor animal quarters at Seton Hall.

All this was a problem for the defense. The 1966 deposition was already in evidence and had been read to the jury. But perhaps the 1976 deposition, or at least the first part of it, could be kept out. The basis for Brown's challenge lay in a statement by Woodcock to Dr. Jascalevich at the start of the deposition on February 4. Woodcock had said that the surgeon was not a "target" of the Riverdell investigation at that time and that there was not yet any indication of a crime's having been committed. "This is not to say that it might not develop further along down the road," the prosecutor added. According to Brown, Woodcock had deceived Dr. Jascalevich and entrapped him into giving the deposition. The defense attorney asked for a hearing, out of the presence of the jury, at which he could call witnesses. Judge Arnold agreed to it.

Joseph Woodcock was the first witness at the hearing. Brown asked the former prosecutor, who was now practicing law in Hackensack, about his involvement in the case from the moment in August of 1975 when I came to his office and asked to see Calissi's old file on Riverdell. Woodcock said that while he had a half-dozen brief conversations with me in succeeding months, he had virtually no first-hand knowledge of the case until I gave him a copy of Dr. Jascalevich's 1966 deposition, which was missing from the prosecutor's file. He recalled that

Detective Chief Richard Kikkert read the deposition and then he did, too. It was that document, he said, that "triggered" his decision to renew the Riverdell investigation. Hadn't Woodcock asked me where I got a copy of Dr. Jascalevich's 1966 deposition? Brown asked. Yes, the witness said. But I "invoked the normal reporter's privilege so we did not make any further inquiry with respect to that."

More to the point of the hearing, Woodcock testified that while Dr. Jascalevich was "center stage" in his investigation before February 1976, he did not regard the surgeon as the "target" until some time between February 4 and March 1976, when he received a report indicating the presence of curare in Nancy Savino's body. "The thrust of the investigation in January 1976 was to determine whether or not those unexplained deaths were homicides. The prosecutor's office does not investigate people, they investigate crimes. The first thing that you have to do is to determine whether a crime has been committed."

"I didn't ask you for a lecture," Brown said.

Cross-examining her former boss, Moses emphasized that neither Woodcock nor anyone on his staff had subpoenaed Dr. Jascalevich in 1976 or asked him to voluntarily "come into the office" to give a deposition.

ARNOLD: Well, let me ask Mr. Woodcock something: how did he happen to come in?

MOSES: How did he happen to come in? That is the best question of the day, Judge.

WOODCOCK: I received a call from Mr. Anderson, who indicated to me that he represented Dr. Jascalevich. After that telephone conversation, he came to my office and offered to have Dr. Jascalevich come in to testify—well, let's say to have his deposition taken . . . [as] in '66 . . . in an effort to clear up any questions we might have.

Woodcock said that he warned Dr. Jascalevich of his rights to avoid self-incrimination on February 4, 1976, because of the possibility that the surgeon might ultimately become the target of the Riverdell investigation.

ARNOLD: Let me ask you one thing, Mr. Woodcock. When Mr. Anderson came to see you, did he mention he was coming because of *The New York Times* article?

A: I am sure that was the thing that triggered his phone call to me because he had been involved with the case back in '66.

MOSES: And despite the fact that certain articles had appeared in *The New York Times,* he still wanted to come in and bring his client in. Isn't that true?

A: That is correct.

13

Ray Brown was foraging for evidence of collusion between Woodcock and me. Clearly, he was going to call me as a witness at the hearing to determine whether Dr. Jascalevich had been tricked by the prosecutor in 1976; if nothing else, he could use it as a dry run for my testimony later in the trial. I didn't think my appearance was relevant to the hearing. But within the confines of what I believed to be my constitutional and statutory rights as a reporter, I was prepared to answer the subpoena for oral testimony that I had received in March. What neither I nor *The Times* was prepared for was the notice we received on May 23, 1978, from Acting State Supreme Court Justice George Roberts in Manhattan.

Justice Roberts informed us that four days earlier, Judge Arnold had invoked an interstate compact and requested the New York courts to subpoena certain materials for him from me and *The Times*. The materials included all notes of interviews, memoranda, pictures, recordings, and "other writings" relating to a list of 193 potential witnesses for the Jascalevich trial, and "contractual information relating to the above." Judge Arnold's request was based solely on an affidavit by Brown on May 17 that "all" the materials were "critical" to his client's defense. The affidavit was no more specific than the judge's request to Justice Roberts. In support of the need for everything, the affidavit cited only one document—Lee Henderson's statement to me, the guts of which *The Times* had long since published.

I was stunned by the scope of the subpoena. With Judge Arnold's support, Brown was attempting to subpoena all the information that I had gathered on the Riverdell story; in effect, he was asking for my

desk. The request made no distinction between published and unpublished material, or between confidential and nonconfidential material. Just give me everything, Judge Arnold was saying, and, "by hearing or otherwise," he would decide what to turn over to Brown. Surely
the judge—and Brown—knew that *The Times* and I would oppose so
sweeping a subpoena as a violation of the First Amendment and of
New Jersey's "shield" law protecting reporters—and as a "fishing expedition" that would be invalid even if the rights of the press were not involved. But maybe that was Brown's game; maybe he was counting on
our opposition to further delay the trial and to suggest that *The Times*
and I were hiding something.

As for Judge Arnold, he had already made known his views of our
position. In his opinion barring me from covering the trial, he said that
"the rights of the press under the First Amendment can never exceed
the rights of a defendant to a fair and impartial trial." Presumably that
now meant that Brown could rummage at will through my files. How
ironic, I thought. Brown had labeled me an "agent of the prosecutor";
now he wanted to make me an agent not of *The Times,* but of the defense. All the notes I had gathered for *The Times,* and had never
shown Woodcock or anyone else, would presumably now belong to
him, and perhaps to Moses as well. Judge Arnold, in his sequestration
opinion in March, had not ruled on New Jersey's forty-five-year-old
shield law, which was amended in 1977 to make it one of the strongest
laws of its kind in the nation. But it seemed that he had made up
his mind about that, too. In his request for my materials, and those
of *The Times,* he noted that "there appears to be no privilege" under
the shield law "that can prevent the withholding of these documents." I
found that a rather queer and dogmatic interpretation of a statute that
said that a reporter "has a privilege to refuse to disclose . . . to any
court" either the source of any information or "any news or information obtained in the course of pursuing his professional activities,
whether or not it is disseminated." The only exceptions occurred when
a reporter had "waived" his rights, or had concealed from his source
the fact that he was a journalist, or had been eyewitness to, or involved
in, physical violence or property damage. I had waived none of my
rights, and Judge Arnold had not ruled to the contrary. The first thing
I did when I walked into Woodcock's office in August 1975 was to introduce myself as a reporter for *The Times.* And of course I had not
witnessed any of the events at Riverdell Hospital in 1965 and 1966.

There was something else that bothered me on May 23, 1978. No
one—not Judge Arnold, nor Ray Brown—had approached me and
said, "We need something so that Mario Jascalevich can get a fair trial,
and we're pretty sure that only you've got it. That's all we want, apart

from your oral testimony, and we'll identify it for you. We understand the importance of confidentiality to reporters; after all, lawyers regularly protect the confidences of their clients. So if you've got a problem, if you think your ethics as a journalist will be compromised, let's talk about it before there's any confrontation, particularly at this stage in the trial. We can all try to be reasonable." Nothing like that had happened. Instead I had been served directly with an order, and an order for everything.

Justice Roberts said there would be a hearing on Judge Arnold's request in Manhattan Supreme Court on May 31.

On May 24, I was called as the last witness at the "target" hearing in Hackensack. Floyd Abrams, my attorney, was then in California on a case, and I was accompanied to the hearing by three other lawyers. Two of them—Gene Scheiman and Faith Wender—were associates at Floyd's firm. The third lawyer with us that morning was Peter Banta, a partner in the Hackensack law firm of Winne, Banta, Rizzi & Harrington. Banta's firm, which represented the *Bergen Record,* was brought in by *The Times* because of the firm's experience in Bergen County and its familiarity with New Jersey press cases and court procedure.

When we arrived at the courthouse, the lawyers went into Judge Arnold's chambers for a conference. I was standing in the hallway near the judge's chambers when Stephen Delaney, a private investigator for Brown, walked over and slapped a new subpoena against my chest. I let it drop to the floor, as Gene had instructed me to do.

"I don't mean any discourtesy," I said to Delaney, as he retrieved the folded paper.

"That's all right," he said. "You're not accepting this?"

"I'm not accepting anything," I replied. I was in New Jersey only in response to the March subpoena and, legally, this was neither the time nor place for the defense to take advantage of my presence by serving me again. Henry Furst, Brown's assistant, thought otherwise. He took the subpoena from Delaney and tried to shove it in the breast pocket of my suit jacket. I moved away and, once again, it hit the floor. "Well, you get the point," Furst said, picking up the subpoena.

I later learned that this subpoena was also for "all documents, notes" and so forth in connection with the Jascalevich case. But Judge Arnold told Scheiman that he would not enforce it because of the manner in which it had been served in the courtroom. The judge was content to have the New York courts get the materials for him.

While I was waiting for the lawyers to finish with Judge Arnold, I chatted briefly with some of the reporters who were covering the trial. From what I had heard, Brown had been the darling of the courthouse press corps when the trial started. His hyperbole made "good copy"; he regaled the reporters, during recesses, with his legal exploits; he occasionally took them to lunch or for drinks. But lately, I gathered, the "treatment" was wearing thin. Brown had accused "the press"—not just *The Times*—of being "as vicious as the prosecutor," and individual reporters who wrote articles that were not to his liking were no longer "Walter Lippmanns." They were now from *"Pravda."* Once, David Bird wrote a long, front-page story describing the atmosphere and antics in and about Judge Arnold's courtroom. Brown was enraged. When Ted Rohrlich of the *Record* said that he wished he had written the piece by the *Times* reporter, Brown told him that "this trial separates the pricks from the princes." In open court the defense attorney charged that Bird's article "borders on the scurrilous." It was written, he said, "by a reporter who violated every confidence I've ever heard of."

I was sure that Bird hadn't violated any confidences. I was also pleased to know that a reporter's failure to keep his word would offend Brown.

The trial reporters had drifted into the courtroom when Brown emerged from Judge Arnold's chambers and, without so much as a nod, passed by me and disappeared into the men's room. Instantly I decided to follow him. I couldn't believe that Brown swallowed his own rhetoric about me—"miscreant purveyor of irresponsible journalism" and the like—and I was curious to see his reaction if we were alone. As I opened the door to the bathroom, he was standing by the corner urinal, his back to me. There was no one else present, and he looked over his shoulder when I spoke up.

"I thought I'd say 'good morning' to you, even if you may not want to say 'good morning' to me. I'd also like to tell you that my motives in this case are pure."

Brown laughed and, to my surprise, praised the "great job" I had done as a reporter. He said he didn't doubt my motives and that I shouldn't feel personally responsible that publicity had led to "grief" for his client. "I'm not blaming you for that."

"Well, that's not what I've heard," I said.

"Oh, no, you're a reporter doing your job, and I'm just trying to do mine. I'm no genius, but I try."

As he washed his hands, Brown said the only "bad" thing he had heard about me was my "intellectual arrogance." But he said that half-kiddingly, too. I remarked that I was sorry he had excluded me from covering the trial because I recognized "talent wherever I find it," and I would have liked to have seen him in action. And then he surprised me again. Keeping me out of the courtroom, he said, *"was* a stroke of genius. Well, not genius but . . ."

Brown threw about 100 questions at me in court that day, and I answered some eighty-five of them. Citing the First Amendment and the New Jersey shield law, I declined to answer a dozen questions that involved confidential information or sources, or information that I had gathered as a reporter but had not printed. I was anxious not to appear evasive—I realized that some people would misinterpret a refusal to answer even one question, particularly in a trial where the defendant faced so grave a penalty as life imprisonment. At the same time, I was determined not to undercut my rights as a reporter—in this or any other matter. These same rights, I knew, were my only protection against the ominous threat posed by the blanket subpoena for my notes and other documents.

So I took what seemed to be the only course available to me on May 24, 1978; I exercised my rights, but I exercised them sparingly. Under questioning by Brown, I acknowledged that I had given Woodcock a copy of Dr. Jascalevich's 1966 deposition, and I said that was all I had given him. I testified that I had spoken to Woodcock a half-dozen times, and I confirmed the accuracy of the statements by the prosecutor that I had published in 1976. I admitted having examined the Riverdell file at least several times in 1975 and having seen tapes in it, one of which I tried without success to have played by the prosecutor's office on a Walkie Recordall I brought from New York. But I said I had never had custody of the file or the tapes in it. And though I was unaccompanied on my visits to the narcotics task force building, I had the impression that I was being "monitored" by the detectives there.

When court broke for lunch, Scheiman and Banta stayed behind to speak to Judge Arnold. Faith Wender and I were standing by the rear door of the courtroom waiting for them when Dr. Jascalevich came out. "Man," he said in a quivering voice, "you're in trouble." I was taken aback, less by his implicit threat than by the sudden change in his demeanor. While I was on the stand, he looked utterly relaxed, as if he were a spectator at the trial rather than the defendant. Now, just a moment later, he was shaking.

During my testimony, Brown repeatedly sought to have Judge Arnold rule that I was unprotected by the New Jersey shield law. But the wider Brown's questions ranged, the more Moses disputed their relevance to the hearing. And soon the judge was agreeing with her. Who had given me Dr. Jascalevich's 1966 deposition? Had I recommended Dr. Baden to Woodcock? Did I receive any materials from Charles Umberger, the New York toxicologist? Had I contracted to write a book about this case? The defense lawyer wanted all of these questions, and more, answered immediately. But for now, Judge Arnold said, "I am not concerned whether he is going to write a book or not." And the other questions, he noted, were also irrelevant "to whether Mr. Woodcock was focusing on the defendant" when he took his deposition on February 4, 1976. Brown could ask me these questions later in the trial, the judge said. "I want you to understand that I am not ruling that he may not have to answer these questions at a subsequent time."

I nearly dozed off on the drive back to New York. Not having testified before, I hadn't appreciated how demanding an experience it could be. I didn't envy the witnesses who had to recall events of twelve years ago. But my own situation was complicated by another factor: I had to think twice every time a question was put to me. First, what was the answer? Then, were any confidences involved? Judge Arnold had allowed me to stop and consult my lawyers freely, but I didn't like holding up the proceeding and these interruptions only added to the tension. I thought of what Brown had said to me in the men's room that morning, that he was just doing his job as I had done mine. His job as an advocate and my job as a reporter were hardly the same. And as long as he wanted me to surrender an entire file, my job wasn't over.

Summing up the hearing the next morning, Brown argued that the "publicity generated by *The Times* in articles of early 1976 had forced Dr. Jascalevich to give a deposition to Woodcock. "I feel sick," the defense attorney said. Woodcock was "an absolute liar" who had "played with the press and lied to the defendant" about whether he was the target of the Riverdell investigation on February 4, 1976. Moses countered by saying that "there's one liar here—the defendant." She said that Dr. Jascalevich's conflicting statements about where he was doing dog research in 1965–66 showed that "he just wasn't doing it." And the surgeon knew, as early as February 4, she said, that he might become the target of Woodcock's investigation. "He's sorry now," Moses said, "but it's too late."

It wasn't too late. Judge Arnold ruled that the February 4 deposition could not be placed before the jury unless the defendant took the stand. The judge said there was no question that Woodcock had informed Dr. Jascalevich of his rights on February 4; in fact, the surgeon had "voluntarily waived" those rights when he appeared with Anderson. "I'm sure that Prosecutor Woodcock, in his judgment, felt [at that stage] that no crime had been committed, and he might very well have felt that the defendant wasn't a target . . . Now, from the technical nicety, the prosecutor may have been right. But I have to look at all of the facts as they come out before me in court." Woodcock had seen the old Riverdell file by February 4, Judge Arnold reasoned, and—like Dr. Jascalevich himself—he knew who had been the target of Calissi's investigation in 1966. But Dr. Jascalevich "might very well have thought, after ten years, that he was not any longer the target, particularly since the prosecutor told him he wasn't." If Woodcock hadn't said anything to the surgeon on February 4 about being a target, "the Court, I don't think, would be too concerned about it. But this was an expression saying you are, in effect, not a target." The judge rejected Moses's argument that the February 4 statement was admissible unless Woodcock had deliberately misled Dr. Jascalevich. "I don't think that as long as it has the effect of being a ruse, whether one had intended to do it or not, in my mind, doesn't make any difference."

Judge Arnold held that the second part of Dr. Jascalevich's deposition, on March 3, 1976, could be introduced into evidence. In that part, the surgeon was questioned about the deaths of Frank Biggs, Margaret Henderson, and Carl Rohrbeck.

Moses attempted to appeal the decision, but at that time, the rules of the New Jersey Supreme Court barred such an appeal by the State during a trial. (A year later the rule was changed, making an appeal possible.)

Judge Arnold's decision wasn't the only blow to the prosecution on May 25, 1978, but the effect of the second setback was less certain than that of the first.

With the hearing over and the jury back, Moses called the first of three witnesses who had worked at Pollak Hospital in 1965–66. Robert DeSantis testified that he was employed at both Pollak and Seton Hall in those years. He said that he would anesthetize dogs in the morning at the Seton Hall animal quarters and then take them to the third-floor cardiology lab at adjacent Pollak Hospital. Between 4 and 7 P.M., he would remove dead dogs from the table in the cardiology lab and return them, through a tunnel that connected Pollak and Seton Hall, to the animal quarters.

It was on cross-examination when DeSantis said that "some" of the dogs at Pollak were alive after the day's experiments, but he was not asked whether he then destroyed them.

BROWN: Now was it possible for a doctor to tip someone and get a dog at the end of the day?

A: Yes, of course.

If Brown was expecting that answer, Moses wasn't. And she was as chagrined as Brown had been when earlier in the trial, Father Doyle testified that he preferred Dr. Harris to Dr. Jascalevich as a surgeon. Brown chose not to press his good fortune with DeSantis, but Judge Arnold wanted to make sure he had heard right.

ARNOLD: Excuse me. Did you say it was possible to tip someone and get a dog?

A: Well, yes, you know, why not?

Brown finished up in a minute or two. "No further questions of the good gentleman," he said.

DeSantis was Moses's witness again, and the prosecutor went straight to the issue of tips. Paradoxically, Dr. Jascalevich's statement to Woodcock that he had done dog research in 1965–66 at Pollak had just been declared inadmissible. The only statement in evidence was the one in which the surgeon told Calissi that he had done the work using curare at Seton Hall.

Q: Who was there [at Pollak] at the end of the day working with the dogs, other than yourself, Mr. DeSantis?

A: Nobody.

Q: Well, who would it be possible to tip other than yourself?

A: I wouldn't know.

Q: Was anybody else there?

"No," said DeSantis, repeating that he was the last person out of the lab.

On recross-examination, Brown brought out that DeSantis occasionally took off afternoons on Wednesday, the day of the week that Dr. Jascalevich claimed he did his experiments. Someone else, the witness said, would cover for him then. Neither Brown nor Moses asked who that might be.

Moses's last two witnesses from Pollak were Timothy Regan, the director of the third-floor cardiology lab, and William Burke, the heart specialist on whose dog Dr. Jascalevich worked on November 2, 1966. As they had told Calissi's detectives, both doctors testified that they had never seen Dr. Jascalevich at Pollak Hospital before that afternoon. Nor did they know of any dog handler at Pollak except DeSantis.

At the hearing in Manhattan Supreme Court on Judge Arnold's subpoena request, Henry Furst, Brown's assistant, again depicted me not as a reporter, but as an "investigator" who had collaborated with Woodcock and Dr. Baden and the state of New Jersey. Furst distorted both my position and the testimony that I had given the previous week in Hackensack. He told Acting State Supreme Court Justice Harold Rothwax that I had obtained the Walkie Recordall in New York "for the prosecutor," rather than, as I had testified, for myself. Although I had testified that the only item I ever gave Woodcock was a copy of Dr. Jascalevich's 1966 deposition, Furst stated that I had "delivered to the prosecutor 'items that had originally been in the file.'"

Among other things, Furst referred to a three-page, single-spaced letter that Moses had written to a New Jersey appellate judge in 1977 explaining the considerations that prompted Woodcock to reopen the Riverdell case. In two sentences of the letter, Moses said that "the results of *The New York Times* inquiry were made available to the prosecutor. It was thus determined that there were certain items which were not in the file of the prosecutor." But apart from Dr. Jascalevich's "missing" deposition, no "results" of the *Times*'s inquiry had been turned over to Woodcock. Perhaps Moses's use of the plural "results" was merely inadvertent. Or perhaps she meant that the prosecutor had gleaned additional information from my stories in early 1976. I certainly didn't know.

Furst also told Justice Rothwax that the prosecution's curare experts were "engaged in one of the greatest forensic mistakes ever perpetrated." And in my notes, he said, the defense might find the motive for those scientists "to produce such a result."

Scheiman, in his argument, stressed the seriousness of the issues raised by the subpoena request and the magnitude of the materials sought. Besides the First Amendment and the New Jersey shield law, he said, I was protected by the New York shield law which stated that "no professional journalist" shall be held in contempt "by any court . . . for refusing or failing to disclose any news or the source of any news coming into his possession" in the course of doing his work. All of these issues, Scheiman said, should be dealt with by a New York court before I was compelled to surrender any notes in another state.

On June 2, 1978 Justice Rothwax ruled that I was not entitled to such a substantive hearing in New York. Under the terms of the interstate compact, he said, "the court of the requesting state properly determines whether the witness or document sought" is needed. Moreover, Justice Rothwax said, the New Jersey courts were bound to give me a hearing on "all issues of privilege, statutory, and constitutional"; and whatever rights I enjoyed in New York would be afforded me across the river. The judge signed a subpoena ordering me to produce for Judge Arnold on June 6 "all statements, pictures, memoranda, recordings, and notes of interviews of witnesses for the defense and prosecution" in the Jascalevich case, "as well as information delivered to the Bergen County prosecutor's office and contractual information relating to the above." Compliance with this subpoena, Justice Rothwax said, would not cause me "undue hardship."

In her opening statement to the jury in March, Moses had promised to establish that the five patients whom Dr. Jascalevich was accused of murdering had died "as a direct result of the injection of curare," a drug normally foreign to the body. Now she had to deliver on that promise.

The first of her half-dozen medical and scientific experts was Michael Baden, who, after the short tenure of Dominick DiMaio, had just been named the acting chief medical examiner of New York City. Dr. Baden, who was now also the chief pathologist for the congressional inquiry into the assassinations of John F. Kennedy and Martin Luther King, Jr., was scheduled to testify twice at the Jascalevich trial: once to discuss his own findings on the exhumed bodies and, later, to render an expert opinion on the deaths summarizing the findings of the prosecution's toxicologists.

After detailing the medical reasons that led him to recommend exhumation of the five Riverdell corpses, explaining the general effects of curare, and outlining autopsy procedures, Dr. Baden described the varying conditions of the bodies when they were disinterred in 1976; the examinations he had made of the remains, including microscopic analysis of tissues; and the conclusions he had formed.

With respect to Nancy Savino, Dr. Baden found "no adequate reason or cause of death present." The cause of death listed for Margaret Henderson in 1966—acute hepatic necrosis—was "in error," he said, and no cause was established by her reautopsy a decade later. The cause of Frank Biggs's death was also "not identifiable or explainable" in 1976, according to the witness. Dr. Baden said the 1976 autopsy on Emma Arzt showed no evidence of a heart attack and "no obvious reason for her death." Carl Rohrbeck, Dr. Baden testified, "could have died from the hardening of the artery described by Dr. Denson" [in 1965], but "this was not necessarily a cause of death . . . because there are many people with worse coronary disease who are alive." Leafing through their hospital charts, Dr. Baden testified that none of the five patients had received curare during surgery at Riverdell; Rohrbeck, he noted, hadn't even been operated on. Only two of the patients had been given a muscle relaxant, according to the records, and in both instances it was succinylcholine chloride. That drug, Dr. Baden said, "has properties very similar to curare, but it is in no way chemically related to curare . . . nor would [it] be confused toxicologically with curare."

Brown cross-examined Dr. Baden for more than three days, but won few concessions from the pathologist. Dr. Baden acknowledged that he had never seen Rohrbeck's heart, which was not returned to the body after the 1965 autopsy, and he repeated that Rohrbeck "could" have died as a result of arteriosclerosis. It was also "possible" that Mrs. Arzt had died from a heart condition, but that cause, the witness said, "was not persuasive to me." Well, Brown asked, what about the possibility that Miss Henderson had succumbed to a pulmonary embolism? That, Dr. Baden said, was a "reasonable clinical guess," but it was not supported by the autopsy.

Brown didn't try to convert Dr. Baden to the idea that a distended bladder had led to Biggs's death. But wasn't it reasonable to conclude that Biggs had died of a fatty liver associated with excess fluid in the lungs? Biggs's liver, Dr. Baden said, was not "healthy," but considering the fatty changes that could be expected from the deficiencies of his ulcer diet, it was "normal." It was not as fatty, in Dr. Baden's opinion, as Dr. Markley indicated. And if Dr. Markley—and Dr. Gillson along with him—had thought "the liver abnormality they were looking at was important," Dr. Baden said, "they would have made that the cause of death rather than to attempt to explain it by a vasovagal reflex action from a distended bladder, which is a unique explanation." The vagus nerve, Dr. Baden observed, "doesn't connect with the bladder."

Brown's cross-examination with regard to Nancy Savino centered on the possibility that the child had died of peritonitis, that the fluid in her abdominal cavity was not the result of a ruptured mesenteric cyst and was, in fact, infectious. Like Stanley Harris, Dr. Baden rejected this proposition. The chylous fluid in this case, he said, was "noninfectious," and the removal of the cysts in surgery "definitely" eliminated the source of the child's disease. "The baby was getting better because whatever was causing the problem was removed."

BROWN: That's your interpretation. Suppose this baby—

BADEN: That's the heart of the matter.

Q: Suppose this baby had an infection and died of peritonitis? Wouldn't that change your entire view of this case?

A: Of course it would.

Q: All right.

A: But she didn't have an infection. She didn't have—

Q: That's what you say.

Ever since the defense toxicologist, Frederic Rieders, had reported that curare was destroyed by embalming fluid, Brown had maintained that any curare discovered in the tissues of the five Riverdell bodies had gotten there after exhumation. But whereas Dr. Rieders—who had himself found curare in a sample of Nancy Savino's liver by means of mass spectrometry—didn't speculate on how the drug could have gotten into the tissues following disinterment, Brown did.

The defense attorney told Judge Arnold that the presence of curare in any of the bodies "can only be explained by outright fraud or possibly gross negligence." Brown demanded a hearing—before Moses offered any toxicological evidence—to determine whether curare could survive in embalmed and buried tissues over ten years, and whether the state's tests, chiefly radioimmunoassay (RIA) and high-pressure liquid chromatography (HPLC), could identify the drug even if it were stable under those conditions.

Here was a frontal assault on the state's case. Brown and Moses both knew that if the prosecution's curare results were thrown out, Judge Arnold would consider dismissing the indictment against Dr. Jascalevich. Moses told the judge that the test results were admissible because the RIA antibody-antigen test and HPLC were "standard methods, used widely throughout the field" in recent years. But if there were to be a hearing, she said, it should focus on the reliability of those tests, not on a "matter for the jury" like the stability of curare. "Any other conclusion would encourage the use of novel poisons to commit murder," she said, "and would be devastating to the cause of justice." Brown's charges of fraud or negligence, Moses added, "indicate the length to which the defendant will go to explain away the finding of curare in the liver of Nancy Savino" by his own toxicologist.

Judge Arnold granted a hearing, which yielded conflicting opinions between prosecution and defense experts on virtually all but two points: neither RIA, nor HPLC, nor any other test had been used before this case to trace curare in exhumed bodies; and scientific literature did not describe the stability of the curare molecule in embalmed tissue, whether fresh or decomposed. Citing higher court decisions, Judge Arnold held on June 20 that New Jersey law required two elements for the admissibility of scientific test results: that the tests be "proven to have a high degree of scientific reliability" and that they be administered by "qualified persons." In this case, he said, there was "no doubt" that the prosecution's tests were performed by "highly qualified" scientists. He also believed that the procedures used by the state's experts produced results that were "reasonably reliable for consideration by the jury." The results, he ruled, were admissible.

The curare results that Moses laid before the jury in succeeding weeks were mainly the product of a four-step "analytical system" settled upon by Richard Coumbis, New Jersey's chief toxicologist, and Leo Dal Cortivo, chief toxicologist of Suffolk County, New York. The two prosecution experts had agreed in 1977 to place their emphasis on a system that combined RIA and HPLC. Dr. Coumbis would obtain curare antibodies from the Roche Institute of Molecular Biology, and run the RIA tests in his own lab in Newark. Dr. Dal Cortivo would do the HPLC tests on a new liquid chromatograph in his Hauppauge, Long Island, lab. In HPLC, a substance is injected into the port of a stainless-steel column and, under the influence of chemically coated beads, is propelled through that column. Different compounds pass through the column at different speeds, and these "retention times" are recorded as peaks on a graph by an ultraviolet sensing device. In step one of the Coumbis-Dal Cortivo system, Dr. Coumbis did a "direct" RIA on the extract of a piece of tissue from one of the exhumed bodies; that tissue sample was consumed in the process. In step two, Dr. Dal Cortivo took another piece of tissue from the same body organ and, much as he had done in his thin-layer chromatography studies in 1976, removed thousands of acidic and basic compounds from the tissue sample. In step three, he subjected the remaining extract to HPLC, at a pressure of 800 to 900 pounds per square inch. If the recorder registered a peak consistent with the known "retention time" of curare, the toxicologist collected, in a beaker, the effluent leaving the column at that point. He further purified the effluent by separating out other molecules from what, presumably, was curare. This "eluate," which looked like plain water, was placed in a vial and coded numerically and turned over to Dr. Coumbis. For comparison purposes, Dr. Coumbis was given an eluate of "gunk," or effluent gathered from other peaks in the HPLC run. The New Jersey toxicologist was not told initially which vial contained the eluate that appeared to be curare. In step four, Dr. Coumbis performed RIA tests on the various eluates. All the "gunk" eluates showed negative by RIA, as they should have. If the "curare eluates" were positive by RIA, Dr. Coumbis and Dr. Dal Cortivo concluded with "reasonable scientific certainty" that curare was present in those tissue samples. Any single test that indicated curare—whether RIA or HPLC—was regarded as no more than "presumptive" evidence.

By this system, the toxicologists told the jury in late June and early July 1978, they had identified curare with "reasonable scientific certainty" in the liver tissue of Nancy Savino and Frank Biggs. They said they had also found curare by both HPLC and RIA in the kidney tissue of Carl Rohrbeck, but because the first step in their system had been left out with respect to the kidney, they preferred to use the terms "strong scientific evidence" or "reasonable scientific evidence" rather than "reasonable scientific certainty." In one step of the RIA testing, Dr. Coumbis said he found "presumptive" evidence of curare in Biggs's kidney and Rohrbeck's "liver area," while Rohrbeck's cartilage proved negative. Five RIA's on Nancy Savino's liver—performed on separate occasions in 1977—were positive for curare, as were two on her lung, two on her muscle, three on her urinary contents, and one on her eye, Dr. Coumbis testified.

Because of the poor quality and small quantity of specimens available, Dr. Dal Cortivo did no work on the badly decomposed body of Margaret Henderson. Although Dr. Coumbis said he obtained a positive RIA on a single run of Miss Henderson's spinal cord tissue, his findings on Miss Henderson were "inconclusive."

Neither Dr. Dal Cortivo nor Dr. Coumbis found curare in the body of Emma Arzt, although a positive RIA had been reported on the woman's liver in 1976 by Dr. Richard Matteo at Columbia University.

Dr. Dal Cortivo also testified that in the presence of a defense expert, he analyzed seven of the vials removed by Calissi from Dr. Jascalevich's locker number four on November 1, 1966. All, he said, were positive for curare.

To buttress the toxicologists' testimony, Moses called Dr. Sydney Spector, the Roche Institute pharmacologist who had helped create the antibody that would bind with the curare molecule in the RIA. Dr. Spector said the antibody possessed "a great deal of specificity . . . our studies indicated that if you modify that molecule slightly, the antibody rejected it; it did not find it." The pharmacologist also said that his experience was limited to the measurement of curare in body fluids such as blood and urine. He would insist on confirming the RIA result with another kind of test. And on cross-examination, Dr. Spector said that both HPLC and RIA were "very good presumptive evidence," but for conclusive identification, he would use mass spectrometry—the chemical "fingerprint" test.

Moses next called Dr. David P. Beggs of the Hewlett-Packard Company. Dr. Beggs said that in February and April 1976—soon after the state of New Jersey ordered a mass spectrometer from Hewlett-Packard —Dr. Coumbis came to him at the company's lab in Avondale, Pennsylvania, and asked him, as a courtesy, to test a number of tissue extracts by mass spectrometry. The witness described the mass spectrometer as "one of the most sensitive and specific analytical machines" used to "identify complete unknowns." Dr. Beggs said he eventually learned that the extracts were of tissues from the bodies of Nancy Savino, Frank Biggs, and Emma Arzt. With "reasonable scientific certainty," Dr. Beggs testified, he found curare in the liver of Nancy Savino. Her right elbow and lung indicated the possible presence of curare. Overall, the Biggs and Arzt specimens also suggested the presence of curare, but because of background "interferences" on the spectrum of peaks formed by the mass spectrometer, the drug could not be definitely identified. With regard to Biggs and Arzt, he said, "the results are not as definite as I would like, so I would need confirmatory tests." Dr. Beggs did not analyze tissues from Margaret Henderson or Carl Rohrbeck.

On cross-examination, Dr. Beggs conceded that the results he obtained on the Biggs and Arzt specimens could have come from any one of about twenty-five compounds related to curare. But he said he knew of no compound other than curare that would register on the mass spectrometer in the manner of Nancy Savino's liver specimen. Brown attacked Dr. Beggs for handling his analysis as "a business-related mercantile problem." The witness, Brown said, was "a chemist who works in industry and for industry"—a man who had no experience "in courts of law where a person's life is at stake." When Moses interjected that hospitals used mass spectrometers "all the time," applying the same standards as Dr. Beggs, Brown replied that "hospitals don't necessarily treat life and death, Judge."

MOSES: They don't? What else do they do, Judge?

BROWN: They treat for doctors' purposes so they can make money most of the time. That's what they treat for.

Dr. Dal Cortivo, on cross-examination, said that he ran a number of "controls" during his HPLC work, including fresh and "putrified" tissue. "There are no absolutes in science," the toxicologist told Brown on July 10. "You know that. But in my opinion, the probability of this being something other than curare is reasonably remote."

With Dr. Coumbis, Brown hammered away even harder on the subject of "controls" and on the quality of the RIA testing. Dr. Coumbis said that, to monitor his experiments, he had used water and water spiked with curare; tissues from two embalmed, but unburied, bodies; and tissues from two embalmed bodies that had been exhumed, one after 10 months in the ground and the other after four years. Yet Brown didn't let the toxicologist forget what he had said during the hearing that preceded the curare testimony—that this was a "unique" case and he didn't have "appropriate" controls for it. Dr. Coumbis explained that all he meant by the statement was that it was impossible to replicate the exact conditions of the bodies that had been buried for ten years, and he had to make do with what was "available." But Brown said that wasn't good enough; there were no "appropriate" controls, he kept repeating. "There is one Mr. Brown today," Dr. Coumbis finally rammed back. "There is no one like him present, and there is no one like him in the future. That's what I mean by unique."

"Well put!" said Moses, as the courtroom dissolved in laughter.

"My grandson," Brown scoffed, "might not agree with that."

14

On the afternoon of June 2, a few hours after Acting State Supreme Court Justice Harold Rothwax signed the subpoena for my notes and other materials, I was called to a meeting in Abe Rosenthal's office at *The Times*. Sydney Schanberg, the new metropolitan editor, and Peter Millones, an assistant managing editor, were joined by Gene Scheiman and James Goodale, the *Times*'s executive vice president for legal and financial affairs. Rosenthal, who was now the executive editor of the paper, was plainly troubled by more than the subpoena for my notes.

His concern focused on a U. S. Supreme Court decision two days earlier. In a case involving the Stanford University student newspaper, the Court had ruled 5 to 3 that police could make a surprise raid on a newsroom—or on the home or office of any innocent person—if they had a court-approved warrant to search for evidence of a crime by someone else. A subpoena, which could be contested in court before anything was seized from the newspaper or other innocent party, wasn't necessary. Rosenthal wasn't comforted by the Court's assurances that warrants had to have a reasonable basis and that newsrooms weren't being singled out. He took the Court's ruling as yet another judicial attack on the independence of the press, particularly on its ability to maintain confidential relationships with news sources.

Rosenthal had spent some twenty years as a reporter and fifteen years as an editor, and few things, he said, surprised him anymore. But he had not expected to see the day when the Supreme Court would sanction police raids on newspapers. Nor had he expected to see a judge permit so broad a subpoena as the one served on me; as far as Goodale knew, it was the most sweeping subpoena ever served on an

American reporter. Rosenthal recalled that a year or so earlier, *The Times* had reluctantly complied with a subpoena to turn over a photograph needed in a murder trial. The picture of a bullet hole in a wooden railing, which had been taken by a *Times* photographer, supposedly showed the angle at which the alleged slayer of a policeman was firing. *The Times* had the only copy of the picture. The prosecutor subpoenaed it, and a judge upheld the subpoena. But that subpoena, for a specific, key item that couldn't be obtained elsewhere and that did not implicate confidential sources, was very different from the indiscriminate subpoena in the Jascalevich case; the Jascalevich subpoena had to be fought as "a matter of principle." *The Times* couldn't serve as an adjunct to defense attorneys or prosecutors or judges, Rosenthal said. Until recently the paper would have advised its reporters not to take the stand even to authenticate or verify articles that had been published. "Well, we seem to have gotten into doing that," Rosenthal admitted, "but we've got to draw the line. We're not going to become part of the very judicial process that we're expected to cover. We have to make our position very clear. Especially in this climate."

Goodale turned to Scheiman and told him to file an appeal immediately, starting with the courts in New York.

I came away from that meeting more impressed than ever with Rosenthal. He had always had a remote quality about him and, after he became the top editor at *The Times,* he seemed all the more distant. More than a few reporters resented his ambition and his brooding nature, and of course, he held tremendous power over the assignments and careers of everyone in the newsroom. But I admired Rosenthal precisely because he was rarely satisfied, because he considered shoddy reporting a personal insult, and because of his devotion to *The Times.* He measured himself by the quality of this newspaper. And anything that impaired the ability of its reporters to gather legitimate news and present it to the public was anathema to him. His experience as a correspondent in communist Poland had taught him not only about the terror and cynicism in totalitarian societies; it had fortified his belief in the importance of a free and diverse press.

Of the American press he had few illusions; there were publications, shallow or strident or both, that he wouldn't read, much less work for. In the years since 1963, when he returned from abroad, he had seen the demise of a number of large-city newspapers and the dwindling of competition in many smaller communities. Many newspapers that remained economically viable weren't spending enough money to do their jobs right, and many, with the growth of television and newsweeklies, were cutting back on national and foreign news. But on the whole, Rosenthal felt, American newspapers and magazines, television and radio, were providing more vital information to more people than ever before; and the press, having withstood the anti-intellectual agitprop of the Nixon-Agnew Administration, was more iconoclastic.

In 1978 Rosenthal was alarmed that the most damaging attacks on the independence of the press were coming not from politicians or from people who, as he put it, simply "hate the dentist rather than the toothache" but from judges and lawyers, people who were traditionally wedded to the concept of a free and vigorous press. It was a sad turn of events, he thought, and a dangerous one. By "gagging" the press or parties to a trial, by sealing court records, or by closing pretrial court proceedings where the great majority of criminal indictments are disposed of, judges were increasingly influencing the content or timing of press reports about the criminal justice system. In effect, the bench and the bar were telling the press what not to print.

Conversely, by subpoenaing reporters in cases where they were neither plaintiffs nor defendants, lawyers and judges were attempting to force out information that the press chose with good reason to withhold, information often obtained in confidence, or already deemed inaccurate or unreliable. The Supreme Court, under Chief Justice Warren E. Burger, had substantially affirmed the right of the press to be free of "prior restraints"—injunctions against publishing information already in hand. The Court had also upheld the right of the press to refrain from printing what it didn't want to and to print, without fear of civil liability, information that had been made public in court records. Moreover, the Burger Court had invalidated two state laws that made it a crime for the press to print the name of a juvenile who had been arrested and to print secret information about alleged judicial misconduct.

But Hugo Black and William O. Douglas had retired, and in 1978 the press had few constant champions on the Court. William J. Brennan, Jr., and Thurgood Marshall were acutely sensitive to First Amendment issues, and Potter Stewart was especially sympathetic to the press. But the Court, at least to Rosenthal, lacked a strong center that was committed in legal and constitutional philosophy—as well as votes—to press freedom. Most of the justices, for example, took the view that the press had no greater right than the public at large to inspect prison conditions. Indeed, the Court held that neither the press *nor* the public had any First Amendment right of access to prisons or, more generally, any sources of information within the government's control. The Supreme Court had agreed to review a decision by New York state's highest court holding that pretrial hearings in criminal cases "are presumptively to be closed to the public" and the press when, in the judge's opinion, news reports would threaten the impaneling of an impartial jury; but Rosenthal had little hope that the Court would overturn this ruling. Nor was he optimistic about the Court's decision to review a federal ruling in New York that protected a reporter in a libel suit from being forced to reveal his "state of mind" —his thoughts and opinions and newsroom discussions during the preparation of a disputed story. The Supreme Court wouldn't have taken this case, Rosenthal reasoned, unless it intended to modify or reverse the lower court decision.

But no aspect of the new climate in the courts so disturbed Rosenthal, and many other journalists, as the proliferation of subpoenas on reporters. Until the 1960s prosecutors and defense attorneys seldom subpoenaed journalists to testify about stories they had covered, and reporters who felt ethically bound to protect confidential sources or information had little difficulty in doing so. In fact, it was not until 1958, in a defamation suit against the Columbia Broadcasting System by singer Judy Garland, that a journalist felt the need to argue in court that she had a First Amendment right to refuse to identify confidential sources. The journalist, *New York Herald Tribune* entertainment columnist Marie Torre, lost the argument in the U. S. Court of Appeals in New York and spent ten days in jail rather than disclose to Miss Garland the name of the CBS network executive who had allegedly criticized the singer. But the court's ruling—that freedom of the press "is not an absolute" and "must give place under the Constitution to a paramount public interest in the fair administration of justice"—hardly resolved the confidentiality issue. Miss Torre had to provide the name of her source, the Court said, because it "went to the heart" of Miss Garland's claim against CBS, and Miss Garland "had met with singular lack of success" in obtaining the name from CBS officials. Even so, the Court of Appeals recognized a reporter's First Amendment right to a confidential relationship with a source and observed that "we are not dealing here with the use of the judicial process to force a wholesale disclosure of a newspaper's confidential sources of news, nor with a case where the identity of the news source is of doubtful relevance or materiality." In those circumstances, the First Amendment argument might prevail, implied Judge Potter Stewart, who wrote the Torre opinion shortly before his elevation to the U. S. Supreme Court.

In the decade following the Torre case, about a dozen subpoenas were served on journalists. Reporters who protested these subpoenas on First Amendment grounds generally fared no better than Marie Torre and, like her, they were unsuccessful in getting the Supreme Court to review their cases. Then the dam broke. With the country split over the Vietnam War, with the growing militancy of blacks and other minorities, with turmoil on the campuses and in the streets, many lawyers and government officials came to view the press as a repository of information that could be useful in court. Between 1968 and 1970, an estimated 150 subpoenas were issued for testimony and for unpublished materials, often including unused television "outtakes" and confidential notes about the activities of dissidents. Then in 1972 the Supreme Court, for the first time, took up the matter of a reporter's "testimonial privilege" under the First Amendment.

Actually, the Court reviewed several cases together. One involved Earl Caldwell, a reporter for *The New York Times*. He was subpoenaed before a federal grand jury in San Francisco in 1970 to testify about his conversations with members of the Black Panther Party, which he was covering. (Originally, the government subpoenaed Caldwell's notes as well, but after Caldwell and *The Times* objected, that demand was dropped.) Moving to quash the subpoena, Caldwell argued that journalists had a "qualified" privilege under the First Amendment to protect unpublished information and sources unless the government could meet a three-part test: that the information was demonstrably relevant to a clearly defined inquiry; that the inquiry was likely to turn up material information; and that the information was unobtainable by means "less destructive" of press freedom. (The reporter's argument was not unlike Judge Stewart's opinion in the Torre case twelve years earlier). The District Court in San Francisco accepted much of Caldwell's argument; while Caldwell had to appear before the grand jury, he had a First Amendment privilege not to reveal information given to him unless it was for publication and not to disclose confidential information or sources until the government showed a "compelling and overriding national interest . . . which cannot be served by alternative means."

The Times was satisfied by this landmark ruling, but Caldwell wasn't. Appealing the decision, he said that—except for what he had already printed—he had no information that wasn't now protected by the District Court order. But his mere appearance at a secret grand jury session, he argued, would cause the Black Panthers to distrust and avoid him and would ultimately impede the flow of news to the public. The grand jury would gain nothing from his appearance, he said, but he would lose his sources. The U. S. Court of Appeals in California agreed with Caldwell and excused him from even appearing before the grand jury until the government showed a "compelling need" for his presence. To destroy Caldwell's capacity as news gatherer in exchange for a "barren performance" before the grand jury "hardly makes sense," the Court of Appeals said. But the government appealed to the Supreme Court.

The other cases that the Supreme Court consolidated with Caldwell's were on appeal by journalists. One case concerned Paul Pappas. A television reporter at a time of disturbances in New Bedford, Massachusetts, in 1970, Pappas was admitted to Black Panther headquarters on condition that he would not reveal what he saw or heard except for an anticipated police raid. The raid didn't occur, but Pappas was later called before a state grand jury. He answered questions about what he had observed outside Panther headquarters but, invoking the First Amendment and the new Caldwell decision in California, refused to disclose what he had observed inside. Massachusetts' highest state court ruled against him, saying "there exists no constitutional newsman's privilege, either qualified or absolute, to refuse to appear and testify before a court or grand jury."

The third case considered by the Supreme Court involved Paul Branzburg, a reporter for the *Louisville Courier-Journal.* In 1969 and in early 1971, Branzburg used confidential sources to write stories about illicit drug use in Kentucky. Summoned before state grand juries, he refused to breach any confidences, including the names of persons he had seen—and whose hands had been photographed—making hashish. Branzburg claimed protection under the First Amendment and Kentucky's shield law for reporters. And like Pappas, he cited the Court of Appeals ruling in Caldwell's case as a basis for quashing the subpoena against him. Kentucky's highest state court rejected Branzburg's argument and remarked that the Caldwell decision was "a drastic departure from the generally recognized rule that the sources of information of a newspaper reporter are not privileged under the First Amendment." Kentucky's shield law protected Branzburg from having to disclose confidential sources, the court said, but not if he personally observed illegal drug use or other criminal acts.

On June 29, 1972, the U. S. Supreme Court ruled against the reporters, 5 to 4.

In his opinion for the Court, Justice Byron R. White said "the issue in these cases is whether requiring newsmen to appear and testify before state or federal grand juries abridges the freedom of speech and press guaranteed by the First Amendment. We hold that it does not . . . We do not question the significance of free speech, press, or assembly to the country's welfare. Nor is it suggested that news gathering does not qualify for First Amendment protection . . . [But] it is clear that the First Amendment does not invalidate every incidental burdening of the press that may result from the enforcement of civil or criminal statutes of general applicability." In particular, Justice White continued, reporters had no First Amendment right to withhold information about crimes they had witnessed.

The press, the justice observed, had flourished since the founding of the country without constitutional or common law protection for news sources, and "the evidence fails to demonstrate" that without such protection now, "there would be a significant constriction of the flow of news to the public." Admittedly, he wrote, the reporters were seeking a qualified, not an absolute, testimonial privilege. But the administration of even a limited privilege "would present practical and conceptual difficulties of a high order," including the defining of newsmen, Justice White contended. Of course, the justice noted, Congress or the states were free to enact shield laws for reporters and "we are powerless to bar state courts from responding in their own way and construing their own constitutions as to recognize a newsman's privilege, either qualified or absolute."

Chief Justice Burger and Justices Harry A. Blackmun and William H. Rehnquist joined, without separate comment, in Justice White's opinion.

Justice Stewart, writing for himself and Justices Marshall and Brennan, dissented. He accused the Court of inviting law enforcement officials "to undermine the historic independence of the press by attempting to annex the journalistic profession as an investigative arm of government." The right to publish, Justice Stewart wrote, was central to the First Amendment and basic to the existence of a constitutional democracy. But no less important was a right of "some dimensions . . . to gather news." And that right, in turn, implied "a right to a confidential relationship between a reporter and his source."

"It is obvious that informants are necessary to the news-gathering process as we know it today. It is equally obvious that the promise of confidentiality may be a necessary prerequisite to a productive relationship between a newsman and his informants." Justice Stewart warned that "an unbridled subpoena power—the absence of a constitutional right protecting, in *any* way, a confidential relationship from compulsory process—will either deter sources from divulging information or deter reporters from gathering and publishing information . . . especially in sensitive areas involving government officials, financial affairs, political figures, dissidents, or minority groups that require in-depth, investigative reporting." The justice pointed out that the "long-standing rule making every person's evidence available to the grand jury is not absolute," and was limited by constitutional rights against self-incrimination and illegal searches and seizures, as well as by testimonial privileges involving such relationships as husband and wife, lawyer and client, doctor and patient, and priest and penitent. A reporter's "constitutional right to a confidential relationship with his source" was surely as important as these other rights and privileges, Justice Stewart wrote, because it "functions to insure nothing less than democratic decision making through the free flow of information to the public." The problem, the justice concluded—much as he had in the Torre case in 1958—was to strike a proper balance between the rights of the press and the public interest in the efficient administration of justice.

"No doubt the courts would be required to make some delicate judgments in working out this accommodation," Stewart observed. "But that, after all, is the function of courts of law. Better such judgments, however difficult, than the simplistic and stultifying absolutism adopted by the Court in denying any force to the First Amendment in these cases."

An even stronger dissent was registered by Justice Douglas, who maintained that a reporter enjoyed complete immunity from appearing or testifying before a grand jury. "The press has a preferred position in our constitutional scheme, not to enable it to make money, not to set newsmen apart as a favored class, but to bring fulfillment to the public's right to know," Justice Douglas wrote. The role of the press was to facilitate effective self-government by exploring events, telling the people "what is going on," and exposing "the harmful as well as the good influences at work. There is no higher function performed under our constitutional regime." But if the press cannot guard its sources when necessary, "if what the Court sanctions today becomes settled law," the justice warned, "then the reporter's main function in American society will be to pass on to the public the press releases the various departments of government issue," and the public will be the victims. Justice Douglas also derided the balancing approach advocated by some of his brethren on the Court—and by *The Times.* "Sooner or later," he wrote, "any test which provides less than blanket protection . . . will be twisted and relaxed so as to provide no protection at all."

Justice Lewis F. Powell, Jr., broke the 4 to 4 deadlock on the Court, giving the crucial fifth vote to Justice White. But Justice Powell wrote a brief concurring opinion "to emphasize what seems to me to be the limited nature of the Court's holding. The Court does not hold that newsmen, subpoenaed to testify before a grand jury, are without constitutional rights with respect to the gathering of news or in safeguarding their sources . . . Indeed, if the newsman is called upon to give information bearing only a remote and tenuous relationship to the subject of the investigation, or if he has some other reason to believe that his testimony implicates confidential source relationships without a legitimate need of law enforcement, he will have access to the court on a motion to quash, and an appropriate protective order may be entered. The asserted claim to privilege should be judged on its facts by the striking of a proper balance between freedom of the press and the obligation of all citizens to give relevant testimony with respect to criminal conduct," the justice wrote. And that balance should be determined on a case-by-case basis. "In short, the courts will be available to newsmen under circumstances where legitimate First Amendment interests require protection."

The *Branzburg* vs. *Hayes* decision—the only time the Supreme Court has ruled on a reporter's testimonial privilege—was so narrowly decided that Justice Stewart suggested the vote was really "4½ to 4½." Many press lawyers agreed with Justice Stewart's assessment in 1972 that Justice Powell's opinion gave some hope for reporters in the future. The contest wasn't over; if anything, the issue of confidentiality had been thrown back to the lower courts where, according to Justice Powell, each case should be decided on its own merits.

And there were plenty of cases. A tally by the Reporters Committee for Freedom of the Press, a Washington-based research and legal-aid group, showed about 500 subpoenas on journalists between 1970 and 1976, with the number increasing. Many of those subpoenas were "washed out" by informal compromises or the dropping of government investigations. In some instances the subpoenas simply weren't pursued; in others, the reporter chose to testify. But in those cases where the subpoenas were actively opposed, reporters did much better than might have been expected from Justice White's opinion in Branzburg. Citing Justice Powell's opinion and even some of the limiting language of Justice White's, and often applying the elements of Justice Stewart's test, judges frequently recognized a qualified First Amendment privilege of reporters to refuse to disclose confidential sources and information. This was particularly true in civil cases where reporters weren't party to the litigation, and in criminal cases where trial (rather than grand jury) appearances were at issue. Criminal defendants who asserted a Sixth Amendment right to command evidence in their favor had a notably lower rate of success than prosecutors in obtaining court orders for disclosure by journalists.

Another outcome of the Branzburg decision was a movement to increase statutory protection for reporters. An effort to pass a federal shield law in 1973 floundered when the journalistic profession couldn't agree on its terms or its value. Some members of the press thought that any law, like any "balancing" test, would only subvert the First Amendment. But in the aftermath of Justice White's reference to shield laws, seven more states enacted such measures, bringing the total to twenty-six; and ten states—including New Jersey—substantially strengthened existing statutes. Some of these laws provided a qualified privilege for reporters to withhold sources or information from courts and state agencies; others, like the law in New Jersey, were intended to provide virtually absolute protection. But with state courts often construing these laws narrowly, the more effective shield proved to be the Powell-Stewart formulation of the First Amendment. Not that that shield was impenetrable. Between 1972 and 1978, some forty reporters were held in contempt of court, and more than a dozen were jailed for refusing to reveal confidences. The Supreme Court declined to hear any appeals from these reporters.

Abe Rosenthal watched these developments after Branzburg and worried. Whatever his regrets regarding some of Nixon's appointees to the Supreme Court, and whatever his disagreements with individual lower-court judges, he believed in the courts as an institution and as an instrument of democracy. But a free press was another such instrument, he felt, and no less critical. And when its independence was challenged—as it was being challenged anew by the subpoena in the Jascalevich case—it had to be defended. Once, when U. S. Circuit Court Judge Harold R. Medina wrote an article urging the press to "fight like tigers" for its rights, Rosenthal sent him a one-line note. "I love you," it said.

After the meeting in Rosenthal's office on June 2, 1978, I went up to the *Times*'s legal department and got copies of the Supreme Court's Branzburg decision and the Court's new decision allowing surprise police raids of newsrooms. As I was leaving the *Times* building I ran into Lesley Oelsner, a reporter who had covered the Supreme Court, and she cracked a joke about the lack of shower facilities in jails. But unlike a few months back, when Artie Gelb gave me the book *I Chose Prison,* I wasn't laughing now. On my way home that evening, I stopped by a supermarket and loaded up with empty cardboard boxes. After dinner, I filled the cartons with my notes and documents from the Riverdell Hospital story and arranged to have them moved from my apartment and stored in places where they couldn't be traced.

By midnight I was in bed with a beer and the *Stanford Daily* and Branzburg decisions. Rereading Branzburg reminded me that neither Earl Caldwell (who was no longer working for *The Times*) nor Paul Pappas had testified after the Court's ruling; the grand juries in their cases had been dismissed by the summer of 1972. Paul Branzburg, who had left Louisville for a job with a Detroit newspaper, was sought by Kentucky authorities, but the governor of Michigan refused to extradite him. So he didn't testify either.

I didn't know Paul Branzburg, but I could empathize with him. During 1973 and 1974, when I was covering the "drug beat" for *The Times,* I had interviewed any number of people who were illegally

using or pushing drugs—much as Branzburg had done in Kentucky. I
didn't have these meetings because I was a citizen, and I certainly
didn't have them for the purpose of helping the police nab a few drug
dealers; I couldn't have had them at all under that condition. I had
these meetings because I was a reporter who was trying to understand
and write intelligently about a subject of public concern. I didn't think
I could do that by confining myself to the views of officialdom, within
or outside the government, and neither did *The Times*. It was my job
to enlarge, not constrain, public knowledge. It was my job to draw on
as many sources as possible, to evaluate them *all* with care, to select
material, and to lay it before the public. The final judgment was the
reader's.

I couldn't agree now with Justice White's opinion in Branzburg
anymore than when I first read it. Every reporter recognized an obligation to provide legal evidence in matters that were not related to his
news gathering. It wasn't the reporter who was special; it was the work
that he did on behalf of the public—the editorial process. Justice
Stewart put it very well when dissenting in the *Stanford Daily* case:
"Perhaps as a matter of abstract policy, a newspaper office should receive no more protection from unannounced police searches than, say,
the office of a doctor or the office of a bank. But we are here to uphold a
Constitution. And our Constitution does not protect the practice of
medicine or the business of banking from all abridgement by government. It does explicitly protect the freedom of the press." Justice White
was right in saying, in Branzburg, that the American press had
flourished for two centuries without claiming constitutional protection
for news sources. But he downplayed the fact that until recently, reporters had had little problem protecting sources. The justice was also
right in saying that only a small percentage of news sources were
implicated in crime. But he was wrong in predicting that relatively few
journalists would be directly affected by the Branzburg decision. The
decision was now being applied as much in the context of civil and
criminal trials as in the context of grand jury investigations, even where
reporters had not witnessed crimes.

In my situation, Branzburg was regularly cited by Ray Brown, and
Judge Arnold took Justice White's opinion as gospel. But I wanted
some of the "proper balancing" of interests of which Justices Powell
and Stewart had written. Maybe, at a hearing, Brown could meet the
standards of relevance, exhaustion of alternate means, and "compelling
and overriding interest" that Justice Stewart had urged, and that other
courts had adopted. Maybe, in the end, I would be required to turn
over some unpublished materials. But surely that wouldn't entail my

surrendering an entire file, and I hoped it would avert a clash over the identity of confidential sources.

The New York appellate courts ruled that Justice Rothwax's order, which ran against *The Times* as well as me, was not appealable in New York and that any motion to quash the subpoena from Dr. Jascalevich had to be made in the state where the subpoena originated. In late June, Gene Scheiman went out to Hackensack and met with Brown, Moses, and the judge in Judge Arnold's chambers. At first Brown objected to Moses's presence; then he wouldn't sit on the same couch with her. Gene took the seat next to the prosecutor and, after outlining his objections to the subpoena, asked Brown what he was looking for and whether it was possible to narrow the scope of his demand. "I will not limit anything," Brown replied. "I will not limit anything. I want to see it all."

On June 22, Scheiman formally moved to kill the subpoena. The brief he filed presented substantially the same arguments that he had advanced before Justice Rothwax: this "wholesale disclosure" violated my constitutional and statutory rights as a reporter; Brown hadn't made a showing of "materiality, relevance, and necessity" for my notes and documents, and hadn't shown that my information pertained to the "core" issue in the case or wasn't available elsewhere. The subpoena had been "improvidently granted," Scheiman asserted, and could be "easily disposed of" because it was too sweeping. I supplied an affidavit stating that my notes included "confidential materials and sources." Brown countered, in his brief, by saying that I was "a central figure in the processes that led to Dr. Jascalevich's indictment" and that during my inquiry into the Riverdell affair, I had interviewed many people who later testified at the Jascalevich trial. "To suggest that such information is not material is an absurdity," Brown said. Under Branzburg and other decisions that conformed to Justice White's opinion, I had no right to withhold any of my file, he continued. And while the New Jersey shield law said that I didn't have to provide any confidential information "to any court," that statute had to bow to Dr. Jascalevich's Sixth Amendment constitutional guarantee to a fair trial.

On June 30, 1978, Judge Arnold denied the motion to kill the subpoena, saying that he would not rule on the key issues raised by *The Times* and me until he could examine, "in camera" (in private), all the items covered by the subpoena. Only then could we have a hearing. "This Court is being asked to make a decision in a vacuum," the judge said. "When the [notes and documents] are produced . . . this Court may well decide to quash the subpoena. When the notes are produced, this Court will give the applicants a full hearing as to the materiality of the subpoena, its scope and contents" and "will also decide if the items are barred by the shield law" or for any other reason. Come up with the file by July 3, Judge Arnold said, or face contempt charges.

Scheiman quickly turned to the Appellate Division of the New Jersey Superior Court, arguing that Judge Arnold had ample authority to kill such an "exploratory type" of subpoena without seeing the file and that by viewing it prior to any kind of hearing on the basic issues, the judge was invading the very rights that were protected. "Mr. Farber and *The New York Times* do not contend that they are the sole and exclusive judge of what is relevant and what is privileged," Scheiman told the Appellate Division. "This, of course, becomes at an appropriate time the province of the Court." But the procedure adopted by Judge Arnold, he said, would totally emasculate the statutory and constitutional newspaperman's privileges.

Both the Appellate Division and the New Jersey Supreme Court declined to hear our appeal. And on July 11, Scheiman took the matter to the U. S. Supreme Court, where it landed in the lap of Justice White. Justice White observed that motions to quash subpoenas are not usually appealable in the federal courts, and he couldn't predict "with confidence" that the Court would now vote to take an appeal. "The applicants insist that as a constitutional matter, the rule must be different where . . . the subpoena runs against a reporter and the press, and that more basis for enforcing the subpoena must be shown than appears in the record. There is no present authority in this Court that a newsman need not produce documents material to the prosecution or defense of a criminal case," the justice went on, citing the Branzburg decision, "or that the obligation to obey an otherwise valid subpoena served on a newsman is conditioned upon the showing of special circumstances. But if the Court is to address the issue . . . it appears to me that it would prefer to do so at a later stage in these proceedings." Justice White refused to delay Judge Arnold's order, and the next day Justice Marshall would decline as well. "There are, of course, important and unresolved questions regarding the obligation of a newsperson to divulge confidential files and other material sought by the prosecution or defense in connection with criminal proceedings," Justice Marshall said. "It may well be, moreover, that forced disclosure of these materials, even to a judge for in-camera inspection, will have a deleterious effect on the ability of the news media effectively to gather information in the public interest, as is alleged by applicants." But since there was an "ongoing criminal trial" and no contempt citations had as yet been made, the justice said, this was not the time for the Supreme Court to consider intervening.

I was talking to Rosenthal in his office when Warren Hoge, the deputy metropolitan editor, popped in with a wire-service dispatch from Washington and reported that Justice Marshall had just turned us down. "So what else is new?" Rosenthal sighed. Hoge left as Rosenthal took a call from the *Times*'s Washington bureau. Rosenthal hadn't expected any relief from the Supreme Court—neither had Scheiman nor I—but now that the *Times*'s editor was hearing the bad news from Washington, he looked more distressed than I had ever seen him. He listened in silence, and hung up.

"Well, Myron, it seems that we'll never get a hearing on this thing unless you're held in contempt, or we're held in contempt, or somebody is. Anyway, that's it, and I don't want you to think you've got to become a martyr. *The Times* will support you, whatever you want to do, but you have to make your own decision now. Nobody here is going to tell you that you have to go to jail."

"That's okay, Abe," I said after a moment. "I want to see this through."

Rosenthal reached for some water as Jim Goodale, the *Times*'s counsel, came in. "Jim," he shouted from the kitchenette next to his office, "we're going all the way. We've been saying all these things in these confidentiality cases, and we've been making out a position, and we've got to show that we mean it. What's our next move?" Goodale grinned at me, and at the white chalk stripes running down his own suit. "Are you sure you're the one who ought to go in?" he said. "I'm the one who's ready."

I stepped out of Rosenthal's office to call my wife and overheard some editors asking the brand of tobacco I smoked. They were getting ready, too. There was no answer at home.

A contempt hearing was held two days later, on July 14, before Judge Trautwein in Hackensack. Scheiman was arguing along with everything else that I had been improperly served with the subpoena for notes; he had recommended that I not attend the hearing. But Judge Trautwein was incensed by my absence. "It seems to me," he scolded Scheiman, "that a responsible reporter in a case of this type, with a man's life and liberty at stake, would not choose to hide behind the technical niceties of legal service of process . . . the Court cannot help but feel that *The New York Times* is hiding behind the skirts of Myron Farber, and those skirts are becoming more and more soiled day by day." Before adjourning the hearing, the judge issued a bench warrant for my arrest. That night someone taped my picture to a wall in the *Times*'s newsroom. *"Wanted,"* read the handwritten caption.

On July 18, Justice Rothwax in Manhattan ordered me to appear in Hackensack—"I assume you know where that is," he said. Scheiman and I drove over, and during brief proceedings before Judge Arnold and Judge James I. Toscano, bail was set at $10,000 to insure my return for the next part of Judge Trautwein's contempt hearing. At the annex to the Bergen County Jail, I was placed in a locked, yellow-wire cage with two other men. One of the men, who might have been in his midfifties and who was dressed in rough workpants and a loose shirt, was mumbling to himself. He had been arrested for drunken driving and was going to be released on $250 bail, if he could raise it. He had already put together $106 and was sure that his sister would supply the rest. His main problem seemed to be getting his sister to the jail, and I listened when he was allowed to call her on the pay phone. "The jail . . . the jail," he kept saying. "Everybody knows where it is . . . it's the jail." But his sister didn't know where the jail was, and in his exasperation he dispatched her to the wrong address.

The other man being booked with me, a New Yorker, wore a stylish blue blazer and white ducks, and appeared to be in his late forties. When his chance came to use the phone, he pleaded with his mother for understanding.

"Mother, now don't get too excited. I'm in jail. Mother, it was the inevitable end. I knew it. There was a warrant out, and I was walking down Main Street in Hackensack . . . No, not now, Mother, I can't. I'm in jail. I'll come to see you as soon as I get out. O.K., dear? . . . O.K. Now, please, Mother, don't worry. Give my regards to Broadway."

The Times posted my $10,000 bail within an hour, and after being fingerprinted and photographed, I was released.

The next day, Judge Trautwein reconvened the contempt hearing, and he went after Scheiman again. Gene was in Washington that morning, with the judge's permission, and Faith Wender was substituting for him. Suddenly Judge Trautwein indicated that he would no longer allow Scheiman to represent me and *The Times* in his court—he saw a potential "conflict of interest" with Gene representing "both clients." Faith asked the judge to postpone any action until Scheiman's return in the afternoon, and eventually the judge dropped the matter altogether. But first he lectured the twenty-six-year-old Wender. "My dear girl," he said, "I want you to remember this: Your firm is in this courthouse through the courtesy of the Court . . . We have many able-bodied, well-educated, competent New Jersey attorneys." Faith, an ardent feminist, cringed at being called a girl. I was squirming, too.

The hearing wound up on July 24, and there wasn't an empty seat in the courtroom. Among the spectators, I noticed, was Dr. Jascalevich, whose trial had been recessed for the day. Judge Trautwein seemed so eager to sentence *The Times* and me that he began doing so before finding us guilty. Correcting himself—"I am putting the cart before the horse"—he rendered the verdicts and asked me whether I had anything to say.

"Are you all right?" Gene whispered, putting his hand on my arm.

"I'm fine," I said a little nervously, rising and taking from my pocket a statement I had drawn up:

I would like to explain to the Court, and to the public, why I am refusing to surrender my reporter's file on the case of Dr. Mario E. Jascalevich. As serious as this matter is, and as highly technical as are the legal arguments, my position is not all that complicated. What is at issue here is not Dr. Jascalevich's right to a fair trial; he has access to the same people that I interviewed, and more. Nor is the issue my "right" to place myself above or outside the law. I have no such right, and I seek none. The issue, I believe, is the right of the public to be informed through its press, in accordance with the First Amendment of the United States Constitution.

I have been a newspaper reporter for fifteen years, twelve of them with *The New York Times*. Like anyone who has been a journalist that long, I have embraced certain standards. They are accuracy, fairness, impartiality, thoroughness. I have tried to live up to those standards.

In 1975, having become an "investigative" reporter at *The Times*, I was asked to look into a case of thirteen allegedly suspicious deaths at a New Jersey hospital a decade earlier. In this connection, I spoke to many people, and I sought to interview Dr. Jascalevich. He did not respond to my repeated requests for an interview. In early 1976, I began writing stories about the case. By then, the deaths were being independently investigated by the Bergen County prosecutor, and the prosecutor exhumed five of the thirteen bodies. The case was presented to a grand jury, and subsequently a five-count murder indictment was handed up. I was not called as a witness by the grand jury, and my notes, which have never been shown to anyone, were not subpoenaed. I have never met or spoken with the grand jurors, just as I have had no contact with the petit jurors who are now sitting. Indeed, having been listed as a witness by the defense, I was barred from attending the trial or covering it as a reporter. In May, I was called to testify at the trial, and I appeared. I answered some questions and declined to answer others that would reveal confidential sources or information given to me in confidence.

Some weeks ago, in enforcing a defense subpoena, the trial court ordered me to turn over to it all my notes, documents, and other materials relating to the case. In effect, the order commands me to violate confidences that

I received in my effort to learn, and report, the truth about this case. And this I cannot do. I gave my word that I would respect these confidences, and I gave it in what I believe to be the public interest. I am the custodian of that word today as yesterday.

I deeply appreciate how much our civilization, and civility, depends on order and the rule of law. I am not a fanatic or an absolutist, and like all men who daily submit to reason, I have been torn by doubt on many matters. But not on this matter. I believe the First Amendment means what it says about freedom of the press and that it was annexed to the Constitution with full knowledge that an unfettered but responsible press was crucial to our nation. The benefit was to the public, not to the press. I did not join my profession to cloak myself in the First Amendment or to flaunt it. Few journalists do. But I cannot cast aside my obligations as a reporter simply because they are being contested. The inevitable result of my compliance with this order would be my conversion into an investigative agent for the parties to this case. This is not what Madison and his contemporaries had in mind for the press, nor is it what the legislatures of New Jersey, New York, and other states intended when they passed statutes protecting newsmen's confidential materials. If I give up my file, I will have undermined my professional integrity and diminished the credibility of my colleagues. And, most important, I will have given notice that the nation's premier newspaper is no longer available to those men and women who would seek it out—or would respond to it—to talk freely and without fear.

A reporter has only so many tools with which to work. His strength lies in his readiness and ability to reach out and listen to people on every side of an issue, people with greatly varying views of "the truth" or the facts. But, sometimes, people who have done no wrong yet who have information that is useful to a rounded understanding of an issue are reluctant to speak out. They may be afraid of losing their jobs, or incurring the displeasure of a governmental agency, or drawing unaccustomed attention to themselves or to their families. They may agree to provide information only on a confidential basis. And if I, as a journalist, accept information on those terms, I cannot disavow that agreement later. Not without destroying my integrity. If I was willing to permit any devaluation of my ethical currency, I would soon find that my worth had eroded completely. And I could not work that way.

Your Honor, Dr. Jascalevich says that the material in my possession is "critical" to his defense. But he is mistaken. The deaths for which he is charged occurred in 1965 and 1966, and, as the Court well knows, I have no first-hand knowledge of them. Nor have I seen the bodies that were exhumed for the tissues that were tested for curare. There is nothing in my notes that would establish the defendant's guilt or innocence for the trial court, and there is certainly nothing that would lend credence to his theory that he is being framed. For more than twenty-one weeks, Your Honor, witnesses have trooped across the courtroom to tell, under oath, what they know about the lives and deaths of Nancy Savino and the others. No one is in hiding. And I respectfully submit that it is to their testimony, and to the testimony of others to come, that the Court must look to find the truth.

Thank you, Your Honor.

Judge Trautwein, a big man who looked even more imposing in his black robes, leaned over the bench: "Thank you, Mr. Farber. I have only one comment to make to you. What you have to say has considerable merit . . . but it seems to me that somewhere within the whole fabric of constitutional protection and statutory newsman's privilege, there has to be some person or body or tribunal that can say, 'Mr. Farber, we don't suspect your integrity at all, but let's take a little peek . . . to see whether or not what you say is the truth . . . We have a criminal trial that has progressed for over four and a half months. As I have said time and time again, this is holding it up. If Mr. Brown isn't entitled to [the notes] so be it, let's get it over with. If he is, it seems to me it would be a grave injustice to go on with this trial depriving the defense of something they think they need . . ."

Scheiman was on his feet. "Your Honor, may I briefly respond . . . *The Times* has not said nor has Mr. Farber said that at no time in the future [a] court may look at any documents . . . We have simply asked that preliminary rulings be given as to overbreadth, indeed to avoid the constitutional confrontation with which we are now faced, and I would ask the Court to consider that in any imposition of sentence."

The Times was fined $100,000 as a criminal penalty and, as a civil or "coercive" penalty, an additional $5,000 each day until it complied with Judge Arnold's order. I was fined $2,000 and sentenced to the county jail until I complied with the order. I was then to serve an additional six months as a criminal penalty.

The next thing I knew, Ray Brown was objecting, as a "matter of conscience," to my being imprisoned, and Judge Trautwein was waving him off. "I am not asking your advice on whether to give him a sentence." I looked quizzically to Gene, and out of the corner of my eye, I saw a uniformed guard coming at me with handcuffs.

15

Testimony in the Jascalevich trial had continued during the struggle over my notes, and by mid-July Moses had only two witnesses left: Francis F. Foldes, an anesthesiologist who had studied curare for many years, and Dr. Baden, who was to make his second appearance on the stand. Brown argued that he needed my notes to attack Dr. Baden's credibility on cross-examination and to present the defense case; if the notes weren't produced, he wanted Judge Arnold to dismiss the indictment against Dr. Jascalevich. The judge reserved decision on the request but he warned that if the trial went on much longer and the jury dipped below the legal minimum of twelve members, a mistrial might well result. A second juror had been excused in June, leaving the panel at sixteen, and "if some of these jurors get sick," the judge warned Moses and Brown, "we will be running into all kinds of difficult problems. Now, one boy is scheduled to go to college in August, and I'm going to let him go . . . And there are going to be other problems."

Actually, the problems had already started. The jurors had expected to sit for no more than three months; when that estimate proved unrealistic, Judge Arnold had indicated that the trial would be over in July. A number of the jurors who worked were suffering financially from the length of the trial—the jurors were being paid five dollars for each day they sat, plus two cents a mile for travel expenses, and that hardly covered their morning coffee and buns and their lunches. Employers were not required by New Jersey law to hold the jobs of workers who were selected for jury duty and, as early as May, Judge Arnold had to assuage disgruntled bosses. "Tough luck," one of the jurors sighed when the judge told him that his employer had promised to be patient. Nor were some jurors happy about postponing summer vacation plans. One woman had saved up for years for a visit to Hawaii, and she recovered her deposit on the trip only after Judge Arnold intervened. Frustrating, too, was the amount of time the jurors spent, not in the courtroom listening to testimony, but in the cramped jury room off the judge's chambers. Whenever Judge Arnold felt the jury shouldn't hear something, which was often, the panel was dispatched to its headquarters, to play pinochle or Scrabble, to pitch pennies, to read, to toss Teflon balls at a board, or to pick cabins on a diagram of the *Titanic* that one of the jurors (who also baked cheesecakes for fellow jurors' birthdays) had pinned to a wall. In court the jury was generally attentive. Periodically, though, a panelist would have to be nudged back from slumber.

Judge Arnold also appeared to nod off from time to time, much as he had done at the outset of the trial. And as then, he would lose the thread of testimony. On one occasion, Moses and Brown discussed with the judge the reluctance of a witness to fly up from Florida; she wanted her husband to drive her to New Jersey. But three days later, when the Floridian's name arose again, Judge Arnold asked whether she was alive. On another occasion, the judge sustained an objection because the witness on the stand mentioned the name of a nurse who, according to the judge, hadn't testified yet. But the nurse, as Brown and Moses were quick to remind the judge, had already appeared. "She has?" the judge asked. After another witness testified at length about Frank Biggs's operation at Riverdell, the judge interrupted: "I just want to ask one question. Was this on Mr. Frank Biggs this occurred?" And when Dr. Baden, in the fourth month of the trial, reviewed Biggs's death and testified that the patient couldn't have died of a "vasovagal reflex," Judge Arnold wanted to know "what chart is that, Arzt?"

BADEN: No, Biggs.

MOSES: Biggs.

BROWN: Biggs.

As late as June, the judge was still calling Moses "Mrs. Brown."

"Moses, Moses," the prosecutor cried on June 9, throwing up her arms in exasperation.

BROWN: Thank God, Judge.

MOSES: Goes both ways, Your Honor. Both ways. The name is Moses, Judge.

Another aspect of the trial that hadn't changed was Brown's pummeling of Moses. The defense attorney, a man of extraordinary stamina who kept in shape by jogging afternoons in a Hackensack park, seldom let up on his adversary, who was more self-assured and a dozen pounds lighter than in February. With her "third-year law school tricks" and her "obvious ineptitude," the prosecutor was "absolutely ridiculous," Brown would sneer in court. "Common sense goes out the window when she opens her mouth . . ."; Moses was "a professional liar . . . the lowest form of life I've seen in a courtroom," Brown said. She ought to resign, she ought to be ". . . disbarred." Deploring Brown's "incredible shenanigans," Moses appealed to Judge Arnold. But if the judge considered these personal attacks reprehensible, he did no more about them now than he had done in March.

"How many times are you going to allow him to call me dishonest?" Moses finally beseeched the judge.

"As long as she's dishonest," Brown broke in.

"Now," said the judge, "I've told both of you."

Moses wasn't without some support. Early in the trial a young wino wandered into the court and began cheering for the defense. "Why don'tcha' siddown?" he once yelled at the prosecutor. But as the trial progressed, the wino realized that it offered a choice of underdogs, and one afternoon he confronted Moses in the courthouse corridor. In his hand was a bouquet.

Francis Foldes, an authority on muscle relaxants and former chairman of the anesthesiology department at Montefiore Hospital in New York, supplemented Dr. Baden's testimony about the effects of curare by recalling his own self-experiment with the drug, under the watchful eyes of colleagues. "My eyes drooped," the anesthesiologist told the Jascalevich jury. "I couldn't focus. I couldn't swallow my saliva. [My] grip strength . . . decreased almost to zero." Dr. Foldes said that if a patient was given a normal dose of curare during surgery and wasn't ventilated, he would die in three to eight minutes, depending on his physical condition. If curare was injected into an intravenous tubing, he testified, death would ensue in four to twelve minutes. The rate of the paralysis would depend on the dose of the drug, the speed of the injection, and the volume in which the curare was dissolved. A live person, Dr. Foldes said, would excrete between 75 and 90 percent of a dose of curare within twenty-four hours, mostly through the urine. After the initial loss, he went on, a relatively high concentration of curare appears to be retained in the liver and kidney because those organs "have a very good blood supply and originally a lot of it goes there."

Based on his review of various records and the toxicological findings, Dr. Foldes said that it was his opinion, with "reasonable medical certainty," that Nancy Savino, Frank Biggs, and Carl Rohrbeck had died of curare poisoning and that if curare was administered, it was given intravenously. It was "ridiculous," he said, to contend that Biggs's death was related to a distended bladder. Rohrbeck, he conceded, could have died from a sudden coronary occlusion, but his heart condition was also "compatible with life. There are millions of people walking around with this condition." The witness said that although Emma Arzt had suffered two "bouts" of "some form of respiratory depression," he could not say with reasonable medical certainty what had caused her death. There was "no evident cause of death" for Margaret Henderson.

Moses wanted to elicit from Dr. Foldes an opinion of Dr. Jascalevich's alleged 1965–66 dog research using curare. Judge Arnold barred the opinion unless the defendant took the stand.

On cross-examination, Brown revived his argument that the prosecution's HPLC-RIA "system" could not provide definitive evidence of curare, particularly if the RIA tests lacked appropriate controls. Dr. Foldes said he would "put a little less stress on [the RIA findings] than I would if I had the impossible—namely, the appropriate control, an exhumed, embalmed body who was injected with curare ten years ago, embalmed, and left in the ground." But on a statistical basis, he said, the two-test combination was sufficiently reliable for him. Dr. Foldes said it wasn't necessarily true that a person who received curare would be cyanotic. If Nancy Savino appeared pale rather than blue after death, he said, it might have been because she received a massive dose of curare and died very quickly—or because she was conscious or sleeping lightly, and her body emitted a "violent sympathetic discharge," producing paleness. The witness agreed that peritonitis, if so severe that it caused shock, could also account for paleness. Brown suggested that Biggs couldn't have died from curare because he received artificial respiration for twenty minutes after his attack—enough time to dissipate the lethal effect of curare. But Dr. Foldes said that Biggs's records did not really establish how well he was breathing during that period, or how long.

BROWN: Doctor, please. You mean they were giving [oxygen], but he wasn't getting it?

FOLDES: There isn't anything that says he's getting it. Just like they don't say whether they have an airway or they don't have an airway. You can put a resuscitator on your face and push it, and you wouldn't get any oxygen.

* * *

Q: Well, does [the chart] say he was unconscious for twenty minutes, or conscious for twenty minutes?

A: It doesn't say one way or the other.

Q: It says he was breathing for twenty minutes.

MOSES: It doesn't say that.

A: No, it doesn't say that in the record.

"I give up, Judge. No more questions," said Brown, calling Dr. Foldes "a quack."

Dr. Baden resumed the stand on July 21, 1978, to give his final opinion on the causes of death of the five Riverdell patients. Considering the toxicological results, as well as other factors he reviewed in his earlier testimony, Dr. Baden said that Nancy Savino, Frank Biggs, and Carl Rohrbeck each died of curare poisoning. Incorporating Dr. Coumbis's work, Dr. Baden was also prepared to say that Margaret Henderson had died of curare poisoning. But Judge Arnold ruled that Dr. Coumbis's tests alone were inadequate—"you can't use presumptive evidence in a murder case, dear," he told Moses. Dr. Baden then testified that Mrs. Henderson's death was "undetermined." Emma Arzt, the pathologist said, died of a "respiratory arrest of undetermined cause."

Moses began to ask Dr. Baden about the manner of death of each patient, starting with Rohrbeck. But as soon as Dr. Baden described Rohrbeck's death as "homicidal," Brown objected. Judge Arnold agreed with Brown; the manner of death, the judge said, was a question for the jury, not the expert, to decide.

MOSES: Dr. Baden, is the drug [curare] produced naturally by the body?

BADEN: [Curare] is in no way produced by the human body.

Q: Could the death of a person as a result of [curare] poisoning come from natural cause?

"No," said Dr. Baden after Brown's objection failed, "it could not come from natural causes."

Although Brown protested that he shouldn't have to cross-examine Dr. Baden without benefit of my notes, Judge Arnold ordered him to go ahead. Every legal means had been exhausted to obtain the notes, the judge said, and if they were produced later, Dr. Baden could be brought back as a witness.

So Brown dug into the "ambitious" medical examiner—"the hotshot from New York"—whom he had tried to depict as a co-conspirator with Woodcock and me. Hadn't Dr. Baden, as early as 1973, provided information to me for the "severed head" and other stories that "assailed" Milton Helpern, then his boss? "I have talked to [Dr. Helpern's] widow," Brown said. [Dr. Helpern had died in April 1977.] No, replied Dr. Baden, he was not the source for those stories, which embarrassed the office as much as Dr. Helpern. Hadn't Dr. Baden removed an old file on the Riverdell case from Dr. Helpern's office before the latter's retirement in January 1974—a file containing materials from Calissi's 1966 investigation? No, said Dr. Baden, he had "absolutely" never seen such a file and knew nothing of the Riverdell affair until late 1975. Moreover, he wasn't aware until after he came into the case that Dr. Helpern had been consulted a decade earlier. Well, hadn't Dr. Baden known me for five years; wasn't I his friend? No, said the witness, he knew me only as a reporter, and not one with whom he had a personal or confidential relationship. Woodcock hadn't told him that I had been allowed to see Calissi's old file in Hackensack in August 1975, and I never gave him anything related to the Riverdell case. The pathologist wasn't sure whether he talked to me in December 1975, but after the first of the exhumations in January 1976, many reporters called him. When appropriate, he answered their questions. "It was not to [Farber] alone. It was to reporters in general," he said.

Regarding the curare tests Dr. Baden said that appropriate controls for RIA were a matter of "interpretation when you are dealing with ten-year-old tissue." While RIA and HPLC might separately "pick up decomposition products" in old tissues, the witness conceded, using them in conjunction and on the "same specimen proves beyond a reasonable doubt that the drug is there."

BROWN: Even though each is presumptive in its own sphere?

BADEN: Yes, strong presumption, but I didn't want to go on strong presumption in arriving at a conclusion. That is why we persisted in doing these tests long after the grand jury.

Of all the body organs examined by the toxicologists, none had been more comprehensively analyzed than Nancy Savino's liver, and none had been more consistently positive for curare. In fact, every laboratory that had tested the child's liver tissues—including the laboratory used by the defense—had reported positive results. Curare had been identified by thin-layer chromatography (Dr. Dal Cortivo, Suffolk County, N.Y.); direct RIA (Dr. Matteo, Columbia University; Dr. Coumbis, New Jersey); HPLC (Dr. Dal Cortivo); HPLC-RIA combination (Dr. Dal Cortivo, Dr. Coumbis); and mass spectrometry (Finnegan Corporation, California; Dr. Beggs, Pennsylvania; Dr. Rieders, Pennsylvania).

Now Brown turned to the subject of Nancy Savino's liver and, without putting it in so many words, suggested a theory to account for the uniform curare results. The liver, he implied, had been spiked with curare shortly after the child's exhumation and reautopsy by Dr. Baden at the New York medical examiner's office on January 13, 1976.

Like her other organs, Nancy Savino's liver had been removed on January 13 in full view of a half-dozen medical and law enforcement officials and immediately examined, weighed, and described for the autopsy report. The liver was photographed, and a piece of the organ was cut away for microscopic analysis. According to Dr. Baden, the remainder of the liver was placed in a container, labeled, and locked in a freezer with the child's other organs by Donald Hoffman, the office's senior toxicologist. Only Dr. Hoffman had a key to that freezer, Dr. Baden testified, and the toxicologist did not open the freezer until three days later, when Dr. Baden gave some liver and other tissue to Dr. Dal Cortivo. The freezer was opened again on January 20, 1976, when Dr. Coumbis received liver and other tissue. Both Dr. Dal Cortivo and Dr. Coumbis signed receipts.

Brown offered no evidence to support the notion that the liver was adulterated. Nor did he explain how any curare added to the liver after its removal from the body would have been distributed throughout the organ, as in life. But he handed Dr. Baden a list of Nancy Savino's organs that had been drawn up at the 1976 autopsy by Dr. Hoffman, and he noted that the liver was not on the list. Why not? he asked. Didn't the liver's absence from the list indicate a delay between the time the organ was removed from the body on January 13 and the time it got into the freezer? Not at all, said Dr. Baden. Dr. Hoffman's list, dictated to a stenographer, inadvertently excluded several of Nancy Savino's organs, not just the liver. But he himself had given the liver to Dr. Hoffman at the autopsy, and "it went into that freezer on January 13 with the other organs" of the child.

The only other witness who had been questioned about the handling of the liver on January 13, 1976, was Dr. Coumbis, who was present at the autopsy. Dr. Coumbis said that he saw Dr. Baden give the liver and other organs to Dr. Hoffman, and he saw Dr. Hoffman place them in the freezer.

On July 27, 1978, after twenty-two weeks of testimony by fifty-eight witnesses, Moses rested her case. Brown moved to have the indictment dismissed on the grounds of insufficient evidence, and Judge Arnold threw out two of the five counts of murder. The prosecution had failed to prove that Margaret Henderson and Emma Arzt had died of curare poisoning, the judge said. If the jury chose to interpret all the evidence so far in a light most favorable to the state, he said, it could properly convict the defendant of murdering Nancy Savino, Frank Biggs, and Carl Rohrbeck. So those charges stood.

"No cuffs! No cuffs!"

The voice of County Sheriff Joseph Job boomed across Judge Trautwein's courtroom on July 24. "No cuffs—no, sir!" the sheriff shouted at the guard who was approaching me. Job pushed his way through the reporters who were scurrying for the door and led me to a corner of

the courtroom. "Take it easy," he said. "Let's wait till the crowd goes."
I was too stunned to reply. I had expected to be sentenced to jail, but I
had never thought that I would be given six months in addition to the
"coercive" term. I had also hoped that my jailing would be delayed
pending appeal, that I would be freed on bail. But Judge Trautwein
had just said no to that, and everything was happening very fast. I felt
terribly winded, and I kept thinking that I had almost been handcuffed.
Why would that guard want to handcuff me? Was I running away? Was
I a criminal?

"All right, let's go," said Job, taking my elbow. I was anxious not to
appear dejected, and I steadied myself as we went into the corridor. It
was filled with people and one of the first faces I recognized was that of
Lou Raino, process server for Ray Brown.

"Lou," I said, managing a smile, "are you coming after me again?"

"Why do you say that?" he asked. "I admire you for standing up for
your principles. I've done it all my life."

As soon as we got out of the courthouse, I discovered that the sheriff
had his own plans for me. Instead of putting me behind bars, at 3:15
P.M. he ushered me into a fully furnished apartment in the jail complex. The apartment, he explained, came with his title, and he rarely
used it. I was to stay here, at least for the balance of the day. "Maybe
your lawyers can do something for you by then," Job said. "Meanwhile
I want you to be comfortable. I'll have some food brought up to you.
Do you drink milk?" I assured the sheriff that I drank milk and that I
was more than grateful for his kindness.

"Don't worry," he said, "you're a respected member of the community, and you'll be treated like one here."

Job left as Peter Banta, one of my lawyers, arrived. Banta said that
Gene Scheiman was on his way to Newark to ask the Appellate Division of Superior Court to release me, and to hold up the fines on *The
Times,* pending our appeal of the contempt citations. "We ought to
know something today," he said.

As Banta left, the sheriff returned with four deputies—and two gallons of milk. Either Job took milk drinking very seriously, or he expected me to be around for a while. The sheriff showed me through the
apartment and said I was free to use the phone. He also jotted down
the number of a detective I should call if I wanted anything. Before
departing with his deputies, he proudly identified his wife and children
and relatives in the many photographs on the living room table.

I called home and spoke to my wife, Sabine, who had already heard
from Syd Schanberg at *The Times.* Sabine believed in what I was doing
as much as I did, and after all that had happened in the last few
months, she wasn't surprised to find me in jail. But that didn't lessen

her fury. "Peanuts!" she said. "These judges would rather have you selling peanuts than doing your kind of work. They make me sick. Trautwein, Arnold—they'll hang together forever. Calissi and Galda with them. God, what a bunch of judges in one place." I tried to calm her, mentioning Gene's efforts in Newark, and the apartment arrangement; I even threw in the air-conditioning. But she wasn't easily consoled. I told her that I would speak to the kids later, but she should reach my mother in Baltimore as quickly as possible. I didn't want her jolted by a news report. She had already been upset by Judge Trautwein's remark about my "soiled skirts." "What's going on up there?" she had asked.

After a dinner of creamed chicken, I turned on the local television news. The reports of my jailing were mixed with news that Billy Martin had been forced out as manager of the New York Yankees and that a patient at Hackensack Hospital had been found to have Legionnaire's Disease. Martin, I knew, lived in Hackensack and was a local hero. But I was more interested in the local contagion of the disease that had killed more than a score of people in Philadelphia the previous summer. Legionnaire's Disease, I imagined, did not respect jail walls. On the CBS network news at 7 o'clock, Roger Mudd said that the Appellate Division in Newark had temporarily reduced the fines against *The Times,* but I was to stay in jail until that court could consider my case on its merits, which might be two months down the road. So that was it, I thought. Gene had lost in Newark, and I was going to need a lot more than two gallons of milk.

Around 9 o'clock Sheriff Job bustled in. "Now, don't get your hopes up," he said, "but Justice Pashman wants you in his chambers right away." Scheiman, Job told me, had raced back from Newark and taken his case before Pashman, who was one of seven justices of the state Supreme Court and who had an office in the Bergen County Courthouse. I remembered Pashman, and I wondered whether he remembered me. I had called him that night in November 1977 when the Bergen *Record* mistakenly reported the justice as having said that Dr. Jascalevich wouldn't be brought to trial because of a time limit on murder prosecutions. Pashman hadn't been happy at my waking him.

I grabbed Gene's outstretched hand as I walked into the justice's chambers and Pashman, who looked very relaxed in a golf sweater, slacks, and white sneakers, directed me to a seat. Brown was across the room. Pashman, who had come from home to listen to Gene, said he was going to release me, pending a conference of his Supreme Court colleagues the following day. But he wanted my assurance that I would report to Sheriff Job's office at 11 A.M. to await the court's determination. I was delighted to oblige.

As we were leaving, I told Brown that I was sorry he continued to portray me as a conspirator against his client. "I want you to know, man to man, that I could not do that. I'm just not that way."

"Mr. Farber," he said, "I believe you. But maybe I have a larger perspective on this case."

With only Justice Pashman dissenting, the New Jersey Supreme Court ordered me back to jail on July 25, 1978. The court refused to pre-empt the Appellate Division and deal immediately with my substantive arguments. But it agreed to delay my rejailing while I turned again to the U. S. Supreme Court. So, in late July and early August, I was a free man. I soon discovered that in the public mind, I had been transformed from an individual to a case, from a reporter to a cause. My jailing had received wide attention in newspapers and on television and radio, and I found myself being stopped on the street and waved at and pointed to. "Aren't you the man who said 'No'?" I was asked on Third Avenue in Manhattan. "Right on!" shouted a man on Park Avenue, raising his clenched fist. Pleased and a little embarrassed, I shouted back. And I stopped to talk and, occasionally, I raised my fist, too. I was gratified to see that many people realized this was a public issue, not an issue for the press alone.

At home, Sabine pinned to a corkboard an observation by Albert Camus: "a free press can of course be good or bad, but most certainly, without freedom, it will never be anything but bad." We tried our best to explain to our children why I had been sent to jail, and why I might have to go again. We were not certain what Christophe, who was four years old, understood; we didn't want to give him the impression that he ought to dislike judges just because he loved his father. Delphine, who was nearly eight, was naturally excited by all the hubbub—by seeing my picture on the *Times*'s front page; by meeting Barbara Walters at the ABC-TV studios; by having her own picture taken on the set of the "Today Show" and seeing it in the New York *Daily News* and *The Washington Post*. She listened closely as my wife and I talked at home about the Constitution and the First Amendment and the role of the press in a country like the United States. Delphine had always been proud of the fact that I was a reporter, and Sabine and I were sure that she grasped what we were saying. One morning, while I was being interviewed by a television reporter in the newsroom of *The Times*, the reporter suddenly asked Delphine what she thought of my being jailed. The camera was rolling and she looked straight into it.

"You've got to do what's right," she said.

The *Times* newsroom was a somber place during those days. The contracts between the city's newspapers and their unions had expired in March, and negotiations weren't going well. Many people at *The*

Times, including Abe Rosenthal, thought that a strike was imminent. Rosenthal had other problems, as well. A group of women employees had brought a sex discrimination suit against *The Times,* and if it wasn't soon settled out of court, a bitter public brawl was certain to follow. Then there was the matter of the court in Russia. In mid-July I had received a cable from the *Times*'s Moscow bureau, conveying "all sympathy and support" for my position in New Jersey. "The Moscow bureau is with you," the cable said. But several days later Craig Whitney of that bureau had his own troubles. A Moscow City Court found him guilty of libeling Soviet television officials and ordered him to retract an article questioning the veracity of a dissident's videotaped "confession." When Whitney refused, it appeared that he might be expelled from the Soviet Union. Instead he was fined $72.50, plus court costs. The disparity between that sum and the fines in New Jersey was not lost on *The Times,* nor on me. I wasn't paying the $5,000-a-day (the $100,000 flat sum had been temporarily set aside by the Appellate Division), but I was greatly bothered by it. One afternoon I mentioned my concern to Rosenthal. He froze.

"Every penny *The Times* has ever made it has made because of the First Amendment," he said. "And if we have to, we'll spend every last penny for the First Amendment. So don't ever talk to me again about the fines. You forget about that."

As far as I knew, that was also the sentiment of Arthur O. Sulzberger, the *Times*'s publisher. When the fight thickened, "Punch" Sulzberger asked for a general explanation of the materials I was holding. Through Rosenthal, I had provided that. When I was jailed and the paper was fined on July 24, Sulzberger issued a statement saying that *"The Times* will, of course, support Myron Farber as he maintains the confidentiality of his sources. This is what a free press is all about. And if Judge Trautwein decrees that *The Times* pay $5,000 a day for this privilege, so be it. Bad law doesn't last very long." The publisher followed up by sending a plant to my wife and me. "Just to let you know that everyone at the paper is behind you," the note said.

Of the telegrams and letters that filled my mailbox in late July, the one I appreciated most was from a former New York state official. After considerable agonizing, he had once given me invaluable information in confidence on another story. He said that he had read my statement to Judge Trautwein in an English-language newspaper in South America. "I never doubted for a moment that you meant it . . . when you said you'd go to jail if necessary to protect my confidence. Hang in there, and don't let the bastards wear you down. In my opinion you are dead right, and your stand for the First Amendment is one of the few encouraging things that has happened lately."

On July 28, Scheiman asked Justice White to hold up all penalties against *The Times* and me until the New Jersey appellate courts ruled on the substantive issues we had raised, or until the Supreme Court could consider taking the case. "To this day," Scheiman said in his brief, we "have not been afforded a hearing by any court" on our First Amendment or statutory claims. If the only way to obtain a decision on those claims was to be held in contempt and then appeal, Scheiman said, it was "approaching the unconscionable" to permit severe fines and incarceration while the courts deliberated. Scheiman also argued that "in-camera" inspection by a judge of "confidential materials for which we seek First Amendment protection deprives the press immediately of such protection in the supposed course of determining whether such protection exists . . ." "The judiciary, after all, is a branch of government," he said. Brown responded by informing Justice White that *The Times* and I were engaged in a "groundless, blatant attempt to mislead the Court and the country" and to make it impossible for Dr. Jascalevich to get a fair trial. Woodcock and Dr. Baden and I had "concocted charges of murder against an innocent citizen for pecuniary gain" and to advance our careers, Brown reiterated. "The central issue before this Court, then, is whether Myron Farber and *The New York Times* can abrogate the power of the courts to decide the validity of a subpoena and substitute their private conception of materiality and privilege for the judgment of a court of law."

On August 1, Justice White turned us down. As he had two weeks earlier, he indicated that we were coming to the High Court prematurely. The contempt citations notwithstanding, he was unconvinced that four justices—the required number—would vote "at this time" to accept the case for review. He himself saw nothing wrong with an "in-camera" inspection by the trial judge, followed by a hearing "on all issues of federal and state law." On August 4, Justice Marshall also declined to hold up the penalties against *The Times* and me. He, too, was unpersuaded that four justices would agree to review the case "in its present posture." But unlike Justice White, Justice Marshall said that were he "deciding this issue on the merits," he would not have allowed my jailing and the *Times*'s fines before the New Jersey Appellate Division had ruled on the "important" questions we presented. "Given the likelihood that forced disclosure even for in-camera review will inhibit the reporter's and the newspaper's exercise of First Amendment rights," he said, "I believe that some threshold showing of materiality, relevance, and necessity should be required." The record indicated that Judge Arnold had failed to make these "independent determinations," Justice Marshall said, and Brown's "conclusory assertions" were "insufficient to justify a subpoena of the breadth of the one involved here."

Two hours after Justice Marshall's decision, I was behind bars in the Bergen County Main Jail, a sixty-eight-year-old fortress that a county study commission had recently declared "unfit for human habitation."

The Main Jail, which could have served as a set for a Jimmy Cagney movie, had five circular tiers of cells, most of which were now empty. The jail had actually been closed by Sheriff Job in 1977 after it was declared obsolete. Its inmates, most of whom had been convicted of drug-related offenses, had been transferred to the ten-year-old annex a half mile away. The annex didn't have many maximum security cells —more were being built—but it had outdoor recreation areas, a gymnasium, a library well stocked with law books, a chapel, a hospital ward, workshops, and a mess hall. The Main Jail, which was connected to the courthouse by tunnels and elevators, lacked all these facilities. It was one row of bars after another, and little else. It had been temporarily reopened to house inmates whose conduct at the annex was "not acceptable," or who were thought to be dangerous, or who needed "protection" or were awaiting trial or sentencing, or were in transit between state or federal prisons. Most of these inmates occupied individual cells. But a score of "work-release" inmates, who were allowed to hold jobs during the day, slept in a dormitory. No one occupied the "green room" of the Main Jail, the tiled isolation cell on the top tier that was equipped only with a recessed ceiling light and a hole in the floor. That room had been shut tight after reports that prisoners there had been stripped, beaten and doused with high-pressure hoses. The reports were unconfirmed.

Of course, both the Main Jail and the annex were very different from the sheriff's apartment. Job would have preferred my being returned to his apartment during my incarceration, but he was up for re-election in the fall and couldn't afford any charges of favoritism toward me. He gave me a choice of being housed in the Main Jail or the annex, but he clearly considered it wiser, and safer, for me to stay in the Main Jail, close by his office. I thought it best to take his advice. Job selected a cell for me on the second tier, in what had once been an infirmary wing, and he had the floor scrubbed with disinfectant. Most of the graffiti were removed from the cream-colored walls; the real holdout was a swastika. The cell was about fourteen feet long, eight feet wide, and twelve feet high. The paint on the ceiling, particularly around the fluorescent lights, was flaking. The bed had metal slats instead of springs and was covered by a thin green mattress. A piece of tin, screwed to a wall over the sink to serve as a mirror, had been so badly scratched by my predecessors that it was useless. A square wooden table was near the window, and Job added an office chair and a gray metal folding table for the typewriter he permitted me. The sheriff said that unlike the cells of most of my fellow inmates, my cell would not be locked and I was free to move along the fifty-foot corridor of my cellblock. I could also take my meals in a kitchenette off the guards' desk with two trusties who enjoyed the same privilege. One was Ron, a thirty-nine-year-old former town manager in Bergen County who was serving two to three years for fraud. The other was Bob, a fifty-six-year-old former councilman of another town who was serving five to seven years for perjury.

After a dinner of franks and beans, I was invited to join a gin rummy game that must have begun when the jail was opened in 1910. I hadn't played the game since high school, but I was paired with Ron, and as luck would have it, we drubbed Bob and another inmate. Ron was immensely pleased. "The Farb is here!" he goaded Bob, who grumbled over every loss. "Start with twenty. The Farb is here!" At 2 A.M. we called it quits. "You'll do your time standing on your head," Ron assured me on the way to our cells. "They can't hold you for long." I thanked him for his good cheer, though I didn't share it. The Appellate Division in New Jersey had just decided that it wouldn't hear my appeal until September 18, nearly seven weeks away.

Seven weeks seemed like a very long time. I unpacked a few jeans and shorts and polo shirts from my overnight bag—Job had said I could wear my own clothing—and put a picture of Sabine and the kids on the table. Already there was a note from a radio reporter reminding me that on this day, 243 years earlier, John Peter Zenger had been acquitted of libel charges in New York, much advancing the cause of press freedom. Next to the note was a telegram from some friends in New York, proposing a hacksaw-laden cake. I wondered whether a guard had read the telegram. During the evening I had noticed two signs by the guards' desk. "If you can keep a cool head in these times, perhaps you don't understand the situation," one sign read. The other, more official looking, announced that "All Inmates Housed at the Main Jail Are Escape Risks."

Around 3 A.M. I switched off my light and lay down on the bed. My cell was hot and damp; for a half hour or so, I simply stared at the ceiling. In the darkness of that steel box, I felt quite alone. More than I had for many years.

The first week I was in jail I had a steady stream of visitors. Reporters and television correspondents poured into the jail for interviews, and the sheriff, standing ramrod at my side, basked in the publicity. Of the hundreds of letters that I received, some were opposed to my position, or to me. "I hope you remain in jail for some time. You have some wrong ideas of what is a free press . . ." "Who died and appointed you God?" "Reporters are nothing more than shills—and ill-mannered, loutish shills at that. More power to Burger and his Burger bits . . ." "Ho-ho-ho. *The New York Times* reporting the news impartially? Ho-ho-ho. We recognize b.s. when we hear it . . ." "If you can live with the thought that possibly you had a part in sending an innocent man to jail for life, you can live with it. *The Times* couldn't care less." And an antismoker warned that I was destroying not only my "body chemistry" but also my "credibility." Was I refusing to turn over my file "for the same reason you suck on a pipe?" he asked.

Some of the mail—including a letter from an unabashed sixth-grader who asked to borrow all my notes—was from students who were already planning papers on my case. Prisoners in other jails wrote, some merely commiserating, others asking for help even while I myself was behind bars. Other people offered legal advice or detailed their own grievances against the judiciary. Some sent checks of $1.00 to $1,000 to defray the fines against *The Times* (all the checks were returned); others, including a descendant of Andrew Johnson who asked President Carter to pardon me, passed along copies of letters they had written elected officials on my behalf. Reporters who had been previously jailed for protecting the confidentiality of their sources sent letters of support, as did a California psychiatrist who had been briefly imprisoned for refusing to disclose information about a patient. A Florida librarian who had refused to provide the Federal Bureau of Investigation with information about a patron observed that "even a few people of your resolution can make a tremendous difference." An Episcopal rector in Bergen County, expressing his concern about interference with "privileged communications" between clergymen and parishioners, enclosed a sermon he had delivered assailing my confinement.

Apparently the statement I had made at my sentencing had been widely printed, and many of my correspondents referred to it. "Your statement . . . is correct, and for all our fallen comrades in all the wars, I salute you," a disabled veteran wrote from Syracuse, New York. "Keep the flag high and don't let some judge grab it from you." A rural Pennsylvania resident offered a petition signed by 190 of her neighbors. "I feel he is fighting not just for his rights but for mine. I am afraid for my children and grandchildren if we lose freedom of the press. We are going to lose many more freedoms with it . . ." "Your statement touched me so much that I have to write you," said a New Hampshire woman. "I very much appreciate what you are doing for yourself and for all of us. You read the First Amendment much more accurately than the judge . . ." "You are not only standing up for your profession but also for me and all the public. I am twenty years old and hopefully have many years to live in this country. I am aware that when the time comes that reporters are no longer able to assure confidentiality of their sources, the public will no longer be informed on important matters."

Toward the end of that first week, "Meet the Press" called Sheriff Job and asked whether I could be the guest on its Sunday program, live from the jail. The sheriff had no objection, but Judge Arnold did. The request was vetoed, and Judge Arnold ordered a crackdown on my "special privileges." Reporters were no longer allowed to interview me in jail, and with the exception of my lawyers, the only visitors I was permitted were members of my family—and then only for brief periods twice a week. Not knowing how long I would be in jail, I thought it best for Sabine and the children to go to her family in France for a much-needed vacation. Sabine had just been out to see me. When she was admitted to the jail, one of the guards told her, "If it was up to me, he wouldn't get anything but his underwear." It was an unnecessary remark, and both Sabine and I were irritated by it. But in fact, things were taking a turn for the worse in jail, and I wanted Sabine to take the kids away.

The day after they left for France, *The Times* and the other New York papers were struck, adding to my gloom. The arrival of *The Times* at the jail each morning had been a high point of my day. Not only did the paper give me some idea of what was happening beyond the jail walls, it also reminded me of the purposefulness of my action. And it was good company, an old friend. Now, for the first time since I had worked for *The Times,* it was not publishing.

Two days after the strike began, I had problems of another sort. On August 8, Gene Scheiman had filed a habeas corpus petition in Federal District Court in Newark, seeking my release until I was given a hearing by New Jersey courts on my First Amendment rights. The habeas corpus proceeding—used when a person believes he has been confined without due process of law—was a natural route for Scheiman to take. It was also a course urged upon *The Times* by Griffin B. Bell, the Attorney General of the United States. Bell, a former federal appeals court judge, had run into Jim Goodale, the *Times*'s counsel, just after my jailing. Bell said he couldn't understand why I was in jail and he wasn't—an observation that others were making, too. The previous month, during a civil trial in New York, Bell had been held in contempt of court for refusing to turn over to the Socialist Workers Party the files on eighteen unidentified informers who had spied on the small Trotskyite group for the FBI. But enforcement of the contempt citation had been held up pending appeal. Bell told Goodale there was no question in his mind that I ought to be "out on habeas corpus," and he even suggested that Goodale read some of the habeas corpus opinions he had written when he was on the bench.

On August 11, I was taken to Newark for the argument before Federal District Judge Frederick B. Lacey. It was a disaster. Following Brown's lead, Judge Lacey focused almost entirely on the fact that I had agreed two years earlier to write a book about the Riverdell affair. I was "standing on the altar of greed," I had "rendered evil," I had "misled judge after judge," including two justices of the U. S. Supreme Court, Judge Lacey said. Unlike Paul Branzburg, I had become an "investigative arm of the state" and had "joined forces against a defendant." Surely, the judge went on, I had disclosed "all or substantially all of the alleged confidential information and unpublished notes" to Doubleday & Company, Inc., my publisher—"demolishing" any claim I had under the First Amendment. "Here's this manuscript, floating around somewhere, and it would solve all our problems," Judge Lacey said. "Let's get a hold of this manuscript." At Brown's bidding, Judge Lacey put me on the stand.

"Where is your manuscript?" Brown roared. It was the first and only question. I had no intention of disclosing the whereabouts of the material I had written, which was being held, in a sealed box, by a friend who also had some of my notes. When Judge Lacey ordered me to answer the question, I offered to retrieve the manuscript. That wasn't good enough for Brown or the judge. So to avoid a federal contempt citation, I took the only alternative available to me—I withdrew my habeas corpus petition. That was acceptable to Judge Lacey, who said he had intended to leave me in jail anyway.

I was furious at Judge Lacey. My plans to write a book—known to Brown and mentioned by him in court papers and arguments for months—had no relationship to whether I was being confined illegally, and certainly nothing to do with the fight *The Times* and I were waging over Brown's subpoena. Although Judge Lacey had me on the stand, he took no testimony from me with regard to the origin or history of the book or the contents of my incomplete and unedited draft chapters. And his facts and conclusions, derived mainly from contractual correspondence Brown had just subpoenaed from Doubleday, were all wrong. The judge brushed off the fact that I had not even contemplated writing a book until after my *Times* stories ran. And he completely dismissed Scheiman's rejoinder that I had never agreed, "by contract or otherwise," to reveal confidential sources to Doubleday or in the book. "Well, of course, that's implicit in the contract," Judge Lacey said. But he was wrong, as mistaken as when he described me—without benefit of any evidence—as an "investigative arm of the state."

Gene and Abe Rosenthal and Jim Goodale were equally outraged by Judge Lacey's handling of the habeas corpus petition—and said so publicly. "It was the most surprising moment in my practice of law," Goodale told me. Privately, we all agreed that something had to be done to deflate the extraneous issue of "the book." So from my jail cell, I made arrangements for Gene to receive a copy of the manuscript. I also wrote a letter to Judge Arnold who, when I was before him in May, ruled out questions about my book plans. "With this letter," I began, "I am turning over for your inspection a copy of that part of the draft book manuscript on the Jascalevich case that I have thus far completed and furnished my editor at Doubleday & Company, Inc. . . . Contrary to the charges made against me, there is nothing sinful about a journalist writing a book about his experiences. The tradition is as old as journalism itself . . . The issue here is not whether I am writing a book or what is in it. The issue is whether an American journalist who did nothing more than perform his job, in what he perceived to be the public interest, can be forcibly converted into an investigative arm of the defense or the prosecution. I showed no one—no one—my confidential notes.

"I make no apologies for my stories," I continued. "I make no apologies for later entering into a contract to write a book whose only function can be to inform the public. I make no apologies for being paid for my honest labor." With the seven chapters I enclosed a chronology setting forth my involvement in the book project from its inception.

On August 16, Gene took all this material to Judge Arnold. "I predict they'll never look at this manuscript," Gene said, leaving the jail, "and I hope that'll be remembered in the future." Gene was right. Judge Arnold asked Brown whether he would accept the manuscript, and Brown said, "No, sir . . . We want everything." Later Brown blasted my offer as a "publicity gimmick." Beware, he said, of "Greeks bearing gifts." The envelope containing the seven chapters—the manuscript that Judge Lacey said "would solve all our problems"—was eventually taken by Judge Arnold. But he never opened it, and ultimately it was returned to me.

After the flap over the book, Floyd Abrams resumed an active role as chief attorney for both *The Times* and me. Floyd, who had been consulting with Gene Scheiman all along, had just won dismissal of a suit against the National Broadcasting Company by a California girl who claimed that four juveniles had been prompted to rape her by an NBC television drama that depicted a similar rape scene. But no sooner was Floyd back from San Francisco than another episode occurred—this time in Judge Trautwein's courtroom—that left me wondering whether I would ever get out of jail. It was every bit as incredible as Judge Lacey's tirade a few days earlier.

The Times had been paying $5,000 a day for civil contempt because it had refused to release its own file of documents on the Riverdell matter. That small file—separate and distinct from the notes and other materials that I, as a reporter, held—related primarily to the *Times*'s initial involvement in the story. When Floyd discovered that it merely duplicated information recently furnished to Brown by Doubleday, he turned over the documents to Judge Arnold and asked Judge Trautwein to purge *The Times* of contempt and terminate the daily fine. During a two-day hearing Katharine Darrow, assistant general attorney of *The Times,* testified that when a *Times* reporter was subpoenaed, *The Times* relinquishes to the reporter "all ownership interest" in notes he possesses "and leaves all decisions as to the disposition of the notes to the reporter." That, she said, was a long-standing policy of the paper. When Judge Trautwein persisted in suggesting that *The Times* could force me to give up my notes, Abrams said the paper would not act against me. "It will not dismiss or threaten to dismiss Mr. Farber"— Judge Trautwein had once said that *The Times* could fire me—"and with all real and deep respect for this Court," Abrams went on, "if it must continue to pay the fine in support of Mr. Farber, it is prepared to do so."

At the end of the hearing, Judge Trautwein rejected the *Times*'s application to be freed of the $5,000-a-day fine. The paper's refusal to order me to yield my notes made "a joke of good faith" and was "a convenient way to defeat the Sixth Amendment rights of a defendant in a criminal trial," he said. It was an illegal "duck the subpoena and lay on the reporter" policy. As for the documents *The Times* had now given to Judge Arnold, they were "worthless . . . It defies reason, common sense, and probability that a newspaper . . . would have the effrontery to turn over this useless material and say we have complied" with the subpoena. "The files of *The New York Times* were clearly and unequivocally sanitized. I don't know whether there was a break-in or what happened, but the sanitizing must lay at the feet of *The New York Times.*" The judge said there had been "much talk about the imperialism of the judiciary in this state . . . I say this is an imperialistic press asserting itself."

In New York, Punch Sulzberger was boiling. "The unfounded attack on the integrity of *The Times* is a graphic example of the appalling state of justice with which *The Times* has been confronted since the Dr. Jascalevich trial began," the *Times*'s publisher told reporters. "Dismayed that the *Times*'s files contained no information of relevance to the case—something, by the way, we have told the court before—

Judge Trautwein then accused *The Times* of 'sanitizing' its files before turning them over. This is flatly untrue."

By the third week in August, I was becoming stir crazy. I couldn't accustom myself to being locked up, and each day seemed longer than the last. In my mail, which now included letters from a number of foreign countries, was a postcard from a Canadian who recalled Bertrand Russell's observation that "Everyone should try to spend some time in jail, as it is the only place to catch up on one's reading." But I didn't find that to be true. Whenever I tried to concentrate on a book, my mind wandered back to my own plight. I thought it would divert me to answer my mail, but every time I finished one note, I was swamped with new letters. And the heat in the jail was so intense that I could hold a piece of stationery by my fingers and watch it wilt.

Between the heat and the slamming of cell doors when breakfast was served at 6:30 A.M., I wasn't getting much rest. In the evening, after they were strip-searched for drugs and alcohol, I would chat with the work-release prisoners who had been out during the day. I would tire myself playing cards with Ron and Bob. But occasionally, when I had just managed to fall asleep, lights would bathe my cellblock and I would hear the slow footsteps of the guard who was afraid of ghosts. Some of the guards swore that the jail was inhabited by ghosts of former inmates, particularly one who had hanged himself around 1976. It was no laughing matter to them, not after midnight, and the recent suicide of another prisoner hadn't helped things.

The weekends were especially bad. On weekdays I could always hope that some court would decide to release me, pending my appeal; on weekends there was no hope. On weekdays the parking lot below the window of my cell was filled with cars, and I could watch the courthouse employees and others traipsing about. It was on one of those days, when I was drawn to the window by some shouting, that I noticed Dr. Jascalevich waiting to be picked up. But on weekends, the parking lot was deserted. Even the Good Humor truck, whose familiar ring brightened my day, was gone.

The inmates in the cell to my right were changed regularly, and I had little conversation with them. One, I was cautioned, was an informer. To my left, in a corner cell bereft of amenities, was Boris, the thirty-one-year-old unemployed landscaper who was awaiting trial on charges of beating his mother to death. "I've got a sea of troubles," Boris told me, and nothing was truer than that. Night and day this gaunt, pale-eyed figure raged against the people who were going to "exterminate" him, who were going to burn him alive and dispatch his remains to the moon. "Scientists," he assured me, "have been talking about it. But Shakespeare always said, 'Cursed be he who moves my bones.'" Boris advised me to give up reporting and become a naturalist. "There's nothing like nature's music," he said, "the bee, the bird, the wind. I'd like to get up in the mountains where the air is clean. All I've been given by the world is chiding and criticism. I'd like to be able to write well; I want to be written in the book of life. I want to leave something behind. But, Myron, they want to eliminate me."

And in a way they did. But one night I was sure that Vinnie, another inmate, was going to do the job for the state. "Hey, Guinea," Boris had yelled, "you want to fuck me up the ass?"

"You say that again, and I'll bust your fucking face," Vinnie shot back.

Boris shut up. No one in the jail, which was littered with raunchy magazines, talked about sex—except in the past and future tenses. I longed for my wife. And I was mortified, stepping into the shower room one evening, when another prisoner said, "Nobody's giving out anything tonight, Farber. If you want to get laid, go elsewhere."

Across the hall from Boris, in a cell that had recently been occupied by a military school cadet who had fatally shot his parents and two younger brothers while they were sleeping, was Paul—a forty-three-year-old German travel agent who spoke ten languages. In our conversations, Paul never referred to the sodomy charges on which he was being held. All he said was that he had been in Bergen County for one night in May on his way back to Germany from Mexico. "I'm not here for no reason," he said. "Definitely I did something. But not what I'm accused of." Paul said that he had a wife and son in Frankfurt, but they didn't know where he was or that he was in trouble, and he hoped he would be deported before his family was the wiser. Meanwhile he was listening to Italian broadcasts on a portable radio, writing an autobiographical novel, and reading whatever the library at the jail annex sent him—books such as *Men at Work in New England* and *Astronaut's Nurse*. Paul regarded his jailers as "very simple people," to be pitied. Once he showed me an excerpt from a *Playboy* interview with Muhammad Ali. "The warden of a prison is in a worse condition than the prisoner himself," Ali was quoted as saying. "While the body of the prisoner is in captivity, the mind of the warden is in prison!" Paul cited these words approvingly but, like us all, he really envied the warden's freedom. "I can't understand it," he would protest. "I haven't been let out of this place for three months. But I'm not going to flee—I'm not an aggressive person."

Early one evening in late August, Ron and Bob and I were driven to the annex for some yard exercise. It was the first time I had been out of the Main Jail since my appearance before Judge Lacey. When we were led out the door of the sheriff's office, facing the Hackensack Green, I nearly swooned at the intoxicating odor of freshly cut grass. The only sound was that of a lawn mower. I grasped a railing and moved slowly down the steps, letting my eyes adjust to the sunlight that cast a mellow golden glow over the Green. Across the way I could see the squat building where, exactly three years earlier, I had examined Calissi's old file on Riverdell Hospital. It seemed so much longer than three years ago.

At the annex, I ran. I ran and ran in circles, and over the barbed wire, I watched the small planes that were lifting off from nearby Te-terboro Airport, and I watched the cars that were speeding along an elevated portion of Route 80 toward New York. I was dizzy, and I wasn't sure whether it was from the running or the thought that one of these days, I would be going home.

The most promising development after the Lacey fiasco came from an unlikely source—John J. Degnan, the attorney general of New Jersey. In July, on Judge Arnold's order, Degnan's office had urged that *The Times* and I be convicted of criminal contempt. But now that I was incarcerated and *The Times* was paying a civil penalty of $5,000 a day, Degnan himself was apparently having second thoughts about the manner in which my case had been handled; and he was looking for a means of "de-escalating" the conflict.

"This case presents questions of great public importance," the attorney general wrote to New Jersey's Appellate Division on August 18. "The proceedings to date have generated an unfortunate confrontation between the values of a free press and a fair trial." Degnan proposed that the Appellate Division immediately send, or "remand," the matter back to Judge Arnold. And before viewing any of my notes, even in private, Degnan said, Judge Arnold should conduct a hearing to determine whether I was protected by the New Jersey shield law or had waived my "privilege"; whether Brown's subpoena was reasonable in scope; and whether the notes sought by Brown were really "material and relevant" to Dr. Jascalevich's defense. In substance, the attorney general pleaded for the very hearing that *The Times* and I had asked for before we were convicted.

On August 25, the Appellate Division rejected Degnan's proposal—without comment. But the attorney general, charging that "the failure to remand this matter has created an unnecessary collision course," appealed to the state Supreme Court. On August 30, the Supreme Court of New Jersey reversed itself and took the case away from the Appellate Division. It would review the case itself, without delay. Until it came to some decision, the *Times*'s fines were suspended—and I was a free man.

Within the hour, Abe and Gene and Floyd were barreling down the corridor of my cellblock. Boris was shouting that he would "fix this world good. I am the Chosen One; mark those words on your forehead, Paul. Mark those words on your forehead."

Abe threw his arms around my neck. "C'mon," he said, "let's get out of here."

"What is at issue here is this," Abrams wrote to the New Jersey Supreme Court. "In the midst of a criminal trial, a sweeping subpoena was issued to a newspaper and one of its reporters; when they sought to challenge the breadth of the subpoena, they were told, in effect, that the price of any hearing on their challenge was to be required *first* to turn over to the court all the documents which might be responsive to the overbroad subpoena. When they sought to challenge on First Amendment grounds turning over unpublished and confidential sources and information, they were told that to be heard on their constitutional challenge, they must *first* deliver the materials for inspection by the court. When they urged that a New Jersey statute, less than a year old in its current form and deliberately sweeping in its scope, states that a journalist may 'refuse to disclose . . . to any court' confidential sources and 'any news or information obtained in the course of pursuing his professional activities whether or not it is disseminated'—they were told that they must *first* 'disclose . . . to any court' *all* their confidential material in order to receive a hearing as to whether such material need be disclosed at all! . . . But such a price for a hearing," Abrams continued, "is totally destructive of First Amendment values—not to say the explicit language of the New Jersey shield law—without being necessary to protect Dr. Jascalevich's Sixth Amendment rights." Judge Arnold didn't need, and couldn't demand, a reporter's file to interpret the law. It was not *The Times* and I "who have taken rigid and unyielding positions in this case," Abrams wrote; "it is Dr. Jascalevich and it is the Superior Court."

Brown contended in his brief to the court, that an "in-camera" inspection of my notes by Judge Arnold was "a sensible accommodation to the competing interests in this case," and less than he wanted. Nor, he said, was such a review precluded by the shield law, which couldn't be applied "absolutely" or "mechanistically." In truth, Brown charged, *The Times* and I didn't want a hearing; we wanted "total immunity" from being subpoenaed. It was only our "refusal to participate in the judicial process after numerous appeals have been denied" that deprived us of a hearing, he wrote. We were acting in "bad faith"; our real "object and desire" was to avoid a hearing because it would expose our "true relationships and motivations."

During the oral arguments in Trenton on September 5, which Punch Sulzberger attended along with a lawyer representing thirty-three major news organizations that supported the *Times*'s bid for a hearing by Judge Arnold, Brown said that he would match his concern for the First Amendment "with any man's" and suggested that Attorney General Degnan was playing politics. "I wonder why we're here," said Brown, professing to lack "the erudition and distinction" of his opponents. This was not a "shotgun" subpoena and I was a "government agent . . . There is a reporter who has turned over to the prosecutor but won't turn over to me . . . all we ask, praise God, is that a judge sit and say give the same thing to the defense."

Justice Pashman asked Brown to cite a hypothetical set of facts where the shield law could be invoked by a reporter.

"Well," said Brown, "it can be pleaded if he keeps sacrosanct and private all those things that the shield law reserves to him." But this was "not a question of the shield law," he went on. "It's a question of a great newspaper saying we're not going to conform; we're going to make the law, and you, Mr. Judge, have no business telling us that you will hear all these arguments after you have examined" the notes.

Brown wound up with an attack on those who would "revile and ridicule" Judge Trautwein and Judge Arnold. "I tell you, gentlemen, it is true that we're locked in battle down there. And the kind of hearing I've heard outlined here will take weeks, and then when you get through there will be appeal on top of appeal. So I pray that Judge Arnold in his wisdom, and I tell you the man knows what he's talking about, be given at least the respect he's been denied here today."

Abrams told the justices that he wasn't reviling anyone. If somehow or other I had waived my privileges under the shield law—and Abrams didn't think I had—let Judge Arnold rule on that at a hearing. Noting Brown's implication that I might have items "missing" from Calissi's old file, including the tape of the meeting between Dr. Jascalevich and Riverdell's directors on November 2, 1966, Abrams said that I would willingly surrender "anything" I had from the prosecutor's office. "Mr. Brown tells us that a central tape is missing. He can ask for that tape. I can represent it makes no difference; that if Mr. Farber had that tape, he would turn it over. But the point is terms and specificity; there are ways to deal with a problem like that—a missing tape, photographs, material from the prosecutor's files."

"Are you saying now," asked Chief Justice Richard Hughes, "that Mr. Farber and *The New York Times* would turn over that piece of evidence despite the New Jersey shield law?"

"That kind of material, I'm positive," said Abrams; the law didn't prohibit a reporter from voluntarily giving something up. His point was that Brown should be specific about what he wanted. And "when he doesn't know enough" to be specific, he couldn't make up for it by demanding an entire file. Quite apart from my First Amendment rights, Abrams said, I was no less entitled to stand behind the reporter's shield law than a lawyer was entitled to stand behind the attorney-client privilege or a priest behind the priest-penitent privilege—privileges that were also embodied in New Jersey statutes. I was entitled to assume the constitutionality of the shield law. If the court were now to declare the reporter's privilege unconstitutional in the face of a defendant's Sixth Amendment rights—something no judge had yet done—then the previous contempt citations should be dismissed.

"The premise of many of the questions of this court this morning," Attorney General Degnan said, "is that defendant Jascalevich has a Sixth Amendment right to rummage through a reporter's file. I suggest to you, Your Honors, that that is not so in New Jersey." Even laying aside the shield law, he said, "a trial court subpoena must be specific with reasonable certainty and there must be a substantial showing that [the items sought] are relevant and material" to the defense. "Quite simply, as a result of the trial court's ruling . . . we sit here in the dark not knowing what need exists or how a particular document or category of documents may be relevant or material, or even whether the [shield law] privilege applied or has been waived."

But suppose, a justice asked Degnan, that a defendant "does not in fact know or is unable to produce proof to demonstrate" the exact relevance of items believed to be held by a reporter. And suppose the items are truly relevant to the defense. "Is it your position that the price, if you will, of the First Amendment is that we permit the sequestration and the secretion of that evidence?"

"If the alternative to that is the granting of every subpoena for every reporter's file in every criminal case, which I suggest to you will happen," said Degnan, "then the answer to that is yes."

"Let's say that the court decides to remand," Chief Justice Hughes said, "and at the hearing the intransigence of *The Times* and Farber . . . continue in full flower. What does a judge do then?"

"Then," replied Degnan, "a legitimate contempt citation does lie there, and that avenue is open to this court."

The court reserved decision.

16

When Brown wasn't in one courtroom demanding my notes, he was in Judge Arnold's court presenting the defense case to the jury. Brown had already laid out the major elements of the defense case in legal motions, in his opening statement, in hearings on the admissibility of the state's curare tests and other evidence, and in twenty-two weeks of cross-examining prosecution witnesses. On August 1, 1978, after Judge Arnold dismissed the murder charges involving Margaret Henderson and Emma Arzt, Brown began to flesh out his case through his own witnesses. Now it was Moses's turn to cross-examine. And within a day, Brown was disparaging her efforts.

"Her cross stinks," Brown remarked during a conference at the bench at which he accused Moses of planning to bring him, after the trial, before the ethics committee of the county bar association, of which her husband was a member.

Brown's first witnesses were four former Riverdell employees: a nurse, two nurse's aides, and a laboratory technician.

NANCY SAVINO

Barbara Kenderes, a lab technician who now lived in Florida, was called to refute prosecution testimony that Nancy Savino was found dead as early as 7:30 A.M. on March 21, 1966, rather than at the 8 A.M. time on her chart; and that Dr. Jascalevich was across the hall from the child's room, and in street clothes, when his assistance was sought.

Mrs. Kenderes, whose last name in 1966 was Spadaro, said that it was about 8 A.M., ten minutes after she reported for work, when she was unable to awaken Nancy, and about 8:02 or 8:03 when she was told, at the nurses' desk, to summon help from Dr. Jascalevich in the operating room. The witness said she phoned the operating room and asked for Dr. Jascalevich, who came on the line and identified himself. After hanging up, Mrs. Kenderes recalled, "I looked at the clock on the wall and I noticed it was five minutes past eight, and after that, I don't remember what I did." She said she did not see Dr. Jascalevich anywhere near Room 211 that morning.

The witness testified that Herman Fuhr, the operating room technician who dropped by Nancy's room on the morning of March 21, 1966, later told her that he had left the child alive at 7:40 A.M. Fuhr himself had testified that it was 6:40 A.M. and that he began work in the operating room at 7 A.M.

Mrs. Kenderes also said that when she was unable to rouse Nancy, the child's face was "white," not blue, and not at all unusual for "a little white girl."

On cross-examination, Moses emphasized Mrs. Kenderes' statement to the grand jury in 1976 that she was "approximating" the time she phoned Dr. Jascalevich.

Q: In other words, you did not look at a clock when you were at the nurses' station; you were approximating the time.

A: I did not remember looking at a clock, when I went to the grand jury. I didn't know what questions they would ask me. I didn't know the times were that important. When defense counsel called me—

Q: He told you what questions he was going to ask you?

A: No, he stressed . . . he asked me to come, and I expressed a reluctance to come, and he stated the times were very important, to please go back . . . in my mind to make sure it was accurate. I did, and I remembered five after eight.

Wasn't it true, as a Miami private investigator had written to Brown after interviewing Mrs. Kenderes in April 1978, that she was in a "state of shock" after finding Nancy, so upset that she had to be sent home from work that day?

A: I don't remember anything that happened after I called Dr. Jascalevich.

Q: You were in a state of shock, were you not?

A: I don't remember.

Moses handed the witness a copy of the letter to Brown.

Q: Does it refresh your recollection as to whether you were in a state of shock on that day?

A: Yes, ma'am. It says that.

Q: Is it true? You were in a state of shock that day?

A: Well, these are not my exact words . . . I'm sure I was upset. I don't know [if] in a state of shock . . . I really don't remember after calling Dr. Jascalevich—I don't remember anything I did, how I felt. I'm sure it was an upsetting experience, learning she was dead.

Q: In other words, actually you don't recall if you were in a state of shock because you don't remember anything.

A: Yes, ma'am.

Mrs. Kenderes could not remember having ever seen Nancy before that morning.

Q: You would have nothing to compare, then, Mrs. Kenderes, whether her color differed from the color she had the day before?

A: I had nothing to compare. I don't remember.

And wasn't Nancy the first patient the witness visited on March 21, 1966, Moses asked. Yes, Mrs. Kenderes replied.

Q: You had no idea then what happened prior to that time. Isn't that so?

A: That is so.

FRANK BIGGS

Betsy Fairley, a nurse's aide, testified that on the night of Biggs's death, August 28, 1966, she was giving "evening care" to patients in a room along Biggs's corridor. She said she started about 8:45 P.M.; although she was not assigned to Biggs, she saw co-workers in Room 210 performing the same duties. Shortly after 9 P.M., the witness said, she was walking past Biggs's room to fetch linens when a nurse appeared at the door and said something was wrong. Mrs. Fairley went into the room, where there were "quite a few people," including several patients. "Mr. Biggs was lying in the bed, he was white in color, and he wasn't moving," she testified. She also said that when she was preparing Biggs's body for the morgue, she noted that "his stomach was slightly swollen."

*　*　*

The witness, who finished with Biggs about 10 P.M., said she did not see either Dr. Jascalevich or Dr. Stavrand, Biggs's physician, along the corridor. Or any other doctor.

On cross-examination, Mrs. Fairley admitted that she couldn't have seen "anything that would have gone on in the corridor" or in Biggs's room after she started work at 8:30 or 8:45 P.M. because she was taking care of patients in another room. Moreover, she couldn't recall the name of her partner that night; whether it was 9:05 or 9:15 when she first went into Biggs's room; who, if anyone, was assisting Biggs during the few minutes she stood there; or whether Biggs had an intravenous tubing attached to his arm. She saw no one giving artificial respiration, she said, and she had never seen Biggs before that night.

* * *

Q: Did the distention or swelling that you saw in the nude body of Mr. Biggs [later] equal that of a four-month pregnancy?

Over Brown's objection—"every lady is different, Judge"—Mrs. Fairley said that Biggs's appearance did not resemble "a pregnancy-type condition." The witness also said she did not disconnect any intravenous equipment when she was preparing the body for the morgue.

Q: Do you recall . . . whether or not you saw a catheter or any items that are used to remove urine from the bladder?

A: No, I don't remember seeing one.

Q: Were there any large amounts of urine or fluid in the bed?

A: I don't remember.

On redirect examination, Brown brought out that Mrs. Fairley had told Moses's investigators, as early as 1976, that Biggs was very white and that his bladder seemed swollen and somewhat distended. Then Moses had a parting shot.

Q: You also said [in 1976] that it did not resemble a pregnancy condition. Is that right? Is that correct?

A: That is what I said.

CARL ROHRBECK

Claire Hartman, a nurse's aide, and Genevieve Darcy, a nurse, were called by Brown to testify about events that preceded Carl Rohrbeck's death on the morning of December 13, 1965.

Mrs. Hartman told the jury that between 7:30 and 7:40 A.M. she noticed a light flashing above the door to Room 207. With another nurse's aide named Mrs. Herles, she said, she ran into the room. Rohrbeck's "hands were moving," Mrs. Hartman testified. "His eyes were up in his head. He was panting very badly. His condition and color was pale, and his perspiring was very, very bad."

"We must get help," Mrs. Hartman remembered saying to Mrs.

Herles, who left to get aid at the adjoining nurses' station. As she herself was leaving Room 207 to tend to a sick baby, Mrs. Hartman said, Mrs. Herles was returning with Annette O'Brien, the nurse in charge that morning.

Mrs. Hartman said she did not see Dr. Jascalevich in the area.

On cross-examination, Mrs. Hartman said she had never seen Rohrbeck before this incident. She stayed in his room, at the foot of his bed, for no more than a few minutes. And at that time, she testified, Rohrbeck did not have an intravenous infusion running.

Moses showed Mrs. Hartman the nurse's notes on Rohrbeck's chart for that period. They had been written by Mrs. O'Brien, who testified, during the prosecution's case, that she had spoken to Rohrbeck around 7:20 A.M. and he "appeared to be relaxed, not complaining, oriented, alert."

MOSES: Do the notes indicate that Dr. Jascalevich was visiting at 7:30? Do the notes indicate that?

HARTMAN: It says 7:30, yes.

Q: Do the notes further indicate that at 7:40 Mrs. McKeon [the operating room nurse] was notified of postponement of surgery until further medical evaluation obtained?

A: I don't know about that.

Q: I am just reading what the notes say . . . Do the notes further indicate that at 7:45 an I.V. of 5 percent dextrose and water, 1,000 cc, [was] started by Dr. Jascalevich in [the] right arm? Do the notes indicate that?

"It says that," Mrs. Hartman conceded. But still, the witness added, she "absolutely" did not see Dr. Jascalevich.

Q: So, then, it's possible that when you went into Mr. Rohrbeck's room, it was after 7:45 when he left?

BROWN: I object to that.

ARNOLD: I sustain the objection. Mrs. Moses, you went over this.

Mrs. Hartman went on to say that Rohrbeck's bed was "flat," not on an angle, and that she saw only one of the patient's hands moving.

Q: Which hand?

A: The left hand.

Q: Where was it going?

A: Well, it was just—

Q: He was having difficulty in moving that hand?

A: Just moving like—a person would in distress move their hand.

Q: Did he clutch his chest?

A: No.

Q: Did he scream out in pain?

A: Not in my presence, no.

Q: Did he in any way move his hand to his throat or his chest?

A: No.

Q: In fact, he didn't raise his hand at all?

A: No.

Q: Did you notice that he had a neck vein jumping in his neck? Did you go to his neck?

A: No, I wouldn't say—I wasn't in there long enough to notice anything more than what I did with the panting.

Q: The panting, you remember that.

A: Yes.

Q: That's what really sticks out in your mind, isn't it?

A: Yes.

Q: The breathing, the panting?

A: Yes.

Genevieve Darcy, under questioning by Brown, said that when she reported for work about 7:30 A.M. on December 13, she heard Rohrbeck was in "bad shape," and she went in to see him. "There was a man laying very pale and very weak . . . very pale," she recalled. Rohrbeck spoke to her in a weak but coherent voice. At that time, Mrs. Darcy said, he had an intravenous infusion running.

Mrs. Darcy said that she walked out of Room 207 and met Dr. Jascalevich in the hall. He was writing in a little book he often carried with him when making rounds. The surgeon, she testified, said that he was thinking about canceling Rohrbeck's surgery, and she said that was a good idea. Together they returned to Room 207 and looked at the patient. Dr. Jascalevich then decided to postpone the surgery. "We walked out together, and . . . he said, 'I am going to tell the operating room.' He walked around and up to the operating room." Mrs. Darcy said that she went to the nurses' station to tell "the girls" that Rohrbeck's operation had been put off, and then she returned to Room 207 to inform the patient. And "I saw that he was—I thought he was dead."

BROWN: Could you describe his appearance?

DARCY: He was laying in bed, and I thought him—he was pale and he looked dead.

Q: What did you do then?

A: I ran out and told the girls that he was dead, and ran up the hall and said, "The patient—your patient has died."

Q: Did Dr. Jascalevich ever say to you the patient was dead?

A: He wasn't. He was alive when Dr. Jascalevich was there.

Q: Did you ever see Dr. Jascalevich do anything to this man in terms of anything at all?

A: When I was with him, no.

Mrs. Darcy said that when she went to inform Dr. Jascalevich of Rohrbeck's death, she heard two men arguing in the hall. But the only voice she recognized was that of Dr. Sklar, Rohrbeck's physician.

Q: After you had come to this point and told them that Mr. Rohrbeck was dead, what else did you observe, if anything?

A: I don't remember.

The witness said it was only a matter of minutes between the time she first visited Rohrbeck and the time she found him "in a grotesque —you know, in a death shape" with his head "fallen to the side" and his arm hanging out.

ARNOLD: Excuse me. Do you know what was the first time when you said he was speaking to you that you were in there?

A: When I came in?

ARNOLD: Approximately what time was it?

A: It was right after I came on duty, Doctor, Father—

ARNOLD: I'm not a doctor.

BROWN: You have been a doctor and a priest.

ARNOLD: I make the mistake, so don't feel badly.

MOSES: It's the robe, Judge.

Mrs. Darcy repeated that the time was approximately 7:30 A.M.

On cross-examination, Mrs. Darcy said that, when she first saw Rohrbeck, he was "lying still."

MOSES: You didn't see him panting heavy, did you?

DARCY: No.

Q: You didn't see him perspiring, did you?

A: No.

* * *

Q: Did he do anything which would indicate to you he was in severe pain?

A: I said there was no urgency.

Q: There was nothing that you could see?

A: No, he was a weak man laying there.

Q: Lying still?

A: That's right.

Q: The I.V. was running?

A: Yes.

Q: This is between 7:30 and 8 A.M. in the morning. Other than that, you can't pin it down further?

A: No.

Mrs. Darcy said that just before she left Rohrbeck and encountered

Dr. Jascalevich in the hall, the patient asked her if he was going into surgery, and she said she would find out.

Q: [Dr. Jascalevich] said to you, "I am contemplating canceling surgery"?

A: Yes.

Q: In other words, he hadn't made up his mind at that point?

A: That's right.

Q: You assumed that he had been in the room already.

A: Yes.

Mrs. Darcy said that when she and Dr. Jascalevich went back into Room 207, they stayed in the middle of the room. The surgeon, she testified, did not examine Rohrbeck at that time.

MOSES: Did he take his pulse?

A: No.

Q: Did he check his heart with a stethoscope?

A: No. He didn't touch the patient.

Q: Did he go over to the side of the bed?

A: He didn't go that far.

Q: He just looked at him?

A: Yes.

Q: Did he speak to him?

A: No.

Q: He said nothing to him at all?

A: No.

Q: So if he testified under oath and gave a statement under oath that he told Mr. Rohrbeck—

Judge Arnold sustained Brown's objection.

The witness said that she did not think Rohrbeck was in "imminent danger" at that stage. "He was in poor shape for surgery, but for death —I didn't think it was going to happen."

Q: There was no sense of urgency whatsoever in the defendant's attitude, was there?

A: No.

In response to Moses's questions, Mrs. Darcy said that Dr. Jascalevich hadn't mentioned either a jumping vein or the rales he allegedly had heard in the patient's chest. She said that she had not seen Mrs. Hartman or Mrs. Herles—or anyone else—in Rohrbeck's room when she was there with Dr. Jascalevich. When she returned to Room 207 shortly thereafter and found the patient "in a relaxed position of death," she did not take his pulse or temperature, or apply artificial respiration or heart massage. After running to the nurses at the station —"they went right in"—she continued on to the operating room, where she told Dr. Jascalevich and Dr. Sklar of the death.

Q: And Dr. Sklar came back?

A: Yes.

Q: Did Dr. Jascalevich come back to see the patient?

A: I have no idea. I can't remember anything that happened after it.

On redirect examination, Brown stressed that Mrs. Darcy had told Moses's investigators in 1976 that Rohrbeck was "pale" on the morning of his death.

Q: Did you see him at any time other than pale?

A: No.

Q: Did you ever see him when he was blue?

A: No.

To support Dr. Jascalevich's contention that he had experimented on dogs in 1965–66, as well as in 1963–64, Brown called Alfred Stoholski and Eve Gordon Arons, two former associates of Dr. Umberger, who had died in December 1977. In 1966 Stoholski was the criminologist who had examined some of the seventy-one items taken by Calissi from Dr. Jascalevich's locker number four at Riverdell on November 1, as well as some of the nineteen items the surgeon gave to the prosecutor two days later. Mrs. Arons was a serologist who worked with Stoholski and Dr. Umberger in 1966 in the New York medical examiner's office.

Stoholski's testimony consisted largely of a review of the two Allied lab reports of February 19, 1967: Moses's cross-examination centered on the witness's competence. The prosecutor made much of the fact that Stoholski lacked a college degree and challenged his ability, in 1966, to distinguish dog hairs from other hairs.

Mrs. Arons testified that Dr. Umberger had given her a number of items belonging to a "doctor in Bergen County" in 1966, including a vial of blood, gauze pads, tweezers, clamps, syringes, scissors, and rubber gloves. The serologist said that her test on the vial of clotted blood "absolutely" indicated that it was dog serum. On cross-examination, Mrs. Arons said the blood was no more than five weeks old when she tested it. And Moses suggested that the blood came, not from anything in Dr. Jascalevich's locker number four but from a vial in the Horn & Hardart "research bag" that the surgeon had given to Calissi on November 3, 1966, the day after his visit to Pollak Hospital to work on a dog.

Brown also brought on Judge Calissi and Judge Galda. Calissi testified that as prosecutor in 1966, he "adopted the suspicions of the doctors [who came to him] for the purpose of the investigation, because that is the nature of the beast. That is the prosecutor. He has to be suspicious; otherwise he isn't going to be investigating anything." As

time went on, Calissi said, all but three or four of the deaths he was reviewing were "explained away logically or medically," and he then
"ran into a stone wall" over the issue of finding curare in embalmed
bodies. On cross-examination, Moses asked whether Calissi would have
gone to a grand jury with the remaining "unexplained" deaths if curare
had indeed been found in their bodies. But Brown objected to the
question, and Judge Arnold sustained the objection.

Moses asked Judge Calissi to look at the lab report on the research
items Dr. Jascalevich had given to him on November 3, 1966. Among
the items listed were four jars to which adhesive tape was fixed. In each
instance, according to the report, the tape was labeled "Seton Hall
Research ⅍101" with additional references to numbers of dogs.

MOSES: As a result of sending detectives to the College of Medicine,
were you able to ascertain whether or not there was a Seton Hall Project 101?

BROWN: I object; it is irrelevant and immaterial.

MOSES: You see it on the first page?

BROWN: I object. There is no such thing as Project 101. That is a
fiction of her imagination.

MOSES: That is right, there is no such thing as Project—

"There is nothing on that item that refers to any project," said
Brown, adding that Dr. Jascalevich did not prepare the lab report.

MOSES: Judge Calissi, let me get something straight. The items listed
here [on the lab report], were those items handed in by the defendant
in the Horn & Hardart bag?

A: I testified to that before.

Judge Galda testified that on the afternoon of November 2, 1966, he
listened to the tape of the meeting that morning between the Riverdell
directors and Dr. Jascalevich. Dr. Jascalevich, the witness said, complained about "insufficient work-up" on some patients and operations
that were too long, and he "berated the doctors for incompetency."

Galda said that after receiving the Allied lab reports in late February
1967, "we continued to check out various items."

Q: And what happened then, if you can tell us?

A: Well, the areas we were exploring in connection with this case
suggested that there was no—nothing that we had suggested that this
matter should be presented to a grand jury.

Judge Galda finished testifying on August 29, 1978. That same day
Judge Arnold excused a juror whose health, according to his doctor,
was being affected by the long trial. The jury was now down from eighteen members to thirteen. Increasingly worried that the figure might slip
below twelve, Judge Arnold cautioned the jurors against "getting sick

on us . . . It's quite important," he reminded them. "Take very good care of yourselves."

The defense position was that Nancy Savino, Frank Biggs, and Carl Rohrbeck had died natural deaths at Riverdell Hospital. Through his cross-examination of Dr. Baden and other prosecution witnesses, Brown had already suggested that the Savino child died of infectious peritonitis; Biggs, of a fatty liver related to lung congestion; and Rohrbeck, of heart disease. In Dr. Baden's opinion, they had all died of curare poisoning.

To counter Dr. Baden's testimony, Brown called the defense pathologist, Henry Siegel, a former deputy chief medical examiner of New York who had retired in April 1978 after eight years as medical examiner of Westchester County, New York. Dr. Siegel, whom Brown had consulted in another case around 1974, had been advising the defense lawyer on the Riverdell deaths since the spring of 1976; as an expert witness, he was also allowed in the courtroom, and he had spent some eighty to ninety days at the Jascalevich trial, listening to testimony. Although he had not been present at the reautopsies Dr. Baden performed on the exhumed bodies at the beginning of 1976, Dr. Siegel had received the reports on those examinations plus virtually all the clinical, pathological, and toxicological data on the patients that was available to the prosecution experts.

Dr. Siegel testified that Frank Biggs died of "massive pulmonary congestion and edema" caused by his fatty liver—"it all goes back . . . to the fatty liver" which, the witness said, can lead to "sudden and unexpected death."

The pathologist also said there was nothing in Biggs's chart to support the idea that he had been poisoned by curare, and it was impossible for Biggs to have been blue all over, as Dr. Stavrand had testified. Even in cases of hanging or strangulation or choking, Dr. Siegel said, "the most one sees in the dead body, in the fresh dead body, is cyanosis of the head, the shoulders, the fingernails and toenails."

Dr. Siegel rejected the prosecution's claim that it had discovered curare in Biggs's tissues. "This application of this combination of RIA and HPLC is a unique experiment, [and] at the present time it's not accepted in the scientific community as valid and of scientific certainty," he said. But assuming curare was, in fact, in the tissues, "the mere presence . . . in no way is a factor in this man's death without my knowing the amounts [so] that I can make an estimate of the pharmacological or clinical effects of the drug on the man. It may be present in trace amounts and not have any effect on him at all. And the other main reason is that after examining the entire record and the slides, I have found an adequate, competent, producing cause of death, and the reason for it."

Carl Rohrbeck, Dr. Siegel testified, died of occlusive coronary arteriosclerosis; the left anterior descending branch of his heart—"really the key artery"—was blocked at "the key point." The fact that there was no evidence at the 1965 autopsy of a fresh infarction would "absolutely not" change his opinion. "We know why they died," Dr. Siegel said, referring to people who succumbed to conditions such as Rohrbeck's. "They died of heart disease. But why they died at that time, why they didn't die the day before, why they didn't die two weeks later—that we don't know." The "pitting edema" in Rohrbeck's ankles on the day of his admission was a sign of his heart condition, the witness said. And given Dr. Jascalevich's stated reason for canceling Rohrbeck's operation the next morning, the surgeon's decision to start an intravenous infusion when he did was consistent with good medical practice. "It's a clinical judgment, and here's a man who's had nothing by mouth."

As with Biggs, Dr. Siegel discounted the prosecution's curare findings on Rohrbeck.

Nancy Savino, Dr. Siegel said, died of acute diffuse peritonitis, an infection that he said was present not only throughout her intestine but was also affecting other parts of her body. Dr. Harris's operation, he said, removed "the root" of the child's illness; but the peritonitis, caused by bacteria, remained. Although peritonitis had not been described by Dr. Markley in the naked-eye or microscopic portions of Nancy's 1966 autopsy, Dr. Siegel said, he himself had found evidence of infection in slides that were saved from that postmortem.

The courtroom lights were lowered, and using a pointer, Dr. Siegel interpreted a series of blown-up transparencies and photographs made from the 1966 microscopic slides.

Dr. Siegel also flashed three slides from Dr. Baden's 1976 reautopsy of Nancy Savino and said the slides, according to his interpretation of Baden's testimony in June, represented "different areas" of the small intestine—not simply the site at which Dr. Harris had operated. On each of the slides, Dr. Siegel pointed to bluish dots that he called "inflammatory cells." And this, he said, "is the picture of acute peritonitis . . ."

BROWN: Was that peritonitis treated properly in order that her death be prevented?

SIEGEL: She died.

The witness said that if Nancy Savino were pale at the time of her death, that would be inconsistent with curare poisoning: "the prime thing is cyanosis, and this child had pallor." He would accept the prosecution's discovery of curare in Nancy Savino by mass spectrometry, rather than RIA and HPLC, although "a more complete mass spectrometry could have been done." But still, the pathologist said, the tests "do not tell me how much was found, and that is very, very important."

Laden with medical books and aided by an associate of Dr. Baden, Moses cross-examined Dr. Siegel for five days. It was a fight all the way. Dr. Siegel repeatedly said that he couldn't answer Moses's questions because they made "absolutely no sense" or were "silly" or "absurd." Moses, he groused, was not a good lawyer, and she was asking "tricky" questions and trying to mix him up. "You don't know anything about operating rooms . . . You don't know what you are talking about," Dr. Siegel would chide the prosecutor. ". . . I will teach you some correct medicine."

Moses charged that Dr. Siegel was a know-it-all whose "mind is made up. He is an advocate, Judge, not a scientist . . . He is so emotionally highly involved." The prosecutor was critical, too, of Dr. Siegel's tendency to answer questions with an explanation.

MOSES: Yes or no, sir. Does the [Savino] temperature chart show normal?

A: I cannot answer this stupid question like this.

ARNOLD: You answer it. No more.

Q: Does the temperature chart show normal?

A: It went down.

ARNOLD: Yes or no; yes or no, Doctor. Does it show normal?

A: On the chart the temperature went down to a point which can be called normal.

ARNOLD: All right.

Displeased, Brown asked the judge, at one stage, how he could allow Moses to restrict Dr. Siegel's testimony. How could he allow the prosecutor to demand a yes or no answer? "Who," Brown wanted to know, "is running the courtroom, first of all?"

ARNOLD: I am, and sit down.

Brown often hurried to Dr. Siegel's aid. Dr. Siegel, he said, "knows more about medicine than anybody else in the world," and, if he was laughing on the stand, he was only laughing at Moses, "and I think that is justified." "You cannot get anything but dirt from a dirt hole," Brown said of the prosecutor. When, over Judge Arnold's ruling, Moses pursued Dr. Siegel about whether he would accept a certain medical book as an authority—Brown intervened to say that "she has no respect for the Court or anyone else."

MOSES: He's getting so excited.

BROWN: I think it is an abomination to have her in the courtroom.

ARNOLD: There's no excuse for that, Mr. Brown.

BROWN: I think there is.

Again when Moses was questioning Dr. Siegel about the elements of a physical examination, Brown said he was getting a "headache."

MOSES: I know Dr. Siegel finds it amusing, but someone [Biggs] died here, Dr. Siegel, and I wish you would listen carefully and answer the question.

BROWN: Do you think that is proper, Judge. Did you hear that? How come you don't hear?

ARNOLD: I can't hear because you were shouting.

BROWN: I wasn't shouting when she said it.

ARNOLD: If you had been quiet, maybe I could hear what she is saying.

Cross-examining Dr. Siegel about Nancy Savino, Moses pressed her view that the child did not have acute peritonitis, a generalized infection. Dr. Siegel conceded that after surgery, the Savino child did not display the classical signs or symptoms of peritoneal infection, but that, he said, was "not the picture that one finds on those having acute diffuse peritonitis who come into the receiving ward. It is a classical picture that one uses to teach . . ."

MOSES: Dr. Siegel, as a result of the operation, was not the child recovering and all the signs and symptoms which would indicate that she was recovering were normal?

SIEGEL: She was not recovering. She died from it . . . She died. She was in extremis.

But after surgery, Moses asked, were there any clinical signs of symptoms of acute diffuse peritonitis?

A: Yes, because I saw it.

Q: Look at the chart?

A: The autopsy showed it.

Q: Is there any clinical sign or symptom that this child had acute diffuse peritonitis?

A: All right, it is an incomplete chart, okay?

MOSES: Judge, he is not answering the question. Would you direct the witness to answer the question.

BROWN: He has answered the question.

ARNOLD: I will allow him to answer it.

Q: Do you see one clinical sign or symptom after—

ARNOLD: You mean before death?

MOSES: After the surgery, Your Honor.

ARNOLD: After the surgery.

A: No.

Q: None?

A: No. But it is an incomplete chart.

Q: That is your opinion?

A: Yes.

Q: During the course of that chart, though, the vital signs are reported on Sunday, the twentieth, were they not?

Dr. Siegel conceded that point to Moses, but stressed that ". . . it is the whole clinical judgment you have to go through." An extended effort by Moses to show that Nancy Savino's peritonitis was nothing more than a routine inflammation restricted to the surgical site got nowhere with Dr. Siegel. "I am only making sure that the truth comes out," he said.

With respect to Carl Rohrbeck, Moses raised the possibility that the patient did not have a dominant left coronary artery, and, therefore, the occlusion of that artery was less crucial than Dr. Siegel—and thirteen years earlier, Dr. Denson—had indicated. Dr. Siegel said he couldn't tell from the report of Dr. Denson's autopsy in 1965 whether Rohrbeck had a left coronary artery preponderance, as most people do, but it didn't matter: the seventy-three-year-old patient had died of coronary atherosclerotic occlusion.

The witness granted that "pitting edema" of the ankles could be a sign of illness other than heart disease, but in Rohrbeck's case, he said, he had discounted all of the other possibilities.

Referring to the testimony of nurses O'Brien and Darcy, Moses asked Dr. Siegel whether he would agree that Dr. Jascalevich's examination of Rohrbeck on the morning of his death was "not the equivalent of the appropriate diagnosis of congestive heart failure." "Absolutely not," said the witness. Moses also asked whether there was anything in Dr. Jascalevich's handwriting on the chart to indicate that he had checked Rohrbeck's pulse on December 13. "No particulars," Siegel answered.

Q: So the last known particulars of this decedent, sir, as noted in the record, are normal; are they not?

BROWN: This is the most irresponsible examination—

ARNOLD: I will allow it.

Q: Did Dr. Jascalevich include any of those particulars in his notations?

A: They could have been included in his conclusions. I don't know.

Q: Will you answer the question yes or no?

A: He didn't spell it out one by one, because he did it in the admission history and the physician signed it.

But if a patient were exhibiting signs of heart failure, Moses asked Dr. Siegel, wouldn't it be standard medical practice to order an electrocardiogram?

A: Yes.

Q: Is it not true that . . . the next most important thing would be to give [a] diuretic or some digitalis to the patient, depending on the signs he was exhibiting?

That was a "purely clinical judgment" on the part of the physician, Dr. Siegel said, and as far as the EKG was concerned, it had been ordered the previous day by Dr. Jascalevich and had not been done. If it had not been ordered in "a man of this age," he would have wondered about it.

Q: So generally speaking, you would wonder about it, but in this case, you say you don't have any questions about it. Is that your testimony?

A: That is right because it was ordered.

Q: Would you review the chart and see once again if there is anything ordered [by Dr. Jascalevich] after the surgery was canceled other than the intravenous.

A: If it was—if nothing was ordered after the operation and there was a short period of time, I wouldn't think anything of it.

Q: Do you see anything in the chart, and I am strictly referring to the chart, which indicates that anything was done other than the defendant starting an intravenous of 5 percent glucose and water on Mr. Rohrbeck after there is an indication in the nurse's notes that he decided to cancel the surgery?

A: That is correct.

Q: Nothing else is done?

A: That is right.

With regard to Frank Biggs, Moses and Dr. Siegel clashed over the condition of the patient's liver from the time he entered Riverdell and even before. The witness conceded that albumin and globulin liver-function tests were "within normal limits" preoperatively; that neither Dr. Briski nor Dr. Jascalevich had indicated seeing any problem with the liver during surgery; and that there was no note on the hospital chart suggesting jaundice or edema. But Dr. Siegel said a "whole battery" of other liver tests should have been performed before surgery on Biggs, who, he maintained, had "advanced" liver disease.

But, Moses asked, if Biggs had advanced liver disease, wouldn't the autopsy have shown a change in the size of the liver and the spleen?

SIEGEL: No.

MOSES: Never?

A: I did not say that.

Q: And in this case of advanced liver disease, both the spleen and the liver are normal size, according to the report?

A: That is right.

And wasn't it true, Moses suggested, that a narcotic or a respiratory depressant would produce the same type of lung edema that was described in Dr. Markley's autopsy report on Biggs in 1966?

A: Not necessarily.

Q: But it could be true. That would be a fair statement, wouldn't it?

A: It is possible, yes.

Moses pressed Dr. Siegel further: didn't the autopsy report also indicate that there was no free fluid and no blood in the peritoneal cavity?

A: That is correct.

Q: In your knowledge, sir, isn't it true that a sign of liver disease is ascites, or fluid in the peritoneal cavity?

A: In advanced liver disease, it may or may not be present.

What of the curare? Assuming that curare had been found in the bodies of Nancy Savino and Frank Biggs and Carl Rohrbeck, wouldn't its presence be a "more compelling" cause of death than whatever natural disease existed? Moses asked. How important was the amount "when curare is found in the body of someone who did not receive a therapeutic dose and when someone does not produce it naturally?"

Dr. Siegel said he preferred to answer by way of illustration. "A person can take a drink of beer, one ounce of beer, step outside, and get killed. That is, by an auto or shot or anyway you will. I will find alcohol in him. Am I going to say he is drunk or he died of acute alcoholism? Of course not. That is why in my paper—I am sorry—that I presented in New Zealand, I said heroin is being used so much that people can die from other causes and yet we will find it in the body. Another example is you can smoke a cigarette and then 'go into the atmosphere' where nobody is smoking, and I can detect nicotine in your urine two days later. That doesn't mean that you are being affected by the nicotine, nor does it mean that you have died of nicotine."

Q: Dr. Siegel, aren't you now comparing apples and oranges, sir, to use your phrase?

A: I am just giving examples.

Q: Are you saying, sir, that the finding of curare in a body is similar to the finding of alcohol in the body after someone had a few drinks? Is that what you are saying?

A: I am just giving an example . . . Traces of any substance mean nothing without my knowing what the clinical picture was . . . One must know the whole picture before evaluating.

Moses invited the witness to "look at the whole picture" with regard to Rohrbeck. Was there any explanation in his hospital chart to account for "those traces of curare"? Brown objected to the question, and Judge Arnold said he didn't understand it.

ARNOLD: There is no evidence by the chart of any curare being given to anybody.

MOSES: That is the point.

ARNOLD: What is the point?

Moses tried explaining the point to the judge, and again Brown objected. Dr. Siegel, Brown told the prosecutor, "doesn't accept the strange tests that your strange scientists produced . . . There is no way to find an explanation of curare from the chart."

"That is the point," Moses said. "There is no way." Consider the autopsy reports and any of the circumstances surrounding Rohrbeck's death, she went on. What explained the presence of any curare in that patient's body?

With the jury excused, Brown said "they spiked it." But when the jury came back, Dr. Siegel offered other theories. The witness, who agreed that curare was not produced by the living body, had already testified on direct examination that "there are certain plants, even in this area, that produce curarine-like substances . . . it's important to have adequate controls of the soil" surrounding the graves. Now he said that curare "could have been generated from the decomposing and autolyzing tissues present in the soil that will produce tubocurarine [curare]. And in doing the tests—there were no adequate controls in doing the tests and also in doing the tests tubocurarine was present [and] being used as a controlled substance while the tests were being done."

Well, said Moses, what scientific literature set forth the bacteria theory? Was the soil to be found in New Jersey and New York? (Rohrbeck had been buried in New York.) What was the name of the bacteria? Did it grow normally or under special conditions? Was it affected by temperature? Dr. Siegel said he didn't know the answers, but he would check the literature. How about the plants then? Dr. Siegel couldn't specify the plant, which, he said, was of the genus *Erythrina*. Where does it grow in this area? Moses asked. In New Jersey? In New York? "In the Northeast someplace. I don't know. As I said, I'm not a botanist . . . I read it in one of the books." Which book? "I forget because this goes back two years." Could Dr. Siegel get the book?

SIEGEL: Your Honor, this is such a waste of time, but [if] it has to be done I will do it.

MOSES: Judge, would you instruct the witness to answer the question.

*   *   *

Assuming, Moses said, that Dr. Coumbis testified that he did an RIA test on the dirt from the body and the grave site of Mr. Rohrbeck and that he got a negative finding . . . would that not indicate that there was nothing in the soil which produces a curare or curare-like substance surrounding the grave?

A: It would indicate that at that time there was no tubocurarine present in the soil . . . Whether these plants were present ten years before, I don't know.

Q: Are you saying, sir, then there is a change in the soil of New York and the cemetery over the last ten years?

A: I have no information on that.

Three days later, Dr. Siegel reported that he was unable to find the book he had read on the plant. However, he had found a reference showing that the *"Erythrina* plant" grew in tropical and subtropical regions.

Q: Which, of course, excludes this area?

A: Yes, yes.

As far as the bacteria was concerned, it didn't produce curare; it broke it down. And the work was done in Germany.

Q: And so Dr. Siegel, the question I am going to ask you is this: Are there any bacteria that produce curare that grow in the soil or in the body?

A: I have not come across any.

Moses turned to Dr. Siegel's statement that curare could have been generated by "decomposing" tissues.

Q: Do you know in general whether the molecule curare, generically known as curare, is produced by the decomposed body?

A: Do I know?

Q: Yes.

A: No, I do not know.

And assuming that Dr. Coumbis and Dr. Dal Cortivo "both did extensive extract procedures up to eight stages and assuming that these extract procedures purified the tissue upon which they were going to perform their tests," what "was left in that extract which could account for the presence of curare other than curare itself?"

A: What compounds are left?

MOSES: Other than curare.

BROWN: Will you quiet her and let him answer. This is an outrage. She won't let him answer the question.

ARNOLD: This is Mrs. Moses's cross-examination like you had yours.

BROWN: I have never interrupted a witness to be afraid of his answer.

A: There may be many compounds, but I cannot name them specifically.

Q: Can you name any of the compounds other than curare which would produce the result and which would lead Dr. Coumbis to give the opinion with reasonable scientific certainty that there was curare present in that eluate?

BROWN: I object. She has to justify an incompetent scientist, and I object to that question.

ARNOLD: I will allow it. Go ahead . . . Can you name what other compounds there would be?

A: What other enumerable compounds that would give the same test?

ARNOLD: Yes.

A: No.

Finally, Moses asked about the curare results on Nancy Savino, including the mass spectrometry test. But Dr. Siegel insisted that peritonitis killed the child.

Q: In other words, the presence of curare in the body of this child would not lead you to say she died of curare poisoning?

A: Without knowing the amounts. Because trace amounts mean nothing . . .

Q: Does everybody have trace amounts of curare in their body?

A: As far as I know, no.

Q: No further questions.

Frederic Rieders, the toxicologist who had performed various curare tests for the defense, followed Henry Siegel to the stand. Dr. Rieders, who had been chief toxicologist of Philadelphia for fourteen years before starting a private laboratory in 1970, was highly critical of the prosecution experts' use, in this case, of radioimmunoassay and high-pressure liquid chromatography. As techniques for identifying "unknown" substances in bodies that had been embalmed and buried for ten years, RIA and HPLC were "fleas" compared to the "elephant" of mass spectrometry, Dr. Rieders said. HPLC, he told the jury, was a technique for "separating" out and measuring a "known" substance, and RIA "doesn't identify a substance for you. It tells you that it may be present." Dr. Rieders said that he had used RIA in his lab for a year in the mid-1970s—not involving curare—but had abandoned the technique because it could give "unfounded" results. In the circumstances of this case, he said, even the combination of HPLC and RIA was "improper." At best the combination offered "a somewhat better presumption of the possibility of the presence" of curare, but in "no shape or form" did it provide "a confirmed, positive identification that what was found is, in fact, curare rather than something else which has nothing to do with curare." On the other hand, the witness said, mass spectrometry "is an identifying method, specifically. It is used to identify a substance as a substance, in contrast to virtually innumerable other substances."

Dr. Rieders said that based on his experience and review of the literature relating to curare—even before he conducted tests on the tissues of the Riverdell patients—he had concluded that curare was "unstable in tissue and breaks down rapidly and continuously," and that curare placed in a body that was then embalmed and buried would not "survive in any form in which it is identifiable at the end of ten years as curare."

Brown skipped over Dr. Rieders's own discovery of curare in Nancy Savino's liver—tests done by mass spectrometry in January 1978—and asked the toxicologist about the series of experiments he had conducted in February and March 1978 on embalming fluids that were similar to those used on the bodies of the Riverdell patients in 1965 and 1966. Dr. Rieders said he had undertaken the tests for two reasons: to see whether the embalming components contained any substances which might give a molecular "fingerprint" like curare and be mistaken for the drug, and to see whether the addition of curare to small amounts of embalming fluids precluded detection of the drug. The embalming fluids—chiefly special glacial, which prevents rapid putrefaction of tissues, and Micotrol, which softens tissues—don't really mimic curare on the mass spectrometer, Dr. Rieders testified. But when he added curare to the embalming fluids, he said, the embalming components "interacted" with the drug and, by altering its molecular structure, caused the curare to "become something else"—to "disappear" as curare. To confirm the mass spectrometry results, the witness went on, he turned to another technique. After adding curare to the embalming fluids, he let the mixture sit at room temperature in glass test tubes for seventy-two hours. Then, using certain controls, he put the mixture on thin-layer chromatography plates to observe whether the nitrogen-bearing part of the curare molecule would still react to iodaplatinate spray. Once again, he found that the embalming materials had "broken down a substantial portion" of the curare, causing the drug to "vanish." Dr. Rieders showed the jury photographs of the chromatography plates. "And, of course," he said, "my conclusion based on that was that if that much is destroyed in seventy-two hours, that over a period—as I was asked in this case—over a ten-year period, that no conceivable amount of curare could remain in the body . . . no amount that I can conceive that could be injected into a living person" from 10-cc vials of the drug. Even in plain water, Dr. Rieders said, curare had started to break down after seventy-two hours. And this, he said, corroborated the literature—that curare was stable only in a hydrochloric acid solution.

After Dr. Rieders and Dr. Siegel conferred in Stockholm with Bo Holmstedt, the Swedish toxicologist, Dr. Rieders ran tests on water and "juice" squeezed from tissues of Nancy Savino, Frank Biggs, and Carl Rohrbeck—tissues that had been kept frozen since the exhumations in 1976. Once the tissues were thawed out and pressed, Dr. Rieders said, he added curare to the juice as well as proportions of embalming fluids that "are actually used" in the embalming process. After an hour, and then after sixty hours, the solutions were examined by thin-layer chromatography. And here again, the toxicologist testified, the mixtures "progressively and extensively destroy curare, break it down into unrecognizable curare-like fragments." Half the curare, he estimated, was destroyed by the tissue juices alone in three days, while the embalming fluids worked even faster on the drug.

Finally, Brown came back to Dr. Rieders's mass spectrometry tests, in January 1978, on the tissues of the Riverdell patients.

In these tests, Dr. Rieders said, he had found no curare in samples of Biggs's liver and diaphragm or in Rohrbeck's liver (just as he had not detected curare in the tissues of Margaret Henderson and Emma Arzt). And he had found no curare in a 4-gram specimen of Nancy Savino's muscle. But two tests on 5-gram samples of the child's liver produced a complete mass spectrum that "matched excellently" that of curare. Dr. Rieders estimated that the liver contained about 200 nanograms of curare per gram of tissue—a "substantial amount" of "positively identified" curare.

Q: Now, Doctor, from your experience as a toxicologist, can you tell us if there is any significance in your finding in the tissue of the liver, *d*-tubocurarine [curare] and none in the muscle of the same body?

A: In my opinion, there is considerable significance.

Q: And what is the significance, sir?

A: That there is a tremendous inconsistency, if this were to originate from curare that had been administered to an individual, that a clearly recognizable quantity, of the order of 200 to 300 nanograms—two- to three-tenths of a microgram—per gram be present in the liver, and none at all in the muscle. That is just not the way the circulation works. When you get something into the circulation, it's distributed throughout the body, and there is a relationship between concentrations in the different tissues. If you find it in one, it's present in the others, too.

Q: Doctor, from your experience as a toxicologist and pharmacologist, can you describe for the jury—can you characterize the aspect of the *d*-tubocurarine in the liver as pure, as diluted, or whatever?

A: Well, the tubocurarine which I saw through mass spectrometry was so clearly recognizable that I am reasonably certain that it was, in fact, unchanged, pure tubocurarine, and not fragments of tubocurarine, and not something like tubocurarine that had changed, but, in fact, there was unchanged, pure tubocurarine present in the liver specimen. And not in the muscle.

Q: In view of your experiments showing, in your opinion, that curare, if it had been put into this body prior to death, would have been destroyed and would not appear at the time of exhumation, in view of the fact that you found nothing in the muscle, but the type of curare you found in the liver was pure, do you have an opinion as to whether or not you can tell us when you believe that curare had to be put in that body?

MOSES: I object to that, Judge. How can he tell?

ARNOLD: I'll allow it.

MOSES: On what basis, Judge? On what basis, Judge, can he anticipate and answer the question?

ARNOLD: Well, his experiments—as a result of his experiments. I'll allow it.

A: That this did not occur either prior to death or up until or after the body got back out of the ground ten years later. That means this could not have been present in a body in the ground for ten years after embalming, so it must have been introduced into the body or into the specimen, for that matter—I mean, I don't know which—after it had been removed from the ground. I'm reasonably certain that it couldn't have been there at the time of exhumation.

How much curare, Brown asked, would have to have been put in a body ten years prior to exhumation if 200 nanograms per gram of liver tissue could be detected after disinterment?

Dr. Rieders got out of the witness chair and drew a string of figures on a blackboard. Basing his calculation on a half-life of curare of seventy-two hours, he said the amount was "pretty darn close to infinity"; more curare "than there's curare in the whole world. One gram [of tissue] would have been surrounded by a bulk of curare which is as big as the state of New Jersey."

Moses began her cross-examination by suggesting that Dr. Rieders had been "stuck" with his early curare finding in Nancy Savino's liver and that all his subsequent tests, up until the fourth month of the trial, were an effort to explain away that discovery. The prosecutor, who brought out that Dr. Rieders had billed Brown for about $28,000 of work so far, spent several days assailing those tests. Dr. Rieders said that when he tested the curare in embalming fluids by mass spectrometry in February 1978, about half the curare appeared to have been destroyed by Micotrol; about 90 percent, by special glacial. The figures were only estimates. Wasn't it possible, Moses asked, that "interfering substances" in the embalming fluids had merely "masked" some of the curare? "It's possible," said Dr. Rieders. "I didn't think that was the whole answer, although it might have been part of the answer." Wasn't it possible that extreme heat and oxygen and accelerated chemical reaction in the metal rod, or "probe," that contained Dr. Rieders's solutions caused some loss of curare even before the probe was inserted into the mass spectrometer? "Anything is possible, but I don't think so." Couldn't some of the curare have escaped detection through a phenomenon known as "entrainment," in which portions of the curare molecule were carried off the probe before the mass spectrometer had a chance to analyze the solutions? "It's possible, yes. I don't think so in this case." In the thin-layer chromatography tests in March 1978, wasn't it possible that curare had "complexed" with dye in the embalming fluids and been "absorbed" onto the glass tubes that sat in a closet for seventy-two hours? Wouldn't that explain the failure to see some of the curare? "I am reasonably certain that this is absolutely not the case," the witness replied. The curare that was no longer visible on the TLC plates, he said, was "actually destroyed."

Q: Doctor, did you take any special care before the curare was destroyed, as you said, did you take any special care to prevent this phenomenon of absorption to take place?

A: No, because it does not play any role in the destruction of curare, in my opinion. It is the actual breakdown of the molecule itself by water, in embalming fluids, in tissue fluids and with the exception of the conditions that I had outlined earlier, curare is an unstable compound, unless it is dry, acid, and with preservative.

But wasn't the basis of Dr. Rieders's estimate of curare destruction in March 1978 simply an "eyeball" look at the thin-layer chromatography plates? Yes. And in the tissue juice tests in May and June 1978, didn't he also "just eyeball" the plates? "Yes, and I took photographs."

Q: The photographs don't do anything in regard to a determination of quantity, do they?

A: Well, they do a lot in terms of having someone else look at it and say how much does it look to you.

Q: But you were the one who was giving an opinion, were you not?

A: Oh, yes.

And in the tissue juice tests, did Dr. Rieders really know the amounts and ratios of embalming fluids that had been used more than a decade earlier on the bodies of Nancy Savino, Frank Biggs, and Carl Rohrbeck? No, not for those specific bodies, the witness said. He had asked for that information but couldn't obtain it. And with respect to the curare he had found in Nancy Savino's liver by mass spectrometry in January 1978, wasn't that actually a tiny amount—a gram being about one thirtieth of an ounce; and a nanogram, one thousandth of one millionth of a gram. Two hundred nanograms—"it is a very small amount?" Moses asked.

A: Yes, it is.

Q: Minuscule. Is that correct?

A: Depends. By modern standards, it is no longer minuscule, since now we have methods which can detect one atom.

Q: In this regard, sir, would you consider it a large or small amount?

A: With respect to this case, [a] horrendous amount.

Q: And this was the horrendous amount which you said was pure, unchanged tubocurarine? Is that correct?

A: It came across as a very well identified tubocurarine and therefore not partly altered.

Q: And your theory is it had to have gotten into the liver after the exhumation, isn't that correct?

A: Well, sometime, yes.

Q: Can I ask you, sir, do you know the mechanism by which it got into the liver after the body had been removed from the ground?

A: I have no idea. There is no way that I could possibly know how that happened, not necessarily even how it was done, but how it happened.

Q: And you're basing then—

A: I can only speculate.

Q: You are speculating?

A: I could only speculate. I wouldn't know.

Q: You are speculating then, sir, in regard to when the curare got into the liver?

A: No, I am not . . . I am reasonably certain that there was none in it at the time of exhumation. How it got in afterwards, I really have no idea. It could be an accident; it could be sloppiness; it could be anything. I don't know.

Bo Roland Holmstedt, whose work as a toxicologist in Sweden included considerable experience with mass spectrometry, backed up Dr.

Rieders's testimony. Based on Dr. Rieders's tests and his own review of the scientific literature, Dr. Holmstedt told the jury that there was "no way" curare could survive for ten years in an embalmed and buried body. Dr. Holmstedt challenged a prosecution expert's statement that Frank Biggs's liver was "possibly positive" by mass spectrometry; the finding, according to Dr. Holmstedt, was negative. As far as Nancy Savino's liver was concerned, if curare had been detected in her liver by mass spectrometry, there was "no reason" why Dr. Rieders shouldn't also have found it in her muscle. Dr. Holmstedt said the use of radioimmunoassay and high-pressure liquid chromatography, even in combination, was "insufficient" to establish the presence of an unknown substance, especially if the substance wasn't quantified.

Q: Why is that?

A: Because any number of presumptive tests can be coupled, but they do not lead to positive identification.

On cross-examination, Moses asked whether a molecule of curare that had been in the ground for ten years was any different, any more or less "pure," than a molecule of curare that had been freshly added to tissue. "Hardly," Dr. Holmstedt replied. A solution might be of varying purity, but "a molecule is a molecule." And because the human body didn't produce curare, the prosecutor went on, wasn't it possible to determine its presence by "qualitative analysis," rather than by measuring quantity? "Provided you have the correct method," the witness said. Well, if curare couldn't last for ten years in an embalmed and buried body, Moses asked, "how did it get there?"

A: It's not for me to say.

The last of the defense's scientific witnesses was Valentino Mazzia, a Colorado professor who was formerly chairman of the anesthesia department at New York University. Dr. Mazzia said the hospital records of Nancy Savino, Frank Biggs, and Carl Rohrbeck were "absolutely" inconsistent with death by curare. And he agreed with the causes of death cited by Dr. Siegel.

On cross-examination, Dr. Mazzia said that he had not considered the testimony by prosecution experts that they had found curare in the patients' tissues. But those findings, he said, would not have changed his opinion. The anesthesiologist also acknowledged that in an initial report to Brown two months before the trial, he had not listed liver disease and pulmonary edema as the cause of Frank Biggs's death nor peritonitis as the cause of Nancy Savino's.

Was it possible, Moses asked, that someone who lacked oxygen could be pale rather than blue or cyanotic? Yes, said Dr. Mazzia, but not under the conditions Moses was describing.

Q: Well, sir, I ask would you accept Professor Nickerson's chapter in Goodman and Gilman [*The Pharmacological Basis of Therapeutics*] as an authority on this subject?

A: Absolutely not.

Q: Well, let me try another one, there's a smaller volume, sir, would you accept as an authority in the field of physiology or respiration, Professor Julius H. Comroe, Professor of Physiology at the University of California?

A: No.

Q: When you say that the statement I made that stress or circumstances would cause, through various physiological responses, a paleness rather than a blueness of the skin, when you say you don't agree with that, could you tell us what authority you are relying on that is in a published text or a medical journal or something of that sort?

But Dr. Mazzia said he was relying primarily on his own experience and "that of my colleagues." He wouldn't recognize any book on medicine as an authority because a book was "fixed in time." Not Schwartz's *Principles of Internal Medicine,* not Adelson's *Pathology of Homicide,* not the *Physicians' Desk Reference,* and not others that Moses tossed out on the subjects of anesthesia for children and clinical diagnosis and forensic pathology.

17

The case for the defense was almost over. The New Jersey Supreme Court had yet to rule on Brown's subpoena of *The Times* and me, but on September 13, 1978, the defense attorney called Joseph Woodcock to the stand and began laying the last pieces of his case in place.

Brown's questioning of the former prosecutor retraced the ground covered during the hearing in May on the admissibility of Dr. Jascalevich's 1976 deposition. Woodcock said that none of the conversations I had had with him in the fall of 1975 were "confidential" and that the "only thing we received from Myron Farber" was a copy of Dr. Jascalevich's 1966 deposition. He also denied that I had played any part in his decision to enlist the aid of Dr. Baden.

Well, asked Brown, had he discussed "Dr. Baden coming into the case" with me?

A: With Mr. Farber?

Q: Right.

A: No.

On cross-examination, Woodcock said that at his instruction, Chief Kikkert had prepared an inventory of the file and examined the file before and after my use of it. The file was "intact."

Why, Moses now asked, had Woodcock revived the Riverdell case? Because the contents of the file and Dr. Jascalevich's 1966 deposition "required" it.

MOSES: And wasn't it your duty as prosecutor of Bergen County to investigate anytime questions are raised into deaths, whether or not they are suspicious?

BROWN: May we ask him if it's his duty when *The New York Times* tells him to do it?

ARNOLD: I'll allow it.

MOSES: Would you explain what the duty of the prosecutor is?

A: Mrs. Moses, the duty of the prosecutor is to investigate matters dealing with crimes, suspicions of crimes, and that has nothing to do with who brings the information to the office, be it *The New York Times*, the *Daily News*, whether it is a convicted criminal. The prosecutor has a responsibility of taking the investigation and going forward.

And after the Riverdell case was reopened, Moses continued, was there a "veil of confidentiality" over that investigation?

A: There's no question about it.

And wasn't it the results of that investigation that were presented to the grand jury and that led to the indictment of Dr. Jascalevich?

A: That's true.

MOSES: No further questions.

By September 18, when Brown called me to the stand, I had been out of jail for nearly three weeks. My family was back from France, and my children were in school, but I was practically living with my lawyers. Even when I was calling someone else, I tended to dial Floyd's number or Gene's by mistake. *The Times* was still on strike in September, but I had crossed the picket line on several occasions to confer with Abe Rosenthal or the *Times*'s legal staff. Except for a handful of editors and reporters, who were doing everything from writing stories for the *Times*'s news service to sorting huge satchels of mail, the newsroom was deserted. Rosenthal himself, who was suffering from a torn knee cartilage, hobbled about on a cane.

Abe and I tried not to dwell on the prospect of my returning to jail, but we both knew it might happen. If the New Jersey Supreme Court decision was unfavorable, we would again appeal to the U. S. Supreme Court. But I might very well be rejailed pending any action by the High Court, and the outlook in Washington, as we all knew, wasn't bright. At the American Bar Association convention in August, Fred Graham of CBS News had asked Chief Justice Burger whether he had "any concern in view of recent events about apparently escalating tensions between the judiciary and journalists."

BURGER: No, I don't see it. I don't see any problems.

GRAHAM: Well, in view of the fact that a journalist is in jail now, and that's rather unusual, that is a problem.

BURGER: Well, I suppose a lot of people have been in jail, including judges sometimes. I don't think there's too much to worry about. The problem will work itself out.

Particularly galling to me was a report in the September 12 issue of *Esquire* magazine in which legal columnist, Steven Brill, recalled a conversation with the chief justice on August 4. Burger, according to Brill, had laughingly remarked about my being imprisoned that day. "Well," the chief justice reportedly said, "do you think you have special privileges like this guy Farber does?"

Now, on the morning of September 18, my "special privileges" were again an issue. This time it was my raincoat. I owned only one coat, an old but beloved raincoat, and I didn't want to lose it. So when I arrived for court, I looked for a safe place to hang it, and the only place I could find was the anteroom between Judge Arnold's chambers and the courtroom. Someone associated with Brown must have noticed, because the defense attorney complained to Judge Arnold. And as soon as court opened, he renewed his objection.

BROWN: Mr. Farber came into your chambers, he hung up his coat, he took whatever liberties may be described, and apparently he has special privileges. I also make a motion—

ARNOLD: Please hold it up. I was in my chambers and I did not know he had done this. I did not know he had hung up his coat there, and I was surprised when you told me.

BROWN: I want to put it on the record. The judge was in chambers and had no knowledge of it at all.

Judge Arnold also wanted to put something on the record. He had received letters "pro and con on the freedom of the press," and he was sure the lawyers had too, and he was going to ask for "additional security because of the fact that the issue before the Court this morning might emotionally arouse someone to the extent that they might commit violence."

There wasn't any violence during my three days on the stand, unless it was Brown's effort to weave me into the "conspiracy" against Dr. Jascalevich. The defense attorney started by dwelling on the fact that when I had visited Hackensack in the late summer and early fall of 1975 to examine the old Riverdell file, I had signed "official" in the registry book at the narcotics task force office. I tried explaining that I had put down "official" under the heading "purpose of visit" so as not to arouse the interest of detectives who might be in touch with reporters for the *Bergen Record*. I preferred that only Woodcock, who had allowed me to see the file, knew my identity as a *Times* reporter. When Brown cut me off, Moses objected.

MOSES: Let him explain, Your Honor.

BROWN: Is she counsel for Mr. Farber?

MOSES: No, counsel for the state of New Jersey and trying a murder case, Your Honor.

ARNOLD: Mrs. Moses, I will not have any foolishness today. Step up here, both of you.

"You both come on real quick, and I am advising you both that I am trying to avoid it," the judge whispered. "Don't make any remarks about each other. We will not do it and make a fool of ourselves in front of everyone here in this courtroom today."

While Judge Arnold rapped the lawyers, I surveyed the courtroom from the witness chair. There wasn't an empty seat in the spectators' or press rows. I looked for the face of the woman who had written and then come to *The Times* in 1975 about the hospital deaths. She had been in court when I was on the stand at the hearing in May, outside the presence of the jury. I didn't see her now. Brown knew her name, but I didn't think he would call her as a witness. That wouldn't fit in with the theory that he wanted the jury to buy, that Woodcock and I and Dr. Baden and Dr. Harris and Dr. Lans and others had cooked up a plot against Dr. Jascalevich in 1975. I wondered whether the jurors gave any credence to Brown's conspiracy charge, or whether they had read or heard of my jailing. They weren't supposed to follow any news reports of the trial, but they weren't sequestered. I couldn't tell anything from their faces. They were expressionless, all of them.

Q: Mr. Farber, did you misrepresent yourself as an official when you signed that book?

A: Yes, sir, I did.

Q: You submitted a fraud when you signed that book?

A: No, sir.

Q: Did you tell an untruth when you signed as an official of the County of Bergen?

A: Only to the degree that it is on the paper.

Q: Well, what you signed there is not true?

A: Mr. Woodcock knew I was not an official.

What, Brown asked, had Woodcock and I discussed in the fall of 1975? "Did you, after you worked on the file, give facts which you found in the file to Mr. Woodcock?"

A: No, sir.

Q: You never discussed the facts as you found them in the file with Mr. Woodcock?

A: I don't believe I did. Primarily what I was discussing with Mr. Woodcock, at one point, was why Dr. Jascalevich's [1966] deposition wasn't in the file.

I went on to say that Woodcock and I had mostly discussed the New Jersey legislature, of which he had been a member.

Q: Not the matters garnered and gleaned from the files that you gleaned?

A: No.

Q: Not at any time?

A: It is possible . . . I may have said something about the file, but primarily we talked about the county, the legislature. And he didn't talk to me after a while at all.

I had never been out to Bergen County before that time, I recalled for the jury. So Woodcock and I had chatted about "why Paramus had a lot of shopping centers instead of celery farms today," things like that.

Q: Never about the case?

A: I tried to say to you before, it is not inconceivable, in the middle of that, that something was said about the case. It was not of any consequence.

Q: But your mission in talking to Mr. Woodcock was not about the case, but talking about shopping—

A: What did he know? Mr. Woodcock was not here in '66.

Q: Did you give him the benefit of your examination of the file? Of course he wasn't here in '66, that is why.

A: Mr. Brown, my audience is the *New York Times*'s readers.

Q: I know. Did he discuss with you his political intent to run for governor as a result of this case . . . Did he discuss with you his plans to run for governor at that time?

A: No, sir, he did not.

Brown tried, in another way, to link me to Woodcock. According to a bill or invoice of the Miles Reproducer Company in New York, I had "recommended" that Woodcock's office rent a Walkie Recordall to play the tapes in the old Riverdell file. But I didn't make that recommendation, I testified. When I rented a Recordall from Miles in 1975 and took it to Hackensack, I said, I paid for it. And it was for my purposes as a reporter, not for the purposes of the prosecutor's office.

But hadn't John Fischer, an employee of Miles, phoned me, and hadn't I "instructed" him to bill the prosecutor's office for a Walkie Recordall?

A: No. Mr. Fischer said to me he was fixing the machine, and I said who are you fixing it for, and he said the Bergen County prosecutor's office. I said bill them, don't bill me.

Through introduction of my July 1976 contract with Doubleday & Company, Inc., Brown brought out the fact that I was writing a book about the Riverdell case and that I was to receive, over a period of some years, a $75,000 advance against royalties. Moses briefly cross-examined me when the contract was offered in evidence. Wasn't it true, she asked, "that it is not unusual for people who work for newspapers or magazines, doing investigative reporting, to write books about the reporting they have done."

"Many times," I answered over Brown's objection.

Brown also harped on the fact that in the spring of 1976, Warner Brothers had proposed to buy the film rights to the book I had decided to write. Wasn't it true, Brown pressed me, that payments under the Warner Brothers "contract" were contingent on Dr. Jascalevich's indictment and conviction? No, I said, I had no "contract" with Warner Brothers or any film studio. When Warner Brothers submitted a draft proposal that contained references to Dr. Jascalevich's indictment or conviction, I rejected it outright—"I gave up that money and you know it," I said to Brown.

Again, Moses cross-examined. Why had I not signed the film contract?

A: Well, number one, I found it repugnant that . . . whoever wrote the draft, had tied a contract that they were posing to me to anyone's indictment or conviction. I intended to write a book about the subject of what happened at Riverdell Hospital regardless of anyone's indictment or conviction, or regardless of anything else. I thought it was an intriguing case of public importance.

BROWN: I object to this . . . It sounds like a lecture from a divinity student.

I went on to say that I had never authorized anyone to negotiate a contract based on an indictment or conviction and that I was confident that Lucy Kroll, my literary agent, was not responsible for the Warner language.

MOSES: Do you have any idea, sir, as to who did the drawing up of this draft of the contract which you did not sign?

A: I don't have the foggiest idea.

Judge Arnold ruled that while Brown could question me about the Warner draft, it could not be admitted into evidence of the basis of my testimony. "He knew nothing about this, and there hasn't been anything else established to the contrary," the judge said.

I knew, sitting in that witness box, that Brown would not call anyone from Warner Brothers or Mrs. Kroll, who had already testified at the hearing before Judge Lacey in August that I would "not tolerate" the Warner draft. Nor was Brown going to call Matthew Lifflander, although I testified that the New York lawyer and friend of Dr. Lans was the source of my copy of Dr. Jascalevich's 1966 deposition to Calissi. In recent months Lifflander had said publicly that he was the source of the deposition, and I confirmed it for the jury. But Brown wasn't going to call Lifflander or anyone else whom he thought would hurt his case. Nor was he going to ask me in front of the jury, as he had during the evidentiary hearing in May, whether I had recommended Dr. Baden to Woodcock. Knowing the answer, he wasn't going to ask the question. Instead, he stressed that I had known Dr. Baden since 1973 and had spoken to the pathologist in 1975 before Woodcock had. Brown also resurrected the charge by Milton Helpern, the late chief medical examiner of New York, that Dr. Baden was the source of the "severed head" story I had written in November 1973. It so happened that Brown's investigator, Stephen Delaney, had worked on a criminal case mentioned in that story, for another lawyer. And I had spoken to Delaney in 1973. Now, with Delaney standing by his side in Judge Arnold's courtroom, Brown fired away at me.

Q: Did you in '73 speak to Stephen Delaney and say that Dr. Baden was your private source of information from the office of the medical examiner of New York and that you and Dr. Baden were working together to disgrace Dr. Helpern?

"Absolutely not," I shot back.

Q: Did you in 1973 receive the information that you got in the . . . case from Dr. Baden.

A: I did not.

Moses was on her feet. This line of questioning, she said, was "disgraceful" and irrelevant. No, no, said Brown, it was all pertinent. "We will show the continuing relationship between that man on the stand and Dr. Baden and we will show certain other matters. We will call Mrs. Helpern and it will all be pertinent."

I wasn't sure whether to believe what I heard. Brown was really reaching.

Brown was reaching, too, when he asked me about Barbara Spadaro Kenderes, the Riverdell lab technician who was unable to awaken Nancy Savino in 1966. The defense attorney had made much recently about my telephoning Mrs. Kenderes in the spring of 1976; he had even sent a telegram to Justice Marshall of the U. S. Supreme Court to say that my "collaboration" with the prosecution was borne out by the fact that "the only person she [Mrs. Kenderes] had given her private number to in connection with this case was the Bergen County prosecutor's office." Yet I had managed to call her, Brown advised Justice Marshall. Now the defense attorney raised the subject with me.

Q: From whom did you get Mrs. Kenderes' phone number?

A: A former Riverdell Hospital employee.

Not from materials belonging to the prosecutor's office? No, I repeated.

Brown may have been even more disappointed when he asked me whether I had spoken to Dr. Baba, the former Riverdell Hospital anesthesiologist. Yes, I said, I had spoken to Dr. Baba once, by telephone in early January 1976. I had meant to go see him, but he died shortly thereafter in a house fire. I had no notes of our one conversation.

Q: Did he tell you anything with respect to the use of curare in the hospital and the doctors who used curare at Riverdell Hospital?

A: You mean legitimately or illegitimately? He had an opinion on both.

Q: What did he tell you about the doctors who used curare at Riverdell Hospital with respect to the years 1965 and 1966? For instance, did he tell you that Dr. Harris used it?

When Moses objected, Brown protested that both the prosecutor and Judge Arnold were trying to "dictate" the questions he could ask. "I expect and I will ask my questions as I see fit."

Q: Did you ask Dr. Baba as to whether or not curare was used in the hospital, at Riverdell?

A: Yes, I did, sir.

Q: And did he reply to that?

A: Yes, he did.

Q: What was his reply?

A: He thought some patients had been murdered at Riverdell Hospital with curare.

Brown's jaw went slack. "He did?"

A: Yes, sir.

Q: Did he tell you that curare was used in that murder?

A: He thought so.

Q: Did he tell you that?

A: Let me try to recall the context. As you well know, I have been working on—

Q: Just tell us what he told you.

A: I asked him whether he had ever used curare at the hospital.

Q: What did he say to you?

A: He said that he did not.

Q: Did you ask him whether Dr. Harris used curare at the hospital?

A: I know I then asked him did he know of anyone who used curare at the hospital.

Q: Did he say he knew of anyone who used curare in the hospital?

A: He said he couldn't speak for Dr. DeMarco, but he didn't think [Dr. DeMarco] used curare either.

Q: Did he tell you whether or not any other doctors used curare in the hospital?

A: He thought perhaps Dr. Jascalevich had.

Q: He thought he had used it in operations, or he had thought he used it to murder people?

A: To murder people, Mr. Brown.

Q: Did he tell you whom he had used it to murder?

A: No, I think it was just a discussion of the unusual, so-called unusual and unexplained deaths at the hospital. He was under the impression that some of the people were murdered.

Slowly, Brown moved toward me. Around Moses. Past the jury. He was shouting as his face neared mine.

Q: Did he tell you who the people were?

A: I don't think we ever got that far.

Q: Didn't you ask him who was murdered?

A: I spoke to him on the fourteenth. I had intended to go see him.

Q: Did you ask him on the phone?

A: No, I didn't.

Q: Did you report that interview to the prosecutor?

A: No, I don't believe I ever mentioned it.

Q: You never told the prosecutor that Dr. Baba, an anesthesiologist, said that this man murdered people who were not named?

A: . . . I would have no reason to tell the prosecutor. The prosecutor then opened an investigation of the case; he did his work and I did mine.

Brown dropped Dr. Baba.

During my testimony I disclosed that I had photocopied many of the documents in Calissi's file in 1975, and at Brown's request, I agreed to turn over to him whatever I had reproduced. In all likelihood the defense had received copies of those documents from the prosecution after Dr. Jascalevich's indictment; certainly it was entitled to them. But if Brown wanted to compare what I had with what the prosecution had given him, I would voluntarily comply. Floyd Abrams and I were both anxious to demonstrate my reasonableness, especially in response to a limited request and one that didn't compromise confidential sources. Of course, Brown didn't stop there. Again he demanded all my notes and other materials. Again I refused to produce them. Again, Judge Arnold said that he wouldn't give me a hearing until the notes were shown to him. We were back to where we had started. And as the judge himself pointed out, we still didn't have a ruling from the New Jersey Supreme Court.

The decision came down the next day, September 21, 1978. By a 5 to 2 vote, the state Supreme Court upheld the contempt convictions and ordered me back to jail unless I submitted the subpoenaed materials to Judge Arnold within five days. The majority, in an opinion written by Justice Worrall Mountain, said that reporters had no First Amendment privilege to withhold properly subpoenaed confidential information and sources. "The reason this is so," Justice Mountain wrote, "is that a majority of the members of the United States Supreme Court have so determined," in the 1972 Branzburg case. ". . . Thus we do no weighing or balancing of societal interests in reaching our deter-

mination . . . The weighing and balancing has been done by a higher
court." Although the Branzburg case involved a grand jury subpoena,
Justice Mountain noted, "it follows that the obligation to appear at a
criminal trial on behalf of a defendant who is enforcing his Sixth
Amendment rights is at least as compelling." The New Jersey shield
law, the majority held, was "entirely constitutional." But where that
law "collides" with the rights of a defendant under the Sixth Amendment and its similarly worded counterpart in the New Jersey Constitution, the statute "must yield."

The Times and I had insisted all along that we were entitled to a
"full hearing on the issues of relevance, materiality, and overbreadth of
the subpoena," the majority said. "We agree." But *The Times* and I
had "aborted" that hearing by refusing to let Judge Arnold see my
notes—"such an in-camera inspection is not in itself an invasion of the
statutory privilege." In any event, the majority continued, the court was
now ruling that judges *in the future* had to make a "preliminary determination" on the necessity of a reporter's notes *before* the notes were
turned over to anyone, including the judge. A defense attorney would
have to satisfy the judge "by a fair preponderance of the evidence, including all reasonable inferences, that there was a reasonable probability or likelihood that the information sought by the subpoena was
material and relevant to the defense, that it could not be secured from
any less intrusive source, and that the defendant had a legitimate need
to see it or otherwise use it." Only then, the court held, could a reporter be forced to show his notes to a judge.

Justice Mountain wrote that Judge Arnold hadn't followed such a
procedure or "articulated" any findings. But there was nothing to be
gained, he added, by requiring the judge to start over again. Judge Arnold's knowledge of the Jascalevich case "and of the part Farber had
played was intimate and pervasive. Perhaps most significant is [Judge
Arnold's] thorough awareness of Farber's close association with the
prosecutor's office since a time preceding the indictment." Citing a
half-dozen examples from Brown's brief to the state Supreme Court,
Justice Mountain said it was "perfectly clear" that the defense attorney
could meet the new "threshold" test. Indeed the court was now super-
seding Judge Arnold and ruling that Brown had met the test.

In his dissent, Justice Alan Handler said he was in substantial accord
with much of the majority's reasoning. But he would impose a more
rigorous "threshold" test than the majority and insist that it was
adhered to meticulously. And that, he said, was hardly what had happened here. The orders originally signed by Judge Arnold indicated
"some likelihood that some material sought is relevant; they yield only
a bare conclusion as to its necessity, are silent as to alternative sources,

and are indifferent as to matters of overbreadth, oppressiveness, and unreasonableness," Justice Handler observed. And for the state Supreme Court to conclude otherwise on the basis of "hypothetical findings extrapolated from only a small part of a huge record would be a flight of fancy."

Justice Pashman would also have vacated the contempt citations. "Farber has . . . never received the hearing to which he is constitutionally entitled. I find it totally unimaginable that the majority can even consider allowing a man to be sent to jail without a full and orderly hearing at which to present his defense. Mr. Farber probably assumed, as I did, that hearings were supposed to be held and findings made *before* a person went to jail and not *afterwards*." In considerable detail, the justice described the kind of hearing that was mandated in a clash between a reporter and a criminal defendant, before any in-camera inspection.

"Throughout all stages of the proceeding," Justice Pashman said, "the judge should constantly keep in mind the strong presumption against disclosure of protected materials. All doubts concerning disclosure should be resolved in favor of nondisclosure."

As a result of the decision, reporters were now assured of some kind of hearing by New Jersey trial judges, although the effectiveness of the hearing procedure remained to be seen. But I was to be denied that. My "hearing" had been conducted behind the closed doors of the New Jersey Supreme Court, and I had lost. If this was "equal protection" under the law, if this was "due process," then I didn't understand those constitutional guarantees at all.

Something else troubled me as I read the state Supreme Court's decision. The majority said that it's opinion was "not to be taken as a license for a fishing expedition in every criminal case where there has been investigative reporting, nor as permission for an indiscriminate rummaging through newspaper files." But what else was the court sanctioning here? The New Jersey Supreme Court didn't have the full record of the Jascalevich case before it; all it had were a few excerpts selected by Brown. Most of Brown's half-dozen examples, including the business about Barbara Kenderes' "private, unlisted" phone number, were factually incorrect or misleading. They would have been shown to be at any fair hearing. Yet New Jersey's highest tribunal was using these assertions to justify the exposure of a reporter's entire file, including confidential notes.

A few hours after the court's decision was rendered, Floyd Abrams advised Judge Arnold that I would not produce my file "at least until there was a definitive ruling" by the U. S. Supreme Court. The decision of the state Supreme Court, Abrams said, was "a sad disservice to the

First Amendment" and "in our view, a violation of the state shield law."

Brown, who intended to re-call me as a witness, asked that the trial be briefly delayed, to see what happened in Washington. Without my file, he said, the defense was frustrated, left "dangling in the wind." No, countered Moses, it was the jury that was dangling; she worried constantly about "automobile accidents" or some other mishap that might disable a juror or two. Judge Arnold granted Brown's motion.

As court adjourned, the judge asked Brown whether he intended to put Dr. Jascalevich on the stand.

BROWN: I can't tell you at this time.

ARNOLD: All right, that's all I wanted to know. I have asked the question.

MOSES: Your Honor, could you ask Mr. Brown when he will let the Court know that decision.

BROWN: Wait a minute. I'll tell you what the defendant will state. He states that he will refuse to answer.

What about Farber? the judge mused. "After everything is said and done and Farber says no, what happens then?"

BROWN: It is fascinating.

MOSES: Take him out and whip him until he gets the documents?

ARNOLD: You can't beat him. I guess he'll go to jail.

John Stasse, Sheriff Job's chief aide, was in the corridor as Floyd and I made our way out of the Bergen County Courthouse. "Should we dust off the furniture?" Stasse asked me.

"Not yet," I said. "But I wouldn't put the rag away."

On the morning of September 26, Abrams filed our petition with the U. S. Supreme Court. Abrams argued that *The Times* and I had been convicted of contempt in violation of our due process rights under the Fourteenth Amendment of the U. S. Constitution; that the New Jersey Supreme Court had unconstitutionally nullified "large portions, if not all" of the shield law by mistakenly holding that the reporter's testimonial privilege—if not the statutory privileges pertaining to the lawyer-client, doctor-patient, priest-penitent, and other relationships—"must yield" to the Sixth Amendment; and that the state Supreme Court had misinterpreted the Branzburg decision with regard to the First Amendment and ignored the "pivotal" opinion of Justice Powell in that case. Since 1972, Abrams wrote, many state and federal courts had "applied the principles enumerated by Justice Powell and recognized the need for First Amendment protection of confidential materials, unless overcome by a compelling showing of necessity." That, for example, was the ruling of the Wisconsin Supreme Court as recently as June 1978, in a case in which a murder defendant subpoenaed a reporter to obtain the name of a confidential source. The reporter was not forced to divulge the source.

Finally, Abrams urged the Supreme Court to take our case because the subpoena was "so plainly overbroad that there is no basis at all for permitting the findings of contempt to stand." Abrams cited a 1951 Supreme Court decision vacating a contempt citation, in which the Court said, "One should not be held in contempt under a subpoena that is part good and part bad. The burden is on the court to see that the subpoena is good in its entirety, and it is not upon the person who faces punishment to cull the good from the bad."

The New Jersey Supreme Court had given me until 4 P.M. on September 26 to surrender my file. But forty-five minutes before that deadline expired, Justice Stewart stepped in and, "pending further order of this Court," held up all penalties against *The Times* and me. There was no telling yet whether the Supreme Court would grant "certiorari" and agree to rule on the issues we had raised.

For ten days we didn't hear anything from the Supreme Court, and unable to concentrate on anything but our appeal, I became increasingly restless. The strike at *The Times* dragged on, but even if the paper had been operating, I couldn't have gotten much work done. I made two trips to the West Coast, one for a "media and the law" conference at the *Los Angeles Times* and the other for the annual meeting of the Associated Press Managing Editors Association, which gave *The Times* and me its 1978 freedom-of-the-press award. I was barraged with questions about the case, and for the most part, people were supportive. One woman in Los Angeles startled me by saying that she had named her new puppy "Farber."

But it was also clear at these meetings that some editors and reporters and press lawyers wished we hadn't gone up to the Supreme Court. This, they said, was the "wrong" court, an unsympathetic court that might take a bad decision in New Jersey and make it worse for the entire nation. Better to wait for a simpler case, a case with what lawyers call a more favorable "fact pattern," a case that wasn't cluttered with allegations of conspiracy. Or better still to stay away altogether from Chief Justice Burger, Justice White, and some of their brethren.

I couldn't share this view. The issues in my case affected the public and the press everywhere, and the Supreme Court was the national court. I had too much respect for the Court, as an institution, to fear it. The Court might lack a Holmes or a Brandeis, and it might be led by a man who allowed himself to be amused by my plight, but it was still the Supreme Court. I just couldn't believe—perhaps I just didn't want to believe—that the Court would be sidetracked, much less taken in, by the nonsense about a conspiracy between *The Times* and the prosecutor's office. The Court might not agree with me on the First Amendment, or the shield law, or "due process." But those were the constitutional issues that *The Times* and I were presenting, and if the Court accepted our case for review, those were the issues it would have to confront. So let it rule, I thought. If it were not my case now, in 1978, it would soon be another reporter's.

On October 4, the attorney general of New Jersey, John Degnan, joined in our request for a Supreme Court review. Degnan asked the Court to determine "whether First Amendment rights must be balanced against Sixth Amendment claims with respect to materials subpoenaed from members of the news media and, if so, the constitutional nature of the 'balancing test' to be applied." The same day, in Hackensack, Judge Arnold agreed to a defense request for a second short delay in the trial. Court had begun late that morning anyway; one of the jurors had been in an auto accident. Fortunately, she was uninjured.

On Friday, October 6, the Supreme Court granted a motion by Brown to vacate Justice Stewart's order of September 26. The Court did not say whether it would ultimately take my case and rule on the substantive issues. But in response to Brown's argument that maximum pressure be exerted on me while the trial lasted, the Court removed Justice Stewart's ban on enforcement of the New Jersey Supreme Court decision. I was to report to Judge Trautwein the following Tuesday, October 10.

On the morning of October 10 I again refused to turn over my file. And Abrams informed Judge Trautwein that *The Times* would not direct me to do so. "Think it over," the judge told me. If the file wasn't produced within two days, I was going back to jail.

From Judge Trautwein's courtroom I went upstairs to Judge Arnold's. Re-calling me to the stand, Brown focused on an article I had written on March 7, 1976, in which I reported that curare had been detected in the tissues of Nancy Savino. I attributed the information then to unnamed "law enforcement" sources. Who, Brown now asked, were those sources?

A: I decline to answer that on the grounds of my First Amendment rights and my rights under the shield laws of New Jersey and New York.

Now the lines were really drawn. No notes were involved here. This was a classic example of a reporter, in oral testimony, protecting confidential sources.

Maybe, said Judge Arnold, he should give me a hearing—"then, after the hearing, tell him to answer." Maybe, Brown replied; but according to his reading of the New Jersey Supreme Court decision, a hearing for me was "unnecessary." "Mr. Farber cannot raise the First Amendment. That's been disposed of, because in the language of the opinion, when the Sixth Amendment and the shield collide, the shield has to go, and it already has gone." Abrams said that if my refusal to answer Brown's question wasn't still covered by the shield law and by the "threshold" test imposed by the state Supreme Court, "I don't know what is."

Moses, for her part, said that Brown's question was irrelevant to the issue of Dr. Jascalevich's guilt or innocence. "I think the issue, Judge, is the defendant is trying very hard to take our eye off the main ball . . . The defendant is trying very hard to introduce collateral issues and to, in effect, try Mr. Farber . . . The prosecutor initiated an investigation. There was no cooperation [with *The Times*] after the investigation was initiated."

Judge Arnold held that I had waived my testimonial privilege, not only by signing a book contract, but by disclosing "all" my confidential sources to Woodcock. "I made a note at one time and he testified—he said, 'I discussed with Mr. Woodcock what I found outside the file.' It seems to me he was telling Mr. Woodcock information other than what is in the prosecutor's file, and this was a waiver of the privilege of the subject matter."

Abrams was aghast at this distortion of my testimony.

"Your Honor," he said, "then I would respectfully move . . . to call Mr. Farber and ask him in front of you whether he disclosed to Mr. Woodcock any confidential sources."

ARNOLD: I'm not going to do that because that's what he testified to. Whether he changes his mind isn't going to make any difference.

ABRAMS: May I have the transcript citation?

ARNOLD: I don't know where it is. I just took it from my notes. If I had it, I'd give it to you. It can be found in there someplace."

Of course, it couldn't be found in the record. I hadn't revealed any confidential sources to Woodcock, and the whole burden of my testimony was to the contrary. The judge also refused to permit Floyd to call experts from the publishing industry who could testify that my Doubleday contract did not require the disclosure of confidential sources. "I don't think that's indispensable for my disposition of the matter, Mr. Abrams."

When I came back into the courtroom—I had been sent out during the "hearing"—Brown repeated his question about the "law enforcement" sources. Once more I declined to answer, and Judge Arnold cited me for contempt of court. I answered the great majority of the questions that followed, many of which had to do with my Doubleday contract, but I refused to identify any confidential sources or, again, to turn over my notes. The result was eighteen more contempt citations.

Q: You're willing to talk, but not to show the notes to indicate what you actually wrote at the time?

A: I'm willing to tell the truth in this courtroom.

Q: I didn't ask you that. You wouldn't surrender the notes?

A: I will not surrender the notes.

Brown asked Judge Arnold to dismiss the remaining counts of the indictment against Dr. Jascalevich because *The Times* and I had failed to provide the file. But the judge said he would deal with the motion when the testimony for the defense was completed.

As soon as Moses asked me, on cross-examination, why I had interviewed "scores" of people during my investigation, Brown demanded a mistrial. Judge Arnold called the lawyers up to the bench and warned Moses that she was "flirting with a mistrial" if she was "trying to lead this witness into having him give his opinion as to the guilt or innocence of this defendant." Maybe, the judge told Moses, "you better confer with your witness before—"

MOSES: It's not my witness. It's the defendant's witness, Judge. I am on cross-examination.

ARNOLD: There was close cooperation—

MOSES: There was not close cooperation, and I regret the Court making findings of fact which have no basis. I regret it.

After the sidebar, I testified that the purpose of my interviews "was to learn the truth about the matter that I was looking into."

Q: Did you ever investigate anything at the request of Prosecutor Woodcock?

A: This was for *The New York Times*. I didn't do anything for Mr. Woodcock.

Q: Were you ever paid anything by Prosecutor Woodcock for anything?

A: Of course not.

My cell had sunk into squalor. It was just being vacated, on October 12, by another prisoner, and it stank. There was no furniture except the bed, and the sheets looked as if they hadn't been changed since my departure on August 30. The floor was a mosaic of used coffee cups, cigarette butts, and crumpled centerfolds from porn magazines. Ron, who was both happy and sorry to see me back, helped me find some disinfectant and, together, we mopped up. I took a nap—the jail was infinitely cooler than it had been in August—and after showering, I sat down to a dinner of grilled cheese sandwiches. Gabe Iapella, a guard, tried to console me. "I never thought they'd have the balls to put you back," he said. But Captain Larsen, my head jailor, disagreed. "The betting," he said, "is 8 to 5 that you'll do the full six months after the trial." Ron introduced me to a new prisoner—"one of the best check writers around," he called him—and after dinner the new man joined Ron and Bob and me in the ever-running jailhouse gin rummy game. We must have been playing for an hour or so when there was an awful scream from the tier above us.

"Hey, Gabe, get your fat ass up here. And bring an umbrella. I got something for you, Gabe. I'll bet Myron Farber isn't eating this shit!"

"Is that Boris?" I asked.

"Not Boris; Boris is still next to you," said Ron. "Boris doesn't say a word these days. That's a new guy, a screamer. Screams all the time."

"Hey, Ron," the voice screeched, "I want to register to vote. Hey, where's my cigar. Give me a Joe Job campaign sticker. I love Joe Job."

"Home, sweet home," I sighed.

Brown, too, was mopping up—with Stephen Delaney, his investigator, and Beatrice Helpern, Milton Helpern's widow and former secretary. Contradicting my testimony, Delaney told the jury that in 1973 I had identified Dr. Baden as the source of my information on the "severed head" story. Mrs. Helpern testified that as early as 1967 Dr. Baden had asked her about an "enormous" file that Dr. Helpern kept on his office windowsill, and she had told Dr. Baden that it was "a no-case." The file, she said, contained the Riverdell materials that Matthew Lifflander had sent her husband in 1966, and after Dr. Helpern's retirement in 1974, it could not be found. The defense attorney did not ask Mrs. Helpern whether Dr. Baden knew the subject matter of the file.

On the morning of Friday, October 13, Brown rested his case. Dr. Jascalevich would not take the stand in his own defense.

Moses moved, immediately, to call a rebuttal witness, Werner U. Spitz, the chief medical examiner of Wayne County (Detroit), Michigan. Spitz was the co-author of a standard work on forensic medicine and had been cited as an expert by both Brown and the defense pathologist, Henry Siegel. After Dr. Siegel's testimony in August, Moses had brought Dr. Spitz to New York, and the pathologist had examined microscopic tissue slides and other materials that figured in the Jascalevich trial. Now he was prepared to testify, among other things, that Nancy Savino could not have died of peritonitis and that her tissue slides showed no cause for death.

Brown would have none of it—if Dr. Spitz took the stand, he said, he would cross-examine him "as long as the courthouse stands." Judge Arnold vetoed Dr. Spitz. The rebuttal, he said, would be repetitious. And what's more, two of the thirteen jurors had just informed him that if the trial continued, they "wanted off."

Over the weekend I gave a lot of thought to Captain Larsen's remark. My indefinite jail term, for civil contempt, would end with the end of the trial. But only then would my six-month term for criminal contempt begin. Unless the Supreme Court intervened, I was going to see a great deal of this jail—and I had already had my fill. The screamer hadn't let up, prompting another inmate to warn him that when he landed in "the big house," there would be "1,200 hard-dick men waiting to see if you can shake your ass as fast as you can run your mouth." Undaunted, the screamer smashed the light in his cell with a bed slat and, having stuffed his toilet with paper and oranges, managed to break an old water main. Water poured down from his tier to mine and rapidly began to rise. Ron and I and some of the others switched off the electricity, retrieved the mops, and ran around in our shorts, with buckets. The screamer was clinging to the bars of his cell, laughing hysterically while the guards struggled to get him into a straitjacket. "Hey, I can't swim," he yelled. "It's getting deeper in here."

It was definitely getting deeper. Ron and Bob hoped to be paroled by Christmas, and both were nervous. Paul, the German, had yet to be deported and was morose. And Boris was altogether different than I remembered him. No longer did he rant; no longer did he threaten Paul or the rest of us. Boris was now on trial for the murder of his mother, and he was wasting away. On October 16 Boris took heart from the election of a Pole as Pope, telling me that he, too, was Polish. Plaintively, he asked me that night whether John Paul II's elevation was a good omen for him. Maybe, he said, it "meant something."

"Sure, Boris," I lied. "It's the best kind of sign."

"Are the leaves outside changing color, Myron?"

I was surprised not to know.

Later, when the cellblock was otherwise silent, I heard Boris reciting a lovely Irish toast. "May the road rise up to meet you," he was saying. "May the wind be always at your back . . . May God hold you in the palm of His hand."

The next day, October 17, Judge Arnold denied Brown's motion for a directed verdict of acquittal. After Moses argued that the defense "has everything the state has," the judge observed that I had answered "a considerable number" of questions during my testimony and the court had done everything within its power to obtain my notes and other materials. Dr. Jascalevich's fate would have to be decided by the jury.

After lunch on October 18, Brown angled a lectern into position before the jury and launched into a 7½-hour summation. From time to time, as he referrred to the 395 exhibits or the testimony of the 76 witnesses, he would wave an item from the documents heaped high on an evidence table next to the lectern. An indictment, Brown began, was "of itself but a piece of paper." But the indictment in this case was something more—an indictment encouraged by Farber for "money," an indictment brought by Woodcock to satisfy his "political ambition," an indictment pursued by Moses, who was "rotten to the nines" and who "should be in jail." And it all went back to 1966. "What happens when people die and people sue?" Brown asked. "Well, the best defense in the world is to get the prosecutor to go forward for you and to prove that someone else killed them with curare." Dr. Harris and "his good friend" Dr. Lans "know in their hearts" that Nancy Savino was "a very sick little girl," Brown went on. But they had to "protect themselves," and like Dr. Sklar and Dr. Frieman, they had a "vested interest in the conviction of Dr. Jascalevich. They have a vested interest because it takes the monkey off their backs. It protects their precious profit-making operation, the hospital." Having failed in 1966, Brown said, the frame-up was revived in 1975, when Dr. Baden gave Woodcock "a guarantee." "This was an ad in *The New York Times:* bring your exhumed bodies to me, and I'll give you a conviction. Come across the river . . . We'll find curare. We'll find curare . . ."

The prosecution's curare tests, the defense attorney continued, were speculative at best. High-pressure liquid chromatography and radioimmunoassay were each means of arriving at "presumptive" results and, as Dr. Spector had testified, these two presumptives still don't provide positive identification. And what about quantification, which the state hadn't done? "If you don't know the amount of the drug, how can it be a lethal dose?" No, said Brown, the prosecution hadn't reckoned on the scientific team put together by the defense, a team that proved that the patients had died of natural causes, a team that demonstrated that curare would not last in embalmed and buried bodies. They were experts who had come to Hackensack, not for glory, not for money, but because they were "scientifically indignant."

"This is not the era of Sherlock Holmes," the defense attorney added. "These are not the curare murders. This is a time when the memories of Biggs and Savino and Rohrbeck deserve to be honored. But would that honor be the finding without proof by a reasonable doubt by techniques that you must question because they have been questioned not by me—it is my job to examine but not necessarily to question—but by scientists of stature." The jury had the right to infer that the curare discovered in Nancy Savino's liver by the defense had gotten there "by accident or design" during the three days in January 1976 when the liver "was missing," when it was not on Dr. Hoffman's list of organs taken from the body. And could there be "proof beyond a reasonable doubt," Brown asked, when the scientists themselves differed as to the cause of Nancy Savino's death? "Or is there a question upon which even experts differ?"

Dr. Jascalevich, said Brown, was a "highly skilled, very busy, very energetic, very sincere person" who became a "pawn . . . Let's call it a conspiracy, let's call it a common interest with Dr. Baden, with the prosecutor, with Farber and the others; but that's where it lies, and that's why proof beyond a reasonable doubt means so much; it's meant that since the barons wrested it from the King at Runnymede; it's been a long time, but it hasn't changed much and I'm afraid that nothing will."

The defendant, Brown told the jury, by all accounts was a self-effac-ing and "gentle person who did his job." And why would he "do away with patients, especially his own?" It made no sense; there was no reason, no motive. Moses tried "to convince you that the only reason conceivable for such a horrendous act as they were ascribing to him was that he would hold up the appointments of these men, and then so resent them that he would destroy their patients, including his own. In-cluding his own." But the fact of the matter, Brown said, was that Dr. Jascalevich wanted to improve conditions at Riverdell, and didn't wield power there, and moreover, "there's no evidence that he did anything to any one of these patients." Savino and Biggs and Rohrbeck were sick. And to the extent that Dr. Jascalevich was near them, he was try-ing to help. But the prosecution had distorted all that, trying desper-ately, through testimony, to change the times on the charts to fit "with the whole idea of curare." But the times don't fit, said Brown. And the times on the charts weren't reliable, anyway. Even Mrs. Nelson had conceded that "all the times in these charts are inaccurate." "It's a strange thing," Brown lamented. "A man's future depends so heavily on juggling of times because there is no proof."

Why, too, was the prosecution ducking the fact that the patients were pale, rather than blue, when they died? Because paleness runs "con-trary, as you know, to the whole concept that these deaths could have been due to curare . . . Almost like an old school song, blue is the color of curare." Wouldn't it have been "instructive," Brown asked, if the jury could have had the statements of Biggs's and Rohrbeck's roommates at Riverdell, the statements that, according to Judge Galda, were taken during Calissi's investigation in 1966 and placed in the file? Well, those statements were "missing," like other items "so critical that they go to the heart" of the case, Brown said. And their absence "cannot be explained, except in one fashion."

Moses, the defense attorney said, was going to stress two things in her summation: the curare was found in Dr. Jascalevich's locker and that there were inconsistencies—"Lord knows you will find them"—in the depositions the surgeon gave to Calissi in 1966 and Woodcock in 1976. But they were of "absolutely no moment in this case." If Dr. Jascalevich was killing people with curare, Brown asked, would he have left the used vials "in a locker which was open half the time? . . . Would he attempt to harm anybody and commit a crime in the morning with a little girl in Room 211 and with everybody in the hospital up and around and bustling? Does one do that under those circumstances?" No, said Brown, Dr. Jascalevich was using the curare for experiments on dogs, and that was what the defendant had maintained from the outset. Hadn't DeSantis, the lab man, confirmed that it was possible to tip someone and get a dog? " 'Well, yes. Why not?' " he had testified. "Nothing fancy about his language, but earthy and pure." Now "one of the most obvious discrepancies is the fact that [Dr. Jascalevich] felt that he did his work on the sixteenth floor of the hospital known as the main building, Seton Hall, when in fact Pollak was the place where there were dogs at a certain time. The fact is he did his grant work on the sixteenth floor, and he did most of his dogs apparently over at Pollak. But deal with that as you may see fit. There will be those discrepancies because there are many reasons why there are discrepancies."

Brown ended by saying that his effort to obtain my notes was no "ploy" and that Dr. Jascalevich was not the only person on trial in Judge Arnold's courtroom. The defense, he said, had brought the jury more than a defense—it had brought an "offense." And it had done so because this case, "as you know in your bones, is one of the primary cases of this half a century"; and if an injustice is done here, "it will undo what we have striven in this country to build for over 200 and some odd years . . . I regret we're all on trial . . . And I tell you it is no closing statement by a zealous defense lawyer who tells you that this case has significance so great that if you find that on this kind of evidence there's proof beyond a reasonable doubt that this man is guilty, justice will be questioned in this land for another century.

"Please," said Brown, gripping the lectern, "the proof is not here. This man is already destroyed. Let him live out the rest of his life knowing that no nation and that no citizen will stand for combinations of greed and gain and ambition, for Farber's and Baden's and Woodcock's, and that one can expect to receive that at the final and when all is nearly gone that justice says it won't happen here."

Brown was right, Moses began. He was right when he said the defense had mounted an "offense" because "that's what you do when you are cornered. The curare is in the body, and you don't have the facts to do away with those findings. You go out and become character assassins. You look for ways to divert attention . . . This defense, ladies and gentlemen, was especially interesting in light of the events of last week. You know, the World Series was on and the Dodgers were beaten very badly, and instead of blaming themselves, they blamed the press. They blamed the press, and they blamed the field, and they blamed the reporters. But it wasn't the bystanders who lost the games, and it wasn't the reporters who wrote the news who lost the games, and it wasn't the setting that lost the games. It's just so in this instance, ladies and gentlemen. It isn't the hospital that killed these people. It isn't the people who wrote about it that killed these people. It isn't the prosecutor, who is charged, who is charged by law, sworn to investigate crimes, to investigate charges; he didn't kill anybody. Everybody is being attacked, ladies and gentlemen. Everybody is being attacked, but they didn't kill anyone. And I think it is crucial for you to remember that as I continue my summation."

From inside the lectern Moses withdrew three hospital charts and placed them on the railing of the jury box. "You know," she said, "we have been talking about livers and kidneys and bones and everything . . . But I wish you would remember, ladies and gentlemen, this is Carl Rohrbeck right here. This is what we have been talking about. This is a human being. And this is Frank Biggs, this chart. This man, I think, has become real to us. We know more about him than we may know about some members of our own family. This is Frank Biggs. And, of course," said Moses, "this slim few pages is Nancy Savino."

Each of these patients, the prosecutor went on, died "a silent death. There was no crying out; there was no screaming; there was no calling for help." They died "unexpectedly, unexplainedly. They died when they shouldn't have. It was a great shock to everyone when they died, and we also know that one man and only one man was always there. That's what it's all about. That's what this trial is all about, ladies and gentlemen. I wasn't there, Prosecutor Woodcock wasn't there, Dr. Baden wasn't there, even Myron Farber wasn't there. But only one man, Mario E. Jascalevich, was there every time, and I think you have got to think of that. It's crucial."

Reviewing the medical histories of the patients, Moses asserted that the only "logical" cause of death was curare poisoning. Admittedly, she

said, Nancy Savino and Frank Biggs were sick when they came to
Riverdell. But natural diseases hadn't caused their deaths or the death
of Carl Rohrbeck. Sure, defense experts had challenged the prosecution's findings of curare—"they had a mission, they had to wash out
the curare. They had to change the cause of death." But the jury and
the state don't "have to tolerate murder until there's an extensive body
of literature about the lethal agent," Moses said. "You don't give a
freebie because there are no articles written about curare killers. You
take the evidence before you, ladies and gentlemen." The prosecution's
scientific experts were "reasonable. They were honest. When they
didn't find [curare], they told you." And were their results merely
"presumptive," as the defense would have it? Ask yourselves, Moses
implored the jury, and use common sense. What was the chance of mistake "when you have . . . three bodies, two laboratories, three tests?"
Ask yourselves. "I think it must be something like one in a hundred
million, the coincidence of three bodies, two labs, two tests, and in the
case of Miss Savino, you have the mass spectrometry as well . . .
Ladies and gentlemen, the chance is so remote that you have to put it
out of your mind." The defense, too, had found curare in Nancy
Savino's liver, the prosecutor said, and there wasn't "a shred of evidence" that it had gotten there after exhumation. ". . . How can you
ignore," Moses asked the jury, "how can you not find that there is
curare in the body?"

Nor was the "cry of conspiracy" as unusual as Brown had suggested,
Moses continued. It arose regularly in real life, on television, in the
movies—George Raft had "made a career of saying 'I have been
framed.'" But, in this case, the prosecutor said, the conspiracy theory
was an "incredible tale, a tissue of lies." Moses reeled off the names of
twenty-eight persons whom she said Brown had attacked. "Ladies and
gentlemen, don't you find it incredible that all of these people—they
wouldn't fit in a room—that they got together to attack this man."
"Poor Mario," she said mockingly, gesturing toward the defendant.
"Everyone is against him in 1966. Now in 1976 a whole different
group of people because there is no connection." No connection between the Riverdell doctors in 1966 and the "Baden, Woodcock,
Farber conspiracy. No connection whatsoever. In order to accept this
defense you have to believe that there were two separate conspiracies
out to get this man, and you have to believe that every nurse who got
on that witness stand and every doctor who got on that witness stand
and the people from Seton Hall who got on that stand were all out to
get this defendant. That's what you have to believe." If in 1966 the
Riverdell doctors were really interested in their profits, Moses said,
"don't you think the first thing they would do is try to keep the hospi-

tal's name out of the newspapers, to avoid getting the hospital involved in anything that might bring about bad publicity?" It was ludicrous to believe that a decade later, a prosecutor "sworn to do his duty in a county of nearly a million people would go out of his way, ladies and gentlemen, to frame a doctor. It is ludicrous to believe that great newspapers which uncover crimes committed by men in much higher stature than the defendant would be serving to frame this doctor . . . I say to you, ladies and gentlemen, whatever your opinions are, the newspapers or the First Amendment or privilege, anything of that sort, that is not an issue for you to decide because . . . whatever Mr. Farber did, he is not on trial, and don't you think he is."

Moses pointed to curare vials and other items arrayed on the evidence table, items that had been seized by Calissi from Dr. Jascalevich's Riverdell locker number four in 1966.

"It is not only the fact," she said, "that these were sudden and unexpected deaths; it is not only the fact, ladies and gentlemen, that there were no symptoms or signs of disease which the defendant's experts say killed these people; it is not only the fact, ladies and gentlemen, that there were intravenous [infusions] going in each and every instance; it is not only the fact, ladies and gentlemen, that in two of the three cases the people were recovering well from surgery and in the third the man came in for elective surgery and was seen to be feeling well; it is not only the fact, ladies and gentlemen, that curare was never given therapeutically to any of these people; it is not only the fact, ladies and gentlemen, that curare is never produced naturally by the body; it is not only the fact that this defendant either did not do resuscitation or did inadequate resuscitation to these people; it is not only the fact, ladies and gentlemen, that this defendant attempted to cover up what he was doing in the hospital in the statements to Prosecutor Calissi and Prosecutor Woodcock; it is not only the fact that the whole pattern of this conduct of this man was to reserve to himself in the hospital and to make sure everybody knew that he was right, that he was going to decide who would live and who would die; it is not only the fact, ladies and gentlemen, that this pattern of conduct was apparent in every single case, but it is also a fact, ladies and gentlemen, that this man had in his locker number four, eighteen bottles of a drug d-tubocurarine, and he had in his locker empty syringes and loaded syringes never shown to you by the defense attorney during his summation . . . It is the fact, ladies and gentlemen, that he had no valid reason to have this curare in his locker, that he was not, in fact, doing dog research at Seton Hall, Pollak, or anywhere else in 1965 or 1966 . . . You will have the evidence of the statement in front of you where the defendant says I never throw anything away, I keep every syringe and every drug and every vial that I ever used." It would be interesting, Moses said, "to know which dogs wore the cotton and synthetic fibers" that like some dog hairs, were also found on the syringes. And the vial of "dog's blood"? That, the prosecutor said, was "not a vial taken from locker number four" on November 1, 1966. It was a vial "handed in by the defendant himself on November 3, 1966. Trying to cover up, trying to cover up his tracks. Look, I did an experiment." Had Dr. Jascalevich previously worked on dogs at Pollak Hospital? On November 11, 1966, Moses noted, he "told Prosecutor Calissi under oath that he never worked at Pollak Hospital before November 2, the day he ran down to get a dog."

Moses's voice was starting to go. "Ladies and gentlemen," she said, "I can go on and on telling you about all the implausible and incredible concocted lies this man made up to cover for the curare in his locker, to cover up for the murders by poisoning." Please, she beseeched the jury, read all the evidence, read the patients' charts in their entirety, and "please try and organize yourselves in a logical and reasonable way when you deliberate. Take the defendant's own words. He contradicts himself right in the very statement, and when you find the liar, ladies and gentlemen, you have the curare as the cause of death, and you will know that you will serve justice by bringing a finding that the defendant was guilty of the murders of Nancy Savino, Carl Rohrbeck, and Frank Biggs."

Judge Arnold charged the jury on the afternoon of October 23, and after one panel member was designated an alternate, the jury began its deliberations. Forty-five minutes later the jurors adjourned for the night and, under heavy guard, were bused from the courthouse to a motel near Hackensack. From my cell window I could see the television reporters filming the jurors' courthouse exit; some were turning their cameras in the direction of the jail wall. Boris, too, was watching, and fidgeting. His own jury was out, and he was pacing his cell in his sneakers, smoking and drinking one cup of coffee after another. "My jury will decide," he called out, knocking on the wall that separated our cells. "That's justice, isn't it, Myron? Isn't that justice?"

"Yes, Boris, that's the way it's done."

That night there was a bomb scare in the courthouse, and some of the sheriff's aides swept through the jail. "Hey, Farber," the undersheriff shouted at me. "Will you please get out of here?"

The next morning, a half hour after the Jascalevich jury resumed its deliberations, I was told that Judge Trautwein wanted to see me. I shaved and put on the suit I was wearing when I had returned to jail twelve days earlier, and at 10:15 I was led through the tunnel and onto the elevator that connected the jail with the courthouse. There, in Judge Trautwein's courtroom, were Ray Brown and Gene Scheiman and Floyd Abrams and, in the front row of the crowded spectators' section, Abe Rosenthal and Jim Goodale. Before I knew what was happening, Abe hunched over the railing and congratulated me.

Judge Trautwein asked me whether I still refused to turn over my reporter's file.

"Yes, sir," I said, standing up.

"You and only you, Mr. Farber," the judge said, "and the superior being to whom you must answer from time to time, know whether you withheld something from the trial court and judge that would have been of aid in their search for the truth . . . You chose to put your privilege and your concept of your constitutional rights . . . above the rights of the people of this state and the defendant." But now that the case had gone to the jury, he said, there was no longer any point in keeping me in jail. "Where compliance becomes meaningless, continued confinement becomes meaningless." Judge Trautwein ended the fines against *The Times,* which had doled out $286,000, and suspended my six-month sentence for criminal contempt. I was a free man.

Back in the jail I gathered my things together and said good-bye to Ron and Bob and the guards. Boris, they told me, was in court and had just been acquitted of murdering his mother, on the grounds of temporary insanity. As I pushed through the jail doors and joined Abe and the others, I was surrounded by reporters. Yes, I said, I was glad to be leaving. "My family is waiting for me and my work is waiting for me. I'm proud of the work I do," I added. "I was an independent— and, I like to think, honest and hardworking—reporter before the Jascalevich case, and I hope and expect to be in the future."

We piled into a rented station wagon for the trip back to New York, and as we pulled onto the highway leading to the George Washington Bridge, I rolled down the window. It was a grand autumn morning; the air was sharp and the azure sky, cloudless. I felt renewed. North of me, a few miles, was Riverdell Hospital; south of me was Pollak Hospital and the old Seton Hall Medical School. What had happened at those places, a decade ago, was not for me to decide. That was a matter for the jury. I had crossed the bridge to New Jersey in 1975 to pursue a story, and now, after a longer haul than I had ever dreamed, I was coming home. But I couldn't help thinking again of what Calissi had said at the start of his investigation in 1966. "Somebody," he had said, "is lying."

The jury didn't examine any of the exhibits or trial testimony. It deliberated for two hours. At 11:24 A.M. on October 24, 1978, the six men and six women filed into Judge Arnold's courtroom. Antoinette Mazzei, the jury forewoman, rose and, in a barely audible voice, pronounced the verdict three times: "We find the defendant not guilty."

As spectators burst into applause, Dr. Jascalevich reached over and patted Brown's arm. Then he blew a kiss to his wife and, plucking a handkerchief from the breast pocket of his suit jacket, waved at the jury.

"Thank God," he said, "justice was done."

EPILOGUE

On November 27, 1978, the U. S. Supreme Court announced that it would not hear my appeal. As is its custom when declining to take a case, the Court gave no explanation.

A year later the New Jersey shield law was amended by the legislature to codify the safeguards the state Supreme Court had promised to reporters who followed in my wake. The so-called Farber Law, which also provided that defense attorneys subpoenaing reporters generally had to do so before a criminal trial began, was first put to the test in March 1980, when lawyers for four men charged with murder or racketeering subpoenaed two letters sent by a prosecution witness to a reporter for the *Daily Register* of Shrewsbury, New Jersey. After a hearing, the trial judge ordered the reporter, Robin Goldstein, to produce the letters for his private inspection. But in a 6 to 1 decision, the Supreme Court of New Jersey reversed the judge, saying the defendants had failed to prove that the information in the letters could not be obtained from a source other than the reporter. The Sixth Amendment, wrote the new chief justice, Robert N. Wilentz, could not override the mandate of the legislature merely "upon a defendant's unsubstantiated assertion" that the information held by a reporter could assist him. Until the defense met the conditions laid down in my case, and in the new shield law, even the trial judge could not view the letters to Miss Goldstein, the chief justice went on. "To a confidential source, to all confidential sources, the promise of silence is absolute, and *any* breach is a total one."

I could have written those words myself in 1978; in fact, I had said pretty much the same thing to Judge Trautwein before he packed me off to jail. When I read the opinion by Chief Justice Wilentz, I called

Floyd Abrams and kiddingly asked him how Robin Goldstein had managed to triumph 6 to 1 in a court where I had been drubbed 5 to 2.

"Myron," he said, "you died so that she might live."

With reporters and news organizations now receiving hundreds of subpoenas each year, and with journalists still being jailed, the U. S. Supreme Court will one day have to come back to the issues raised in my case. I hope that it does so in the spirit of its 1980 ruling in *Richmond Newspapers* vs. *Virginia* that reaffirmed the First Amendment right of the public and the press to attend criminal trials. By itself, the 7 to 1 holding was unremarkable—criminal trials in America have been public trials since long before the Revolution, and the Virginia trial in this case was closed in its entirety. But perhaps, as Justice John Paul Stevens declared, this was a "watershed" decision. "Until today," he wrote, "the Court has accorded virtually absolute protection to the dissemination of information and ideas, but never before has it squarely held that the acquisition of newsworthy material is entitled to any constitutional protection whatsoever."

Chief Justice Burger, in an opinion in which Justice White joined, was equally expansive. Just as Floyd had done in my case, he cited Justice White's statement in Branzburg that "without some protection for seeking out the news, freedom of the press could be eviscerated." The chief justice also recalled Justice Black's opinion for the Court in 1941 that the First Amendment "must be taken as a command of the broadest scope that explicit language, read in the context of a liberty-loving society, will allow." Virginia's argument that the public and the press didn't have a right to attend criminal trials because there was nothing to that effect spelled out in the Constitution was rejected by the chief justice. "Notwithstanding the appropriate caution against reading into the Constitution rights not explicitly defined, the Court has acknowledged that certain inarticulated rights are implicit in enumerated guarantees." As examples, the chief justice mentioned the right of association and the right of travel, as well as the rights to be presumed innocent and to be judged, in a criminal trial, by a standard of proof beyond a reasonable doubt. None of these rights, he said, appear in the Constitution or the Bill of Rights, but all of them, and more, have been "found to share constitutional protection in common with explicit guarantees." At trials, Chief Justice Burger said, reporters are "surrogates for the public," and while "media representatives enjoy the same rights of access as the public, they often are provided special seating and priority of entry so that they may report what people in attendance have to say." Justice Brennan, in his concurring opinion, also described the press as "agents of interested citizens" who were themselves not present in court. And both Justice Brennan and Chief Justice Burger quoted

Jeremy Bentham, the eighteenth-century English reformer. "Without publicity," Bentham had written, "all other checks are insufficient; in comparison of publicity, all other checks are of small account."

All of this, I think, has a bearing on the issues in my case. A reporter is indeed a "surrogate for the public"—when he is covering *anything*. As early as 1945, earlier in fact, the Supreme Court recognized that "a free press is a condition of a free society" and that the First Amendment "rests on the assumption that the widest dissemination of information from diverse and antagonistic sources is essential to the welfare of the public." I agree wholeheartedly with that, both as a journalist and as a citizen. And I believe that the First Amendment can, and should be, interpreted as providing protection for a reporter's unpublished materials and particularly his confidential notes and sources. It is, of necessity, one of those "unarticulated rights."

Obviously, some lawyers and judges diagree with this view, as do some journalists, historians, and constitutional scholars. It may well be, as some scholars argue, that the press clause of the First Amendment meant nothing more, in 1791, than that Congress could impose no restraints in advance of publication. It may even be that the Bill of Rights was a politically expedient measure by men whose real concern was the ratification of the Constitution, that Madison and his compatriots didn't know exactly what they intended by such guarantees as freedom of speech and of the press. Surely it is true that the First Amendment—then called the Third Amendment—was little debated in the First Congress. Not until 1798, when the Jeffersonians contested the Alien and Sedition Acts, was the First Amendment much explained. But the libertarian view that emerged then—a view that has been validated by the subsequent history of this nation and that the Supreme Court didn't have occasion to interpret until after World War One—comports with the needs of democracy. Not long after the Bill of Rights was approved, John Marshall, later Chief Justice Marshall, wrote to the French Foreign Minister that no right was "more deeply impressed on the public mind than the liberty of the press. That this liberty is often carried to excess, that it has sometimes degenerated into licentiousness, is seen and lamented; but the remedy has not yet been discovered. Perhaps it is an evil inseparable from the good with which it is allied; perhaps it is a shoot which cannot be stripped from the stalk, without wounding vitally the plant from which it is torn." The press today—28,000 newspapers, magazines, and radio and television stations—is quite different from the journals of opinion and the pamphleteering of individual printers of the Revolutionary era. So, too, is the government quite different. But what Marshall said in that letter to

Talleyrand two centuries ago, a letter that was endorsed by Madison himself, could be said now. And that is why I went to jail.

The American press will not fold if reporters are continually subpoenaed and jailed and if newspapers are subjected to huge fines. But the courts will not benefit from all this, and neither will the public. Some reporters will take fewer notes or will hesitate to keep them for future reference—"no notes is good notes," Russell Baker observed after I was jailed. Editors and publishers here and there will kill some legitimate but controversial stories, and other stories won't be assigned in the first place. However they may be fortified by the sight of reporters who kept their word, some sources will inevitably draw back. Not the person who is absolutely driven to tell what he knows, but the other kind of source—the one who confirms and substantiates or refutes, the one who frequently knows the most. In the long run, these developments will erode the quality of news the public receives and will weaken an institution that, for all its "licentiousness," was meant to serve as a watch on government and as a "sentinel over the public rights."

After the Jascalevich trial, jurors said that my refusal to surrender my file had played no part in their verdict. Clearly they had acquitted Dr. Jascalevich because they believed that Nancy Savino and Frank Biggs and Carl Rohrbeck had died of natural causes and that the state had not proven that curare could be present in embalmed bodies after ten years.

Just before Judge Arnold retired, he fined Sybil Moses $300 for refusing to sit down and be quiet the previous March when Ray Brown accused the prosecutor's office of engaging in "chicanery and fraud." Moses eventually left the prosecutor's office to become a state administrative law judge in Newark. Brown lashed out, after the trial, at the "arrogance of power of the big press and the big law firms" who thought "we who argued against them were just New Jersey jerks." The press, he assured his colleagues of the bar, "will continue to do whatever they please, thank God." And the "only way you can get a fair trial against the press is to have an extraordinary lawyer who is tough enough and mean enough to meet them up every alley."

Riverdell Hospital, reorganized under federal bankruptcy laws, changed its name twice after the trial, then finally closed its doors. The several civil suits that had been filed against the hospital and Dr. Jascalevich after the surgeon's indictment were settled out of court. Dr. Harris continued to practice in New Jersey, but Dr. Lans, making good on an idea that he had first considered in late 1966, took up a residency in psychiatry in New York.

Dr. Jascalevich reportedly began covering for other doctors in New York, where he had had a medical license since 1961. The surgeon, and all but one of the twelve jurors who had acquitted him of murder, asked the New Jersey Board of Medical Examiners to restore his New Jersey license pending the outcome of the malpractice hearing that had been recessed in January 1978. The board refused.

In June 1980 the hearing officer concluded that Dr. Jascalevich was guilty, in the J.E. "cancer" case, of negligence "that endangered the health and life of his patient" and that in the T.R. "operative record" case, he was guilty of "unprofessional conduct deserving of censure." But the state's more extreme charges, the hearing officer said, had not been proven by a legal standard of "clear and convincing" evidence. The hearing was the longest license review procedure in New Jersey history. And while Dr. Jascalevich attended each of its thirty-three sessions, he relied entirely on medical experts—including, again, Dr. Siegel—and did not testify in his own defense. Moreover, Brown resisted an effort by the state to call his client. "Not to permit even a shadow of an inference to be drawn from the doctor's failure to take the witness stand would be unnatural and would challenge reason," the hearing officer noted at the end of his 164-page report to the Board of Medical Examiners.

In September 1980 the board unanimously overruled the hearing officer and found Dr. Jascalevich guilty of "gross malpractice or gross neglect and lack of good moral character." A month later, it revoked the surgeon's medical license in New Jersey. Dr. Jascalevich appealed the board's action, but it was upheld in a unanimous decision by the Appellate Division of Superior Court. Judge Sylvia Pressler, writing for a three-judge panel, said the license revocation was not "disproportionate" to the hearing officer's factual findings and that the board had used an appropriate standard of proof. In the case of J.E., Judge Pressler said, Dr. Jascalevich was found, in October 1975, "to have included a postoperative note as to possible cancer when he knew the patient to be cancer-free." In the T.R. case, the judge added, "He was found to have knowingly permitted a forged operative record" to become part of her hospital file. A deliberate falsification by a physician of his patient's medical record, "particularly when the reason therefor is to protect his own interests at the expense of his patient's," must be regarded as gross malpractice, Judge Pressler concluded.

In the fall of 1981, Dr. Jascalevich sold his house in Englewood Cliffs and his office in West New York, and moved back to Argentina.

In January 1982, Governor Brendan T. Byrne of New Jersey pardoned *The Times* and me of our convictions for criminal contempt and returned $101,000 to *The Times,* the full amount he was empowered to give back. Our purpose, he had concluded, had not been "to insult or frustrate the judicial process, but to stand on a noble, if sometimes imperfect, principle."

—New York, N.Y.
April 1982

INDEX